Jerry Cernak

THE LINCOLN-DOUGLAS DEBATES

THE FIRST COMPLETE, UNEXPURGATED TEXT

THE
LINCOLN-DOUGLAS
DEBATES

THE FIRST COMPLETE, UNEXPURGATED TEXT

EDITED AND WITH AN INTRODUCTION BY
HAROLD HOLZER

HarperCollins*Publishers*

HarperCollins books may be purchased for educational, business, or sales promotional use. For information please write Special Markets Department, HarperCollins Publishers, Inc., 10 East 53rd Street, New York, NY 10022.

FIRST EDITION

Designed by Jessica Shatan

Library of Congress Cataloging-in-Publication Data
Lincoln, Abraham, 1809–1865.
    The Lincoln-Douglas debates : the first complete, unexpurgated
text / edited and with an introduction by Harold Holzer. — 1st ed.
        p.   cm.
    ISBN 0-06-016810-2 (cloth)
    1. Lincoln-Douglas debates, 1858. I. Douglas, Stephen,
1813–1861. II. Holzer, Harold. III. Title.
E457.4.L776 1993
973.6′8′0922—dc20   92-53357

93 94 95 96 97 CC/HC 10 9 8 7 6 5 4 3 2 1

For my daughters,

Remy and Meg . . . great debaters

Public sentiment is everything—
he who moulds public sentiment
is greater than he who makes statutes.

—ABRAHAM LINCOLN
*at the first debate
with Stephen A. Douglas,
Ottawa, Illinois,
August 21, 1858*

Contents

Preface

MORE THAN FORTY EDITIONS of the Lincoln-Douglas debates have been published since 1860. But in a sense, this is the first.

The idea—and the need—for this book arose from the effort to put an earlier book to bed. In the course of editing final page proofs for the 1990 volume *Lincoln on Democracy,* an anthology of speeches and writings collected under the direction of Governor Mario Cuomo, I began wondering about the fidelity of some of the texts that for so long had engaged the governor, our team of scholars, and me—not to mention the generations of historians who labored in the Lincoln vineyards before us.

Nagging doubts lingered for good reason: none of the original manuscripts of Abraham Lincoln's pre-presidential speeches has survived. Before entering the White House, Lincoln simply did not think it important to preserve them. Neither, apparently, did anyone else. Thus there is no surviving autograph version of his Lyceum speech, Cooper Union address, or House Divided speech, among other early triumphs.

And most vexing of all, where the fabled Lincoln-Douglas debates are concerned we do not even have any surviving handwritten notes or fragments of unquestionable authenticity. For purposes of assembling *Lincoln on Democracy,* we had relied—like earlier generations of editors—on period newspaper reprints of these speeches, some recorded on the spot by stenographers. But were these records always reliable? True, where Cooper Union was concerned, Lincoln not only supplied a manuscript to the typesetters, he proofread the results. But such was not always the case. Sometimes he had not read from a manuscript to begin with.

Speaking from text, Lincoln was perhaps the most eloquent orator of his age. But as an impromptu speaker, he could be dreadful. Notwithstanding his reputation as an engaging storyteller and spellbinding courtroom lawyer, an unprepared Lincoln could be a surprisingly hapless spouter of hollow banality. What is more, the record of such utterances is inherently suspect, since it relies on shorthand transcriptions, not authenticated texts. As historian Don E. Fehrenbacher discovered only recently—more than a century and a quarter after its delivery—the long-accepted newspaper printing of the House Divided speech featured a transposed, out-of-sequence paragraph that rendered some of its opening thoughts all but incomprehensible.

A review of the rest of the early Lincoln canon shows that even the well-deserved reputation of his Farewell Address to Springfield owed more to the text Lincoln composed after his journey got under way than to the less polished speech delivered to his neighbors and transcribed by the local newspaper while he spoke. Most of the public statements he subsequently delivered from the back of the trains carrying him to Washington, even allowing for his resolve to avoid discussing policy, seem today not only insubstantial but uninspired. They seemed equally so to a number of observers back in 1861. In more skillful hands, such talks might have served to reassure an anxious nation tottering on the brink of disunion and civil war. Instead they placated few, and irked many.

The presidency did little to add luster to Lincoln's rare bursts of spontaneity, now wisely curtailed. Even the twin Union triumphs at Gettysburg and Vicksburg on the eve of Independence Day in 1863 at first elicited only tortured syntax. In an impromptu speech from the White House, Lincoln could disguise neither his exuberance nor his clumsiness as he proceeded to belabor a brilliant idea. "How long ago is it?" he asked, "—eighty odd years—since on the Fourth of July for the first time in the history of the world a nation by its representatives, assembled and declared as a self-evident truth that 'all men are created equal.' " Not until he had four months more to ponder the victories was he able to recraft these thoughts—meticulously writing out several drafts until he was satisfied—into the unforgettable poetry of the Gettysburg Address: "Fourscore and seven years ago, our fathers brought forth upon this continent, a new nation, conceived in Liberty, and dedicated to the proposition that all men are created equal." As Lincoln had conceded at the White House that evening in July, this was "a glorious theme, and the occasion for a speech." But, he admitted frankly, "I am not prepared to make one worthy of the occasion." Unless he carefully wrote out his words in advance, he rarely was.

Seldom did he display these shortcomings more painfully than in responding to calls for one such impromptu speech the evening before he delivered his most famous address. Even in hallowed Gettysburg, Lincoln could do little more than sputter: "In my position it is somewhat important that I should not say any foolish things." To which a voice in the crowd shot back: "If you can help it." Admitted Lincoln in a self-deprecating reply: "It very often happens that the only way to help it is to say nothing at all."

But there were times when Lincoln apparently could *not* help it, and it was the resulting archive of unrehearsed oratorical mediocrity that ultimately drew my attention to the Lincoln-Douglas debates of 1858, surely the most demanding extemporaneous exercise of Lincoln's career. Given his lackluster record in unrehearsed oratory, how did he summon the skill to make cogent, hour-long speeches, along with ninety-minute rebuttals, and thirty-minute rejoinders, in his debates with Stephen A. Douglas? These events offered Lincoln a precious opportunity to reach his widest audience to date, but also posed grave dangers. Even if he was able to read his opening statements directly from text, which no witness ever suggested he did, Lincoln certainly could not hope to anticipate his opponent's rebuttals and prepare rejoinders in advance. Yet the surviving published record of the debates suggests that Lincoln spoke flawlessly, sometimes inspiringly, each time he took his turn against Stephen A. Douglas—exhibiting a facility for resonant impromptu oratory he failed to evidence either before the debates or after. How was this possible?

It seemed likely that the answer might be found in the faded press records of that 1858 campaign season, and that is where the research for this volume began: through the old Illinois newspapers that originally published so-called "exact" transcriptions of each debate; in the letters of both debaters in which they also debated the accuracy of these long-accepted transcripts; and through a prolonged dispute of the day, seldom recalled since, between party-affiliated newspapers, over whose published texts were more reliable. Contained therein was not only the elusive solution to the mystery but a clue to how the unexpurgated speeches could now be resurrected.

The result of the search is this new collection of long-ignored debate transcriptions, assembled for the first time since 1858 in an effort to "hear" again the true voices of these remarkable leaders, just as they were likely first heard in Illinois by the crowds who flocked to listen to them: not in the form of highly polished narrative prepared after the events for newspapers and books but as charged oratory designed to excite and persuade voters.

These hitherto ignored transcripts turn out to shed new light on Lincoln's reputation as a public speaker, while compelling us to use this fresh evidence to reassess Stephen A. Douglas's performance as well. And the texts illuminate more vividly than ever the volatile atmosphere of the debates themselves: the passionate responses by the crowds who heard them, and the debaters' ability to rouse, amuse, and outrage them. Hopefully these unedited words—together with descriptions by period eyewitnesses of the hullabaloo that greeted them—will bring us closer than ever before to the drama of the most important political debates of American history, and the men who conducted them.

This was how they probably sounded, and this is how they should be remembered.

Acknowledgments

THIS PROJECT COULD NEVER have been undertaken, much less realized, without the invaluable help of a number of people whose efforts deserve more gratitude than I can possibly acknowledge adequately here.

First, Thomas F. Schwartz, curator of the Henry Horner Lincoln Collection at the Illinois State Historical Library in Springfield, helped facilitate the research by providing the original Illinois newspaper records that formed the basis for the transcripts reproduced in this volume. I am indebted to him for all his assistance, not to mention his forbearance when smeared xeroxes had to be rephotographed.

Wherever I turned, my colleagues in the Lincoln fraternity were ready and willing to help. My good friend and frequent coauthor Mark E. Neely, the director of the Lincoln Museum in Fort Wayne, supplied both enthusiasm and his usual invaluable critical reading of the text. His suggestions made this a better book. Another close friend, Frank J. Williams, president of the Abraham Lincoln Association, also read the text, and generously agreed to the publication of his wonderful painting of the debaters in action. And Wayne C. Temple of Springfield shared many valuable insights on Lincoln's likely inspiration for the format of the debates.

I could never write about the Lincoln-Douglas debates without gratefully acknowledging too the inspiration provided me over the years by the greatest orator of our own age, Mario Cuomo, for whom I was privileged to work from 1984 to 1992. Not only does his eloquence hark back to an age in which all leaders were expected to inspire with their words, but ever since I first met him in 1977, we have enjoyed sharing our mutual fascination with Lincoln. Running for mayor of New York that year, he objected regularly to the frustrating restrictions of televised candidate debates, citing the Lincoln-Douglas legacy as a lost ideal of political confrontation. I never forgot his words, and it turns out they were right.

I am grateful also to Eamon Dolan, my editor at HarperCollins, who manages somehow to balance a writing stable that embraces historians as well as mystery writers, while maintaining enthusiasm for both. He has my thanks not only for encouraging this effort but for introducing me to the addictive works of another of "his" authors, Tony Hillerman, my hungry consumption of which ironically worked to delay delivery of this manuscript. Thanks also go to a onetime editor at HarperCollins, Amy Gash, who first brought this project to the attention of her former colleagues there; and to my indefatigable agent, Geri Thoma, who saw early and emphatically the value of presenting these long-hidden texts.

As always, I owe the biggest debt to my family for their patience and encouragement. My wife, Edith, not only endured the temporary redecoration of our home with two-by-three-foot copies of nineteenth-century newspapers but gave the text a thorough reading and offered important suggestions for improving it. I owe apologies to my daughters for spending more time with Lincoln than with them this past year; but twelve-year-old Meg managed to start middle school auspiciously without her father's guidance, and sixteen-year-old Remy had no help from me in preparing college applications, save for the writing of checks. She was admitted into Harvard anyway (Robert T. Lincoln's alma mater, I reminded her, to her annoyance), which helped much to assuage my guilt. Both girls also responded usefully to my occasional frenzied pleas for help with synonyms and adjectives I had difficulty recalling, and I hope they will recognize their contributions on these pages.

Finally, I must thank Janice Banks and Vince Lipani for their crucial help, and especially Amy Varney-Kiet, who together with Cecilia Thomas squinted through the agonizing process of typing these debates from the minuscule print of the original newspapers. When she regains both her eyesight and her willingness to read again the materials she helped assemble, I hope Amy will be comforted by the knowledge that this project could not have been accomplished without her.

THE LINCOLN-DOUGLAS DEBATES

THE FIRST COMPLETE, UNEXPURGATED TEXT

INTRODUCTION

"THE PRAIRIES ARE ON FIRE," reported a New York newspaper in 1858, gazing west to take the temperature of the most heated election contest in the nation.[1]

In the summer of that turbulent year, as America slid perilously closer to the brink of disunion, two Illinois politicians seized center stage and held the national spotlight for two extraordinary months. Through the sheer force of their words, personalities, and ideas—not to mention the exuberance of their supporters—they transformed a statewide contest for the U.S. Senate into a watershed national disquisition on the contentious issue of slavery. They attracted tens of thousands of voters to their appearances, and newspaper reprints of their speeches became required reading for hundreds of thousands more. However imperfect that written record was—and its defects are the reason for this book—its immediate influence proved genuine and widespread. The eyes and ears of the entire nation turned to Illinois as the war of words intensified. It was the season of the Lincoln-Douglas debates.

Beginning in August and going on through mid-October, the nationally known forty-five-year-old, two-term Democratic incumbent, Senator Stephen A. Douglas, and his formidable challenger for reelection, ex-congressman Abraham Lincoln, a forty-nine-year-old Republican, met face-to-face publicly on seven memorable occasions before huge, ardent audiences throughout their state. Even as a brutal summer hot spell gave way to chill autumn winds, the enthusiastic partisans of "the Little Giant" and "Long Abe" kept thronging into parched open fields and bustling town squares to witness the remarkable encounters, as these mesmerizing orators argued the future of their troubled country. Through twenty-one hours of speeches, rebuttals, and rejoinders—all punctuated by choruses of cheers and jeers—the tall, awkward Lincoln, and the short, cocky Douglas offered exhaustive variations on their contrasting visions for America, one embracing life, liberty, and the pursuit of happiness regardless of race, the other stressing government by and for white men only, and in perpetuity. By fall, their "thunder tones," as Lincoln described them, were roiling the state and, increasingly, the nation. They galvanized public attention north as well as south, shaking the very foundations of what Lincoln called "the house divided." Entering the fray as rivals for a Senate seat, they emerged as rivals for the highest political prize of all. As the Richmond *Enquirer* seemed to sense early in the campaign, theirs became "the great battle of the next Presidential election."[2]

It all began with a challenge from the challenger. Since launching his Senate campaign in June, Abraham Lincoln had been frustratingly campaigning uphill against a better-financed, better-organized opponent. "His tactics," Lincoln complained of Douglas, ". . . make it appear that he is having a triumphant entry into; and march through the country." In response, perhaps recalling that four years earlier he had held his own while debating Douglas at Peoria over the controversial Kansas-Nebraska Act, Lincoln began trailing the senator through Illinois, responding publicly to his addresses, and thus, by his own account, getting "a concluding speech on him" every time. He heard Douglas speak in Chicago on July 9, and the following night delivered a ringing response from the same spot. And when Douglas spoke in Springfield eight days after that, Lincoln followed him with a lengthy reply only a few hours later. It was, he felt, "the very thing."[3]

But the strategy began wearing thin. There were some occasions on which Lincoln felt constrained not to respond by "feelings of delicacy."

Worse, the opposition press was beginning to ridicule him. Since there were "two very good circuses and menageries traveling through the state," mocked one paper, why not have them "include a speech from Lincoln in their performances. In this way Lincoln could get good audiences and his friends be relieved from the mortification they all feel at his present humiliating position." It was clearly time for Lincoln to try a different approach. The *"offensive"* was better than the *"defensive,"* he admitted to a supporter on July 20.[4]

Then on July 22, the pro-Lincoln Chicago *Daily Press and Tribune* came out with a provocative suggestion: "Let Mr. Douglas and Mr. Lincoln agree to canvass the State together, in the old western style." A few days later, Lincoln issued a formal challenge to Douglas "for you and myself to divide time, and address the same audiences." For his part, Douglas neither needed nor welcomed the proposal; such encounters could scarcely help a well-known incumbent, and they held out the frightening possibility of elevating Lincoln merely by providing him the opportunity to share platforms with him. But "the old western style" also dictated that Douglas could not easily decline, especially once the Republican press began editorializing that a candidate "who refused to speak in that way had no better reason than cowardice" for dodging the challenge.[5]

Still, Douglas did not immediately acquiesce. He seethed that Lincoln had waited until he had crowded his schedule with binding commitments. He fretted that a third candidate might soon enter the race "with no other purpose than to insure my defeat by dividing the Democratic Party for your benefit," he wrote Lincoln, and he was not about to grant to a spoiler "the right to speak from the same stand" too. He was certainly not willing to debate a hundred, or even fifty, times, as Lincoln hoped.[6]

In the end, he had little choice but to "accommodate" his opponent, but Douglas would insist on making the terms: They would meet only once in each of the state's nine congressional districts. And having already spoken—if not jointly, then consecutively—in two of them, with their remarks at Chicago and Springfield, Douglas would now consent only to seven more joint meetings. He also named the venues and dates: the county seats of Ottawa on August 21, Freeport on August 27, Jonesboro on September 15, Charleston on September 18, and then, after another hiatus, Galesburg on October 7, Quincy on October 13, and Alton on October 15. The schedule would leave plenty of room for each candidate to campaign extensively on his own.[7]

For Lincoln, it would have to do. The only thing upon which he insisted now was "perfect reciprocity, and no more. I wish as much time as you, and that conclusions shall alternate. That is all." The idea for rotating the opening speeches may have come from a fifteen-year-old book by Lincoln's pastor friend, Rev. Dr. James Smith. His tome, *The Christian's Defence,* which Lincoln kept in his modest library at home, included copious notes from its author's 1841 debates on religion with a skeptic named C. G. Olmstead. For eighteen consecutive nights, these debaters had taken turns delivering one-hour opening addresses, two-hour rebuttals, and half-hour rejoinders. Lincoln may well have recalled this system of "perfect reciprocity" when he made his arrangements with Douglas in 1858. Whatever the inspiration for the system they ultimately adopted, within days of a chance meeting between the two on the campaign trail, the details were finalized. Each debate would last a total of three hours. The opening speaker would occupy an hour; then an hour and a half would be allotted for a reply, and finally a half hour given to the first speaker for a rejoinder. If there was a slight advantage, it would be Douglas's: he would take the opening and closing positions at the first and final debates, and thus enjoy the last word on four occasions, to Lincoln's three. Even so, to a supporter, Douglas worried: "I shall have my hands full." However imperfectly, however reluctantly, the stage was finally set.[8]

Neither candidate could have been prepared for the overwhelming public response to come. Seldom before or since has political rhetoric elicited such sustained, fevered interest, or exerted such powerful or long-standing influence. Well attended and widely published at the time, reported not only in Illinois but throughout the country, the debates were also destined to be reprinted in their entirety in an edition engineered by Lincoln himself—and in innumerable volumes since. The legendary political encounters quickly earned—and have held ever since—an almost sacred place in both history and folklore. Arguably, the Lincoln-Douglas encounters are the most famous political debates ever held in the United States.

And yet the real Lincoln-Douglas debates have largely been lost to us, almost from the very moment they were conducted. In an effort to showcase the debaters to the best advantage, the raw power and unexpurgated spontaneity of the speakers were permanently sanitized by partisan stenographers, transcribers, and editors. Together they repro-

duced the speeches and rebuttals as they perceived their equally partisan readers wanted them preserved. Inevitably, their approved (and
improved) versions of the debates became the basis of the permanent
historical archive. It would be hyperbolic to suggest that the original
record was suppressed, but inaccurate to deny that it was enhanced.
The truth is, what Lincoln and Douglas said at their seven debates in
1858 was not then, nor has it been since, accurately reported. And what
was printed has never been seriously questioned, perhaps for the reason,
as historian Reinhard Luthin put it, that the Lincoln-Douglas debates
have remained "vastly more admired than read." Or possibly because
readers simply remained ignorant of how the record was assembled.[9]

To understand how and why the distortions originally occurred
requires an appreciation of the political culture of mid-nineteenth-
century America, an atmosphere of enthusiastic, nearly unanimous
public participation so vastly different from our own as to seem by
comparison almost alien.

The mere idea today of summoning thousands of ordinary citizens to
gather together outdoors, unsheltered and, more often than not, unseated, to observe political debates firsthand—much less expecting
audiences to listen attentively to hours of speechifying—borders on the
fantastic. But in 1858, spectators came from all over Illinois, and from
nearby states as well, crowding fairgrounds, village streets, and once a
vacant lot, in towns stretching from the cool northern reaches of the
state near Wisconsin to the steamy river towns bordering the slaveholding South, just to hear a Democrat and a Republican debate slavery.
Difficult as it may be in our more remote television age to imagine such
frenzied public involvement, a century and a quarter ago, especially in
the West, politics still offered sparsely populated communities not only
the opportunity to take sides on crucial issues but their sole access to
grand entertainment as well. Politics provided high drama and spirited
fun to neighborhoods devoid of activities anywhere near as engaging or
exciting. Ministers might hurl fire and brimstone from the local pulpit,
but only on Sundays. The county fair set up only once a year. Visits by
itinerant preachers were rare, and tours by traveling minstrel shows
even rarer. But politics supplied day-in, day-out excitement, and with
it the allure of all the other attractions combined.[10]

Particularly in the small towns that dotted the Illinois prairie, the
pulse of politics and the heartbeat of community life throbbed as one;
election fever was a year-round malady that infected its eager victims

with incurable enthusiasm. Public officials might be revered, voter turnout was nearly unanimous, and politics lured masses of celebrants to barbecues, Fourth of July picnics, fireworks displays, and stem-winder speeches that combined the fervor of the revival meeting, the spectacle of theater, and the passion of neighborly argument. "It is astonishing," one New York journalist marveled after a trip to Illinois, "how deep an interest in politics these people take." Yet even in this intoxicating milieu, Illinois had never experienced anything quite like the Lincoln-Douglas debates. It is somewhat ironic that the same political culture that made the encounters both possible and popular ultimately conspired to make their accurate recording unlikely.[11]

That the campaign between Lincoln and Douglas quickly gripped all of Illinois in its thrall comes as no surprise. But even in Illinois, the impassioned response to the longtime arch-rivals broke new ground. Theirs were not mere political discussions but gala pageants: public spectacles fueled by picnic tables groaning with local fare; emblazoned with gaudy banners and astringently worded broadsides; and echoing with artillery salutes and martial music. On the days the events were staged, roads to debate sites were choked with wagons and horses as whole families crowded onto the scene. Hotels overflowed with guests, and those who could not book rooms slept on sofas in lobbies.

In Ottawa, scene of the first encounter, attendance swelled to more than double the permanent population. They came "by train, by canal-boat, by wagon, buggy, and on horseback." Lincoln arrived on a special train bulging with excited supporters. Douglas led a mile-long procession in a beautifully appointed head carriage, as crowds cheered him "from the sidewalks, from windows, piazzas, house-tops and every available standing point." At the second encounter, at Freeport, an "immense assemblage" of boosters met Lincoln at the depot, feted him at a levee, and "wheeled" him to the debate site in an open wagon drawn by six white horses. When the debates themselves got under way, one correspondent observed virtual "hand-to-hand conflict for even the meagerest . . . standing room." Once the speeches began, partisans interrupted continually with outbursts of applause and cheering, occasional heckling, and frequent shouts of "Hit him again," "That's the Doctrine," and "Give it to Him." At one encounter, a heckler shouted out his opinion that Lincoln was a fool, to which he quickly retorted, to gales of laughter: "I guess there are two of us" (an exchange, predictably, expunged from the record later). Audiences were fed with barbecued meat and ice cream, and both Democrats and Republicans accused each other of "keeping spirits up by pouring spirits down." Inevitably, the scenes that erupted at the conclusion of each event often rivaled the oratory itself for intensity or humor. The rowdiness could sometimes drift over the edge of acceptability: once, between debates, enemies smeared Douglas's carriage with what a horrified journalist could only bring himself to describe as "loathsome dirt," referring undoubtedly to excrement. And on another occasion, Lincoln was unexpectedly borne off by exuberant supporters who failed to calculate their candidate's extreme height, leaving Lincoln's legs dangling un-ceremoniously "and his pantaloons pulled up so as to expose his under-wear almost to his knees." It was not unusual—even after standing on their feet much of the day for the festivities, either denied sufficient food and drink or bloated with an excess of both—for such overwrought partisans to flock to nearby locations once debates ended for still more boisterous celebrations, and sometimes more speeches as well. (Lincoln himself joined an audience after the first debate to hear yet another politician deliver yet another oration.) Even after the orators (and their listeners) were finally exhausted, the townspeople would invariably be kept awake all night by noisy, torchlit parades through the streets.[12]

Within this rollicking atmosphere, the press played a crucial role, but decidedly unlike the one the media perform today. Newspapers were not nonpartisan. They took sides—not only editorially but in day-to-day coverage, aiming not only to report but to persuade. And therein lies the essential clue to the elusiveness of the "real" Lincoln-Douglas debates.

This wildly different journalistic ethic was partly attributable to the economic realities of the newspaper business at midcentury, when the press depended largely on political organizations for survival. Alliance with a political party translated into guaranteed subscribers and lucra-tive legal and governmental advertisements. In return for this lifeblood of patronage, the press was expected to trumpet the party line. Thus the larger towns typically supported two opposing sheets. In Springfield, for example, the Illinois state capital where Lincoln still lived in 1858, and which Douglas had called home years earlier, the Democrats claimed one newspaper, the *Illinois State Register,* while the new Republican party had the *Illinois State Journal.* (Today they are merged, reflective of trends in our own times toward both commercial retrenchment and political neutrality.) Similarly, in the bustling lake city of Chicago, Democrats read the Chicago *Daily Times,* and Republicans the Chicago *Daily Press and Tribune.* In the days before celluloid campaign buttons and bumper stickers testified to political allegiances, Americans made known their party loyalties by the newspaper they carried.

Partisan reporting was hardly confined to the opinion columns. During the debates, newspapers uninhibitedly lauded the candidates of their choice on their news pages and routinely vilified opponents, sometimes poisoning the air with slanders that in earlier times provoked duels and today might inspire not votes but litigation. Their crowd estimates were reliable only in their consistent unreliability, owing far more to fancy, puffery, and exaggeration than to head counting. Accounts of audience response differed markedly according to which journal purported to hear it: to Democratic reporters, Douglas was always vigorously cheered and Lincoln ignored or jeered; Republican journalists heard approbation only for Lincoln and somehow failed to distinguish applause for Douglas. As for the party faithful who turned out to welcome candidates into town, they were always vast in number and uncontrollable in their excitement—that is, if they were being described by the loyal party journal. If the rival newspaper was filing the report, then the Lincoln crowds were inevitably abolitionist, foreign-born, or dirt-poor, and the Douglas boosters Irish, drunk, or both. In these manifestly prejudiced reports, one debater invariably triumphed, while the other not only faltered but sometimes dissolved into tremors or had to be physically restrained from violent interruptions. In a way, the nineteenth-century press functioned much as today's paid campaign "spin doctors" do, dispensing adjective-laden instant interpretation in an attempt to make each defeat seem a draw, each draw a victory, and each victory a rout.

From the outset, the Democratic and Republican journals in Chicago treated the Lincoln-Douglas debates as worthy not only of this intensive and openly biased old-style coverage but also of something relatively new: start-to-finish transcription. As a result, a few days after each debate, citizens throughout the state were able to read, verbatim, the speeches that the respective candidates had offered face-to-face. Or so the readers believed.

Of course, the requisite electronic technology had yet to be developed to record flawlessly what candidates said. Neither audiences nor transcribers enjoyed the benefit of the electronic amplification or access to tape recording we take for granted today. The "recording" process could be daunting. Stenographers hastily took copious notes, transcribers transformed the hieroglyphics into words, and typesetters turned the words into newspaper copy. In a way, the demands placed on the shorthand reporters inhibited subterfuge: facing intense pressure to catch every word, a stenographer hardly had the opportunity to distort or enhance what he was hearing as he labored mightily merely to keep track of the furious pace of debate. But that did not mean transcribers and editors could not introduce such enhancements later.

The record suggests that they did. Somewhere along the fevered trail between stenography, transcription, and composition—even though so-called "overnight" debate reports still took two or three days to get into print*—a transfiguration occurred. On the Democratic side, supportive editors apparently gave careful critical reading to Douglas transcripts, deleting ungrammatical sentences, improving stylistic transgressions, plugging up run-on sentences, and extending fragmentary thoughts . . . and in the interest of time, left Lincoln's portion alone. The Democratic journal would invariably boast a polished Douglas transcript and a rather rough-hewn Lincoln text.

In turn, sympathetic Republican editors were practicing much the same dishonesty in the name of "Honest Abe." Performing comparable cosmetic surgery on the words of their candidate, they subjected his debate transcripts to similarly rigorous editing, this time printing the Douglas texts verbatim, flaws and all. One odd result of the subterfuge was that only Democrats got to read the unexpurgated Lincoln, and only Republicans the unedited Douglas. Around the state and country, like-minded party organs republished the respective Chicago reports without question. Thus the party faithful never really enjoyed unedited print access to the candidate of their choice as he truly sounded in debate. One had to be there.

---

*Overnight transcriptions did not always live up to their name. The debate speeches were not published until two or three days after each meeting, suggesting that ample time was allowed for typesetting—and editing. This was the publishing schedule: Ottawa, August 21, published in the *Daily Times* and the *Press and Tribune* on August 23; Freeport, August 27, published in both newspapers on August 30; Jonesboro, September 15, published in both papers on September 17; Charleston, September 18, published in both papers September 21; Galesburg, October 7, published in both papers on October 9; Quincy, October 13, published in both papers October 15; and Alton, October 15, published in the *Times* on October 17 and the *Tribune* on October 18. Party newspapers across the country in turn reprinted the transcripts based on these Chicago reports.

Issues were never compromised in this enterprise: readers knew these leaders and their views too well. But in the process of bringing order to the chaos of unscripted stump oratory, immediacy fell victim to the demands of high style, and the spontaneous magic of these debates was suffocated. Later, when only the edited adaptations were transferred from newspaper to book, they became an immutable part of the record, enhancements and all.

If such was the case, a modern reader might reasonably inquire, why didn't editors and politicians complain at the time? In fact, they did. The Democrats criticized Republican transcripts of Douglas's speeches because they so obviously lacked the polish *their* editors lavished upon them. And Republicans cried foul over the Democratic record of Lincoln's writings for they, too, appeared without the embellishments they had crafted for them retrospectively. Of course, both sides failed to renounce, or even admit guilt for, the chauvinistic editorial work they were performing for their respective candidates. But how else can we account for the far more realistic texts—complete with pauses, shifts in reasoning, inconclusive thoughts, and colloquialisms—to be found only on the pages of "rival" transcripts: the unedited Democratic version of Republican Lincoln's talks, and the untouched Republican version of Democrat Douglas's (the very texts provided in this book)?

II

The Lincoln-Douglas debates were the first sustained political encounters to inspire so-called "phonographic" reporting, and in this milestone lay the key to their early and enduring fame, as well as their ultimate distortion. At first, the Chicago *Press and Tribune* placed coverage of the encounters solely in the hands of a twenty-four-year-old journalist named Horace White. But White discovered that the Douglas camp had employed two shorthand reporters, Henry Binmore and James B. Sheridan, "whose duty it was to 'write it up' in the columns." White quickly recognized "the necessity of counteracting or matching that force," so the *Press and Tribune* dispatched Robert Roberts Hitt, "the pioneer" of this "new feature in journalism in Chicago," to assume the additional responsibility.[13]

By the time the debates got under way, both newspapers were fully committed to utilizing verbatim reporting and fully organized for prompt transcription and publication. The three men on the cutting edge of the new process have been largely forgotten by history, but they are principal characters in the story of the real Lincoln-Douglas debates.

Henry Binmore of the pro-Douglas Chicago *Times* was a twenty-five-year-old Englishman who perfected a form of shorthand so individualized he boasted that it could not be transcribed by anyone but himself. At the outset of the 1858 campaign, he was employed by the St. Louis *Republican* (another Democratic organ, despite its name), and his reports on Douglas's early speeches impressed the *Times* enough to hire him to record the debates. For backup, the paper imported James B. Sheridan, who perfected his phonographic reporting skills at a special school in Philadelphia, later taking a job with the influential *Press,* a local newspaper whose owner supported Douglas in his political battles with the Buchanan administration. The publisher went on to dispatch Sheridan to Illinois to cover the Douglas campaign, and there the *Times* retained him to help Binmore record the debates.[14]

On the Republican side, transcription became the sole responsibility of Hitt, a twenty-four-year-old, Illinois-born future congressman. Educated at what is now DePauw University in Indiana, Hitt opened his own office in Chicago in 1856 and quickly became that city's leading shorthand reporter, gaining regular employment in the courts and newspapers. He had transcribed Lincoln speeches in the past, and by the year of the debates was serving as official stenographer of the Illinois legislature. Like Binmore of the *Times,* Hitt also had an assistant on the debate trail, but nothing is known about him except that he was a French Canadian named Laramine whose job was to transcribe Hitt's notes.[15]

These phonographic reporters were reliable professionals, but it soon became apparent to politicians and ordinary readers alike that their debate transcripts differed substantially once in print. *Tribune* "verbatim" accounts of the debates magically transformed Lincoln's occasionally bumpy impromptu prose into seamless, cogent writing while presenting Douglas's words as informal and coarse. *Times* reports, in turn, abbreviated Douglas's windier phrases and also diluted some of his venom, frequently deleting the inflammatory adjective from one of his favorite attack phrases, "Black Republican," or changing his use of "nigger" to "negro." When angry Republicans began complaining that their own man was emerging as incomprehensible in the same *Times* renditions, the newspaper snapped back editorially that the Lincoln followers "were ashamed of his poor abilities and wanted to divert attention from them, under the cry of mutilation and fraud." Republican stenographer Hitt may have provided the earliest clue to the origin of such discrepancies when, recalling the debates thirty-five years later, he admitted: "I was employed to report them on the Republican side." That is precisely what he did, just as Binmore and Sheridan did the same for the Democratic side.[16]

Hitt went to his grave insisting that his transcripts of Lincoln's debate speeches were never significantly altered before going to press. "I mention this," he told an interviewer in 1893, "as it was often charged at that time in the fury of partisan warfare that Mr. Lincoln's speeches were doctored and almost re-written before they were printed; that this was necessary because he was so petty a creature in ability, in thought, in style, in speaking when compared with the matchless Douglas." Why, right in the middle of the Quincy meeting, hadn't Hitt faithfully dispatched his assistant to rush the notes for the first half of the debate to Chicago? Far from rewriting it, "I first saw the work printed in a newspaper," Hitt claimed, adding: "Mr. Lincoln never saw the report of any of the debates." Left unanswered was the question of whether either the stenographer or the candidate could reliably prove that no one else subsequently provided such editing—and whether what the *Tribune* ultimately published truly reflected exactly what Hitt had recorded from the speakers' platforms. Survivors like Hitt, called on years after Lincoln's death to feed the public's insatiable appetite for stories about the great man, seldom had anything disparaging to report; but their generosity probably owed more to Lincoln's subsequent elevation to national sainthood than to flawless recollection. For as the rival *Times* saw it back in 1858, these same *Tribune* transcriptions seemed to feature "whole paragraphs of which Lincoln's tongue was innocent."[17]

The Douglas paper launched a campaign to promote its own equally suspect record virtually as soon as the ink had dried on publication of the very first debate. Its highly polished Douglas transcript of Ottawa, they insisted, was "printed . . . literally," explaining: "There is no orator in America more correct in rhetoric, more clear in ideas, more direct in purpose, in all his public addresses, than Stephen A. Douglas. That this is so, is not our fault, but rather it is the pride of the Democracy of Illinois and of the Union." If the Republicans were howling over its version of Lincoln's performance at Ottawa, it was only because "they dare not allow Lincoln to go into print in his own dress; and abuse us, the TIMES, for reporting him literally." The way the Douglas organ saw it, anyone who heard Lincoln at Ottawa "must have been astonished at the report of that speech as it appeared in the *Press and Tribune.*" It went on:

> We did not attempt, much, to "fix up" the bungling effort; that was not our business. Lincoln should have learned, before this, to "rake after" himself—or rather to supersede the necessity of "raking after" by taking heed to his own thoughts and expressions. If he ever goes into the United States Senate—of which there is no earthly possibility—he will have to do that; in the congressional arena, the words of debaters are snatched from their lips, as it were, and immediately enter into and become a permanent part of the literature of the country. But it seems, from the difference between the two versions of Lincoln's speech, that the Republicans have a candidate for the Senate of whose bad rhetoric and horrible jargon they are ashamed, upon which before they would publish it, they called a council of "literary" men, to discuss, reconstruct, and re-write.

The *Times* was adamant. "We never touched a line," it insisted of its Lincoln transcript. Its version of his speech was exactly "as transcribed by the reporter, positively the speech he delivered." Unable to resist adding insult to injury, the newspaper went on to snicker: "Any one who has ever heard Lincoln speak . . . must know that he cannot speak five grammatical sentences in a row."[18]

Without responding specifically to the charge of "raking over" the Lincoln speeches, Republican newspapers went on the offensive. Citing "outrageous frauds," one journal counted 180 "mutilations" in a Chicago *Times* Lincoln transcript, and predicted that "an action for libel would hold against these villains," adding: "They richly deserve the prosecution." To the *Tribune*, "the whole aim has been to blunt the keen edge of Mr. Lincoln's wit, to mar the beauty of his most eloquent passages, and to make him talk like a booby, a half-witted numbskull." As the local *Daily Whig* charged after the Quincy debate, "Douglas carries around with him a reporter by the name of Sheridan, whose business it is to garble the speeches of Mr. Lincoln and amend and elaborate those of Mr. Douglas." A close inspection of the surviving transcripts reveals no such wholesale sabotage, yet even after the October 7 Galesburg debate, the *Tribune* was continuing to insist that the latest examples of alleged *Times* mutilation left Lincoln's words so "shamefully and outrageously garbled" and "emasculated" that if doctoring prose was a crime, "the scamp whom Douglas hires to report Lincoln's speeches would be a ripe subject for the Penitentiary." Their own transcribers, they boasted, were neither "hired puffers nor paid libelers," and their impartial reports had consistently won even Douglas's approval. "No complaint has been entered or exceptions taken to the accuracy and fairness of these reports," the paper contended.[19]

Of course, Douglas's newspaper had in reality been complaining loudly, and three days before the final debate at Alton, protested anew that the *Tribune* was not only routinely marring Douglas's speeches but, just as important, brazenly "re-writing and polishing the speeches of . . . poor Lincoln," who, they jabbed, "requires some such advantage."[20]

The earliest scholar of the Lincoln-Douglas debates saw a simple explanation for the wholesale discrepancies. Edwin Erle Sparks, who researched the transcripts for a useful fiftieth-anniversary edition in 1908, conceded: "Quite naturally the Democratic reporters did not exercise the same care" with "the utterances of Mr. Lincoln as with those of Mr. Douglas, and *vice versa.*" Left unsaid was precisely how such "care" had manifested itself in the bowdlerized partisan records. Citing White's reminiscences, Sparks assigned additional blame to "the lack of accommodations for writing, the jostling of the crowds of people, and the occasional puffs of wind which played havoc with sheets of paper." But Sparks's book presented the resulting "official" transcripts anyway—as have editors and historians ever since—even though it seems clear that behind the old charges of fraud and the shrill protests of innocence, both newspapers did precisely the same thing: they methodically "raked over" their man's flawed transcripts.[21]

Those who benefited the most from "raking over" steadfastly refused to acknowledge its existence, at least where their own words were concerned. But even in denying collusion in the friendly editing of his own transcripts—"The first I saw of my speeches, after delivering them, was in the *Press & Tribune,*" he insisted—Lincoln could not conceal his suspicion that Douglas's "two hired reporters . . . probably revised their manuscripts before they went to press." Lincoln's old friend Henry Clay Whitney remembered that Lincoln was careful never to vouch for the reliability of his *Tribune* record. He was simply willing to see them published "by *accepting* the Tribune's version of *his* speeches, and the

Times' versions of *Douglas'* speeches." Douglas himself pointed out later that the debates had been conducted "in the open air to immense crowds of people, and in some instances, in stormy and boisterous weather, when it was impossible for the reporters to hear distinctly and report literally." In his equally damning judgment, all texts reprinted later in book form were "imperfect, and in some respects erroneous"—including his own. He too yearned for the chance of "revising and correcting" them.[22]

Lincoln had had one such chance in the past, and, revealingly, seized it, demonstrating a perfect willingness to be edited, provided the result could help him. Four years before the debates, the same Horace White took down one of his speeches, displaying "absolute fidelity to ideas," the reporter admitted, but no more than "commendable fidelity to language." Lincoln protested not at all. "Well, those are my views," he drawled when he read the report, "and if I said anything on the subject, I must have said substantially that, but not nearly so well as that." Besides, Lincoln added, he retained "but a faint recollection of any portion" of the speech himself. Like all campaign orations, he explained, it was "necessarily extemporaneous"—just like the debates.[23]

Carefully read, even the newspaper columns themselves occasionally provided such frank admissions. The *Times,* for example, in the midst of maintaining that it had published the debates "exactly as . . . delivered," admitted freely that its proofreader had corrected "wanton violations of the rules of grammar" whenever he could do so "without destroying the sense." By the same token, as an old man, Horace White finally let slip that in proofreading the Hitt transcripts for publication, he had yielded to "the temptation to *italicise* a few passages in Mr. Lincoln's speeches, where his manner of delivery had been especially emphatic." What's more, in those "few cases where confusion on the platform, or the blowing of the wind, had caused some slight hiatus or evident mistake in catching the speaker's words," Hitt further admitted to making a few "changes." How often did the wind blow away a point, or a hiatus drown out a syllogism? White never specified, leaving the unexpurgated "opposition" texts of the Lincoln-Douglas debates the sole source of the elusive answers. The only concession White would offer was that there was "no foundation" for the early charges that the opposition *Times* had mutilated Lincoln's speeches. They simply "took more pains with Mr. Douglas's speeches," he explained, just as the *Tribune* did with Mr. Lincoln's. The gaps in the Douglas transcripts had merely been "straightened out by his own reporters, who would feel no responsibility for the rough places in Mr. Lincoln's"—as if straightening out the "rough places" was truly their responsibility to begin with.[24]

III

Given the partisan atmosphere that dictated the press's unwillingness either to see or to present any evidence of their candidates' flaws, is it possible to know how the debaters really performed on the stump? Happily, contemporaries left a rich archive of reminiscences that captured for posterity the almost comically divergent forms and styles of the tall, angular Lincoln and the short, combative Douglas.

"Two men presenting wider contrasts," a New York newspaperman observed, "could hardly be found as the representatives of the two great parties": Douglas, "a short, thick-set, burly man, with large round head, heavy hair, dark complexion, and fierce bull-dog bark . . . proud, defiant, arrogant, audacious," and Lincoln, "the opposite . . . tall, slender and angular, awkward even, in gait and attitude. . . . In repose, I must confess that 'Long Abe's' appearance is *not* comely. But stir him up and the fire of his genius plays on every feature." Lincoln needed all the fire he could summon to match his incendiary foe. Even Lincoln partisans like the *Tribune*'s Horace White could praise the senator's "unsurpassed powers of debate," admitting: "He could make more out of a bad case . . . than any other man this country ever produced." Another contemporary likened Douglas to a prizefighter, citing his "pluck, quickness, and strength," while Lincoln's friend and biographer Isaac N. Arnold grudgingly credited Douglas with "an iron will" and "great personal magnetism" wrapped up in a style that was "bold, vigorous . . . aggressive and at times even defiant." Arnold had to concede that Douglas was every bit Lincoln's equal—except in "wit and humor," where Lincoln enjoyed "a great advantage." Douglas, in turn, did not underestimate Lincoln. He reportedly confessed that Lincoln's "droll ways and dry jokes" made him nothing less than "the best stump speaker . . . in the West." Concluded the Little Giant: "If I beat him my victory will be hardly won."[25]

Many eyewitnesses to the debates went on to share their personal impressions of the encounters, like the sixteen-year-old boy who wiggled under the legs of some elderly farmers to get close to the speakers' platform at Ottawa. He later remembered Douglas as "leonine" in aspect, looking for all the world like "one born to command." Lincoln, on the other hand, while "gracious and smiling all through his two speeches," seemed "the very opposite in appearance and manner to Douglas." In oratory, the youngster thought Douglas "never lacked for words and uttered them with a force of speech calculated to carry conviction to his hearers. He made few gestures and these were graceful; an emphatic shake of the head and rather long black hair often ended a sentence." Lincoln, in turn, was "fluent, persuasive, and logical" in his presentation. He spoke, Horace White conceded, "in the accent and pronunciation peculiar to his native state, Kentucky": *Mr. Chairman* would come out as *Mr. Cheermun; there* sounded more like *thar.* But Lincoln made up for Douglas's superior elocution with dogged preparation. He wrote out long fragments. He consulted almost daily on the campaign trail with Horace and other party loyalists. Meanwhile, back in Springfield, he kept his law partner, William H. Herndon, "busy hunting up old speeches and gathering facts and statistics at the State Library." Recalled Herndon: "I made liberal clippings bearing in any way on the questions of the hour" and "sent books forward to him" on request. Kept in Lincoln's coat pocket thereafter, "to be drawn upon whenever the exigencies of debate required it," was a six-by-four-inch leather book with a brass clasp, in which Lincoln pasted not only newspaper articles but the second paragraph of the Declaration of Independence, along with a section of a Henry Clay oration and the opening of his own House Divided speech to the Convention that nominated him for Senator—"all the ammunition," Herndon remembered, "Mr. Lincoln saw fit to gather in preparation for his battle with Stephen A. Douglas."[26]

Not even potent ammunition, however, could make up for Lincoln's distinct disadvantages in appearance and manner. One of the last surviving witnesses to the final debate at Alton would recall forty years later "the tall, gaunt" Lincoln at first strikingly "ungraceful in his gestures," quite unlike the "short, thickset, and much more graceful Douglas," who kept Lincoln's House Divided speech in a little notebook of his own, frequently producing it to recite (and assail) his opponent's words in his own vividly contrasting voice and style. Yet even Lincoln's Kentucky twang, the Alton witness insisted, could echo with "an animation that bound the audience with a spell. . . . His tones rang out clear," while Douglas, exhausted by the long campaign, "sounded like . . . a mastiff giving short, quick barks." A small-town newspaper editor who attended the earlier Freeport debate, however, was aghast when he first caught sight of Lincoln in his "rusty-black Prince Albert coat with somewhat abbreviated sleeves." The bizarre image was made even more comical when, every so often, Lincoln would suddenly "bend his knees so they would almost touch the platform, and then . . . shoot himself up to his full height, emphasizing his utterances in a very forcible manner."[27]

To no less discerning—and presumably, hostile—an observer than Harriet Beecher Stowe, Stephen A. Douglas could claim "two requisites of a debater—a melodious voice and a clear, sharply defined enunciation." Another contemporary never forgot the "wrathful frown" Douglas wore in debate, which he punctuated by "defiantly shaking his head . . . clenching his fists and stamping his feet." Hearing the Little Giant, even a Lincoln man would admit to moments when he was "completely carried away with his masterful and fascinating manner." To a young Douglas admirer, the orator cast his spell with a voice that "rose and fell with the effortless volume of a great organ tone." The secret to Lincoln's eloquence, on the other hand, writer George H. Putnam remembered, "lay in the strength of his logical facility, his supreme power of reasoning." But "the first utterance of his voice was not pleasant to the ear," admitted Putnam, "the tone being harsh and the key too high." Only when his speech was well along did the voice gain "a natural and impressive modulation," illuminated by an "earnest look from the deeply-set eyes." Herndon verified that it took several minutes of outdoor public speaking before his partner's voice lost its "shrill, piping, unpleasant" timbre and "mellowed into a more harmonious and pleasant sound." But Lincoln "never acted for stage effect," Herndon added, ". . . never sawed the air nor rent space into tatters as some orators do." Douglas may have "electrified" audiences with his "majestic bearing," but Lincoln won them over eventually with his "logic and appeal to manhood." What was more, observed Herndon, when Lincoln turned during the debates to the subject dearest to him— the Declaration of Independence—"his little gray eyes flashed in a face aglow . . . [and] his uneasy and diffident manner sunk themselves beneath the wave of righteous indignation that came sweeping over him. Such was Lincoln the orator." It took a more impartial observer to notice also that Lincoln sometimes "stopped for repairs before finishing a sentence."[28]

One of the best accounts of the two debaters in action was left by the newspaperman Henry Villard, a Lincoln admirer who covered the encounter at Ottawa, and painted a vivid picture of the combatants in action at their first joint meeting:

> The Democratic spokesman commanded a strong, sonorous voice, a rapid, vigorous utterance, a telling play of countenance, impressive gestures, and all the other arts of the practiced speaker. As far as all external conditions were concerned, there was nothing in favor of Lincoln. He had a lean, lank, indescribably gawky figure, an odd-featured, wrinkled, inexpressive, and altogether uncomely face. He used singularly awkward, almost absurd, up-and-down and sidewise movements of his body to give emphasis to his arguments. His voice was naturally good, but he frequently raised it to an unnatural pitch. Yet the unprejudiced mind felt at once that, while there was on the one side a skillful dialectician and debater arguing a wrong and weak cause, there was on the other a thoroughly earnest and truthful man, inspired by sound convictions in consonance with the true spirit of American institutions. There was nothing in all Douglas' powerful effort that appealed to the higher instincts of human nature, while Lincoln always touched sympathetic chords.[29]

IV

That either candidate could communicate "the higher instincts of human nature"—or make himself understood at all—by the end of the grueling Senate campaign was a tribute to herculean endurance. The debates were even more physically demanding on the speakers than on their audiences, and what's more, the joint meetings constituted only a small part of the rigors they endured. Surviving recollections like Villard's have helped fuel a number of stubborn myths about the debates, including the reigning misconception that the staged encounters constituted the entire campaign for the Senate, and second, that they elevated the level of political debate to a lofty plane: a high-water mark in the golden age of political discourse seldom equaled before or since. Neither legend is supported by the facts.

The formal debates represented only a fraction of the candidates' overall efforts, although no other part of their campaigns attracted nearly as much attention, then or since. Both Lincoln and Douglas stumped the state tirelessly, delivering long orations to large crowds in the nondebate towns, repeating and refining the mantras that would become familiar elements of the speeches and rebuttals at their joint meetings. In all, Lincoln made at least 60 speeches during the 1858 race, and Douglas, by his own count, 130. Both crisscrossed the Illinois prairies until they had covered more than 4,300 miles apiece. Lincoln alone logged 350 miles by boat, 600 by carriage, and 3,400 by rail. Douglas preferred train travel—he had his own special car lavishly fitted out for the purpose, while Lincoln journeyed by ordinary coach. The senator occasionally traveled with his dazzling wife, Adele, and a sole staff aide—a rarity in the 1850s—a male secretary whose presence some detractors found ostentatious enough to report it disparagingly in the press. Lincoln, on the other hand, prudently left his troublesome wife, Mary, at home (she joined him only for the final debate), boasted no retinue of campaign advisers (except for partisan journalists), and seemed content merely to meet strangers and swap stories on the long trips from village to village. Not surprisingly, the challenger spent only $1,000 on his reelection bid, the incumbent a staggering fifty times more.[30]

As for the tone of debate, perhaps the best that can be said is that the meetings offered ideal opportunities for political discourse, but not always the lofty rhetoric such forums might have inspired. The unedited texts of the debates reveal with pellucid new clarity that the level of rhetoric by both of the 1858 candidates was seldom as majestic as folklore suggests. Defining statements, ringing perorations, and new ideas were very much the exception. The speakers attacked each other and defended themselves with biting humor, bitter sarcasm, and hellish fury, but seldom appealed—as generous eyewitnesses remembered— purely to "logic." In fact, the unaltered transcripts seem more star- tlingly than ever to confirm that the majority of time at each encounter was devoted to character attacks and conspiracy charges, replete with personal insults and name-calling, and not to a high-minded explora- tion of issues. In unadulterated form, the speeches seem especially targeted to appeal to their immediate audiences—the excited crowds ringing the speakers' platforms and frequently erupting with hurrahs and harassment—and not to the buyers of newspapers or books. Satisfy- ing reader demands would be left to others, later. Nor did the encoun- ters often provide the elusive "something new" that television so relent- lessly requires of modern political debates before anointing them as newsworthy, much less equal to the Lincoln-Douglas tradition. Excep-

tional interludes occurred—fresh charges, novel rebuttals, soaring perorations, engaging humor, slips of the tongue—but for the most part, the
only "smoking gun" at the Lincoln-Douglas debates was the brass
cannon that the Douglas forces transported to each city and fired noisily
whenever their candidate scored a particularly good "hit" on Lincoln.

Of course, Illinois voters were by then largely familiar with both the
messages and the messengers. Lincoln and Douglas had been arguing
the nuances of their respective positions for years. They had debated
publicly in 1854, when Douglas first championed the Kansas-Nebraska
Act, a law that overturned the thirty-four-year-old Missouri Compromise and opened territories acquired in the Louisiana Purchase to the
possibility of slavery. Then and thereafter, Douglas advocated a credo
known as "popular sovereignty," which held that citizens of every new
territory had the inherent right to vote slavery up or down for themselves. It was, he said, a sacred right of self-government. Lincoln opposed "squatter sovereignty," as he sometimes referred to it derisively,
pointing out that it enabled a small cadre of slaveholders to surge into
a new region and forge a skewed majority for slavery that would
institutionalize bondage long before large numbers of settlers arrived.
Was it fair, he asked, to bind future generations of pioneers to the vote
of a handful of zealots? Lincoln contended that slavery was a wrong
which the nation's founders had earmarked for extinction, that it ought
not to be extended into new territories under any circumstances. Douglas insisted the question was always best left to local areas to decide.[31]

By and large, all twenty-one hours of debate between Lincoln and
Douglas in 1858 radiated from this crucible of contention. The two
never discussed tariffs, land grants, internal improvements, or the growing needs of both farm and factory communities—only the intersecting
crisis points of slavery and union, in all their imaginable variations, save
for one: the future of black people in white America. Of course, all
Illinois voters, and most likely nearly all the people who witnessed the
debates in 1858, were white. And besides, as historian David M. Potter
pointed out, Douglas may have cared a great deal about slavery, but he
cared very little about the slaves. As for Lincoln, facing the prospect of
a free black population in America's future, he could do no better than
admit: "If all earthly power were given me, I should not know what to
do." Nonetheless, Douglas predictably charged that Lincoln was an
abolitionist who covertly harbored sympathy for equal rights for blacks.
Lincoln denied it, and claimed, in turn, to see in popular sovereignty

proof of Douglas's collusion in a plot to make slavery "perpetual and universal." As evidence, he cited not only Kansas-Nebraska but the explosive Dred Scott Supreme Court decision. That landmark 1857 ruling had not only declared that blacks could never be citizens, it opened up the possibility of expanding slavery by affirming property rights of slave owners no matter where they transported their chattel. Douglas supported the decision, despite the fact that it promised to outlaw popular sovereignty in its wake, citing the inviolability of all Supreme Court rulings; Lincoln attacked it as factually flawed and fatally illogical, and urged that the decision be overturned.[32]

When not debating slavery, the candidates occupied much of their debate time haranguing each other on purely diversionary points: Lincoln's earlier opposition to the Mexican War, Douglas's gaffe in erroneously recalling Lincoln's support for a radical Springfield Republican platform he had neither signed nor endorsed (but probably did not oppose), a battle over which of the two was the true heir of the founding fathers or of the late hero Henry Clay, Douglas's so-called moral indifference to slavery, Lincoln's supposed habit of changing his positions to suit different audiences in the northern and southern regions of the state, and a maze of alleged political conspiracies and plots. The debates frequently turned on personal, not political issues, and these distractions have never been more apparent than they are in the unedited transcripts.

Yet the debaters were capable too of examining with passion and persuasiveness both the nation's rich legacy and its imperiled future, drawing strikingly different visions of each. One of the most important—and perhaps the most memorable—ongoing battles of the Lincoln-Douglas debates came over interpreting the Declaration of Independence. To Lincoln, the inalienable rights it guaranteed were designed for every living person, white or black, free or slave, at least as far as they assured the basic opportunity to eat the bread earned with one's own hands. Douglas countered that America "was established on the white basis . . . for the benefit of white men and their posterity forever." He attempted to portray Lincoln as a closet abolitionist masquerading as a moderate. Lincoln answered that it was possible to oppose slavery without favoring "amalgamation"—the period word for race mixing. As the debates progressed, Douglas often resorted to such surly race-baiting that the modern reader may well cringe to see it spelled out on these pages. Still, even Lincoln used the word "nigger" in the encounters, though not as often as his opponent. It is useful to keep in mind that in the Illinois of 1858, racism was firmly institutionalized in law and in the constitution; only ten years earlier, its citizens had voted to bar blacks from its borders altogether. Lincoln and Douglas both reflected prevailing racist views, yet for all their biases and frequent use of ugly words so discordant to modern ears, each candidate stood only on the moderate rim of the political spectrum within his time, place, and party. There were Republicans more progressive (and others more conservative) on race than Lincoln, and Democrats for more reactionary than Douglas.

The debates had political as well as moral dimensions, offering both men the opportunity to fight for the middle ground in the battle for undecided votes in the swing counties of central Illinois. It was a given long before their first meeting that the vast majority of southern voters sympathetic to slavery would cast their ballots for Douglas, and antislavery men in the northern counties, for Lincoln. The election would be decided among those who identified themselves with neither faction.

In this struggle, Lincoln found himself at some disadvantage. Douglas had earlier broken with the pro-Southern wing of his party, and his president, James Buchanan, over the pro-slavery Lecompton Constitution proposed for Kansas. Courageously, Douglas risked his political future to oppose Lecompton on the grounds that an unacceptably small faction had written and ratified it, and that the whole document was not scheduled to be submitted to the people. His stand so impressed voters at home that for a time, there was actually talk of throwing Republican support behind his reelection effort. Lincoln blocked such an endorsement, and now Douglas was fighting desperately to hold together his Democratic coalition, while Lincoln was working tirelessly to ensure the survival of the new Republican party.[33]

To dramatize their differences, Lincoln had launched his own campaign in June 1858 with the most radical statement of his career. "A House divided against itself cannot stand," he declared in Springfield. "I believe that this government cannot endure, permanently, half *slave* and half *free*." From that point forward, Lincoln was compelled to defend his dire prophecy—although he never varied from it—while Douglas, arguing that the nation had indeed long existed "half slave and half free," and could continue to do so indefinitely, was emboldened to paint him as a dangerous disunionist. Apparently, few voters tired of the opportunity to hear these issues argued publicly. Only toward the very end of the schedule did debate attendance plummet. Otherwise, the Lincoln-Douglas meetings, however raucous, redundant, or diversionary, remained irresistible attractions for the people of Illinois at the time, gaining an even greater—some suggest an inflated—reputation for importance in the years since.[34]

The considerable impact of the debates has been further obscured, and perhaps exaggerated, by the stubborn historical suspicion that Lincoln shrewdly used the debates mainly to position himself for the presidency two years later, intentionally sacrificing his chances of victory in the Senate race, but also dooming Douglas's White House hopes in the bargain (for more details, see the Freeport debate). However farfetched, the question lingers at the heart of the overarching, still-debated question of who really won the 1858 war of words, for it deceptively encourages modern readers to forgive Lincoln almost anything he said in 1858 on the mistaken assumption that his tactics were calculated to defeat the dangerous Douglas for the White House two years later. Such an end understandably seems to justify practically any means required to achieve it in the eyes of admirers who cannot help recalling Lincoln the martyr when they should be remembering Lincoln the debater.

On the issue of which debater truly prevailed, most scholars believe, with James M. McPherson, that Lincoln won "in the judgement of history—or at least of most historians." Others, revisiting the debates in the light of twentieth-century mores, find Lincoln's views on race so much more palatable than Douglas's that they award him the decision by default.[35]

The unexpurgated transcripts may make a more informed answer possible. In these texts, the candidates' debating styles seem more starkly at odds than even their political principles: Douglas's fevered, occasionally vitriolic; Lincoln's more casual, sometimes self-deprecating. Douglas emerges the clear victor in at least one category: sustained bombast, a sure crowd pleaser in the 1850s. He also seemed to sense more instinctively when to reach for a concluding argument (one report marveled that he had stopped at the precise moment his time expired), while Lincoln often let his time run down anticlimactically, or halted before he was required to. Douglas played skillfully, if repugnantly by modern standards, to audience racism. And while Lincoln scored more persuasively on moral issues, Douglas seemed the superior in raining blows on his opponent, and also in forging neatly arranged sentences; Lincoln's words simply do not as often scan as coherently. Occasionally an inspired Lincoln did turn an unforgettable phrase that lingers in the mind's ear—as it undoubtedly did for audiences in 1858. And it would not be unfair to note that Douglas's words have similarly failed to endure. "He has no . . . splendid passages, no prophetic appeals, no playful turns," a journalist of the day admitted. "He deals only in argument." As a result, one suspects, his pronouncements are today neither recalled nor quoted. It is Lincoln who gave honor and meaning to the moral wrong of slavery; his views seem more modern, and so does his rhetorical technique. But that impression may rely more on hind-sight than on nineteenth-century sensibilities. The unedited transcripts reveal that it was Douglas who spoke more fluently, not Lincoln; it is difficult to imagine his even pausing for breath between flourishes. Now, as then, choosing a winner is largely a matter of taste, but Douglas's impassioned style may well have suited the age and situation better than Lincoln's amusing informality and clever appeals to logic.[36]

The newly excavated texts do serve to vivify Lincoln's early reputa-tion as a witty stump orator. He is genuinely funny, and his humor contrasts sharply with his opponent's penchant for heavy-handed, bela-bored taunts. But whether Lincoln's droll ripostes proved formidable enough to withstand Douglas's relentless, searing, and usually more cogently phrased attacks is open to question. Listening impatiently to his candidate, one Lincoln supporter longed to "see blood follow every time he closes a sentence." He rarely got his wish. In unedited form, Lincoln's restrained style seems less a match for Douglas's withering frontal assaults than the edited record has long indicated. The judgment is not foolproof, since even the "pure" transcripts reprinted here were in their day subject to question and challenge. But the sustained pattern of attack and parry emerges indelibly here, and the unaltered evidence indicates that Douglas, not Lincoln, was the more agile extemporane-ous public speaker. Writing many years later, Joseph F. Evans, an eyewitness to the Galesburg debate, recalled that "the revised editions of the printed debates" gave "an imperfect idea of their effect upon the audience, as a speech which required an hour and a half in delivery cannot be compressed into five or ten minutes' reading." Besides, Evans incisively noted, "the flavor, spirit and humor has vanished, and the skill of the orator to hold his audience does not appear on the printed page." The fresh perspective made possible by these long-ignored transcripts suggests that purely in terms of performance, not content, Stephen A. Douglas may well deserve what history has denied him: ultimate recognition as the winner of the great debates of 1858. As for the Lincoln texts, here, beyond the sometimes disjointed phrasing, can often be found logic as riveting and moral suasion as soaring as that in his most carefully written speeches as president. And more than a hint of greatness yet to come.[37]

That assessment, and the textual differences on which it is based, may not alter history. But it is possible that in their own time, they might have. Had the subsequently published book version of the Lincoln-Douglas debates featured unedited instead of polished texts, one might logically wonder whether Lincoln's stock among voters outside Illinois would still have risen in almost direct proportion to the volume's staggering 1860 sales. Many historians credit the broad distribution of that book with enhancing Lincoln's reputation; but would the boom have collapsed under the burden of his unedited debate transcripts? Of course, it is impossible to know for sure. But it is not unreasonable to conjecture that Lincoln would have enjoyed considerably less retrospective benefit from the debates had they been republished in the form in which they were originally heard.

In another sense, however, Lincoln nonetheless "won" the debates on three counts—first, merely by engaging his better-known rival (and emerging from the fray a national figure in his own right); second, by curtailing his party's brief flirtation with Douglas as a potential leader; and third, by emerging in edited print far better than he did in person. Whatever his inadequacies of gesture, voice, and syntax in the flesh, the *Tribune* reports and the book they inspired managed successfully to veil them. His choppy sentences were parsed, his roving syntax refined. The edited transcripts made it appear that he had more than held his own with one of the nation's most formidable debaters. Douglas's swaggering grandiloquence, on the other hand, so crackling in the unedited texts, seemed more stilted and purple in the formalized *Times* records. So it is not surprising that Lincoln's edited words went on to help establish him as an important voice for his party. With his speeches in print, local leaders, especially moderates, began talking of him as a favorite son candidate for president, his "House divided" sentiments apparently forgotten. Such approbation constituted a decided triumph for Lincoln, even if the *Tribune* deserved a share of the credit. "Public sentiment is everything," Lincoln had declared in the first debate. "He who moulds public sentiment is greater than he who makes statutes." Thanks at least as much to the edited record as to their stump performances, Douglas returned to the Senate to make statutes, while Lincoln won the battle to mold public sentiment.

Douglas won the debates if they are judged from the immediate political result alone: he was reelected to a third term in the Senate, and Lincoln was beaten. Yet even these results are too complex to be reported without providing some explanation. Not until 1913 did Americans obtain the right to elect their senators by direct popular vote. In 1858, state legislatures still chose U.S. senators, and that is where the Illinois contest between Lincoln and Douglas would ultimately be decided. On election day, no Illinois voters could cast ballots for either candidate directly; there was no so-called "beauty contest." Based on the legislative results and the votes cast for State Treasurer, the best estimates give the Republicans 125,000 votes, to 121,000 for the Douglas Democrats and 5,000 for the Buchanan Democrats. (The vote was closer—124,556 to 122,413 to 5,173—in the race for Superintendent of Public Instruction.) Thus Lincoln men bested Douglas men, although Democrats amassed slightly more total votes than Republicans. In the popular count, it was practically a dead heat, with Lincoln men, perhaps significantly, faring slightly better in those counties that hosted the seven debates.* However, in the all-important contest for legislative seats, forty-six went to Democrats, and forty-one to Republicans.[38]

Here there are further complications: thirteen more legislative seats were not up for reelection at all in 1858, eight of which were Democratic. That ensured a total of fifty-four votes for Douglas and forty-six for Lincoln in the final tally for the Senate. Some historians later claimed that the districts had been gerrymandered to guarantee a Democratic majority, or at least left unchanged despite an outmigration of pro-slavery southerners and the arrival of freedom-loving foreigners; others insist the district lines did not appreciably affect the result. The pro-Lincoln *State Journal* seemed surprised not by losing but "that we made so strong a fight." One thing was certain: the fight did not prove strong enough to unseat the incumbent.

"Let the past as nothing be," Lincoln wrote consolingly to a disappointed supporter a week after his defeat. "My view is that the fight must go on." As for his own future, he pledged to stand "in no one's way" for political office, merely to "fight in the ranks" in behalf of others. Glad as he was that he made the race, he claimed to believe its

*See table, p. 373.

outcome would render him politically extinct. Rather full of self-pity, he told a supporter: "I now sink out of view, and shall be forgotten."[39]

But destiny had different plans for Abraham Lincoln. And after a few more days mired in melancholy, the defeated candidate summoned the foresight to declare that "the cause of civil liberty must not be surrendered at the end of *one,* or even one *hundred* defeats." He assured one sympathetic correspondent, "I am neither dead nor dying." And another who Lincoln knew was "feeling like h--l yet," he encouraged: "Quit that . . . we shall have some fun again." Now beginning to look to the future, he confidently predicted: "Another explosion will come."[40]

The explosion came as prophesied. Lincoln triumphed at the Republican National Convention of 1860, and then Southern Democrats refused to join their Northern brethren in supporting Douglas to oppose him. In the ensuing four-way race for president—but one in which he would have prevailed even if the opposition had united around his old rival—Lincoln defeated Douglas and two others to win the presidency.[41]

No new debates were proposed for the 1860 campaign. Custom forbade it. Presidential nominees were still expected to conduct back-porch campaigns far from the hullabaloo of politics. Although Douglas broke with this tradition to stump the nation indefatigably, Lincoln stayed home, basking in the glow of the frenzied national campaign waged by the party in his behalf. Declaring it "imprudent," as he put it, "to write, or speak anything upon doctrinal points," he encouraged correspondents and visitors alike to reread his old orations, including the Lincoln-Douglas debates. "My published speeches contain nearly all I could willingly say," he declared in midcampaign. It was a wonderful example of subtle self-promotion. As Lincoln well knew, the debates were now available in a book version whose publication he had masterminded himself—a volume that helped elect him, but also helped compound and institutionalize the errors in the old edited transcriptions in the *Times* and *Tribune.*[42]

V

Only a few weeks after losing the Senate race to Douglas, Lincoln was already admitting to "being desirous of preserving in some permanent form, the late joint discussions between Douglas and myself." Before long, he had collected a complete run of transcripts from both the *Tribune* and the *Times* in a scrapbook. Displaying it to an old friend "with great satisfaction," he explained that "he had got a book binder to paste the speeches, in consecutive order, in a blank book, very neatly." He had done even more. "In my own speeches I have corrected only a few small typographical errors," he wrote a prospective publisher (the surviving scrapbook indicates he did a bit more work than he was willing at first to admit). And he offered Douglas, in turn, "the right to correct typographical errors in his, if he desired," alluding again to the old "mutilation" issue by adding: "I think the necessity in his case, would be less than mine. . . . I had no reporter of my own, but depended on a very excellent one sent by the Press & Tribune; but who never waited to show me his notes or manuscripts."[43]

Publishing these speeches directly from their respective party organs, Lincoln was now convinced, "would represent each of us, as reported by his own friends, and thus be mutual, and fair," to the candidates if not to the readers. Editorial comments and crowd reactions would be "rigidly" excluded. By Christmas 1858, he was openly predicting that "there is some probability that my Scrap-book will be reprinted," and the following March several publishers were indeed voicing interest. But one of the contenders soon dropped out of consideration, and while the remaining prospect maintained confidence that the proposed "experiment" would "sell readily and to good profit," Lincoln derailed the project by imposing impractical conditions. He wanted the book to be taken directly from his scrapbook, but he did not want the scrapbook "out of my own control." The publisher had no office in Springfield, but Lincoln suggested it be printed in his hometown "under my own supervision." The title he had in mind was dreadful: *Illinois political canvass of 1858.* These early plans went nowhere.[44]

Not until Lincoln toured neighboring Ohio in the election campaigns of 1859 was the project reinvigorated—and then quite by accident. Traveling that state to stump for Republican candidates, he left the scrapbook behind one day in a hotel room. To Lincoln's immense relief, the landlord retrieved it and sent the prize back to him. But in casting about for its safe return, he intrigued the Ohio Republican chairman, who reintroduced the notion of seeing it published in "authentic and permanent form." The contest for the White House was still a year away, but the state chairman astutely recognized that such a volume could become "essential . . . to the cause." Before long, the scrapbook was in the hands of the Columbus, Ohio, publishers, Follett, Foster & Co., and by the spring of 1860—perhaps even before the Republican National Convention met in Chicago in mid-May—the book was in print and on sale for fifty cents a copy and forty dollars per hundred, promoted as an essential tool for every "thorough and intelligent politician."[45]

But the "mutilation" issue refused to go away. Three months before its publication, word reached the Democrats that Lincoln had amended his remarks for the book. "You labor under a mistake, somewhat injurious to me," Lincoln protested to the editor of the Chicago *Times*, "if you suppose I have *revised* the speeches, in any just sense of the word. I only made some small verbal corrections, mostly such as an intelligent reader would make for himself, not feeling justified to do more."[46]

Lincoln reiterated this defense in a letter reproduced as the opening statement of the book. "The copies I send you are reported and printed, by the respective friends of Senator Douglas and myself, at the time," he wrote, "—that is, his by his friends, and mine by mine. It would be an unwarrantable liberty," he added, "for us to change a word or a letter in his, and the changes I have made in mine, you perceive, are verbal only, and very few in number." Lincoln may have protested a bit too much; a close examination of his well-preserved scrapbook suggests that he made more alterations than could reasonably be called either "verbal only" or "few in number."[47]

Notwithstanding the renewed controversy, the first edition of *Political Debates Between Hon. Abraham Lincoln and Hon. Stephen A. Douglas in the Celebrated Campaign of 1858, in Illinois* quickly became a best-seller. New printings were ordered, sales soon exceeded 30,000, and the publishers did not much exaggerate when they trumpeted: "Every Body Reads Them." As for its impact on the voters of 1860, two influential Lincoln scholars who showed considerable sympathy for Douglas—Albert J. Beveridge and James G. Randall—would use the identical word in conceding that the book successfully "advertised" Lincoln in his race for the presidency.[48]

Understandably, Stephen A. Douglas steadfastly maintained that the permanent record thus enshrined by Lincoln was "partial and unfair." It did not record the debates as he, for one, remembered them; the whole project was an "injustice." Even his own speeches suddenly seemed "ambiguous, incoherent, and unintelligible." Anyone could see, by contrast, that Lincoln's transcripts had been "revised, corrected, and improved." Indignantly Follett, Foster & Co. informed Douglas that in their view, "the speeches of Mr. Lincoln were never 'revised, corrected, or improved' "—at least not "in the sense you use those words." It was the old, familiar story. But by then it was too late to change it. Lincoln had never sought Douglas's permission to publish the debates.[49]

The publishing history of the Great Debates was in fact just beginning. By 1943, thirty-eight separate printings in book form had been recorded, and in 1958, the centennial year of the debates, historian Paul M. Angle put out yet another. *The Collected Works of Abraham Lincoln*, published between 1953 and 1955, included not only Lincoln's debate speeches but also Douglas's, as did Don Fehrenbacher's 1988 anthology of Lincoln's speeches and writings for the Library of America. All these reprintings were slavishly based on the scrapbook texts. The Little Giant's protests notwithstanding, the Lincoln scrapbook had become a permanent part of the historical vocabulary of American politics. For Lincoln students, it earned a status that placed them nearly above reproach: not only had the volume served successfully to introduce Lincoln to voters outside Illinois but, as Carl Sandburg cannily noted, it was also the only book Abraham Lincoln ever "wrote," "edited," and published. Generations earlier, when a journalist visited Lincoln's home shortly after his election to the presidency, he had spied, buried beneath "heaps and hills of newspaper" covering a table in the parlor, the old scrapbook that Lincoln had assembled after the debates. "Excellent reading they are, too," added the reporter, perhaps unaware of the controversy its contents had inspired.[50]

Already forgotten in the afterglow of the 1860 triumph, and long since relegated to the dustbin of history, was the fact that the debate book clearly presented something other than what "earwitnesses" had heard at Ottawa, Freeport, Quincy, and the other towns. Forgotten was the fact that partisan newspaper editors had irretrievably sanitized the texts to begin with, and that Lincoln himself had subsequently done some further damage to the historical record. "These debates are authentic," an advertisement for the original edition blithely declared, explaining—or perhaps thus contradicting its claim—that the texts had been "reported by the friends of each."[51]

And so the debates came down to us, not as they were argued originally but as the debaters and their supporters wanted them to be remembered. To know the real Lincoln-Douglas debates is to know the apotheosis of American political discourse as spectacle—with all weapons loaded, no holds barred, and audiences hanging on every word, unless they were vociferously interrupting to offer comments of their own.

But how to reassemble the "lost" debates? In fact, it proved such a deceptively simple enterprise that it is astonishing that it has never been attempted previously. What historians long enjoyed access to, but seldom consulted, were the Democratic versions of what Republican Lincoln said and the Republican versions of what Democrat Douglas said, unaltered at the time and unedited since. Buried there, then as now, were the real Lincoln-Douglas debates.

VI

As for the saga of Lincoln and Douglas themselves, with the 1860 campaign behind them, there was but a brief coda left before the final curtain fell on their long rivalry. On March 4, 1861, Abraham Lincoln rose on the portico of the U.S. Capitol to deliver his inaugural speech. The lantern jaws were now hidden beneath luxuriant whiskers. Gone were the awkward gestures. The dusty clothes had been replaced by a handsome new suit. But there was still the inevitable stovepipe hat, and as the incoming president glanced behind him in search of somewhere to place it, he saw his longtime opponent leaning forward, hand outstretched gallantly. "Senator Douglas took it with a smile," an onlooker reported, "and held it during the delivery of the Address." That night, Mary Lincoln, the new First Lady, triumphantly entered the inaugural ball on the arm of the man who, legend holds, rivaled her husband not only in politics but also in romance, in the long-ago contest for her affections. As the first chapter of Abraham Lincoln's presidency began, the final chapter of the Lincoln-Douglas competition concluded: the new chief executive returned to the White House to begin his work, while Douglas and Mary danced a sentimental quadrille.[52]

Less than three months later, after undertaking yet another arduous speaking tour, this time to plead for the preservation of the union, Stephen A. Douglas died suddenly in Chicago of complications from rheumatism. He was only forty-eight. Back in Washington, Lincoln solemnly ordered the White House draped in black, and directed that government offices be shut down out of respect. On the day of the Little Giant's funeral, Lincoln would see no visitors. He remained in isolation behind the closed doors of his office, his thoughts surely turning back to the unforgettable summer and fall of 1858.[53]

Lincoln's most famous speeches were before him. His triumphs at Gettysburg and the second inauguration were yet to come. But on that day, the voices of both of the century's greatest debaters were silent.

A WORD ON THE
TEXTS

THE TEXTS PUBLISHED HERE for the first time since 1858 are the unedited transcripts recorded on the spot during each Lincoln-Douglas debate by the *opposition* press. Previous anthologies presented only the much improved, suspiciously seamless versions supposedly recorded simultaneously by each debater's friendly newspaper.

The resurrection of these unexpurgated transcripts will give modern readers long-overdue access to the debates as they were likely heard originally by the multitudes who witnessed the encounters back in 1858. In the process, the historical record will finally be liberated from reliance on texts that long ago were processed through the alembic of hired reporters, sympathetic publishers, and ultimately Lincoln himself, whose editorial hand guided the book-length version that, in turn, has provided the basis of all the published versions since.

But as this project progressed, it became clear that adjustments would have to be made. Short of presenting every word of every transcript of every debate side by side for comparison, each page annotated with footnotes, a compromise system seemed better suited to the effort to exhume these old texts and present them to new readers.

In reading both the Republican and Democratic versions of the debates together, line by line, for example, it became obvious that all too often the various "phonographic experts" on both sides of the contest not only heard things differently but heard different things. Huge discrepancies occasionally leapt from the page and demanded clarification. So in presenting those sections which the two stenographers heard in dissimilar ways, we chose to present *both* versions—with the "friendly" alternative in the form of a bracketed insert. It is instructive that, charges to the contrary, there were only a few occasions to be found in the record of the "emasculation" and "mutilation" reported at the time (readers are alerted to all of them and supplied alternative passages within the text).

Read side by side, the texts often prove startlingly different. One of the most frequently quoted of Lincoln's aphorisms, for example—"he who moulds public sentiment, goes deeper than he who enacts statutes or pronounces decisions," as the pro-Republican press reported it from the first debate at Ottawa—was heard by opposition Democrats there in far less stylish, more truncated prose. It was simply "he who moulds public sentiment is greater than he who makes statutes." Who can say for certain whether the pro-Douglas press fractured Lincoln's wording as he spoke it, or whether pro-Lincoln reporters enhanced it later? But the latter explanation seems more believable.

In another revealing example, Lincoln's well-known comments at the final debate at Alton were again heard quite differently by Republican-hired and Democrat-hired stenographers. As Lincoln's man heard it, he said:

> That is the real issue. That is the issue that will continue in this country when these poor tongues of Judge Douglas and myself shall be silent. It is the eternal struggle between these two principles—right and wrong—throughout the world. They are the two principles that have stood face to face from the beginning of time; and will ever continue to struggle. The one is the common right of humanity and the other the divine right of kings. It is the same principle in whatever shape it develops itself. It is the same spirit that says, "You work and toil and earn bread, and I'll eat it." No matter in what shape it comes, whether from the mouth of a king who seeks to bestride the people

of his own nation and live by the fruit of their labor, or from one race of men as an apology for enslaving another race, it is the same tyrannical principle.

It is a superbly crafted passage. But it is not what the rival press heard at Alton. As the Democratic reporter transcribed it, Lincoln said:

That is the real issue! An issue that will continue in this country when these poor tongues of Douglas and myself shall be silent. These are the two principles that are made the eternal struggle between right and wrong. They are the two principles that have stood face to face, one of them asserting the divine right of kings, the same principle that says you work, you toil, you earn bread, and I will eat it. It is the same old serpent, whether it come from the mouth of a king who seeks to bestride the people of his nation, and to live upon the fat of his neighbor, or whether it comes from one race of men as an apology for the enslaving of another race of men. It is the same old policy. . . .

Again, while the Democratic version lacks polish, it echoes with an impromptu-sounding immediacy lacking in the version published by Lincoln's allies. In the light of its long-delayed exposure, it can clearly be argued that the opposition version of all the transcripts deserve to be included on history's bookshelf, at the very least alongside the editions once approved by Lincoln, Douglas, and their supporters.

True, these newly unearthed rival transcripts may be no more perfectly dependable than the texts produced last century by the candidates' backers, but they may well be no more flawed, either. And it might logically be argued that the unfriendly supporters who transcribed these halting, imperfect sentences were surely no more likely to have altered them out of malice than were the friendly reporters and editors likely to improve theirs out of sympathy.

At the very least, many of the long-ignored turns of phrase revealed in these transcripts open new windows onto how the candidates really sounded. One particularly intriguing example occurs in the first debate when Lincoln refers to Henry Clay, or so we have long thought, as "my beau ideal of a statesman." The phrase has been cited so many times by biographers that it has entered the historical language. But the Democratic Chicago *Daily Times* heard Lincoln say "my beau ideal of a *great man* [emphasis added]," not "statesman." A minor point, but illustrative. How, logically, could the *Times* have flawlessly heard the less coherent French part of that phrase and somehow missed the English part? We cannot know for sure, but at the very least, the discrepancy enlightens us on how Lincoln pronounced his words. Even if he did say "statesman" that day, he evidently emphasized the second syllable, not the first. Clay was not a "*states*man" but a "states*man,*" which makes it easier to understand how one or the other stenographer misheard it. Surely readers deserve to read both versions when transcripts so differ, and on these pages, they will.

On other occasions, friendly editors softened harsh or colloquial phraseology to make it gentler on the eyes of its readers than it had been on the ears of its listeners. The *Press and Tribune,* for example, usually deleted the adjective whenever Douglas railed against "Black Republicans." We chose here to let the blemished transcripts speak eloquently of the drama of the moment, if not the seamless prose of the orators. But again, alternative words and phrases are occasionally provided in brackets for the sake of comparison.

Then there were the moments when crowds erupted into such an avalanche of noise that stenographers confessed, right in their transcripts, their inability to follow whole sentences at a time. In such instances, alternative transcripts become vital tools to fill in blanks, even if the careful reader will wisely question how one reporter could have kept up his work uninterrupted while another confessed himself deafened by ambient sounds.

Where crowd noise is concerned, Lincoln deleted all mention of it from his "scrap-book," an ill-advised decision fortunately overturned by subsequent editors who long ago rescued the cheers and catcalls from obscurity. But in its restored state, even this long-accepted record is problematical. The Republican stenographer always seemed to hear wild, enthusiastic outbursts for Lincoln when the Democratic reporter heard mere applause. And the Democratic stenographer predictably heard frenzied applause for Douglas when the Lincoln reporter remained suspiciously deaf to the approbation. As the *Daily Press and Tribune* complained editorially about the *Daily Times* stenographer in October 1858: "The fellow has even gone the length of suppressing the cheers and applause that so frequently greeted the remarks of Mr. Lincoln, while he has thickly interspersed Douglas' harrangues with such ejaculations as 'Great laughter,' 'Loud shouts,' and 'Tremendous cheers,' when it is notorious that his remarks excited neither the one nor the other."

While it is next to impossible to imagine that the so-called phonographic reporters intentionally mangled opposition texts in the midst of taking rapid shorthand, it does not strain credulity to imagine their being either reluctant to concede audience approval during an opponent's speech or eager to insert evidence of applause that no one else heard when their own candidate was holding forth. Our editorial solution seemed obvious: crowd reactions as interpreted by *both* sides is included in bracketed inserts, the rival paper's first. (Brackets are used throughout, even though the *Times* reported crowd response in parentheses.) Readers will want to judge for themselves which reaction seems more probable, and will likely be amused by the more shameless discrepancies in the "record." (And as a further effort to make all inserts as concise as possible, the newspapers are throughout identified only as the *Tribune* and the *Times*.)

We also let stand a Democratic report from the Ottawa debate that portrayed Lincoln becoming so agitated during Douglas's remarks that he had to be restrained by his followers. The Republican press never reported the incident, and, although obliged later under his own rules for adaptation to use the *Times* clippings of Douglas's speeches in preparing his scrapbook, Lincoln nonetheless deleted all reference to it. But surely such reports deserve again to be mentioned, so they are restored to the text here, carefully annotated to remind readers that the newspapers did not always agree that such incidents occurred, and even when they did, seldom concurred about the details.

In editing these texts, punctuation errors have been cleansed, although several obvious errors have been retained, and identified through the use of *"sic."* Spelling mistakes—especially where proper names were given incorrectly—have been corrected as well. But the fragmented thoughts that came to a halt too soon to make perfect sense, and the long-winded sentences that lurched in one direction and then drifted off uncontrollably in another, have all been retained intact.

So, of course, have proper names. But while midcentury partisans were well acquainted with the political celebrities and political jargon of the day—Lincoln on one occasion elicited a knowing laugh by referring to Douglas, President Buchanan, and Chief Justice Taney respectively as Stephen, James, and Roger—today's readers can hardly be expected to know, for example, that a "Danite" was the period epithet for a pro-Buchanan, anti-Douglas Democrat, or that southern Illinois was then colloquially known as "Egypt." Nor have the more obscure elected officials of the day—even a onetime presidential candidate like Lewis Cass—retained sufficient name recognition to be readily recalled today. To help, where appropriate, editorial identifications have been sprinkled into the text, often enough, it is hoped, to provide context to the material, yet sparingly enough so that interpretation does not lapse into interruption.

Finally, readers will undoubtedly notice that Lincoln preferred to call his opponent *Judge*, not *Senator* Douglas, a reference to the Little Giant's early days on the Illinois bench. The Democratic *Times* frequently referred to him the same way, so the title was not purely pejorative. But Lincoln could not help at one point during the debates reminding the audience that while Douglas deserved credit for bringing about the expansion of the state's judicial system, he had somehow managed to emerge from his public-spirited effort a judge himself. The crowd roared with laughter, in true Lincoln-Douglas debate style.

THE FIRST JOINT
DEBATE AT OTTAWA

Saturday, August 21, 1858

·THE SCENE·

THE FIRST LINCOLN-DOUGLAS DEBATE began late. No one was
prepared for the crush of humanity that poured into the
overwhelmingly Republican village of Ottawa on that searingly hot
day, and no one made adequate provisions to control the crowd.
The result bordered on chaos, and Lincoln later confided of the
"vast concourse of people" that there were "more than could [get]
near enough to hear."

A canal town hugging the Fox and Illinois rivers midway between
Chicago and Peoria in the northern part of the state, Ottawa could
claim a permanent population of at most 7,000. But by debate day,
between 10,000 and 20,000 more—estimates varied wildly—arrived
in town from all directions to fill Ottawa to overflowing.

"Men, women, and children, old, and young," as one reporter
described the arrivals, flooded in on foot, on horseback, in ox-drawn

wagons, in fancy carriages, and aboard huge canal boats
emblazoned with political banners. A fourteen-car special train
hauled in spectators at half fare from Chicago, while eleven extra
cars brought another crowd from Peru and La Salle. By early
morning, the "great multitude" tramping through the unpaved
streets left the town so "shrouded in dust" that the scene looked to
one onlooker like "a vast smoke house."

Then at one p.m., a full hour before the speeches were scheduled
to begin, the throng began surging into the modest public square,
quickly transforming it into "one mass of active life." Most
spectators rushed forward to secure good standing room—no chairs
had been provided, and onlookers complained bitterly about the
"wretched accommodations"—while others brazenly overran the
unguarded speakers' platform. As the audience howled with
laughter, a few daredevils clambered onto its wooden awning,
leaping about recklessly until they came crashing down through the
roof and onto the laps of the few startled dignitaries who had finally
fought their way to their seats.

Under a scorching summer sun, national flags, patriotic bunting,
and motto-bedecked banners fluttered dazzlingly in the hot breeze.
Peddlers hawked their goods at every corner, military units drilled
solemnly, and musicians strained to make their martial tunes audible
over the deafening crowd noise. At regular intervals the overall din
was magnified by an explosion of artillery salutes that seemed to
make the earth tremble. There were only a few trees in the square
to shade the crowd, and tempers flared as hot as the weather: fueled
by an abundant supply of liquid refreshment, Democrats fought with
Republicans and Republicans argued with Democrats, while
overwrought marshals pompously girdled in "partisan" sashes tried
vainly to keep order. "Vanity Fair," one journalist on the scene
marveled, "never boiled with madder enthusiasm."

Lincoln had arrived earlier in the day aboard a seventeen-car
train bulging with supporters. Escorted into town in an
evergreen-laden carriage, he was now resting in the mayor's house.
Douglas made his entrance in "an elegant carriage drawn by six
white horses," at the head of a procession of flag-waving supporters;
he was ensconced at the local hotel. Now the candidates at last
appeared on the scene, inching their way through blocked sidewalks

and toward the stage as the clamor around them intensified feverishly. Cheers echoed through the square as both men ascended the platform. A long half hour behind schedule, the Lincoln-Douglas debates finally got under way at two-thirty p.m.

Douglas was the opening speaker, and he occupied his hour introducing charges with which he would goad his opponent throughout the encounters to come. Lincoln was a dangerous radical. Lincoln had dishonorably opposed the Mexican War as a congressman a decade earlier. Lincoln was conspiring to "abolitionize" the old Whig and Democratic parties. Lincoln's opposition to the Supreme Court's Dred Scott decision, and its ban on citizenship for blacks, would lead to increased black immigration into Illinois. And Lincoln secretly favored a four-year-old set of radical resolutions adopted in Springfield, which called for repeal of the fugitive slave law, the emancipation of slaves in the nation's capital, and other "Black Republican" goals. Douglas ended his searing attack by posing seven pointed questions to his rival, and he challenged Lincoln to respond to each.

Lincoln's unusual stump style provided the audience with a distinct change of pace. Where Douglas had been angry and bombastic, Lincoln appeared relaxed and jovial. He donned spectacles to read from an old speech, jokingly explaining to the crowd that he was "no longer a young man." He teased that the diminutive Douglas was a "great man" and he but a "small man." And he drew roars of laughter in denying Douglas's libel that he had operated a "grocery," or saloon, as a young man in New Salem, by admitting only that he had once worked at "a little still house up at the head of the hollow." Ignoring Douglas's interrogatories, he switched rhetorical gears to dwell eloquently on the original promise of the Declaration of Independence, and reminded the crowd that his political hero, Henry Clay, a slaveholder, never denied its applicability to blacks as well as whites. Still, Lincoln, who seldom used the word "nigger" publicly, used it twice even in progressive Ottawa, whose congressman, Owen Lovejoy, was on race issues the most advanced officeholder in Illinois. Finally, Lincoln brushed aside Douglas's attack on the radical Springfield resolutions by pointing out that he had not even been in Springfield when they were adopted, and had never authorized support for them.

Douglas resumed his fierce attack during his half-hour rejoinder, reminding the crowd that Lincoln had again failed to specifically renounce the controversial Springfield resolutions, and chiding him for refusing to respond to his set of questions. When it was all over, supporters hoisted a surprised Lincoln on their shoulders—in triumph, boasted Republican newspapers later; Democratic journals insisted that the "funeral procession" was organized because Douglas's onslaughts had left Lincoln's "limbs cold" and "his respiratory organs . . . obstructed." In the Louisville *Journal*'s opinion: "If they had foreseen how he would come out in the debate, they would have borne him off before it commenced."

As the Democratic press saw it, Douglas had "electrified the crowd" at Ottawa, while Lincoln "dodged" and looked "embarrassed." Republican journals, on the other hand, thought Lincoln appeared "high toned" and "powerful," and Douglas "boorish" and "cowardly." From faraway New York, Horace Greeley's New York *Tribune* cheered that Lincoln had turned the race into nothing less than "a contest for the Kingdom of Heaven or the Kingdom of Satan—a contest for advance or retrograde in civilization."

But Lincoln's Republican friends at home privately worried that he had appeared far too defensive at Ottawa, and urged him to be more aggressive at the next debate. Law associate Henry Clay Whitney told the candidate bluntly that he had "dodged on the platform," and pleaded with him not to handle Douglas so "tenderly" next time. "You have got to treat him severely," he advised, "& the sooner you commence the better & easier." A debate eyewitness from nearby Tiskilwa agreed that Lincoln had erred in not answering Douglas's Ottawa interrogatories. *"I think that any answer,"* he wrote sternly, *"is better than none."* Bluntest of all was the disappointed editor of the pro-Lincoln Chicago *Press and Tribune*. "For God's sake," pleaded Charles H. Ray, "tell him to 'Charge Chester! Charge!' "

Lincoln himself shrugged off all the criticism, writing in mock relief to a friend: "Douglas and I, for the first time in this canvass, crossed swords here yesterday, the fire flew some, and I am glad to know I am still alive."

The transcripts follow: the pro-Republican Chicago *Daily Press and Tribune*'s for Democrat Douglas's opening speech and rejoinder, the pro-Democratic Chicago *Daily Times*'s for Republican Lincoln's rebuttal.

Mr. Douglas' Opening Speech

At half past two, Mr. Douglas took the front of the platform, amid the cheers of the Hibernians, who had fought their way to the front [such references to the overwhelmingly Democratic Irish, typical in the Republican press of the day, were designed to alarm voters who feared immigration and disliked foreigners—*ed.*], and said:

Mr. Douglas said—Ladies and gentlemen. I appear before you to-day for the purpose of discussing the leading political topics which now agitate the public mind. This vast concourse of people shows the deep feeling which pervades the masses in regard to this question. By an arrangement previously made, we have to-day a joint discussion between Mr. Lincoln and myself as the representatives of the two great political parties in this State and the Union.

Prior to 1854, this country was divided into two great political parties, known as the Whig and Democratic parties—both national and patriotic in their principles—both advocating principles which were universal in their application. An old line Whig could proclaim his principles in Louisiana and in Massachusetts alike. Whig principles were not limited by the Ohio river, nor by the Potomac, nor by the line of the free and the slave States, but applied and were proclaimed wherever the Constitution ruled, or the American flag waved over American soil. [Hear him, and three cheers. —*Times*] So it was and so it is with the principles of the great Democratic party, which from the days of Jefferson until this period, had proven itself to be the historical party of this nation. While the Whig and the Democratic parties differed in regard to a Bank, and in regard to a Tariff, and in regard to Distribution, and in regard to the Specie Circular [President Jackson's 1836 order that the government accept only specie in public land sales—an effort to arrest speculative fever—*ed.*], and in regard to the Sub-Treasury, they agreed on the great question that now agitates the Union, known as the Slavery question. I say that Whigs and Democrats agreed on this Slavery question, while they differed on those matters of expediency to which I have referred.

The Whig party and the Democratic party jointly adopted the compromise measures of 1850 as the basis of the solution of the slavery question in all of its forms. Clay was the great leader, with Webster on his right and [Lewis] Cass [senator from Michigan—*ed.*] on his left, sustained by the patriots in the Whig and Democratic ranks, in devising, and adopting, and enacting the compromise measures of 1850 [an attempted final solution to the sectional crisis, fathered by Henry Clay and championed by Douglas, which its advocates believed would defuse the volatile slavery issue. But more than two thirds of Congress voted against at least some elements of the package, and it managed only to postpone the conflict to come—*ed.*]. Again, in 1851, in Illinois, the Whig party and the Democratic party united in resolutions endorsing and approving the compromise measures of 1850 as the proper adjustment of this question. In 1852, when the Whig party assembled at Baltimore, for the purpose of nominating its candidate for the Presidency, the first thing it did was to adopt the compromise measures of 1850, in substance and in principle, as the satisfactory adjustment of that question.

[Here a number of persons began to applaud, when one strong-voiced applauder, with more enthusiasm than the rest, prolonged the strain until it ended in a melancholy howl, which produced great laughter. —*Tribune;* Here the speaker was interrupted by loud and long continued applause. —*Times*]

Mr. Douglas continued. My friends, silence is more acceptable to me in the discussion of this question than applause. I desire to address myself to your judgment—to your understanding—to your consciences—and not to your passions. I was saying, when the Democratic Convention assembled at Baltimore, in 1852, for the purpose of nominating a candidate to the Presidency, they also adopted the Compromise measures of 1850 as the basis of Democratic action. Thus you see that up to 1853–4, the Whig party and the Democratic party both stood on the same platform in regard to the Slavery question which now agitates the country. That platform was the right of the people of each State and of each Territory to decide their local and domestic institutions for themselves, subject only to the Federal Constitution.

At the session of 1853–4, I introduced into the Senate of the United States a bill to organize the Territories of Kansas and Nebraska on that principle, which had been adopted in the Compromise measures of 1850, approved by the Whig party and the Democratic party and the Democratic party in Illinois in 1831, and endorsed by the Whig party and the Democratic party in the national Conventions of 1852. In order that there might be no misunderstanding in regard to the principle involved in the Kansas and Nebraska bill, I put forth the true intent and meaning of the act in these words: "It being the true intent and meaning of this act not to legislate slavery into any State or Territory, not to exclude it therefrom, but to leave the people thereof perfectly free to form and regulate their domestic institutions in their own way, subject only to the Federal Constitution."

Thus you see that up to 1854, when the Kansas and Nebraska bill [whose "popular sovereignty" provisions had aroused Lincoln to re-enter politics—*ed.*] was brought into Congress for the purpose of carrying out the principles which, up to that time, both parties had endorsed and approved, there had been no division in this country in regard to that principle, except the opposition of the Abolitionists. In the Illinois Legislature, in the House of Representatives, upon the resolution asserting that principle, every Whig and every Democrat in the House voted for that principle. Only four men voted against it, and those four men were Old Line Abolitionists. [Cheers. —*Times*] In 1854, Mr. Abraham Lincoln and Mr. [Lyman] Trumbull [U.S. senator and 1858 Lincoln supporter—*ed.*] entered into an arrangement one with the other, and each with their respective friends, to dissolve the old Whig party on the one hand, and to dissolve the old Democratic party on the other hand, and convert the members of both parties into an Abolitionist party under the name [and disguise —*Times*] of the Republican party. [Applauses and hisses. —*Tribune;* Laughter and cheers, hurrah for Douglas. —*Times*] The terms of that arrangement between Mr. Lincoln and Mr. Trumbull have been published to the world by Mr. Lincoln's special friend, Mr. James H. Matheney [the best man at Lincoln's 1842 wedding—*ed.*], which was that Mr. Lincoln was to have Gen. [James] Shields' [longtime Lincoln foe and Democratic U.S. senator unseated by Trumbull—*ed.*] place—then about to become vacant in the United States Senate—and Mr. Trumbull was to have my place. [Great laughter. —*Times*] Mr. Lincoln went to work industriously to abolitionize the old Whig party all over the State, pretending that he was as good a Whig as he ever was. [Laughter. —*Times*] Trumbull went to work in his part of the State, down in Egypt [southern Illinois—*ed.*], preaching Abolitionism in a milder and a lighter form, and of not quite as dark a color, but yet trying to abolitionize the Democratic party and bring the old Democrats handcuffed, bound hand and foot into the Abolition camp. ["Good," "hurrah for Douglas" and cheers. —*Times*]

In pursuance of that arrangement, the parties met at Springfield in October, 1854, and proclaimed their new platform. Mr. Lincoln was to bring into the Abolition camp the old line Whigs, and transfer them over to [Joshua R.] Giddings [abolitionist congressman from Ohio—*ed.*] and [Salmon P.] Chase [antislavery former senator from, then governor of Ohio, later Lincoln's treasury secretary—*ed.*], Fred[erick] Douglass [the country's best-known black leader—*ed.*], [Owen] Lovejoy [Republican congressman and ardent Lincoln booster; he sat on the speakers' platform during this debate—*ed.*] and [John F.] Farnsworth [congressman from Chicago—*ed.*], who were then ready to receive and christen them into Abolitionists. [Laughter and Cheers. —*Times*] They laid down on that occasion a platform for this new Republican party, which was to be constructed out of the old Whig party and the old Democratic party, by abolitionizing both and transferring them to abolitionism. I have the resolutions of that Convention, which was the first Mass State Convention ever held in Illinois by the Republican party. I now hold them in my hand, and will read a part of the resolutions and cause the others to be printed. Here is one of the resolutions and the most material one of this Abolition platform, under the new name of Republicanism:

2. *Resolved,* That the times imperatively demand the reorganization of parties, and repudiating all previous party attachments, names and predilections, we unite ourselves together in defense of the liberty and constitution of the country, and will hereafter co-operate as the Republican party, pledged to the accomplishment of the following purposes: to bring the administration of the government back to the control of first principles; to restore Nebraska and Kansas to the position of free territories; that, as the constitution of the United States vests in the States, and not in Congress, the power to legislate for the extradition of fugitives from labor, to repeal and entirely abrogate the fugitive slave law; to restrict slavery to those States in which it exists; to prohibit the admission of any more slave States into the Union; to abolish slavery in the District of Columbia; to exclude slavery from all the territories over which the general government has exclusive jurisdiction; and to resist the acquirements of any more territories unless the practice of slavery therein forever shall have been prohibited.

[The resolutions, as they were read, were cheered throughout. —*Times*] [Douglas read only Resolution No. 2, but submitted a total of three resolutions for publication two days later in the *Times,* a clear indication of their editors' collaboration in the effort to enhance the senator's debate texts in print—*ed*.] Now, gentlemen, you have cheered—you Republicans have cheered every one of these propositions [renewed cheers. —*Tribune;* "Good and cheers." —*Times*], and yet I venture to say that you cannot get Mr. Lincoln, your candidate, to come out and say that he is now for each one of them. [Laughter and applause. "Hit him again." —*Times*] That these propositions do one and all constitute the platform of the Black Republican party this day, I have no doubt ["good." —*Times*], and when you were not aware for what purpose I was reading these resolutions, you cheered them as good Black Republican doctrine [cheers. —*Tribune;* "That's it," &c. —*Times*], and yet my object in reading them is to put the question to Abraham Lincoln this day, whether he now stands, and will stand by each article of that creed, and carry them all out. ["Good," "Hit him again." —*Times*] I desire to know whether Mr. Lincoln to-day stands pledged as he did in 1854, in favor of the unconditional repeal of the Fugitive Slave Law. I desire him to answer whether he stands pledged to-day as he did in '54, against the admission of any more slave States, even if the people want them. I want to know if he stands pledged to vote against the admission of a new State into the Union with such a Constitution as the people of that State may see fit to make. ["That's it," "put it at him." —*Times*] I desire to know whether he stands pledged to-day to the abolition of slavery in the District of Columbia. I desire to know whether he stands pledged to abolish and prohibit the slave trade between the different States. ["He does." —*Times*] I desire to know whether he stands pledged to prohibit slavery in all the Territories of the United States, North as well as South of the Missouri Compromise line [36° 30′ latitude—*ed*.]. ["Kansas too." —*Times*] I desire him to answer whether he is opposed to the acquisition of any more territory, unless slavery is first prohibited therein. I want his answer. Your affirmative cheers in favor of this Abolition platform are not satisfactory; but I want Abraham Lincoln to answer these questions, in order that when I trot him down into Lower Egypt [colloquialism for the southern areas of Illinois, whose residents were more pro-slavery than elsewhere in the state—*ed*.], I may compel him to repeat the same. [Enthusiastic applause. —*Times*]

My principles are the same everywhere. [Cheers, and "hark." —*Times*] I can proclaim them alike in the north and in the south, in the east and in the west. My principles will apply wherever the Constitution prevails, and the American flag waves over American territory. ["Good," and applause. —*Times*] I desire to know whether Mr. Lincoln's principles will bear to be transplanted from Ottawa to Jonesboro. I put these questions to him to-day and ask an answer. I have a right to an answer upon these ["That's so," "he can't dodge you," &c. —*Times*] for I quote them from the platform of the Republican party— the platform made by himself and others at the time the Republican party was first formed, and the bargain was made to dissolve and kill off and destroy the old Whig and Democratic parties, and transfer each of their members, bound hand and foot, into the Abolition party, under the directions of Giddings and Chase. [In the official transcript, Douglas or his supporters substituted the name of "Fred" Douglass here, probably hoping it would prove more inflammatory—*ed.*] [Cheers. —*Times*]

In the remarks which I have made upon this platform, and the positions of Mr. Lincoln upon it, I mean nothing personal, disrespectful or unkind to that gentleman. I have known him for nearly twenty-five years. We had many points of sympathy when I first got acquainted with him. We were both comparatively boys—both struggling with poverty in a strange land for our support. I an humble school teacher in the town of Winchester, and he a flourishing grocery [in frontier parlance, a saloon—*ed.*] keeper in the town of Salem. [Laughter. —*Tribune*; Applause and laughter. —*Times*] He was more successful in his occupation than I, and thus became more fortunate in this world's goods. Mr. Lincoln is one of those peculiar men that has performed with admirable skill in every occupation that he ever attempted. I made as good a school teacher as I could, and when a cabinet maker I made the best bedsteads and tables, but my old bones said I succeeded better in bureaus and secretaries than in anything else. [Laughter. —*Tribune*; Cheers. —*Times*] But I believe that Mr. Lincoln was more successful in his business than I, for his business soon carried him directly into the Legislature. There I met him in a little time, and I had a sympathy for him, because of the up hill struggle that we had in life. [Cheers and laughter. —*Tribune*] He was then as good at telling an anecdote as now. ["No doubt." —*Times*] He could beat any of the boys at wrestling— could outrun them at a foot race—beat them at pitching quoits and tossing a copper, and could win more liquor than all the boys put together [Laughter and cheers. —*Tribune*; Uproarious laughter. —*Times*]; and the dignity and impartiality with which he presided at a horse-race or a fist-fight were the praise of everybody that was present and participated. [Renewed laughter. —*Tribune* and *Times*] Hence I had sympathy for him, because he was struggling with misfortune and so was I.

Mr. Lincoln served with me, or I with him, in the Legislature of 1836, when we parted. He subsided or submerged for some years, and I lost sight of him. In 1846, when [David] Wilmot [Pennsylvania senator— *ed.*] raised the Wilmot Proviso tornado [a failed but portentous 1846 attempt to bar slavery from territory taken in the Mexican War—*ed.*], Mr. Lincoln again turned up as a member of Congress from Sangamon District. I, being in the Senate of the United States, was called to welcome him, then without friend and companion. He then distinguished himself by his opposition to the Mexican war, taking the side of the common enemy, in time of war, against his own country. [Cheers and groans. —*Tribune;* "that's true." —*Times*] When he returned home from that Congress, he found that the indignation of the people followed him everywhere, until he again retired to private life, and was submerged until he was forgotten again by his friends. ["And will be again." —*Times*] He came up again in 1854, just in time to make the Abolition–Black Republican platform, in company with Lovejoy, Giddings, Chase and Fred. Douglass, for the Republican party to stand upon. [Laughter, "Hit him again," &c. —*Times*] Trumbull, too, was one of our own contemporaries. He was one born and raised in old Connecticut. Bred a Federalist, he removed to Georgia, and there turned Nullifier, when Nullification was popular. But, as soon as he he [*sic*] disposed of his clocks and wound up his business, he emigrated to Illinois. [laughter. —*Times*] When he got here, having turned politician and lawyer, he made his appearance in 1840–41 as a member of the Legislature, and became noted as the author of a scheme to repudiate a large portion of the State debt of Illinois, and thus bring infamy and disgrace upon the fair escutcheon of our glorious State. The odium attached to that measure consigned him to oblivion for a time. I walked into the House of Representatives and replied to his repudiation speeches until we carried resolutions over his head denouncing repudiation, and asserting the moral and legal obligation of Illinois to pay every dollar of debt she owed—every bond bearing her signature. ["Good," and cheers. —*Times*] Trumbull's malignity towards me arises out of the fact that I defeated his infamous scheme to repudiate the State debt and State bonds of Illinois.

Now these two men, having formed this combination to abolitionize the old Whig party and abolitionize the old Democratic party, and put themselves in the Senate in pursuance of the bargain with each other, are now carrying out that arrangement. Matheny states that the bargain was made, and I understand it from others, and I suppose Lincoln will not deny it. [Applause and laughter. —*Times*] The bargain was, that Lincoln was to have the place of Shields in the Senate, and Trumbull was to wait for mine. [Laughter and cheers. —*Times*] The story goes that Trumbull cheated Lincoln at that time. Trumbull having control of four or five Abolition Democrats, who were holding over in the Senate [state legislators then elected U.S. senators—*ed.*], would not let them vote for Lincoln, and forced the Abolition Whigs to go over to Trumbull, thus cheating Lincoln out of his part of the bargain. [Lincoln indeed turned his support to Trumbull to block Democratic Joel Matteson from election to the Senate, but he denied that a deal had earlier been struck to guarantee both Trumbull and himself Senate seats—*ed.*] Now Lincoln desires that he shall have the place then designed for Trumbull, as Trumbull cheated him and got his place; and Trumbull is now stumping the State, traducing me, for the purpose of securing that position to Mr. Lincoln in order to quiet him. ["Lincoln can never get it," &c. —*Times*] That accounts for the fact that the Republican Convention were compelled to instruct for Lincoln and nobody else when they nominated him. They had to pass a resolution that Lincoln was the first choice of the Republican party. Archy Williams was nowhere—[Orville] Browning was nobody—John Wentworth was not worthy of notice—[Norman] Judd was not to be considered [all fellow Republicans—*ed.*]. They had nobody else in the Republican party except Lincoln, for the reason that Lincoln demanded that they should now carry out the arrangement. ["Hit him again." —*Times*]

Hence, having formed this new party for the joint benefit of deserters from Whiggery and deserters from Democracy—having laid down the abolition platform which I have read—Lincoln now takes the stand and proclaims his abolition doctrine. Let me read a part of it. In his speech to the convention which nominated him for the Senate, in Springfield, he says—"In my opinion the slavery agitation will not cease until a crisis shall have been reached and passed. 'A house divided against itself cannot stand.' I believe this government cannot endure permanently half slave and half free. I do not expect the Union to be dissolved. I do not expect the house to fall, but I do expect that it will cease to be

divided. It will become all one thing or all the other. Either the opponents of slavery will arrest the further spread of it, and place it where
the public mind shall rest in the belief that it is in the course of ultimate
extinction, or its advocates will push it forward until it shall become
alike lawful in all the States, old as well as new, North as well as South."
[Tremendous cheers. Cries of "Good! good!" —*Tribune;* "Good,
good," and cheers. —*Times*] Yes, I have no doubt it is, and I am
delighted to hear you ["you Black Republicans," according to the
Times—ed.] say good. [Good! good! Laughter. —*Tribune*] I have no
doubt that that doctrine expresses your sentiments, and yet I will prove
to you, if you will listen to me, that doctrine is revolutionary, and
destructive of the existence of our government. ["Hurrah for Douglas,"
"good," and cheers. —*Times*] Mr. Lincoln here says that our government cannot endure permanently in the same condition in which it was
made by its framers. It was made divided into free States and slave
States. Mr. Lincoln says it has existed for near eighty years thus divided;
but he tells you that it cannot endure permanently on the same principles and in the same conditions relatively in which your fathers made
it. ["Neither can it." —*Times*] Why can't it endure divided into free and
slave States? Washington, as the President of the Convention, Franklin,
and Madison, and Hamilton, and Jay, and the patriots of that day,
made this government divided into free States and slave States, leaving
each State perfectly free to do as it pleased on that subject of slavery.
["Right, right." —*Times*] Why can't it exist upon the same principles
upon which our fathers made it. ["It can." —*Times*] Our fathers knew
when they made this government that in a country as wide and broad
as this—with such a variety of climate, of interests, of productions, as
this—that the people necessarily required different local laws and local
institutions in certain localities from those in other localities. They knew
that the laws and regulations that would suit the granite hills of New
Hampshire would be unsuited to the rice plantations of South Carolina.
["right, right," —*Times*] Hence, they provided that each State should
retain its own Legislature and its own sovereignty, with the full and
complete power to do as it pleased within its own limits in all that was
local and not national. [Applause. —*Times*] One of the reserved rights
of the States was that of regulating the relation between master and
slave, or the slavery question. At that time—that is when the Constitution was made—there were thirteen States in the Union, twelve of
which were slave States, and one was a free State. Suppose this doctrine

of uniformity—all to be one or all to be the other—now preached by Mr. Lincoln had prevailed then, what would have been the result? Of course the twelve slaveholding States would have over-ruled the one free State, and slavery would have been fastened by a constitutional provision on every inch of the American continent, instead of being left as our fathers wisely left it, for each State to decide for itself. ["Good, good," and three cheers for Douglas. —*Times*] I therefore say that uniformity in the local laws and local legislations of the different States was neither possible nor desirable. If any uniformity had been adopted, it must inevitably have been the uniformity of slavery everywhere, or the uniformity of negro citizenship and negro equality everywhere.

We are told by Lincoln that he is utterly opposed to the Dred Scott decision [divisive 1857 Supreme Court ruling that held that blacks could not be American citizens, and Congress could not bar slave "properties" from the territories—*ed*.], and will not submit to it, for the reason, as he says, that it deprives the negro of the rights and privileges of citizens. That is the first and main reason, he says, for his warfare upon the Supreme Court of the United States, that it deprives the negro of the rights and privileges of citizenship. [Laughter and applause. —*Times*] Now, I ask you, are you in favor of conferring upon the negro the rights and privileges of citizenship? ["No, no." —*Times*] Do you desire to strike out of our State Constitution that clause which keeps slaves and free negroes out of the State, and allow the free negro to flow in ["never," —*Times*] and cover our prairies with his settlements. Do you desire to turn this beautiful State into a free negro colony ["no, no," —*Times*], in order that when Missouri shall abolish slavery, she can send us these emancipated slaves to become citizens and voters on an equality with you. ["Never," "no," —*Times*] If you desire negro citizenship—if you desire them to come into the State and stay with white men—if you desire to let them vote on an equality with yourselves—if you desire to make them eligible to office—to have them serve on juries and judge of your rights—then go with Mr. Lincoln and the Black Republicans in favor of negro citizenship. ["Never, never," —*Times*] For one, I am opposed to negro citizenship in any form. [Cheers. —*Times*] I believe that this government was made on the white basis. ["Good," —*Times*] I believe it was made by white men for the benefit of white men and their posterity forever, and I am in favor of confining the citizenship to white men—men of European birth and European descent, instead of conferring it upon Negroes and Indians, and other

inferior races. ["Good for you." "Douglas forever." —*Times*] But Mr.
Lincoln, following the lead of the Abolition orators that came here and
lectured in the basements of your churches and school houses, reads the
Declaration of Independence that all men are created free and equal,
and then says: "How can you deprive the negro of that equality which
God and the Declaration of Independence awards to him?["] He and
they maintain that negro equality is guaranteed by the laws of God, and
re-asserted in the Declaration of Independence. If they think so, they
ought thus to say and thus to vote.

I do not question Mr. Lincoln's conscientious belief that the negro
was made his equal, and hence is his brother. ["Laughter," —*Times*]
But, for my own part, I do not regard the negro as my equal, and I
positively deny that he is my brother, or any kin to me whatever.
["Never." "Hit him again," and cheers. —*Times*] But he has learned
Lovejoy's catechism, and can repeat it as well as Farnsworth, and could
receive baptism from Father Giddings or Fred. Douglass on Abolitionism. [Laughter. —*Times*] He holds that the negro was [*Times* added:
born his equal and yours, and that he was] endowed with equality by
the Almighty, and hence that no human power alone can deprive him
of these rights which the Almighty has guaranteed to him. I do not
believe the Almighty ever intended the negro to be the equal of the
white man. ["Never, never." —*Times*] If he did he has been a long time
demonstrating the fact. [Laughter. —*Tribune;* Cheers. —*Times*] For six
thousand years the negro has been a race upon the earth, and during
that whole six thousand years—in all latitudes and climates wherever
the negro has been—he has been inferior to whatever race adjoined
him. The fact is he belongs to an inferior race and must occupy an
inferior position. ["Good," "that's so," &c. —*Times*] I do not hold that
merely because the negro belongs to an inferior race, therefore he ought
to be a slave. By no means can such a conclusion be drawn. On the
contrary, I do hold that humanity and Christianity both require that the
negro should have and enjoy every right, every privilege, and every
immunity, consistent with the safety of the society in which he lives.
[That's so. —*Times*] On that point I presume there can be no diversity
of opinion. You and I are bound to extend to every inferior dependent
being every right, every privilege, and every facility and immunity,
consistent with the public good.

Then the question arises, what rights and privileges are consistent
with the public good? That is a question which each State and each

Territory must decide for itself. Illinois has decided that question for herself. We, in Illinois, have provided that the negro shall not be a slave. We have also provided that he shall not be a citizen, but we protect him in his civil rights—in his life—in his person—in his property—while we deprive him of any political right whatsoever, and refuse to treat him on an equality with the white man. ["Good." —*Times*] That policy of Illinois is satisfactory to me. If it were to the Republicans, then there would be no question upon the subject. But the Republicans say that the negro ought to be made a citizen, and when he becomes a citizen, he becomes your equal in all rights and privileges of citizenship. ["He never shall." —*Times*] They assert that the Dred Scott decision is wicked and monstrous because it denies that a negro is or can be a citizen under the Constitution. Now I hold that Illinois had a right to abolish and prohibit slavery as she did, but I hold that Kentucky has the same right to continue and protect slavery that Illinois has to abolish it. I hold that New York had as much right to abolish slavery as Virginia has to continue it. I hold that each and every State of this Union is a sovereign power, with the right to do as it pleases on this question of slavery, and all domestic institutions [the essence of Douglas's doctrine of popular sovereignty, which he championed with the 1854 Kansas-Nebraska Bill, and which Lincoln steadfastly opposed; it held that the people of each territory, not Congress, should be empowered to welcome or bar slavery as they saw fit—*ed.*]. But slavery is not the only domestic relation that comes upon this controversy. The question is far more important to you. What shall be done for the free negro? We have settled the slavery question as far as we are concerned; we have prohibited it in Illinois forever. In doing so, I think we have done wisely, and there is no man in the State who would be more strenuous in his opposition to the introduction of slavery than I would [cheers —*Times*]. But when we have settled it for ourselves, we have exhausted all our power over the subject, we have done our whole duty; we have no right to go further, but we must leave each and every other State to decide for itself beyond our limits. Then the question arises, which shall be our policy in regard to free negroes? We have said they shall not vote. The State of Maine says free negroes may vote. Maine is a sovereign State, and has the power to regulate the qualifications within her limits. While I would not be in favor of conferring the rights of citizenship upon free negroes in our own State, yet I shall not quarrel with the State of Maine because it differs from me in opinion. Let Maine take care of her own negroes and let Illinois alone, and we will let the State of Maine alone. So with the State of New York. She allows the free negro to vote and hold office, provided he owns $250 worth of property, but not otherwise. While I would make no distinction between a negro who held property and one who did not, yet if the sovereign State of New York adjudges to make that distinction, it is her business and not mine. I will not quarrel with her if she does this. She may do as she pleases upon this question, and mind her own business, and we will do the same.

Now, my friends, if we will only act rigidly and conscientiously upon the great principle of popular sovereignty which guarantees to each State and each Territory the right to do as it pleases, instead of Congress interfering, we will be at peace one with another. Why should Illinois be at war with Missouri, or Kentucky with Ohio, or Virginia with New York, merely because their institutions differ? Our fathers intended that these institutions should differ. Our fathers knew that the South and the North, so far apart—differing in climate and production, had different interests requiring different institutions. This doctrine of uniformity of Mr. Lincoln's making all of them conform alike, is a new doctrine, never dreamed of by Washington or Madison, or the framers of the Constitution. Mr. Lincoln and the Republican party set themselves up as wiser than those who made the government. This government has flourished for seventy years upon the principle of popular sovereignty, recognizing the right of each State to do as it pleases. Under that principle, we have grown up from three or four millions to about thirty millions of people. Under that principle, we have crossed the Alleghany Mountains, and filled up the whole Northwest, turning the prairie into a garden, building up cities, and towns, and churches, and schools, and spreading civilization and Christianity where before there was nothing but savage barbarism. Under that principle, we have become from a feeble nation the most powerful nation on the face of the earth. If we still only obey that principle we can go forward increasing in territory, increasing in power, in strength and glory, until the Republic of America shall be the North star that shall guide the friends of freedom throughout the civilized world. ["Long may you live," and great applause. —Times] Then, my friends, why can we not adhere to that great principle of self-government upon which our institutions were originally made? ["We can." —Times] I believe that this new doctrine preached by Mr. Lincoln and this Abolition party would dissolve the Union. They try to array all the Northern States in one body against the South, inviting a sectional war of the free States against the slave States—Northern States against Southern States, to last until the one or the other shall be driven to the wall.

I am told that my time is out. You will now hear Mr. Lincoln for an hour and a half, and then myself for half an hour in reply. [Three times three cheers were here given for Douglas. —*Times*]

MR. LINCOLN'S REPLY

[When Mr. Lincoln rose, there were evident signs of a desire to applaud. —*Times;* Mr. Lincoln then came forward and was greeted with loud and protracted cheers from fully two-thirds of the audience. This was admitted by the Douglas men on the platform. It was some minutes before he could make himself heard, even by those on the stand. At last he said— —*Tribune*]

My fellow citizens: (Don't take up my time)—when a man hears himself misrepresented just a little, why, it rather provokes him, at least so I find it with me, but when he finds the misrepresentation very gross, why it sometimes amuses him. [Laughter. —*Tribune*] The first thing that I find to mention on this occasion that Judge Douglas has mentioned, is the fact that he alleges that Judge Trumbull made an arrangement in 1854, by which I was to have the place of Shields in the United States senate, and Judge Trumbull was to have Judge Douglas' place.— Well, all I have to say is, that Judge Douglas cannot prove that because it is not true, nor nothing like it. [Cheers. —*Tribune*] I have no doubt he is conscientious [Laughter. —*Times* and *Tribune*] in saying so. Again—I am not going to waste much time on this affair—as to these resolutions that he took such a time to read as the platform that the republican party passed in 1854, I never had anything to do with them, and I think Trumbull never had [Renewed laughter. —*Tribune*], and Judge Douglas cannot show that we ever did have, either one of us. Now, I believe this is true about these resolutions.—There was a call for a convention to form a Republican party in Springfield. I think my friend Lovejoy, who is with me on the stand, had a hand in it. I think that it is so, and I think that if he will remember correctly, that he tried to get me into it; and I would not do it. [Cheers and laughter. —*Tribune*] Well, I believe it is also true, as I went from Springfield when the convention was in session. I did not remain, but went to Tazewell court. They had placed my name without any of my authority on a committee and they wrote to me to attend the convention, and I refused to do it. That is the plain truth of the whole thing.

Now all these stories about Trumbull bargaining to sell out the old democratic party, and Lincoln the old whig party—well I have the means of knowing about it, and Judge Douglas may not have the means of knowing about it, and there is nothing of it in the world. [Cheers and

laughter. —*Tribune*] Now, I have no doubt Judge Douglas is conscientious about it. [voices, "that is it—hit him again," &c. —*Times;* Laughter. —*Tribune*] I know that after this, when Mr. Lovejoy got into the
legislature, he complained of me, that I had told him that they were old
whigs in our party, and that old whigs were good enough for us to vote
for, and that some of them had voted against him. A man cannot prove
a negative at all but he has the right to ask the man who asserts a state
of case to prove it. I cannot introduce testimony to show the negative
of this thing, but I have the right to claim that the man who says that
he knows these things, that he should say how he knows them. It is not
exactly satisfactory to me, because he may be conscientious in it.
[Cheers and laughter. —*Tribune*]

Now, I hate to waste my time on some things [*Tribune* substituted
"such things"—*ed.*]. But on the abolition tilt, that the Judge thinks that
I was engaged in, I hope you will permit me to read a part of a speech
that I made at Peoria, which will show altogether a different state of
case. [A voice—put on your specs. —*Times* and *Tribune*] Yes, sir, I am
obliged to do that. I am no longer a young man. [A voice—too young
to get into the senate. —*Times;* Laughter. —*Tribune*]

[Mr. L. here read, for seven minutes, from a speech delivered by him
at Peoria, October, 1854—the intention of which was to show that he
did not entertain the idea of the negro, &c. —*Times;* (The *Tribune*
reprinted the excerpt in full, as follows—*ed.*)]

This is the *repeal* of the Missouri Compromise. The foregoing history may not be precisely accurate in every particular; but I am sure
it is sufficiently so, for all the uses I shall attempt to make of it, and
in it, we have before us, the chief materials enabling us to correctly
judge whether the repeal of the Missouri Compromise is right or
wrong.

I think, and shall try to show, that it is wrong; wrong in its direct
effect, letting slavery into Kansas and Nebraska—and wrong in its
prospective principle, allowing it to spread to every other part of the
wide world, where men can be found inclined to take it.

This *declared* indifference, but as I must think, covert real zeal for
the spread of slavery, I can not but hate. I hate it because of the
monstrous injustice of slavery itself. I hate it because it deprives our
republican example of its just influence in the world—enables the
enemies of free institutions, with plausibility, to taunt us as hypo-

crites—causes the real friends of freedom to doubt our sincerity, and especially because it forces so many good men amongst ourselves into an open war with the very fundamental principles of civil liberty— criticising the Declaration of Independence, and insisting that there is no right principle of action but *self-interest.*

Before proceeding, let me say I think I have no prejudice against the Southern people. They are just what we would be in their situation. If slavery did not now exist amongst them, they would not introduce it. If it did now exist amongst us, we should not instantly give it up. This I believe of the masses north and south. Doubtless there are individuals, on both sides, who would not hold slaves under any circumstances; and others who would gladly introduce slavery anew, if it were out of existence. We know that some southern men do free their slaves, go north, and become tip-top abolitionists; while some northern ones go south, and become most cruel slave-masters.

When southern people tell us they are no more responsible for the origin of slavery, than we; I acknowledge the fact. When it is said that the institution exists, and that it is very difficult to get rid of it, in any satisfactory way, I can understand and appreciate the saying. I surely will not blame them for not doing what I should not know how to do myself. If all earthly power were given me, I should not know what to do, as to the existing institution. My first impulse would be to free all the slaves, and send them to Liberia,—to their own native land. But a moment's reflection would convince me, that whatever of high hope (as I think there is) there may be in this, in the long run, its sudden execution is impossible. If they were all landed there in a day, they would all perish in the next ten days; and there are not surplus shipping and surplus money enough in the world to carry them there in many times ten days. What then? Free them all, and keep them among us as underlings? Is it quite certain that this betters their condition? I think I would not hold one in slavery, at any rate; yet the point is not clear enough to me to denounce people upon. What next? Free them, and make them politically and socially, our equals? My own feelings will not admit of this; and if mine would, we well know that those of the great mass of white people will not. Whether this feeling accords with justice and sound judgment, is not the sole question, if indeed, it is any part of it. A universal feeling, whether well or ill-founded, can not be safely disregarded. We can not, then, make them equals. It does seem to me that systems of gradual emancipation might be adopted; but for their tardiness in this, I will not undertake to judge our brethren of the south.

When they remind us of their constitutional rights, I acknowledge them, not grudgingly, but fully, and fairly; and I would give them any legislation for the reclaiming of their fugitives, which should not, in its stringency, be more likely to carry a free man into slavery, than our ordinary criminal laws are to hang an innocent one.

But all this; to my judgment, furnishes no more excuse for permitting slavery to go into our own free territory, than it would for reviving the African slave trade by law. The law which forbids the bringing of slaves *from* Africa; and that which has so long forbid the taking them *to* Nebraska, can hardly be distinguished on any moral principle; and the repeal of the former can find quite as plausible excuses as that of the latter.

Now, after all the Judge has said of me, the Judge heard me make that speech, he heard me make it four years ago—I may be right or wrong—but I have never departed from that. [Voices—"right," "wrong" &c. —*Times*] I follow on to say that my own feelings will not permit of this.

That I told the Judge four years ago. I think the judge has some reason to know that I was not then engaged in an abolition tilt but I don't mean that the judge shall catechize me. I will have one for one, when the time comes for original ones, but here is one slips out, and I have answered it before mine comes; he has got it without my getting one. [*Tribune* added: "He has got my answer on the Fugitive Slave Law."—*ed.*]

"Again, when they remind me," I am reading still [here the *Times* inserted the last lines of the Peoria extract—*ed.*], "that they are no more responsible for the existence of slavery than we are, I acknowledge their truth; but all this, to my judgment, furnishes no more excuse for permitting slavery to go into our own free territory, than it would for reviving the African slave trade by law. The law which forbids the bringing of slaves from Africa, and that which has so long forbid the taking of slaves to Nebraska, can hardly be distinguished [*sic*] principle. I deny that they can be distinguished at all.—The repeal of the former could find as many excuses as that of the latter."

These are the viewpoints upon the whole subject, upon the institution of slavery, and any system of argumentation that says anything, or that argues me into the idea of perfect social and political equality with the negro, is a species of fantastic arrangement of words by which a man can prove a chestnut horse to be a horse chestnut. [The *Tribune* version of this joke, and the one repeated since, but possibly altered by Lincoln and his editors at the time, was "by which a man can prove a horse chestnut to be a chestnut horse"—*ed.*] [Applause. —*Times;* Laughter. —*Tribune*]

I will say here while I am upon this subject, I have no purpose directly or indirectly, to interfere with the institution of slavery in the states where it exists. I believe I have no lawful right to do so, and I have no inclination to do so. I have no disposition to introduce political and social equality between the white and the black races. There is a physical difference between the two, which in my judgment will probably forever forbid their living together on terms of respect, social and political equality, and inasmuch as it becomes a necessity that there must be a superiority somewhere, I, as well as Judge Douglas, am in favor of the race to which I belong having the superior position; but I hold that because of all this there is no reason at all furnished why the negro after all is not entitled to all that the declaration of independence holds out, which is, "life, liberty, and the pursuit of happiness" [applause; —*Times;* Loud cheers. —*Tribune*][,] and I hold that he is as much entitled to that as the white man. I agree that the negro may not be my equal and Judge Douglas' equal in many respects—certainly not in color, and in intellectual development, perhaps—but in the right to [*Tribune* added "eat"—*ed.*] the bread [*Tribune* added, "without leave of anybody else,"—*ed.*] which his own hand earns, he is my own equal and Judge Douglas' equal, and the equal of every living man.

[Voice, "bully for you," "all right," etc. —*Times;* Great applause. —*Tribune*]

Now, one or two other of these little matters, and I pass on. The judge is woefully at fault again about his early friend being a grocery keeper. [Laughter. —*Tribune*] I don't know that it would be a great sin if I had, but he is mistaken. Lincoln never kept a grocery in his life. [Laughter. —*Tribune*] It is true that Lincoln did work, the latter part of one winter at a little still house up at the head of the hollow. [Roars of laughter. —*Tribune*]

So I think the judge is equally at fault when he charges me when I was in congress, with having opposed the Mexican war. The judge does not make his charge very distinctly—he rather insinuates it, but I will tell you how that was. Whenever the democratic party tried to get me to vote that the war had been properly begun, it could not do it, but when they asked me to give money, or supplies, or land warrants to the soldiers, I gave the same votes as Judge Douglas did, for he was in the other branch. [Loud applause. —*Tribune*] You may think as you please as to whether I was consistent, but when he insinuates that I withheld my vote; or did anything to perplex [the *Tribune* substituted "hinder"—*ed.*] the soldiers, he is mistaken altogether, as an investigation of the record will prove.

I will state, as I have not used so much of my time as I thought I had, perhaps I will dwell a little longer upon some two or three of these little topics that the judge has spoken of. He has read from my speech at Springfield in which I say that "a house divided against itself cannot stand."—Does the judge say it can? [Laughter. —*Tribune*] I don't know—the judge don't seem to be attending to me just now—but I would like to know if it is his opinion that it can. If so, that raises a question of veracity, and it is not a question of veracity, between the judge and I, but the judge has a question of veracity with a somewhat higher character than myself. [Laughter and applause. —*Tribune*] It is not a question between him and me.

Now, I ask your attention to that matter for the purpose of saying somewhat seriously, and not merely for the purpose of fun; and I know the judge will agree with me. We may misapply it as a true maxim, and he may argue that I misapply it. I have then the right, on the contrary, to show that I do not. Now, when he undertakes to show that because I say that, I think this Union cannot exist permanently so divided, when I say this so far as the question of slavery is concerned, that I am in favor of bringing about a dead uniformity, he, as I think, argues very errone-ously, as I will try to show.

Now the great variety in the local institutions of the states spring from the difference of their climates, and they are really the bonds of union between the states, each furnishing the means to supply the wants of the other, they become no apples of discord. [The *Tribune* here added, perhaps later: "They do not make a house divided against itself, but they make a house united. If they produce in one section of the country what is called for by the wants of another section, and this other section can supply the wants of the first, they are not matters of discord, but bonds of union, true bonds of union"—*ed.*] But can this question of slavery be assimilated to these things? I leave it to you to say whether throughout the history of our government, from time to time, has not this institution of slavery always failed to be a bond of union, but on the contrary, proved to be an apple of discord, and an element of discord, in the house [Cries of "yes, yes," and applause. —*Tribune*]; and I ask you to consider whether so long as the structure of men's minds shall continue as God has seen fit to make them, this question of slavery will not continue to be an element of discord in the houses. If that institution is standing in that position, and it will continue to be an element of division [Cries of "Yes, yes." —*Tribune*], if so, then I have the right to say that in regard to that thing, this Union is a house divided against itself, and when the judge reminds me, as I have often said to him, that the institution of slavery has existed for some eighty years in some of the states, while it did not exist in some other[s], I agree to the fact, and I explain and account for the fact by the attitude in which our fathers originally placed it, legislating to put off its source, putting the seal of legislation against its spread, and leaving the public mind at rest in the belief that it was in the course of ultimate extinction. [Applause. —*Times;* Cries of "Yes, yes." —*Tribune*]

But I think lately that he and those who have acted with him have placed that institution on a new basis, one that looks to the perpetuation and extension of it. [Loud cheers. —*Tribune*] While it is placed upon this basis I have said that I believe we shall not have peace until "either the opponents of slavery will arrest the further spread of it, and place it where the public mind shall rest in the belief that it is in [the] course of ultimate extinction; or its advocates will push it forward, till it shall become alike lawful in all the states, old as well as new, north as well as south." [From the House Divided speech—*ed.*]

Now, let me repeat. If we would arrest the spread of it—if we would place it where Washington, Jefferson and Madison placed it, it would be in the course of ultimate extinction, and the public mind would be at rest in the belief of its ultimate extinction. The crisis would be passed; and though the institution might be alive long, and might linger for a hundred years, yet it would be going out in God's own time, in the way that would be best for both the white and the black races. [Applause. —*Times;* Great cheering. —*Tribune*]

A VOICE—You repudiate popular sovereignty, then?

Well, we will talk about popular sovereignty, as you insist upon it. [Laughter. —*Tribune*] What is popular sovereignty? [A voice, "a humbug." —*Times* and *Tribune*] Is it the right of the people to have slavery, or not, if they see fit, in the territories? Is it, or not?

I will state that my understanding is that popular sovereignty, applied to the question of slavery, and as now applied, does allow the people of a territory, to have slavery if they want it, and it don't allow them to not have it if they don't want it. [Applause and laughter. —*Times* and *Tribune*] I don't mean to say that if this vast concourse of people were in the territory of the United States that any one of them are obliged to have slaves if they did not want them, but I do say that if any one among them wants them, there is no one or number of them can keep him from it. [A voice, "Well, you are a fool." —*Times*] Well, that may be, and I guess there are two of us that are that way. [Laughter.]

When I made my speech at Springfield,—that speech of which the judge complains, or from which he quotes,—why, I really was not thinking of this thing that he ascribes to me at all. I had no thought in the world that I was doing anything to bring about the absolute equality of the white and black races. It never occurred to me that I was doing anything to reduce to a dead uniformity all the local institutions of the states; but I must say in justice to the judge, that if I am really doing something that leads to these bad results, it is just as bad to the country, whether I wished it or not; but I ask you, can it be true that placing this institution of slavery upon the original basis upon which our fathers placed it, that it can have any tendency to compel the people of Vermont to raise sugar corn because they can raise it in Louisiana, or to compel the people of Grand Prairie to cut pine logs off the prairie where none grow, because they cut them in Maine[?] [Laughter. —*Tribune*]

The people [*Tribune* had "the Judge"—*ed.*] does not generally claim that he is administering, by his Kansas-Nebraska doctrine, the slavery question upon the basis of the original constitution. I think he says, in one of his speeches, that he saw evidences of a policy to allow slavery to be in existence south of a certain line. Now, I am fighting him upon this original principle. I am fighting in favor of the old principle of Washington, Jefferson and Madison. [Laughter and applause. —*Tribune*]

Now, my friends, I want to attend a little to one or two other things. In that Springfield speech, my main object was to show, so far as my humble self was capable of doing—to arouse this country to the belief—that there was a tendency, if not a conspiracy, to make slavery perpetual and universal in this Union; and having made that speech principally for that object, after bringing forward the evidence that I thought tended to prove that proposition, among other things I went on with this little bit of comment, which I will read to you. I said this:

"We cannot absolutely know that all these exact adaptations are the result of preconcert. But when we see a lot of framed timbers, different portions of which we know have been gotten out at different times and places, by different workmen—Stephen, Franklin, Roger, and James for instance [Douglas, Pierce, Taney, and Buchanan—all collaborators, Lincoln charged, in the conspiracy to nationalize slavery—ed.]—and when we see these timbers joined together, and see they exactly make the frame of a house or mill, all the beams ["tenons" in Lincoln transcript—ed.] and mortices exactly fitting, and all the lengthy ["lengths and"—Tribune] proportions of the different pieces exactly adapted to their respective places, and not a piece too many or too few—not omitting even [the] scaffolding—or, if a single piece be lacking, we can see the place in the frame exactly fitted and prepared to getting such piece in—in such case we find it impossible to not believe that Stephen and Franklin and Roger and James all understood one another from the beginning, and all worked upon a common plan or draft before the first lick was struck." [Great cheers. —Tribune]

When my friend Judge Douglas came to Chicago, on the 9th of July, this speech having been delivered on the 16th of June, he made a speech [the Tribune substituted "harrangue"—ed.] there in which he took hold of this speech of mine, and showing that he had carefully read it, and while he paid [no attention] to this at all, he complimented me as being a most kind, amiable and intelligent gentleman. Notwithstanding I had said this, he goes on and draws out from that speech this tendency of mine to set the states at war, and to set the negroes [the Tribune had "niggers"—ed.] and white people to marrying with one another. [Laughter. —Tribune] Well the next evening after that, as the judge had complimented me as highly as he had, I must confess to my weakness—I was a little taken with it [Laughter. —Tribune], it coming from a great man, and one that the world acknowledges as a great man—I do not speak that in mockery—I was a little taken with it; I was not much accustomed to flattery. I was very much like the hoosier with the gingerbread—he said that he loved it better and got less of it than any other man. [Roars of laughter. —Tribune] Well, as the judge had flattered me as much as he had, I made up my mind that he did not mean to misrepresent me at all, so I went to making a speech, to show him and to convince him that I did not mean all these dreadful things.

As an illustration, I had incidentally said that I claimed "no right, and there ought to be no inclination in the people of the free states, to enter into the slave states and interfere with the question of slavery at all." The judge thereupon, at Bloomington, where I heard him speak, said that I had said that I would not go into the slave states, but that I said I will go on to the bank of the Ohio and shoot over among them. [Laughter. —*Tribune*] Well, he runs on step by step in the race, until he gets on at Clinton to using this form of speech, and says that "unless he shall be successful in firing his batteries, the Union cannot stand." Now, I did not think that was exactly the way to treat a kind, amiable, and intelligent gentleman. [Roars of laughter. —*Tribune*] I thought that if I had asked the judge to show when or where it was that I had said that if I did not succeed in firing into the slave states the Union would be dissolved that he could not do it. I understood well enough, he would say, I did not mean to quote from you. I only meant that this was the result of the argument; but I would have the right to ask it, and I now do ask him. Did you not put it in the form that an ordinary listener or reader of a newspaper would take it as a quotation from me? [Laughter. —*Tribune*]

But I turned in, and, in a speech at Springfield, I thought I might as well attend to my own business a little. I recalled, as well as I could, his attention to this charge of conspiracy to nationalize slavery. I called to his attention, that he had acknowledged that he had twice read the speech, and as he had made public no plea or answer, I took a default upon him and insisted that I had a right to renew the charge of that conspiracy.

Well, ten days afterwards, I met the judge at Clinton—that is to say, I was on the ground, not in a discussion, but I was on the ground to hear him make a speech. He then comes in with his plea to the charge, for the first time, and his plea when it is put in, I believe, as well as I can remember, it amounts to this: that he never had any talk with Chief Justice Taney or the president of the United States, about the Dred Scott decision, before it was made, and that I, Lincoln, ought to know that the man who makes a charge, not knowing it to be true, falsifies as much as he who knows it to be false, and lastly, that he would pronounce the whole thing a falsehood; but he made no personal application of the charge of falsehood—not out of regard for the kind, amiable and intelligent gentleman, but for his own personal self-respect. [Roars of laughter. —*Tribune*] I have understood since—but [turning to Judge

Douglas—*Tribune*] I won't stick the judge to it, if he does not want to have it—he has come up to saying the thing out.

He nods to me—that is so. [Laughter. —*Tribune*] Now it may astonish you that I can keep as good humored as I can, when the judge acknowledges that he is making a question of veracity with me. I know that the judge is a great man [while I am only a small man—*Tribune*], but I feel in my soul that I have got him. [Tremendous cheering. —*Tribune*]

I demur to that plea—I waive all objections because it was not filed until after default was taken, and I demur to it upon the merits. What if Judge Douglas never did talk to Chief Justice Taney or the president until the decision was made? Does it follow that he could not have as perfect an understanding with them without it as with it? But I am disposed to take his denial rather as an answer in chancery, that he neither had knowledge or belief of the existence of any such conspiracy. Now, I ask you, after that is denied, if he had done so, have I not the right yet to prove it on him, and is there not more than the evidence of the two witnesses to prove it, and if it does not prove the existence of conspiracy, does it disturb the facts at all that would run to show that he had been used by the conspirators instead of being the leader of them? [Vociferous cheering. —*Tribune*]

Now, in regard to his reminding me of the moral rule, that persons who tell what they do not know to be true falsify as much as they who knowingly tell a falsehood. I remember that rule, and it should be borne in mind that what I have read to you says that I do not know such a conspiracy to be true; but I say that I believe it, and if he says that I don't believe it, then he says that which he don't know, and falls within his own rule.

As to his statement that if it were not for his self-respect he would call the whole thing a falsehood, or, in plain words, call somebody a liar about it. I want to ask your attention to a little discussion about that branch of the case. I had arrayed the evidence which brought my mind to the conclusion. Now, if in stating that evidence by mistake any part of it was erroneous, it needed but the judge to have pointed it out to me, because I would have taken it back. If I should have brought forward any thing as a matter of fact that is not a matter of fact, and he should point it out to me, it will not ruffle me to take it back, and if he will not point it out to me, or show that I have reasoned falsely, it is not for him to call the kind, amiable, and intelligent gentleman a liar. [The *Tribune* had, "is it not rather for him to show . . . than to call the 'kind, amiable, intelligent gentleman,' a liar?"] [Cheers and laughter. —*Tribune*] If I have reasoned to a false conclusion, it is but the vocation of a very able debater to show the fact in a very amiable way, without cross or ugly language. It is easily done. But I want to ask the attention of the audience to a portion of the Nebraska bill which the judge himself has quoted:

"It being the true intent and meaning of this act not to legislate slavery into any territory or state, but to leave the people thereof perfectly free to regulate their own domestic institutions in their own way, subject only to the federal constitution."

And thereupon the judge instantly began arguing in favor of popular sovereignty, the right of the people to have slaves if they wanted them, and to exclude slavery if they wanted to do so. But, said a senator from Ohio, by the name of Chase, we more than suspect you do not mean that the people shall have the right to exclude slavery if they want to, and if you do not mean it [the *Tribune* says, "if you do mean it"—*ed.*], accept an amendment expressly authorizing the people to exclude slavery. I believe I have the amendment before me:

"The people of the territory, through their appropriate representations, may, if they see fit, prohibit the existence of slavery therein."

I now state it as a fact to be taken back if there is any mistake in it, that Judge Douglas and those acting with him voted that amendment down. [Tremendous applause. —*Tribune*] I now think that those men who voted that down had a real reason for doing so. They know what that reason was. It looks to us since we have seen the Dred Scott decision come, holding that under the constitution the people cannot exclude slavery, it looks to outsiders, poor, simple, amiable, intelligent gentlemen [great laughter, —*Tribune*], it looks as if it was the place left to put that Dred Scott decision in [laughter and cheers —*Tribune*], and now I say again that if there was another and a different reason other than the conclusion that I have drawn, it will avail the judge much more to point out to these people what that good reason was for voting that amendment down, rather than swelling himself and asserting that he may be provoked to call somebody a liar. [Tremendous applause. —*Tribune*]

Again, there is in that same quotation from the Nebraska bill another point. It being not the intention to legislate slavery into any territory or state, I have always been puzzled to know what business the word state had there. Judge Douglas knows, he put it there, he knows what he put it there for. We outsiders could not see what it was put there for. The law that they were passing was not about states, it was making no provision for states. What was it put there for? After seeing the Dred Scott decision, if another shall come holding that they cannot exclude it from the states, we shall find it was the odd half of something, the other half of which was to come in due time. Now I say again if there is any different reason for putting it there, the judge can, in a good humored way, without calling me or anybody else a liar, tell what that good reason was. [Renewed cheers. —*Tribune*]

When the judge spoke at Clinton he was very near making a charge of falsehood against me. He used, as I find it printed in the newspapers afterwards, and as I remember it, the language was very nearly if not quite the same, the following words: "I did not answer the charge before, for the reason that I did not suppose there was an American whose heart was so corrupt as for a moment to believe that such a charge could be true." [A voice, "We knew it to be true, didn't we?" —*Times*] And then the judge after I have dropped a part of the quotation, added that he "had too much respect for Mr. Lincoln to suppose he was serious in making the charge." I confess that I thought that was a curious view, that I had made what he now says, was a serious charge, in fun. [Laughter. —*Tribune*]

Now says the judge, I did not for a moment believe that there was a man in America whose heart was so corrupt as to make such a charge. I hope the judge will not blame me as being the only man in America who has a heart base enough to make such a charge. I hope that he will excuse me if I find out one other who has made a charge something as I have. If I should find one, that one happened to be Judge Douglas himself [who made one—*Tribune*], why then I hope he will consider this question of the deep corruption of hearts which he has thought fit to ascribe to me. [Great applause and laughter. —*Tribune*] In Judge Douglas' speech of the 22d March, 1858, I read—

"In this connection there is another topic to which I desire to allude. I seldom refer to the course of newspapers, or notice the articles which they publish in regard to myself; but the course of the Washington *Union* has been so extraordinary, for the last two or three months, that I think it well enough to make some allusion to it. It has read me out of the democratic party every other day, at least, for two or three months, and keeps reading me out, [laughter,] and, as if it had not succeeded, still continues to read me out, using such terms as 'traitor,' 'renegade,' 'deserter,' and other kind and polite epithets of that nature. Sir, I have no vindication to make of my democracy against the Washington *Union*, or any other newspapers. I am willing to allow my history and action for the last twenty years to speak for themselves as to my political principles, and my fidelity to political obligations. The Washington *Union* has a personal grievance. When its editor was nominated for public printer, I declined to vote for him, and stated that at some time I might give my reasons for doing so. Since I declined to give that vote, this scurrilous abuse, these vindictive and constant attacks have been repeated almost daily on me. There is one article in an issue of that paper which I ask my friend from Michigan to read."

This is a speech made on the 22d March, 1858, and this part begins on page 21. I tell you the place so that you may read the article which [Charles] Stuart [senator from Michigan—*ed.*] read for Judge Douglas. When he got through reading, Judge Douglas sums up, as I think correctly, the views advanced by the *Union:*

Mr. President, you here find several distinct propositions advanced boldly by the Washington *Union*, editorially and apparently authoritatively[,] and every man who questions any of them is denounced as an abolitionist, a free soiler, a fanatic. The propositions are, first, that the primary object of all government at its original institution is the protection of persons and property; second, that the constitution of the United States declares that the citizens of each state shall be entitled to all the privileges and immunities of citizens in the several states; and that, therefore, thirdly all state [the *Tribune* added, "laws, whether organic or otherwise, which prohibit the citizens of one State from settling in another with their slave"—*ed.*] property, and especially declaring it forfeited, are direct violations of the original intentions of the government and constitution of the United States; and, fourth, that the emancipation of the slaves of the northern states was a gross outrage on the rights of property, inasmuch as it was involuntarily done on the part of the owner.

Remember that this article was published in the *Union* on the 17th of November, and on the 18th appeared the first article giving the adhesion of the *Union* to the Lecompton constitution [disputed pro-slavery constitution ratified in Kansas in 1857 after Free Soilers boycotted Constitutional Convention, subsequently approved by Congress but rejected by Kansas voters in 1858; Douglas had split with President Buchanan, a fellow Democrat, to oppose it—*ed.*]. It was in these words:

"KANSAS AND HER CONSTITUTION.—The vexed question is settled. The problem is solved. The dread point of danger is passed. All serious trouble to Kansas affairs is over and gone"—and, a column, nearly, of the same sort. Then, when you come to look into the Lecompton constitution, you find the same doctrine incorporated in it which was put forth editorially in the *Union*. [The *Tribune* version included several Lecompton constitution clauses—*ed.*]

"It will be seen by these clauses in the Lecompton constitution, that they are identical in spirit with this authoritative article in the Washington *Union* of the day previous to its indorsement of this constitution, and every man is branded as a free-soiler and abolitionist, who does not subscribe to them."

It ends at last with this:

"When I saw that article in the *Union* of the 17th November, followed by the glorification of the Lecompton constitution on the 18th of November, and this clause in the constitution asserting the doctrine that no state has a right to prohibit slavery within its limits, I saw that there was a fatal blow being struck at the sovereignty of the states of this Union, a death blow to state rights, subversive of the democratic platform and of the principles upon which the democratic party have ever stood, and upon which I wish it will ever stand."

Now, what was this charge that the judge thinks I must have so very corrupt a heart to have made? It was a purpose on the part of certain high functionaries to make it impossible for any state to prohibit the citizens of other states coming into that state and settling down with their slave property[;] in other words, it was a conspiracy, as I had charged, as my belief, to make the constitution [the *Tribune* has "institution"—*ed.*] national. And now I want to ask your attention to what this is that the judge has done. I know he made that part of his speech ostensibly as a reason why he had refused to vote for a certain man as public printer, but when we get the charge, it is the same charge that I made against him; and now who does he make that charge against? Does he make it against the newspaper editor merely? That it is identical in spirit with the Lecompton constitution, so that the framers of the constitution are brought in with the editor of that newspaper, in that "fatal blow being struck." He does not call it a conspiracy. In his language it is a "fatal blow being struck," and he may, if the word is any better, change the word that I used into a "fatal blow being struck." [Cheers and laughter. —*Tribune*] But we see that he charges that that fatal blow is not being struck by the editor of the *Union*, but by the framers of the Lecompton constitution; but not only so, the article was "authoritative," so by whose authority was it made? Who does he mean? It is by the authority of the president and government—the administration. Is there any question but that this is so? Where is the editor of the *Union*, the framers of the Lecompton constitution, the president, the government, and all the supporters of the Lecompton constitution, in congress and out of it—all are involved in this charge of Judge Douglas of the fatal blow being struck to nationalize slavery. I commend to him the consideration of the question as to how corrupt the heart of a man must be to make such a charge. [Laughter and applause. —*Times;* Vociferous cheering. —*Tribune*]

A VOICE—Are you in favor of the Lecompton constitution?

MR. LINCOLN—And now, my friends, I have but one other branch of this subject that in the limited time we have to speak, I shall touch upon. I have but one other branch to which I will call your attention; then I shall come to a close. It is probable that I shall not actually occupy all the time that shall belong to me, although I would have liked to have talked twice as long. I ask the attention of this community here assembled and elsewhere to the course of [*sic*] Judge Douglas is pursuing every day as upon this question of making slavery national. Not going back to the record and going to the speeches that he made here and elsewhere, I ask attention to that.

In the first place, what is necessary to make the institution of slavery national? There is no danger of the people of Kentucky shouldering their muskets to bring slavery upon us—there is no danger of our going there to make war upon them. [A voice—"You dare not do it." —*Times*] What is necessary to make slavery national? It is simply the next Dred Scott decision—it is simply for the supreme court to decide that no state under the constitution can exclude slavery, just as they and the territorial legislatures cannot exclude it from the limits of the territory. This being true, this being the way as I think that slavery is to be made national, if it is ever to be made so at all, let us consider what Judge Douglas is doing. First let us say that public sentiment is everything [the *Tribune* transcript, with a phrase perhaps written later, added: "With public sentiment, nothing can fail; without it, nothing can succeed"—*ed.*]—he who moulds public sentiment is greater [the *Tribune* has "goes deeper"—*ed.*] than he who makes [the *Tribune* has "enacts"] statutes [or pronounces decisions—*Tribune*]. This borne in mine [*sic;* should be "mind"—*ed.*], and also the additional fact that my friend Judge Douglas is a man of vast influence, and, that it is enough for many men to profess to believe a thing, so that when others find out that he professes it or believes, they take it as a part of their creed. This is the attitude of the party which is, perhaps, as he claims a majority party, who will agree with his sentiments in a political campaign. This being borne in mind, what does the judge do in regard to the Dred Scott decision? He sticks to a decision that forbids the people of a territory to exclude slavery, not because he says it is right in itself, but because it has been decided by a court—because it has come from that court, he, as a good citizen, and you, as good citizens are bound to take it in your political action [as *law*—*Tribune*]—not that he judges of it on its merits, but because the decision of the court is to him a "thus saith the Lord." [Applause. —*Tribune*] He places it upon the ground, and you will bear in mind that this commits him to the next one just as much as this. He does not commit himself to it because of its merits, but because it is a "thus saith the Lord." The next [decision —*Tribune*] will be "thus saith the Lord" [Laughter. —*Times*] as much as this, and there is nothing that can turn the judge away from his devotion to this decision. It is nothing that I point out to him that this great prototype, Jackson did not believe in this way upon the great binding force of supreme court decisions. It is not that I point out to him that Jefferson did not believe in it. I had said that I had heard the judge himself often approve of the opinion of Jackson, but I say he ought to remember better than I, and I will make no question with him; but it still seems that I have heard him do it twenty times. [Applause and laughter. —*Tribune*] I will tell him though that he claims to stand on the Cincinnati platform, and that Cincinnati platform asserts that congress cannot charter a national bank in the teeth of the decision of the court, that congress can charter a national bank. [Loud applause. —*Tribune*] I will remind him also of a piece of Illinois [the *Tribune* added "history"—*ed.*] of the time when the respected party which the judge belongs [to] was displeased with a decision of the supreme court of Illinois, because they had decided that the governor could not remove a secretary of state [the *Tribune* added: You will find the whole story in Ford's History of Illinois—*ed.*], and he will not deny that he went in for overslaughing that court by appointing five new judges [Cheers and laughter. —*Tribune*], and it ended in his getting his name of judge in that very way, thus breaking down the supreme court, and when he tells me about how a man who shall be appointed on such a principle by being questioned, I say judge, you know you have tried it [Laughter. —*Tribune*], and when he seeks [says—*Tribune*] that the court will be prostituted below contempt, I say judge, you know you have been through the mill once. [Great laughter. —*Tribune*] But when I speak of all these things, I cannot make the judge fall loose from his adherence to this Dred Scott decision; if I may say so, and I mean by it no disrespect, he is like some creature that will hang on which he has got his hold to a thing, you may cut his arms and limbs off, and still he is hanging on. He is bespattered from the beginning of his life with war upon the courts, and at last he hangs with desparation [*sic*] to the Dred Scott decision. [Loud cheers. —*Tribune*]

Does not this show that there is a purpose [*strong as death and eternity*— *Tribune*] for which he adheres to that decision upon a principle that will make him adhere to all other decisions coming from the same court? [Vociferous applause. —*Tribune*]

[A HIBERNIAN: Give us something besides Dred Scott. —*Tribune*] [The *Times* made no mention of this interruption by a "Hibernian." Republicans used fear and loathing of Irish immigrants to tar Democrats as often as Democrats used blacks to warn voters against Republicans—*ed.*]

Now, no doubt, you would rather hear something that don't hurt you. [Laughter and applause. —*Tribune*] Now, on another matter, having spoken of this Dred Scott decision, Mr. Clay—my beau ideal of a great man [the *Tribune* had "statesman"—*ed.*] the man for whom I fought all my humble life—Mr. Clay once said of a class of men who, he supposed, would express all tendency to ultimate emancipation that they must, if they would do this, go back to the hour of our own liberty and independence, and muzzle the cannon that thunders its annual joyous return; that they must blow out the moral lights around us; that they must pervert the human soul, and eradicate the human soul and love of liberty, and then, and not till then, they could perpetuate slavery in this country. [Loud cheers. —*Tribune*] To my thinking, Judge Douglas is now, by his example and his vast influence, doing that very thing in this community. [Applause. —*Times;* Cheers. —*Tribune*] When he is saying that the negro has no share in the Declaration of Independence, he is going back to the year of our revolution, and, to the extent of his ability, he is muzzling the cannon that thunders its annual joyous return. When he is saying, as he often does, that if any people want slavery they have a right to have it, he is blowing out the moral lights around us. When he says that he don't care whether slavery is voted up or down, then, to my thinking, he is, so far as he is able to do so, perverting the human soul and eradicating the light of reason and the love of liberty on the American continent. [Enthusiastic and continued applause. —*Tribune*] And when he shall have succeeded in bringing public sentiment to an exact accordance with his own,—when this vast assemblage goes back with these sentiments instilled into them, then it needs only the formality of a second Dred Scott decision, which he is in favor of, to make slavery alike lawful in all the states, old as well as new.

My friends, that ends the chapter; the judge can take his half-hour.

[Mr. Lincoln retired, having spoken less than his time by thirteen minutes. —*Times;* As Mr. Lincoln retired, three cheers were proposed and given with tremendous volume—followed by three more, extending to all parts of the public square. —*Tribune*]

I will now occupy the half hour allotted to me in reply to Mr. Lincoln. The first point to which I will call your attention to [is] what I said about the organization of the Republican party in 1854, and the platform that was formed on the 5th October of that year, and then put the question to Mr. Lincoln whether or not he approved of each article of that platform. ["He answered that already." —*Times*] I have told him that I should call for a specific answer to each of these interrogatories. ["He has answered." "You cannot make him answer," &c. —*Times*] I do not charge him with being a member of the committee that reported the platform. ["Yes, you did." —*Times*] I charge that that platform was the platform of the Republican party, and adopted by them. The fact that it was the platform of the Republican party, is not now denied; but Mr. Lincoln now says that although his name was on the committee, that he don't think that he was there. He thinks he was in Tazewell, holding court. [Disturbance. —*Tribune*; "He said he was there." —*Times*] I ask your silence, and no interruption. I want to remind Mr. Lincoln of the fact that he was here [the *Times* added "in Springfield"—*ed.*], and I will remind him of the fact. ["You can't do it." "He wasn't there," &c. —*Times*] [Here the *Times* reported that Mr. (Joseph O.) Glover, Chairman of the Republican Committee, interjected: "I hope no Republican will interrupt Mr. Douglas. The masses listened to Mr. Lincoln attentively, and as respectable men, we ought now to hear Mr. Douglas, and without interruption." ("Good") Lincoln deleted this pronouncement from his debates scrapbook, and thus it was not published in the 1860 book edition.—*ed.*] The point is this, that after I had made my speech in Springfield in '54, during that fair, he gave me notice that he was going to reply to me on the next day after the notice. I was sick at the time, and I stayed over to hear his reply to me, and to reply to him. On that day, this very convention of which he speaks was to meet in the Senate Chamber, while he was speaking in the house, and when he got through his speech, my recollection is distinct, that Mr. [Ichabod] Codding [prominent antislavery minister and lecturer—*ed.*] walked in, as I took the stand to reply, and gave notice that the Republican Convention would meet instantly in the Senate Chamber, and called upon the Republicans to go into this very convention instead of listening to me. [Three cheers for Douglas. —*Times*]

Mr. Lincoln [interrupting, excitedly and angrily—*Times*]—Let the Judge add that Lincoln went along with them. [This interruption was made in a pitiful, mean sneaking way, as Lincoln floundered around the stand.—*Times*]

JUDGE DOUGLAS—Mr. Lincoln says let him add that he went along with them to the Senate Chamber. I will not add that for I do not know it.

MR. LINCOLN [again interrupting—*Times*]—I do know it.

[According to the *Times:* "Two of the Republican committee here seized Mr. Lincoln, and by a sudden jerk caused him to disappear from the front of the stand, one of them saying quite audibly, 'What are you making such a fuss for. Douglas didn't interrupt you, and can't you see that the people don't like it.'" Lincoln had this entire, astounding report deleted from the 1860 book edition of the debates—*ed.*]

JUDGE DOUGLAS—But whether he knows or not my point is this, and I will yet bring him to his milk on this point. In the first place Mr. Lincoln was selected by the very men who made the Republican organization that day, to make a speech in reply to me—a speech for that party. He was the leader of that party, and on the very day that he made his speech there in reply to me, preaching up the same doctrine of the Declaration of Independence that niggers were equal to white men— that very day this Republican Convention met there. [Three cheers for Douglas. —*Times*] That Convention waited on him after its time of meeting to hear Mr. Lincoln's speech, and then Codding, the leading man, marched in and gave notice, the moment Lincoln was through, that they would proceed, for they did not want to hear me in reply. ["Strike him again,"—three cheers, etc. —*Times*]

Another fact I have here, a newspaper printed in Springfield, (Lincoln's own town,) in October, '54, a few days afterwards, publishing these resolutions, and charging Mr. Lincoln as entertaining those sentiments, and trying to prove that Mr. [Richard] Yates [future Illinois governor—*ed.*], the candidate for Congress, did. Those have been published on Lincoln again and again, and never before has he denied it. [Three cheers. —*Times*] But, my friends, this thing of denial about acting on the committee, is a miserable quibble to avoid the main issue. [applause, "That's so," —*Times*] The main issue is that this Republican platform declares in favor of the unconditional repeal of the fugitive slave law. Has Mr. Lincoln answered that question? [No, no. —*Times*] I called his attention to it, and I predicted that he would not answer it.

[Bravo, glorious and cheers. —*Times*] How does he answer it? He answers by saying, "I wasn't on the committee that wrote it." [Laughter. —*Times*] Then I repeat the next question, about restricting slavery to those States in which it exists. I asked him to answer that—"Is it so, yes or no?" He says, "I wasn't on the committee at the time. I was up in Tazewell."

The next question is to prohibit the admission of any more slave States in the Union. I put the question to him distinctly whether if the people of the Territory, when they had sufficient population to make a State, should make a State recognizing slavery in it, he would vote for or against admission. ["That's it." —*Times*] He is a candidate for the United States Senate. It is possible, if elected, that he would have a vote directly on this question. ["He never will." —*Times*] I asked him to answer me and you whether he would vote to admit to [the *Times* had "a"—*ed.*] State into the Union with slavery or without, as its own people might choose. ["Hear him," "That's the doctrine," and applause. —*Times*] He has not answered that, has he? ["He never will." —*Times*] He has not answered that question. He has dodged that question under the cover of saying he wasn't on the Committee at the time—he wasn't present when the platform was made. I want to know if he were present in the Senate when the State applies for admission with a Constitution acceptable to its own people, will he admit the State if it asks? [That's the question. —*Times*] He avoids the question; [The *Times* here reported: "MR. LINCOLN—interrupting the third time excitedly, No, Judge—(Mr. Lincoln again disappeared suddenly aided by a pull from behind)." Once again the interruption, if it took place as claimed, was expunged from the "official" transcripts published in 1860—*ed.*] at the same time he gives the Abolitionists to understand by a hint that he would not vote to admit such a State. Why? Why, he says that a man who would talk about each State having Slavery as it pleased, was akin to the man who would muzzle the press of the Revolution. [Great laughter. —*Times*] He says that that kind of talk is blighting the glory of this country. What is the meaning of that? The meaning is, that he is not in favor of each State doing as it pleased on the Slavery question. ["Stick it to him," "don't spare him," and applause. —*Times*] And now I tell you, I shall put the question to him again and again, and I want to screw it out of him. [Immense applause. —*Times*]

Again, this platform which was made at Springfield by his own party, when he was its acknowledged head, proves that they will go for abolishing slavery in the District of Columbia. I asked Mr. Lincoln specifically whether he will do that or not, yet did you get an answer from him? ["No, no." —*Times*] He is afraid to answer. ["We will not vote for him." —*Times*] He knows I will trot him down to Egypt. [Laughter and cheers. —*Times*] I intend to make him answer there as well as here ["That's right," —*Times*], and I intend to show the people of Illinois that his object is not to answer on these points. ["Keep him to the point," "give us more," etc. —*Times*]

Again, they go on further, and pledge themselves to exclude slavery from all the territories over which the General Government has exclusive jurisdiction, north of 36 deg. 30 min. [the Missouri Compromise line—*ed.*] as well as south, and south as well as north. Now I want to know whether he is for that prohibition. [He'll never answer and cheers. —*Times*] I want to know these things, and when he answers them, I want to know his opinion on the further point, whether he will redeem the pledge of this platform to arrest the acquisition of any more territory, unless the practice of slavery shall have been therein forever prohibited. I want him to answer that last question—each and all of those questions. They are practical questions—questions upon which the Republican party was formed. They are the fundamental principles of the [*Times* added "Black Republican"—*ed.*] party, and I want to know whether he is the unanimous—the first, last and only choice of that party with whom he don't agree in principle. [Great applause, "Rake him down." —*Times*] He don't deny but what that platform was unanimously adopted by the party—he don't deny but what the man who is not faithful to it is faithless to the Republican party. I want to know whether the Republican party are unanimously in favor of a man who don't adopt their creed or agree with them in their principles? I want to know whether a man who is afraid to avow that he is with them, is the first, last and the only choice of the Republican party. [Cheers. —*Times*]

A Voice—How about the conspiracy?

Judge Douglas—Never mind. I will come to that soon enough. [Bravo, Judge, hurra, three cheers for Douglas. —*Times*]

But the platform not only lays down this, but has the other resolution "that in furtherance of these principles we will use such constitutional and lawful means as shall seem best adapted to their accomplishment, and that we will support no man for office, under the General or State

Government, who is not positively and fully committed to the support of these principles, and whose personal character and conduct is not a guaranty that he is reliable and who shall not have abjured old party allegiance and ties." ["Good," "You have him," &c. —*Times*] Now the Republican party stands pledged that they never will support Mr. Lincoln till he has given pledges for that platform. [tremendous applause, men throwing up their hats, and shouting, "you've got him." —*Times*] And he cannot devise an answer. He has not made up his mind whether he will or not. [Great laughter. —*Times*] He talked about everything else he could think of in order to occupy his hour and a half, and when he could not think of anything more to say, in order to get an excuse for refusing to answer these questions, he sat down before his time was up, and told you so. [Cheers. —*Times*]

Now about this charge of conspiracy. Mr. Lincoln to-day goes on and quotes a part of his speech—a playful part of it—about Stephen and James, and Franklin, and Roger, &c., and said that I did not take exception to that, and did not answer. He repeats that again. That was not what I took exception to. He has a right to use these playful words, and throw his words together as much as he pleases. What I took exception to was this. Afterwards he made a speech in which he said he intended that speech as a charge of corruption and conspiracy between the Judges of the Supreme Court, President Pierce, President Buchanan and myself. That gave the offensive character to the charge. He then said that when he made it, he did not know whether it was true or not [laughter —*Times*], but he said that inasmuch as Judge Douglas had not denied it, although he replied to the other parts of the speech three times, he now repeated the charge of conspiracy on Judge Douglas, and thus turned it into a charge of moral turpitude, and when he put it in that form, I did not say that inasmuch as he repeated the charge merely because I did not deny it—did it on my silence, not knowing it to be true. I would deprive him of the opportunity of ever repeating it again, by saying it was in all its bearings an infamous lie. [Three cheers for Douglas. —*Times*] He says he will repeat it until I will get into answering his folly about Frank [President Pierce—*ed.*], and Bob, and John [perhaps associate justices Robert Grier and John Catron—*ed.*]. He studied that out, and prepared that one sentence, and committed it to memory, to put it in his speech at Springfield, and carries it around now and reads it to the audience to hear how pretty it is. [Laughter. —*Times*] His vanity is offended because I won't go into that beautiful passage about building the house. [Renewed laughter. —*Times*] All I have to say is, I am not green enough to let him make a charge which he acknowledges he did not know to be true and then take up the whole of my time in answering a charge which I know to be false and nobody knows to be true. [Cheers. —*Times*] I have not brought a charge of moral turpitude against him, and when he or any other living man bring one against me, instead of putting myself on the proof and disproving it, I will say it is a lie! [Enthusiastic applause. —*Times*] I have lived twenty-five years in Illinois—I have served you with all the fidelity and ability I know how ["That's so," "Good," and cheers, —*Times*], and he is at liberty to attack my public course and sections, to attack my views and conduct, but when he attacks my moral integrity by a charge of conspiracy between me and Justice Taney and the two Presidents, I repel it. ["Three cheers for Douglas." —*Times*]

Mr. Lincoln has not character enough for integrity and truth, merely on his own *ipse dixit* [a dictum asserted but unproved—*ed.*], to arraign President Buchanan and President Pierce, and the Judges of the Supreme Court, any one of whom would not be complemented if put on a level with Mr. Lincoln. ["Hit him again, three cheers," &c. —*Times*] There is as unpardonable presumption in a man putting himself up before thousands of people, and pretending to think his *ipse dixit* without proof, or fact, or evidence or truth, is enough to break down the character of the purest and best of living men. ["Hear him," "Three cheers." —*Times*]

I must pass on: my time is escaping. Mr. Lincoln wants to know why I voted against Chase's amendment to the Nebraska Bill. I tell him in the first place, the bill already conferred all the power which Congress had, by giving them the whole power over the subject. Then Chase offered a proviso, that they might abolish slavery, which by implication would carry the idea that they could prohibit, but could not introduce it. Gen. Cass, I think, proposed to modify it so that they might either introduce or prohibit slavery and make it fair and equal. Chase refused to modify it in that form, and then Cass and all the rest of us voted it down. [Immense cheering. —*Times*] These facts appear in the journals and debates, where Mr. Lincoln found the charge, and if he had told the truth, there would have been no necessity for me to occupy your time in explaining the charge. [Laughter and applause. —*Times*] Mr. Lincoln wants to know why the word State, as well as Territory, is put in the Nebraska Bill. I tell him it was put there by me, particularly to

meet just such false arguments as he has been introducing [Laughter.
—*Times*]—that not only the Territory should do as it pleased, but that
the State should—that is, it should come in as a State with or without
slavery, as it pleased. I mean to knock in the head these abolition
doctrines of his that there should be no more slave States, even if the
people wanted them [Tremendous applause. —*Times*], and it won't do
for Mr. Lincoln and the [Black—*Times*] Republicans to say that nobody
is against the doctrine of there being any more slave States.

What was the cause of the Missouri Compromise? The people of
Missouri formed a constitution as a slave State, and asked for admission, and the Free Soil party being in the majority, voted her out of the
Union, because she had slavery. Hence this first slavery agitation arose
upon a State and not upon a Territory; and yet Mr. Lincoln don't know
why the word "state" was there. [Great laughter and applause.
—*Times*] The whole abolition agitation arose out of that doctrine of
prohibiting the State from entering in with slavery or without it as it
pleased, and that question is now in this Republican platform of '54—
never been repealed yet—and every Republican stands pledged by the
platform never to vote for any man who is not in favor of that platform;
and yet Mr. Lincoln does not know that there are men in the world
opposed to admitting a State with slavery if they want it, at the same
time that this platform says that they won't receive a State under these
circumstances. [The *Times* added: "He is an ignorant man" (Cheers)—
ed.]

Now, my friends, you see that on these very points I am as far from
bringing Lincoln to the line as I ever was before. He did not want to
avow his principles. I do want to proclaim mine as sunlight in mid-day.
The Democrats in principles are founded—Democracy is founded—in
the eternal principles of truth. [That is the talk. —*Times*] The plainer
those principles are avowed, the stronger the support they will receive.
I only wish I had the power to make them so clear that they would shine
in the heavens, for every man, woman and child to read. [Loud cheering. —*Times*] And the first principles that I would proclaim, would be
in opposition to Mr. Lincoln's doctrines of uniformity between the
institutions of the different States, and would declare in lieu of it the
sovereign right of each State to decide the Slavery question as well as
all other questions for themselves, without interference from any other
State or power whatsoever. [Hurrah for Douglas. —*Times*] When you
will recognize that principle, you will have peace, and harmony, and

fraternity between all the different States of this Union. Till you do recognize that doctrine, there will be a sectional warfare, agitating and disturbing the peace of this country. What does Mr. Lincoln propose? He says the Union cannot exist divided into free and slave States. If it cannot endure thus divided, then he must strive to make them all free or all slave, or be for a dissolution of the Union. [Cries of "he can't do it." —*Times*]

I am told that my time is up, and stop therefore. [Three times three cheers were here given for Senator Douglas. —*Times*]

[At the conclusion of the debate, when Mr. Lincoln walked down from the platform, he was seized by the multitude and borne off on their shoulders, in the center of a crowd of five thousand shouting Republicans, with a band of music in front. The Chicago delegation scattered for the cars, and so ended the GREAT DEBATE. —*Tribune*. But the *Times* reported: "When Douglas had concluded the shouts were tremendous; his excoriation of Lincoln was so severe, that the republicans hung their heads in shame. The democrats, however, were loud in their vociferation."]

THE SECOND JOINT
DEBATE AT FREEPORT

Friday, August 27, 1858

· THE SCENE ·

STEPHEN A. DOUGLAS arrived in Freeport the night before the second great debate to be greeted by "a vast multitude," "a turn-out of torches," and "a salvo of artillery" as enthusiastic as any welcome ever afforded "Napoleon or Victoria." At least, that is how the Democratic press described the reception afforded him there. As a Republican journal scoffed, the so-called parade attracted only "boys" and "loafers," and boasted no more than seventy-four torches at most.

If the latter version came closer to the truth, there was ample reason. The site of the second Lincoln-Douglas meeting, like the first, was a Republican stronghold in the upper regions of the state, six hours by train from Chicago. If the political climate in Freeport was somewhat less radical than in Ottawa (the local congressman, Elihu Washburne, was nonetheless a loyal Lincoln supporter), it made up for the slight disadvantage by geography. The town of 7,000 was situated even farther north than the first debate town—only a few miles south of the Wisconsin border.

Lincoln arrived in Freeport the morning of the debate, aboard a special train filled with his supporters. The crowd of enthusiasts who met him at the depot "roared themselves hoarse on his appearance," an eyewitness remembered, greeting him with a booming cannon salute before escorting him into town.

By noon, both debaters were installed in the same hotel, the elegant new Brewster House, where each was given a welcoming reception. Lincoln could be seen waving periodically from the windows, and one of the last living survivors of the events that day swore he recalled seeing both candidates appear on the hotel balcony "Arm-in-Arm," to roars of approval from onlookers gathered below.

Meanwhile, crowds of enthusiasts were surging into town for the afternoon debate. The Freeport *Journal* had predicted "the largest gathering ever known here," and despite the damp, chilly, overcast day, by noon, as the candidates took dinner, some 15,000 men and women, double the population of the village, had flocked into what some onlookers remembered as a grove—"a vacant lot" was how another eyewitness described it—only "a couple of squares behind" the Brewster House, and not far from the Illinois Central railroad tracks and the banks of the Pecatonica River. There, "in the shadow of two trees," a crude platform had been erected that looked to one observer like a "pyramid of lumber." Again, no chairs or benches had been provided for spectators, prompting anxious "scuffles for position." And again, the uninvited swarmed over the stage and planted themselves stubbornly in the seats reserved for politicians and reporters, refusing to be ousted until the last possible minute.

Lincoln made an uncharacteristically theatrical entrance onto this scene, riding the short distance from the hotel in a box-shaped, horse-drawn Conestoga wagon, seated alongside an escort of "old-fashioned farmers." The emphasis on his frontier roots presaged the "railsplitter" image that would be developed for Lincoln in the presidential race two years later. Douglas had planned a similar ride into the grove aboard his own horse-drawn conveyance—a more elegant one than Lincoln's—but apparently decided instead to walk after observing his opponent's "burlesque." By the time both debaters reached their seats, an "immense throng" encircled the platform, above which bobbed a flotilla of banners

declaring such sentiments as "All Men Are Created Equal,"
"Lincoln the Giant Killer," "Douglas and Popular Sovereignty,"
and "No Nigger Equality."

The striking contrast between the combatants was never more in
evidence. Douglas was dressed "richly" in what one spectator
remembered as "plantation style": a ruffled shirt, a close-fitting blue
coat with shiny buttons, and a "wide-brimmed soft hat." Lincoln, on
the other hand, wore his customary well-worn stovepipe hat, "a
coarse-looking coat with sleeves far too short, and baggy looking
trousers so short they showed his rough boots." Whatever advantage
Douglas enjoyed in dignity, however, may have been reduced when
he was struck rudely in the shoulder by a melon rind during his
speech.

Before the debate could get under way, Lincoln learned that the
Chicago *Press and Tribune*'s "phonographic reporter" had not yet
taken his seat on the platform. "Ain't Hitt here?" Lincoln was
overheard asking. "Where is he?" Ultimately the encounter began in
Hitt's absence; a stenographer in the audience was summoned to
take his place until the frail *Tribune* employee could break through
the crowd and reach the stage.

What followed were the best-remembered three hours of all the
Lincoln-Douglas debates, although, ironically, the fame of the
Freeport encounter is attributable chiefly to a myth. Lincoln opened
the discussion by responding to the seven questions Douglas had
posed the week before at Ottawa, and then turned the tables on his
opponent by asking four interrogatories of his own.

It was the second of these questions that, deservedly or not,
immortalized Freeport. Asked Lincoln: "Can the people of the
United States territory [territories] in any lawful way, against the
wishes of any citizen of the United States, exclude slavery from their
limits prior to the formation of a state constitution?" Douglas had
no problem supplying an answer: Since slavery always depended on
local police laws to sustain a slave code, he replied, a local
legislature could indeed exclude slavery simply by refusing to enact
such laws. The exchange hardly sounds momentous to modern ears,
but legend held that Lincoln shrewdly posed the question in order to
destroy the senator's standing in the South, thereby killing his
chances for the presidency two years later, even if the response
might ensure Douglas's reelection to the Senate. "I am after bigger

game," Lincoln supposedly confided (some heard it as, "I am killing larger game"). "The battle of 1860 is worth a hundred of this."

Hard evidence—or the lack of it—conspires against the folklore. For one thing, Douglas was already on shaky ground with Southerners over his opposition to the pro-slavery Lecompton Constitution for Kansas. As Lincoln put it, "he knows he is already dead there." And as Douglas himself had acknowledged a year earlier of his status among his pro-Lecompton fellow Democrats: "I am an out sider." Besides, others had posed similar questions before and Douglas had answered them in much the same way. Finally, Lincoln was only beginning at this point to earn national attention; to suggest he was already focused on presidential ambitions is ludicrous. Furthermore, a losing Senate race is not ordinarily a stepping-stone to the White House. In fact, the Freeport question might well have been a political blunder for Lincoln, not Douglas. It allowed the senator to broaden his appeal to undecided, moderate Illinois voters, without achieving any positive result for Lincoln. As the stuff of myth, historian David Potter later dismissed the exchange as "one of the great non-events of American history."

Lincoln may have won the Freeport debate anyway—principally by enjoying the first and last word there, which always put the ninety-minute rebuttal speaker at a disadvantage, and by swinging out against Douglas with a new aggressiveness from the outset, as admirers had urged in letters inspired by his comparatively enervated performance at Ottawa. In a letter forwarded to him at Freeport, apparently calculated to inspire him before he took to the platform there, a Cincinnati admirer admonished: "Your [sic] too mild, I fear, on that fellow. You should be more severe . . . give him fits from the word go." And the Press and Tribune's Joseph M. Medill agreed: "You are dealing with a bold, brazen, lying rascal and you must fight the devil with fire!' " Added Medill, "Give him h--l." Lincoln seemed to take the advice to heart.

As for the Little Giant, his performance is best remembered for his scornful charge that when last in town, he had seen black leader Frederick Douglass daring to ride alongside white women in a carriage driven by a white man. "What of it?" someone in the crowd shouted back; but even in pro-Republican Freeport, another voice was heard to cry out: "Down with the negro." Racism still had its following everywhere in Illinois. (Frederick Douglass had four years earlier challenged Stephen Douglas to what he called an "ebony and ivory" face-to-face debate, but the senator refused. "No man of his time," the former slave later charged, "has done more than he to intensify hatred of the negro.")

Newspaper assessments of the Freeport debate were predictably partisan. In a preemptive strike against the opposition transcripts, the Republican organ published a front-page warning within its August 30 coverage of the Freeport debate, under the headline "Look out for More Forgeries." Announced the *Press and Tribune:* "We are informed that Douglas has another great forgery in soak, viz: a mutilated report of LINCOLN's Freeport argument, on the exact plan of Ottawa." Here, the paper charged, was nothing less than a "system of scoundrelism . . . to be pursued THROUGHOUT THE CAMPAIGN." Undaunted, the Democratic *Illinois State Register* declared that Lincoln failed to "recover any of the ground lost at Ottawa," while the Republican *Press and Tribune* insisted that the spectators at Freeport heckled Douglas into submission, adding: "Good for old Stephenson [county]." In Congressman Washburne's view, however, because of the noise, confusion, and dismal weather, "the audience did not take in the vast importance of the debate." The encounter broke up, he wrote later, "without any display of enthusiasm."

The following texts were published by the rival newspapers.

Mr. Lincoln's Opening Speech

[Mr. Lincoln was introduced by Hon. Thomas J. Turner, and was greeted with loud cheers. When the applause had subsided, he said: —*Tribune*]

Ladies and Gentlemen:—On Saturday last, at Ottawa, Senator Douglas and myself first met in public discussion. He spoke an hour, I an hour and a half, and he replied half an hour. It is now reversed. I am to speak an hour, he an hour and a half, and I reply half an hour.

I propose to myself to devote the first hour to the scope of what was brought within the range of his half hour's speech at Ottawa. Of course, there was brought within the scope of that half hour's speech something of his own opening speech. In the course of that speech—the first one—Judge Douglas propounded to me seven distinct interrogatories. In my speech of an hour and a half, in attending to some other part of his speech, I incidentally, as I thought, answered one of his interrogatories. I then distinctly intimated to him that I would answer the other of his interrogatories upon the terms that he would answer as many for me. He made no intimation at the time of the proposition, nor did he, in his reply, allude at all to the suggestion of mine; but I think I do him no justice in saying that he occupied that last half hour of his reply in dealing with me as though I had absolutely and unconditionally refused to answer his interrogatories. I now propose to the judge that I will answer every one of his interrogatories upon condition that he will answer any number from me not exceeding the same number. [Applause. —*Times*] I shall make no objection to the judge saying "yes," or "no" right now, or, if it suits him, to remain silent. I pause for a moment to see how it will be—[a voice—"answer," —*Times*] well, I suppose that I may assume that the judge chooses to remain silent. [Laughter and applause. —*Times*] I now say to you, my fellow citizens, that I will answer his interrogatories whether he answers mine or not. [Laughter. —*Times*] I shall then propound mine and leave them standing for the judge's good pleasure. [Laughter, and a voice, "hit him again." —*Times*] [The *Tribune* had not recorded Lincoln's remarks up to this juncture, explaining: "Owing to the press of people against the platform, our reporter did not reach the stand until Mr. Lincoln had spoken to this point. The previous remarks were taken by a gentleman in

Freeport, who has politely furnished them to us"—*ed.*] Before I enter upon this answering of the judge's interrogatories—

[The *Times* reported: "Here an interruption of some minutes occurred by the uprising of Mr. Deacon Bross, who, perceiving a friend in the crowd, desired that he should come upon the stand. The particular friend of Mr. Deacon Bross having mounted the platform;" (William Bross was an editor of the pro-Lincoln Chicago *Press and Tribune,* but Lincoln deleted all references to his subsequent comments and asides from his debates scrapbook; hence they were not included in the book version of the debates—*ed.*)]

Mr. Lincoln proceeded. I desire to say that I have no secret pledges in connection with my position in this canvass to any man or set of men. That I have supposed myself, since what I consider the organization of the republican party at Bloomington, in May, 1856—I supposed myself bound as a party man by the platform of the party then and since then; and in some of the interrogatories which I shall answer I go beyond the scope of what is within any of the platforms that I allude to, and in doing so I do not know really whether I stand in accordance with the republican party or not.

Having said this much, I will now take up the judge's interrogatories as I find them propounded in the Chicago *Times.* I answer them *seriatim,* and in order that there may be no mistake about it, I have copied in writing the interrogatories, and also my answer to them.

The first one of these interrogatories is in these words. "I desire to know whether Lincoln to-day stands as he did in 1854, in favor of the unconditional repeal to the fugitive slave law." To which I answer: I do not now nor ever did stand in favor of the unconditional repeal of the fugitive slave law. [Cries of "Good," "Good." —*Tribune*]

2d interrogatory: "I desire him to answer whether he stands pledged to-day, as he did in 1854, against the admission of any more slave states into the Union, even if the people want them." I answer I do not nor ever did stand pledged against the admission of any more slave states into the Union.

3d interrogatory: "I want to know whether he stands pledged against the admission of a new state into the Union with such a constitution as the people of that state may see fit to make." I answer I do not stand pledged against the admission of the people of that state with such a constitution as they may see fit to make. [Cries of "good, good." —*Tribune*]

Interrogatory 4: "I want to know whether he stands today pledged to the abolition of slavery in the District of Columbia." I answer, I do not stand to-day pledged to the abolition of slavery in the District of Columbia. [Confusion. —*Times*]

Question 5. "I desire him to answer whether he stands pledged to the prohibition of the slave trade between the different states." I answer, I do not stand pledged to the prohibition of the slave trade between the different states.

Question 6.—"I desire to know whether he stands pledged to prohibit slavery in all the territories of the United States, north as well as south of the Missouri compromise line." I answer, I am impliedly, if not expressly pledged to the belief in the right and duty of congress to prohibit slavery in all the United States territories. [Great applause. —*Tribune*]

[Deacon Bross of the Chicago *Press and Tribune*. Good. —*Times*]

Question 7.—"I desire him to answer whether he is opposed to the acquisition of any more territory unless slavery is first prohibited therein.["] I answer, I am not generally opposed to the honest acquisition of territory, and in any given case I would or would not oppose such acquisition, according as I might think such acquisition would or would not aggravate the slavery question among ourselves. [Cries of good, good. —*Tribune*]

Now, my friends, it will be perceived upon an examination of these questions I answer that so far I have only answered as to whether I was pledged for this, or that, or any other thing. The judge has not framed his interrogatories to ask me anything more than this, and I have answered in strict accordance with his interrogatories, and truly, that I am not pledged at all upon any of the points to which I have answered that I am not pledged; but I am not disposed to hang upon the form of his interrogatories, but I am disposed at least to take up some of these questions, and state what I really think upon them.

I say to the first, in regard to the fugitive slave law, I have never hesitated to say that I think, under the constitution of the United States the people of the southern states are entitled to a congressional fugitive slave law. I have always said that, and having said that, I have nothing to say in regard to the existing slave law further than this, that I think it might have been framed to have been free from some of the objections that pertain to it without at all lessening its efficiency. But inasmuch as we are not in the midst of an agitation in regard to the modification of that law, I would not be the man to introduce it as the subject of a new agitation upon the subject of slavery.

In regard to these other questions of whether I am pledged to the (non)admission of any more slave states in the Union, I state to you freely, frankly, that I should be exceedingly sorry to ever be put in the position of having to pass upon that question. I should be exceedingly glad to know that there never would be another slave state admitted into the Union [applause. —*Tribune*], but I must add in regard to this, that if slavery shall be kept out of the territory during the territorial existence of any one given territo[r]y, and then the people should, having a fair chance and clear field when they come to adopt a constitution, if they should do the extraordinary thing of adopting a slave constitution uninfluenced by the actual presence of the institution among them, I see no alternative, if we own the country but we must admit it into the Union. [Applause. —*Tribune*]

[Deacon Bross, editor of the Chicago *Press and Tribune*—That is the true doctrine! That is popular sovereignty! —*Times*]

Mr. Lincoln continued.—The third interrogatory is answered by the answer to the second, the third being substantially the same as the second, as I conceive.

The fourth one is in regard to the abolition of slavery in the District of Columbia. In relation to that I have my mind very distinctly, whether correctly or not, made up. I should be exceedingly glad to see slavery abolished in the District of Columbia. [Applause. —*Times;* Cries of "good, good." —*Tribune*] I believe that congress possesses the constitutional power to abolish it, yet as a member of congress I should not be in favor, with my present views of interfering, to abolish slavery in the District of Columbia, unless it should be upon three conditions: 1st. That the abolition should be gradual; in the second place, that it should be upon the vote of a majority of the qualified voters within the district, and lastly, with compensation to unwilling owners. With these three conditions, I confess that I should be exceedingly glad to see congress abolish slavery in the District of Columbia, and, in the language of Henry Clay, "sweep from the national capital that foul blot upon our nation." [Loud applause. —*Tribune*]

In regard to the fifth interrogatory, I must say here that as to the question of the slave trade between the different states, while I can truly answer as I have, that I am pledged to nothing about it at all, it is a subject to which I have not given that mature consideration that would make me feel authorized to state a position so as to hold myself entirely bound by it; in other words, that question has never been made prominent enough before me to induce me to investigate the question as to whether we really have the constitutional power to do the thing. I could investigate it if I had sufficient time, and bring myself to a conclusion upon it, but I have not done so. I say so frankly here to you, and to Judge Douglas. I must say, however, that if I should be of opinion that congress does possess the constitutional power to abolish the slave trade among the different states, I should not be in favor of the exercise of that power unless it should be upon some conservative principle, as I conceive it akin to what I have said in relation to the abolition of slavery in the District of Columbia.

My answer as to whether I desire that slavery should be prohibited in all the territories of the United States is fully expressed within itself, and cannot be added to, as I suppose, by any comments of mine.

[Deacon Bross, editor of the Chicago *Press and Tribune*—That will do. —*Times*]

MR. LINCOLN,—and so I suppose in regard to the question as to whether I am opposed to the acquisition of any more territory, unless slavery is first prohibited therein, I suppose my answer to that is such that I perhaps could add nothing to it by way of illustrating it, or making me better understood, than the answer which I have placed in writing.

In all this the judge has me, and he has me on the record. I supposed the judge has flattered himself, that I was really entertaining one set of opinions in one place and another in another that I was afraid of saying in one place what I would not say at another, but what I am saying here, I suppose I am saying in presence of a large audience as strongly tending toward abolitionism as any audience that can be gotten in the State of Illinois. I suppose that if such an audience can be found, I am saying it in the presence of that audience.

I now proceed, my friends, to propound to the judge the interrogatories, so far as I have framed them, and I will bring forward a new installment when I get ready. [Laughter. —*Tribune*] The interrogatories so far as I have framed them, only now reach to number four.

The first one is, if the people of Kansas shall by means entirely unobjectionable in all other respects adopt a state constitution and ask admission into the Union under it before they have the requisite number of inhabitants according to the English bill, to wit; ninety-three thousand, will you vote to admit them? [Applause. —*Tribune*] [The

"English Bill" was Indiana congressman William English's effort to resubmit the controversial, already defeated Lecompton Constitution to the people of Kansas through a technicality: by offering it now as a land-grant resolution. The Republicans—and Douglas—opposed the English Bill in the Senate, but it passed anyway. Then, only three weeks before this debate, Kansas voters again decisively defeated Lecompton by a margin of eight to one—*ed.*]

2. Can the people of the United States territory in any lawful way, against the wishes of any citizen of the United States, exclude slavery from their limits prior to the formation of a state constitution? [Applause, and cries of "that's it," "good," "he won't answer!" —*Times;* Renewed applause. —*Tribune*]

3. If the supreme court of the United States shall decide that states cannot exclude slavery from their limits, are you in favor of acquiescing in adopting and following such decision as a rule of political action? [Applause. —*Times;* Renewed applause. —*Tribune*]

4. Are you in favor of acquiring additional territory in disregard of how such acquisition may affect the nation on the slavery question? [A voice—"better." —*Times;* Cries of "good," "good." —*Tribune*]

As introductory to those interrogatories which Judge Douglas propounded to me at Ottawa, he read a set of resolutions which he said Judge Trumbull and myself had participated in the adoption of in the first republican state convention held at Springfield in October, 1854. He insisted that I and Judge Trumbull, and perhaps, the entire republican party, were responsible for the doctrines contained in a set of resolutions which he read, and it was from that set of resolutions that he deduced, as I understood, the interrogatories which he propounded to me, and using the resolutions as a sort of authority for propounding those interrogatories to me. Now, I say here to you to-day, that I do not answer his interrogatories because of their at all springing from that set of resolutions which he read. I answer them because Judge Douglas thought fit to ask them. [Applause. —*Tribune*] I do not now, nor ever did, recognize any responsibility upon me in that set of resolutions. When I replied to him, or answered him upon that occasion, I assured him that I had never had anything to do with that set of resolutions. I repeat here to-day that I never, in any possible form, had anything to do with that set of resolutions.

It turns out, I believe—it turns out as I believe, that those resolutions were never passed in any convention at Springfield. [Applause. —*Times;*

Cheers and laughter. —*Tribune*] It turns out that they were never passed in any convention, or any public meeting that I had any part in; and I believe it turns out, in addition to all this, that there was not in the fall of 1854 any convention holding a session in Springfield calling it a republican state convention. [Applause and laughter. —*Times*] Yet it is true that there was a convention, or assemblage of men calling themselves a convention at Springfield, that did pass some resolutions—at least I believe this to be true, and so little did I really know of the proceedings of that convention, and what sort of resolutions they had passed, having a general knowledge that there had been such a convocation of men there, that when Judge Douglas read his resolutions I really did not know but they were the resolutions that had been passed there, and it all passed by without my contradicting it. They were so very precise that I could not bring myself to suppose that the judge could bring himself to say what he was saying upon that subject without knowing that it was true. [Cheers and laughter. —*Tribune*] I contented myself upon that occasion with denying, as I truly could, all connection with them, not denying or affirming whether they were passed at Springfield or not. It turns out that they were passed at some meeting held in Kane county. [Renewed laughter. —*Tribune*] Now, I want to say here, that I don't conceive in fair and just minds this discovery relieves me any at all. I had just as much to do with the convention in Kane county as I had with that at Springfield. I am just as much responsible for the resolutions passed in Kane county as for those passed at Springfield.

[Deacon Bross, editor of the *Press and Tribune*,—"that is good." —*Times*]

MR. LINCOLN.—It amounts to just nothing; no more than there would be in regard to the responsibility of a set of resolutions passed in the moon. [Laughter and loud cheers. —*Tribune*]

I allude to this extraordinary matter in this canvass for some further purpose than what I have yet advanced. Judge Douglas did not make his statements upon that occasion as matter that he believed to be true; but he stated them roundly as being true, in such form as I understand to pledge his veracity for the truth of them. When this matter turns out as it does, and when we consider who Judge Douglas is—that he is a distinguished senator of the United States; that he has served nearly twelve years in such capacity, and that his character is not at all limited as an ordinary senator of the United States, but that his name has become of world wide renown; it is most extraordinary, as I think, that he should so far forget all the suggestions of justice to an adversary, or of prudence to himself, as to venture upon the assertion of a thing which the slightest investigation would have shown him to be altogether false; [applause. —*Times;* cheers. —*Tribune*] and I can only account for his having done so upon the supposition that that evil genius which has attended him through his life, giving to him an apparent astonishing prosperity, such as led very good men to doubt of there being any advantage in virtue over vice [Cheers and laughter. —*Tribune*]—I can only account for it upon the supposition that that evil genius has at last made up his mind to forsake the judge, [laughter. —*Times;* Continued cheers and laughter. —*Tribune*] and I may add, while I am upon the subject, another rather extraordinary feature of the judge's conducting of this canvass—as it seems to me, made more extraordinary by this incident.

The judge is in the habit, as I understand, in almost all the speeches he makes, of charging falsehood upon his adversaries—myself and others.

[A VOICE—Come on to free labor; never mind the judge; tell us what you mean. —*Times*]

MR. LINCOLN—I do now ask the judge's attention whether he shall be able at all, in any thing that I have said, to find a justification at all comparing with what we have in this instance against him, for that sort of ugly talk [the *Tribune* substituted "vulgarity"—*ed.*]. [Applause. —*Times;* Cries of "good," "good," "good." —*Tribune*]

I have been in the habit, as I may begin to say now, of charging, as a matter of belief, that in the introduction of the Nebraska bill into congress there was a conspiracy to make slavery perpetual and national. I have arrayed, from time to time, the evidence which I think—I have thought—tends to prove the truth of this charge. I recurred to this in the discussion at Ottawa. I shall not have the time to dwell upon it with very great length; but inasmuch as Judge Douglas, in his reply of half an hour, made some points back upon me in relation to that matter, I propose noticing a few of them.

The judge insists that in the first speech I made, in which I very distinctly made that charge, as I think that he thought for a good while I was in fun. [Laughter. —*Times*] That I was playful, that I was not sincere about it, that he only grew angry and somewhat excited when he found that I insisted upon it as a matter of earnestness, and he says that what he characterizes as falsehood is so far as I implicate his moral character in that transaction. Well I was not—until the judge presented that view—I was not aware that I had implicated his moral character. Now the judge is very much in the habit when he argues me up into a position which I never thought of occupying for myself, of saying that he has no doubt in saying it, he has no doubt Lincoln is altogether conscientious in that matter. Now the judge should remember that I have no doubt *"he* is conscientious in that matter." [Great laughter. —*Tribune*] I can conceive that it is possible for him to conspire to do what he thinks in itself is good and right. I do not find anything really in Judge Douglas' course or argument that is contrary or inconsistent with his belief, of the right to nationalize and perpetuate slavery as being a good and blessed thing [Continued laughter. —*Tribune*], and so I hope he will understand that I do not question that in all this matter that he is conscientious in it. [More laughter and cheers. —*Tribune*]

But to draw your attention to one of the points I made in that case, beginning at the beginning. When the Nebraska bill was introduced, or a short while afterwards by an amendment, it was provided—and I am afraid I shall be offensive to the judge by quoting it again—it was provided, that it be "the true intent and meaning of this act, not to legislate slavery into any state or territory, nor to exclude it therefrom, but to leave the people thereof perfectly free to form and regulate their domestic institutions in their own way, subject only to the constitution of the United States." I have called his attention to the fact, that when thereupon he and his friends began arguing, that they were giving an increased degree of liberty to the people in the territories, over and above what they had formerly on this question of slavery, that it was questioned whether the law was intended to give any additional liberty to the people. To test the sincerity of those who made that argument, Chase of Ohio introduced an amendment in which he made the law, if the amendment was adopted, expressly declare that the people of the territory should have the power of excluding slavery if they saw fit, and this being so, I have asked attention to the fact that Judge Douglas with those who acted with him, voted that amendment down, although it exactly expressed the very thing that they said was the true intent and object of that law, yet when introduced by Chase they voted it down. I have asked attention to the fact that in subsequent times a decision of the supreme court has been made, in which it has been declared that the people substantially as I say—that the people have no constitutional right to exclude slavery, and I have argued and said that white men who had intended that the people of a territory should have the right to exclude slavery absolutely and unconditionally, the voting down of that amendment is wholly inexcusable. It is a puzzle—a riddle that cannot be understood.

But I have said, that with men who did look forward to such a decision as that, who then had it in contemplation that a decision of the supreme court would or might be made in which it should be held that the people could not exclude slavery—I say with such men as that the voting down of that amendment would be perfectly rational and intelligent; it would keep congress from being in collision with such decision when it was made.

Now, anybody can conceive that if there was an understanding or expectation that such a decision as that was to follow, that it would not be a very desirable party attitude to get in for the supreme court. All its members, or nearly all of them belonging to them [the *Tribune* substituted: "to the same party"—*ed.*] to decide one way, when the party in congress had decided the other way, and this being so, it, it would be perfectly rational for men who expected such a decision to come to keep a place in that law for it to come, to avoid such a collision. And after I have pointed that out and have told Judge Douglas that it looks to me that that was the reason why Chase's amendment was voted down, I tell him that as he did it he knows why he did it. If he had a different, better, or other reason than this, he knows what that other reason was and can tell it, and I tell him it will be vastly more satisfactory to the country to give some other intelligent, plausible reason for voting it down than it will to stand upon his dignity and call people liars. [Loud cheers. —*Tribune*]

Well the judge did on Saturday, make his answer to that, and now what do you think that answer was? He says that if I had only taken upon myself to tell the whole truth about that amendment of Chase's that no explanation would have been necessary on his part or words to that effect. Now, I say here that I am altogether unconscious of having suppressed anything that is material to the case; but I am very plain [the *Tribune* substituted "frank"—*ed.*] to say that if there is a sound reason it is altogether fair for the judge to produce it. What reason does he produce? Why, he says, when Chase came forward with his amendment expressly authorizing the people to exclude slavery from the limits of every territory, that Gen. Cass, as the judge thinks, proposed to Mr.

Chase, that if Chase would add to his amendment that the people should have the power to introduce or exclude it, that then they would let it go and, because Chase would not do that—would not accept that as an amendment—they voted it down. I believe I fairly state Judge Douglas' answer. Well, it turns out, I believe, upon examination of the record, that Gen. Cass did take some part in the little running debate that was had upon that amendment of Chase's, and then ran away and did not vote upon it. [Laughter. —*Tribune*] Is not that so? [Applause. —*Times*] So confident, as I think, was Gen. Cass, that there was a snake in it that he choose [*sic*] to run away from it, and upon the call of the ayes and noes, his name does not appear. Of course, that is but an inference on my part, but, at least, his name does not appear.

What I ask attention to this for is this: does that answer of Judge Douglas amount to a satisfactory answer upon that question! [A voice— "no," "that is the question!" cries of "yes," and "no." —*Times* and *Tribune*]

[Deacon Bross spoke. —*Times*]

MR. LINCOLN—There is some difference of opinion, [Laughter. —*Tribune*] but I ask attention a little while, as to whether it amounts to a satisfactory answer.

The men who were determined, as I think, that that amendment should not go in the bill and spoil the place that the Dred Scott decision was to come in, sought an excuse to get rid of it some way, and one of those ways—one of those excuses was to ask Chase to add to his proposed amendment a provision that the people might introduce slavery if they wanted to. Now, they very well knew that Chase wouldn't do it—they very well knew that Chase was one of the men differing from them on the broad principle that freedom was better than slavery, a man who would not consent to place a provision in a law—to pen it with his own hand—to place a provision in a law by which he was to recognize that slavery on the one hand and freedom on the other were equal. When they insisted on that, they well knew that they were insisting on Chase's doing what they knew that he would not do.

But there is another thing about this matter. I have not had a chance of examining the *Congressional Globe* or *Journal* on the subject; but I believe it is true, that the state of the bill at that time, according to parliamentary rule, was such that no member could propose an additional amendment to Chase's amendment. I rather think that is true. The judge shakes his head! Very well, I would like to know then if they wanted Chase's amendment amended in that way. I ask the judge why they did not offer the amendment—why did they stand there dallying and asking Chase to put it there, when they were able to put it there themselves[?] [Laughter. —*Tribune*]

But we will take it on the other ground. Suppose it is true, that there was an amendment to an amendment offered and that Chase's amendment was an amendment to an amendment, then you cannot by parliamentary law pile it on. Suppose that was so all the gentleman [*sic*] had to do was first, to vote Chase's on, and then in the amended form add their own amendment to it. If they wanted it put in that shape, that was all that they had to do, and the ayes and noes show that they were 36 in favor of the bill and fourteen against it; that thirty-six held entire control, they could in some form or other put it in the exact form and shape that they wanted it. They could pass it at any point of time; they could add Chase's amendment, and then it being merged into the bill, they could add another of their own, and put it exactly in the condition they then desired to have it in. They did not do that. They chose to get into a quibble with Chase to get him to do what they knew very well he would not do for his right arm, then they stand upon that—I must say—flimsy pretext, for voting down an amendment that expressed what they argued was the express purpose of their bill, and thus left room for the Dred Scott decision, which goes far to make slavery national in the United States.

I will drop one or two points that I have, because my time will expire. In doing so, I must be allowed briefly to say that Judge Douglas refers to the enormity of Lincoln—an insignificant individual like Lincoln confesses himself to be—upon his *ipse dixit* charging a conspiracy upon a large number of members of congress, the supreme court, and the president to nationalize slavery. I want to say in the first place, that I have not made any charge of this sort upon my *ipse dixit* or upon my word. I have only arrayed the evidence that tends to prove a state of fact, and showing that to the understanding of others. I give you the means of saying whether it be true or not. That is all that I have done. I have not placed it upon my *ipse dixit*.

But again, I want to call his attention to a piece of evidence that I brought forward at Ottawa, showing that he made substantially the same charge against precisely the same men, excluding his own dear self from the category. I want him, if he pleases, to give us some attention to the fact that he discovered that there was, as he said, "a fatal blow being struck," which fatal blow he ascribed in evidence, in an article in the *Washington Union* published by authority. By whose authority? "Are identical with the provision in the Lecompton constitution." Made by whom? The framers of that constitution? Advocated by whom? By all the members of the party in the nation who advocated the introduction of Kansas into the Union under the Lecompton constitution. I have asked his attention to the evidence that he read to prove that such a fatal blow was being struck, and to the fact that he expressed a charge being identical with this one that he thinks is so villainous in me to make, by pointing it not at a newspaper editor alone, but to the president, at all his cabinet, all the members who voted for that constitution and all the framers of that constitution. I must say that in this regard that my *ipse dixit* may not be so great as his, but somewhat reduces the force of his charge. [The *Tribune* substituted: "the *enormity* of my making a like charge against him." (Loud applause.)—*ed.*]

["Go on, Judge Douglas." —*Tribune*] Mr. Lincoln here sat down.

[Senator Douglas' appearance was the signal for three cheers. —*Times*]

Ladies and Gentlemen—The silence with which you have listened to Mr. Lincoln during his hour is creditable to this vast audience, composed of men of various—of all political parties. Nothing is more creditable to any large mass of people assembled for the purpose of hearing a political discussion than that kind and respectful attention that is yielded not only to your political friends, but to those who are opposed to you in politics.

I am glad at last that I have brought Mr. Lincoln to the conclusion that he had better define his position on certain political topics which I called to his attention at Ottawa. He then showed no disposition—no inclination to answer. I did not present to him mere idle questions for him to answer for my gratification. I proposed to lay the foundations for these interrogatories by showing that they constituted the platform of the party whose nominee he is for the Senate. I did not presume that I had a right to catechise him upon every question that I saw proper, unless I showed that his party, or so large a portion of them were in favor of these propositions as to render it the presumption that the resolutions were contained in the party platform. I desired simply to know, inasmuch as he had been nominated as the first, last, and the only choice of his party, whether he concurred with his party in the platform which that party adopted for its government. I will proceed in a few moments to review the answers which he has given to these interrogatories; but in order to relieve his anxiety, I will first respond to those which he has presented to me. Mark you, he has not presented interrogatories which are or ever have received the sanction of the party with which I am, and hence he has no other foundation for them than that they are merely his interrogatories. ["That's a fact." —*Times*]

First: He desires to know whether, if the people of Kansas shall form a Constitution by means entirely proper and unobjectionable, and ask for admission as a State before they have the requisite population for a member of Congress, whether I will vote for the admission. Well, even I regret exceedingly that when he put that interrogatory to me that he did not first answer it himself, instead of leaving us to infer which side he was on. [Good, good. —*Times*] Gentlemen, Mr. Trumbull, during the last session of Congress, voted, from beginning to end, against the admission of Oregon into the Union, although a free State, because she had not the requisite population. [That's it. —*Times*] Mr. Trumbull is in the field fighting for Mr. Lincoln. I would like to have Mr. Lincoln answer his own question, and tell me whether he is fighting Trumbull on that issue or not [Good, put it to him, and cheers. —*Times*], but I will answer his questions. In my opinion, whenever Kansas has people enough to constitute a slave State, she has people enough for a free State. [Cheers. —*Times*] I will not make any exception of Kansas to the other States of this Union. [Sound, and hear, hear. —*Times*] I hold it to be a sound rule of universal application to require Territories to contain the requisite population for a member of Congress before they came into the Union. I made that proposition in the Senate in 1856. I renewed it in the Senate during the last session, by a bill providing that no Territory of the United States should form a constitution and apply to the Union until it had the requisite population. Congress did not adopt my general rule, requiring all the Territories to have that amount of population before they should come into the Union, but did make an exception of Kansas and applied the rule to Kansas alone. I will not stand by that exception. [Applause. —*Tribune;* Cheers. —*Times*] Either Kansas must come in the same as any other State, with whatever population she may have, or the rule must be applied to all the other States alike. [Cheers. —*Times*] I therefore answer at once, it having been decided that Kansas has enough for a slave State, I hold that she has enough for a free State. [Applause. —*Tribune;* "Good," and applause. —*Times*] I hope Mr. Lincoln is satisfied on this question. ["He ought to be," and cheers. —*Times*] And now I would like to get his answer to his own interrogatory, whether he will vote to admit Kansas before she has the requisite population. ["Hit him again." —*Times*] I want to know whether he will vote for the admission of Oregon before she has the requisite population. Trumbull won't. The same reason that commits him against the admission of Oregon commits him against the admission of Kansas ["You've got him," and cheers. —*Times*], and if there is any sincerity or truth in the argument Trumbull made in the Senate against the admission of Oregon, because she had not 93,420 people, although she had more than Kansas, it will apply as well to Kansas as Oregon. He stands by that argument, pledged against Oregon and Kansas both coming in until they have 93,420 inhabitants. I would like Mr. Lincoln to take his own medicine. [Laughter. —*Times* and *Tribune*] I would like him to answer his own question, and then if he differs with Trumbull let him answer Trumbull's argument on the Oregon question, instead of poking his questions at me. ["Right, good, good," laughter and cheers. —*Times*]

The next question Mr. Lincoln propounded to me is, "Can the people of a Territory exclude slavery from their limits by any fair means, before it comes into the Union as a State." I answer emphatically, as Mr. Lincoln has heard me answer a hundred times, on every stump in Illinois, that in my opinion the people of a Territory can by lawful means exclude slavery before it comes in as a State. [Cheers. —*Tribune;* Enthusiastic applause. —*Times*] Mr. Lincoln knew that I had given that answer over and over again. He heard me argue the Nebraska Bill on that principle, all over the State in 1854 '5 and '6, and he has now no excuse to pretend to have any doubt upon that subject. Whatever the Supreme Court may hereafter decide as to the abstract question of whether slavery may go in under the Constitution or not, the people of a Territory have the lawful means to admit it or exclude it as they please, for the reason that slavery cannot exist a day or an hour anywhere unless supported by local police regulations [Right, right. —*Times*], furnishing remedies and means of enforcing the right to hold slaves. Those local and police regulations can only be furnished by the local legislature. If the people of the Territory are opposed to slavery they will elect members to the legislature who will adopt unfriendly legislation to it. If they are for it they will adopt the legislative measures friendly to slavery. Hence, no matter what may be the decision of the Supreme Court on that abstract question, still the right of the people to make it a slave Territory or a free Territory is perfect and complete under the Nebraska Bill. I hope Mr. Lincoln will deem my answer satisfactory on this point. [Deacon Bross spoke. —*Times*]

In this connection I will notice the charge which he has renewed about the Chase amendment. I thought that I had, at Ottawa, chased that amendment out of Mr. Lincoln's brain [laughter, —*Tribune*], but it seems that it still haunts his imagination, and he is not yet satisfied. I had supposed that Mr. Lincoln would be ashamed to press that question further. He is a lawyer; he has been a member of Congress; yet he has occupied your time, and amused you, by telling you about the rules of parliamentary proceedings. He ought to have known better than to have tried to palm off that miserable humbug upon this intelligent audience. ["Good," and cheers. —*Times*] Now the Nebraska bill provided that the legislative power and authority of the said Territory should extend to all rightful subjects of legislation consistent with the organic law, and the Constitution of the United States. It did not make any exception of slavery, but gave all the power that it was possible for Congress to give without violating the Constitution, to the territorial legislature, with no exception on the subject of slavery at all. Hence that bill, in and by itself, gave to the people of the territory the full power and the full authority over the subject of slavery, negative and affirmative, to introduce or exclude, so far as the Constitution of the United States would permit. What more could Mr. Chase give by his amendment? [The *Times* added: "Nothing"—*ed.*] Yet he offered his amendment for the identical purpose that Mr. Lincoln is using it for—to allow demagogues in the country to try to deceive the people. ["Good, hit him again," and cheers; Deacon Bross spoke. —*Times*] His amendment was to this effect, that the legislature should have the power to exclude slavery. Gen. Cass suggested, "Why not give them the power to introduce as well as exclude slavery?" The answer was, they have already got the power in the bill to do both. Chase was afraid his amendment would be adopted if he put in it the alternative so as to make it fair both ways, and he was not willing to have it adopted. He wanted it rejected. He offered it simply to make capital out of it on the stump, that the people might be deceived in public meetings, at least that small politicians in the country might use it for this purpose, and Mr. Lincoln is carrying out the plan admirably. ["Good, good." —*Times*] Mr. Lincoln knows that that bill, without Chase's amendment, gave all the power which the Constitution of the United States would permit. Could you confer any more? ["No, no." —*Times*] Could you go beyond the Constitution of the country? That bill made the full grant. There was no exception upon slavery one way or the other, but we left that question as we did all other questions, to be decided by the people themselves just as they please. I will not occupy time on that question. I have argued it before, all over Illinois. I have argued it in this beautiful city of Freeport. I have argued it at the north and at the south, in the east and in the west, avowing the same sentiments and the same position. I was not afraid to avow my sentiments up here for fear I would be trotted down into Egypt [the informal name for southern Illinois, where antiabolitionist sentiment ran strongest—*ed.*] [Laughter. —*Tribune;* Cheers and laughter. —*Times*]

The third question Mr. Lincoln presents is this: If the Supreme Court of the United States shall decide that a State of this Union cannot exclude slavery from its own limits, will I submit to it. Now I am amused that Mr. Lincoln should ask such a question. ["A school boy would know better." —*Tribune* and *Times*] As a school boy would know better, gentlemen, the object of that question is to cast an imputation on the Supreme Court. Mr. Lincoln knows there was never but one man in America claiming any degree of intelligence or decency, who ever for a moment pretended to that doctrine. It is true that the Washington *Union,* in an article published on the 17th of last December, did put forth that doctrine, and it was in reply to that article in the *Union* that I denounced the Washington *Union* in the Senate last year in the speech which Mr. Lincoln now pretends was against the President. The *Union* had put forth the doctrine that slavery had a right to go into the free States, and that any provision in the constitution or laws of the free States of the country was null and void. I denounced it on the Senate floor. I was the first man that ever did denounce it. Trumbull, and [William H.] Seward [senator from New York, and early favorite for the 1860 Republican presidential nomination—*ed.*], and [John F.] Hale [generally considered the first antislavery candidate ever elected to the U.S. Senate—*ed.*], and [Henry] Wilson [Massachusetts senator who changed his name from Jeremiah Colbath upon launching his career as a legislator twenty-four years earlier—*ed.*], and the whole Black Republican side of the Senate, were silent. They left it to me to denounce it. [Cheers. —*Times*] What was the reply made to me on that occasion. Mr. Toombs, of Georgia, got up and undertook to read me a lecture upon the ground that I had deemed it worthy of notice, to even reply to such an article as that in the *Union,* and declared that there was not a man, woman or child south of the Potomac in any slave State who did not repudiate any such doctrine. Mr. Lincoln knows that that reply was made on the subject a year ago, and now he wants to put the question, Suppose the Supreme Court of the United States shall decide that the States can't exclude slavery from their limits, would I sanction it? He might as well ask you, Suppose Mr. Lincoln should steal a horse, would I sanction it? [Laughter. —*Times*] It would be as gentlemanly in me to ask him what, in the event of his stealing a horse, ought to be done, as for him to ask me such a question. He throws an imputation upon the Supreme Court of the United States, that they would violate the Constitution of the country. I tell him that such a proposition as that is not possible [Cheers. —*Times*], but it would be an act of moral treason—an act that no man on the bench could ever descend to. Why,

Mr. Lincoln himself would never so forget himself in his partisan feelings as to be guilty of an act of that kind. ["Good, good." —*Times*]

The fourth question is, Are you in favor of acquiring more territory, without regard to how it may affect the country on the slavery question? That question is very ingeniously and cunningly put. [Deacon Bross here spoke, *sotto voce*,—the reporter understanding him to say, "Now we've got him." —*Times*] The Black Republican party, in their creed, laid down the proposition that under no circumstances would we acquire any more territory, unless slavery be first prohibited in the country. I ask Mr. Lincoln whether he is in favor of the proposition. [Addressing Mr. Lincoln:—*Times*] Are you against any further acquisition of territory under any circumstances, unless slavery is prohibited? That he didn't like to answer. I ask him if he stands up to that article in the platform, and he turns around, Yankee fashion, and, without answering it himself, asks me: Are you opposed to admitting a slave Territory? [Good. —*Times*] I answer him that, whenever it becomes necessary for our growth and progress to acquire more territory, I am for it without reference to the question of slavery, and when we have got it, that we leave the people in the Territory free to do as they please—either to make a slave Territory or a free Territory, just as they choose. [Applause. —*Tribune;* Here Deacon Bross spoke, the reporter believing that he said, "That's bold." It was said solemnly. —*Times*] It is idle to tell me, and to tell you, that we have territory enough now. Our fathers supposed that we had enough when we acquired the territory only to the Mississippi River; but in view of the growth and expansion of the country, we were satisfied that we needed more territory, and we acquired the Louisiana Territory, including the west bank of the Mississippi River to the British Possessions. Then we acquired Oregon, and then California and New Mexico. We have enough now for the present, but this is a young nation and a growing nation. It swarms as often as a bee hive, turning out a new swarm every year, and they must have new hives in which they may gather and make their honey. [Good. —*Times*] In less than fifteen years the same ratio of progress that has distinguished this country for the last fifteen years, would occupy every vacant foot of land between this and the Pacific Ocean under the government of the United States and will you not continue to increase after that time as well as now? I tell you to increase, to multiply, to expand, is the law of this nation's existence. [Good. —*Times*] You cannot limit this great country by mere boundary lines, saying thus far thou must go and no further. Any one of you, gentlemen, might as well say to his son, twelve years of age: "You are now big enough; you mustn't grow any larger," and, in order to prevent growth, put a hoop around him to keep him to his present size. What would be the result? Either that hoop must burst and be rent asunder or the child must die. [Laughter. —*Times*] So with this great nation. With our national increase that is going on with a rapidity unknown in any other part of the globe—with a tide of immigration that is fleeing from despotism in the Old World, and seeking refuge in our own—there is a constant outpouring into this country that requires more land, more territory upon which to settle, and just as fast as our interests, our destinies and our necessities require additional territory—in the South or in the North, or in the islands of the Ocean—I am for it. And when we get it I will leave the people of each Territory free, according to the Nebraska Bill, to do as they please on the subject of slavery and every other question. [Good, good, hurra for Douglas. —*Times*] I trust now that Mr. Lincoln will deem himself answered on these few points. He racked his brain so much in devising these few questions that he exhausted himself, and had not strength enough left to invent another [Laughter. —*Times*], but as soon as he can hold a council of his advisers, by getting Lovejoy, and Farnsworth [Cheers. —*Tribune*], and Giddings, and Fred. Douglass together, he will then frame and propound the other interrogator[ies]. [Good, good, &c. Renewed laughter, in which Mr. Lincoln feebly joined, saying that he hoped with their aid to get seven questions, the number asked him by Judge Douglas, and so make *conclusions* again. —*Times*] I have no doubt you think they are all good men—good Black Republicans. [White, white. —*Times; Tribune* omitted last phrase] I have reason to recollect that some people in this country think that Fred. Douglass is a very good man. The last time I came here to make a speech, while I was talking on the stand to you people of Freeport, as I am today, I saw a carriage, and a magnificent one too, drive up and take its position on the outside of the crowd, with a beautiful young lady on the front seat, with a man and Fred. Douglass, the negro, on the back seat, and the owner of the carriage in front driving the negro. [Laughter. —*Tribune;* Laughter, cheers, cries of Right, what have you to say against it, &c. —*Times*] I witnessed that here in your town.

A VOICE—What of it?

JUDGE DOUGLAS—What of it! All I have to say is this, if you Black Republicans think that the negro ought to be on a social equality with young wives and daughters, and ride in the carriage with the wife while the master of the carriage drives the team, you have a perfect right to do so. [Laughter. —*Tribune;* Good, good, and cheers, mingled with shouting and cries of White, white. —*Times*] I am told also that one of Fred. Douglass' kinsmen, another rich black negro, is now traveling this part of the State making speeches for his friend Mr. Lincoln, who is the champion of the black man's party. [Laughter. —*Tribune;* "White men, white men," and "what have you got to say against it." "That's right," &c. —*Times*] All I have got to say on that subject is this, those of you who believe that the nigger [the *Times* substituted "negro"—*ed.*] is your equal, and ought to be on an equality with you socially, politically and legally, have a right to entertain those opinions, and of course will vote for Mr. Lincoln. ["Down with the negro," no, no, &c. —*Times*]

I have now a word to say on Mr. Lincoln's answer to the interrogatories contained in my speech at Ottawa, and purporting to be replied to here to-day. Mr. Lincoln makes a great parade of the fact that I quoted that Black Republican platform of 1854 as having been adopted at Springfield, whereas it turns out to have been adopted at other places than Springfield. Mr. Lincoln is great in the particular spots at which a thing is to be done. He thinks the platform was not adopted at the right spot, like the Mexican war, which in his opinion was unjust and infamous because the first blood was not shed at the right spot. So in regard to this particular spot at which these particular resolutions were adopted. Now all I have to say on that point is this: that if I was mistaken about that spot at which the thing was done, Mr. Lincoln was also mistaken, for he did not know but what it was the particular spot. Now I will show you, if it is a mistake (and when I get down there I will investigate it and see if it is a mistake as to the place), I will show you how I was led into it. In 1856, Major [Thomas L.] Harris, a member of Congress from this State, and Mr. [Jesse O.] Norton, a Representative member from the Joliet district in this State, got into political discussion, in the course of which, Major Harris quoted these identical resolutions as the Republican platform, stating that they were adopted at the first Black Republican State Convention [the *Times* omitted "Black" from many of these references—*ed.*] ever held in Illinois. The other day, when I thought I would make these resolutions the foundation for propounding the question to Mr. Lincoln, whether he now stood on the platform of the party, I wrote to Charles Lanphier, editor of the Springfield *Register,* stating that I understood that Major Harris was lying sick in that term, and calling his attention to Major Harris' speech containing these resolutions, and asking him to call on Major Harris, and find out and let me know the time and place of holding the convention which adopted them. I received in reply from Mr. Lanphier a copy of the *State Register,* printed at Springfield, Illinois, (Mr. Lincoln's own town,) bearing date on the 16th of October, 1854, only eleven days after the convention to which Mr. Lincoln refers had adjourned, in which I found a statement in these words, which I will read:

"During the late discussion in this city Lincoln made a speech, to which Judge Douglas replied. In Lincoln's speech he took the broad ground that, according to the Declaration of Independence, the whites and blacks are equal. From this he drew the conclusion, which he several times repeated, that the white man had no right to pass laws for the government of the black man without the nigger's consent. This speech of Lincoln was heard and applauded by all the Abolitionists assembled in Springfield. As [So] soon as Mr. Lincoln was done speaking, Mr. Coddington arose and requested all the delegates to the Black Republican Convention to withdraw into the Senate Chamber. They did so, and after long deliberation they laid down the following Abolition platform as the platform on which they stood. We call the particular attention of all our readers to it."

It thus sets out word for word the identical platform which I quoted at Ottawa [Cheers. —*Times*], and I read it from that newspaper printed in Mr. Lincoln's own town only eleven days after the convention itself was held. Now, Mr. Lincoln says that these resolutions were not adopted at this place, and tries to avoid the force of these revolutionary principles contained in that platform by the allegation that they were not adopted at that time and place. Well, I will read them to him now, but I wish to read them now from another paper, and say whether they will be denied. This platform which I now read to you was adopted in the various counties in the various Congressional Districts throughout the north end of the State. It was adopted in the north in every county that gave a Black Republican majority to the[ir] member of the legislature; here is a man [pointing to Mr. Denio, who sat on the stand near Deacon Bross—*Times*] who knows as well as any living man that was the creed of the party at the time. I would be willing to call [Cyrenius B.] Denio [a state representative from Jo Daviess County—*ed.*] as a witness, or any other honest man belonging to that party, to say whether these were the principles of the party at that time. I will now read the resolutions adopted at Rockford, on the 30th of August, 1851, at the Congressional Convention which nominated [Elihu B.] Washburne [pro-Lincoln Illinois congressman who earlier had briefly flirted with the idea of wooing Douglas to the Republican side—*ed.*], and on which resolutions you elected him to Congress.

Resolved. That the continued and increasing aggressions of slavery in our country are destructive of the best rights of a free people and that such aggressions cannot be successfully resisted without a united political action of all good men.

[Cries of "All right," "All right." —*Tribune*] You say that is all right. Now for the next.

Resolved. That the citizens of the United States hold in their hands, peaceful constitutional and efficient remedy against the encroachment of the slave power, the ballot box and, if that remedy is boldly and wisely applied, the principles of liberty and eternal justice will be established.

[Loud Cheers. —*Tribune*]

Resolved. That we accept this issue forced upon us by the slave power, and in defense of freedom will co-operate and be known as Republicans, pledged to the accomplishment of the following purposes:
To bring the Administration of the Government back to the control of first principles; to restore Kansas and Nebraska to the position of the territories; to repeal and entirely abrogate the Fugitive Slave Law.

A VOICE—That's all right.

JUDGE DOUGLAS—That's all right you say. Mr. Lincoln tells you he is not for it, and yet it is all right. Here is the next purpose to which you Black Republicans are pledged by this platform.

VOICES—White Republicans! White! White!

JUDGE DOUGLAS—Wait until I read it. The next is "To restrict slavery to those States in which it exists; to prohibit the admission of any more slave States into the Union." ["Good," "Good." —*Tribune*] You answer by a loud voice that is all right. "To exclude slavery from all the Territories over which the general government has jurisdiction, and to resist the acquisition of any more territory unless the introduction of slavery therein forever shall be prohibited." You think that is a good platform, don't you? ["Good enough." "All right." —*Tribune;* "Yes. Yes, all right," and cheers. —*Times*] Then, if you do approve it now, and if it's all right, you won't join with those men who say I libel you by calling this your platform [the *Times* substituted "principles"—*ed.*], will you? ["Good, good, hit him again," and great laughter and cheers. —*Times*] Now, all that Mr. Lincoln complains of is that I do him and you injustice, by saying that this was the platform of your party. [Renewed laughter. —*Times*] I am told that Washburne made a speech last night in Galena, in which he abused me awfully for bringing to light this platform on which he was elected. [The *Times* added: "He thought that you had forgotten it, as he and Mr. Lincoln desire to." (Laughter.)—*ed.*] He didn't deny but what he subscribed to what you adopted—but what he was pledged to it, but it is not fair to call it up, and remind the people that this is their platform. [Here Deacon Bross spoke. —*Times*] I am glad to find that you are more honest in your Abolitionism than your leaders, by avoiding that it is your platform and all right. [Laughter. —*Tribune;* Laughter, "you have them, good, good." —*Times*] Now I will read another resolution:

> *Resolved.* That in furtherance of these principles we will use such constitutional and lawful means as shall seem best adapted to their accomplishment, and that we will support no man for office under the General or State government who is not positively committed to the support of these principles, and whose personal character and conduct is not guaranty that he is reliable, and shall abjure all party allegiance and ties.

[The *Times* added a final resolution in its transcript, which Douglas evidently did not read at the time: "*Resolved,* That we cordially invite persons of all former political parties whatever in favor of the object expressed in the above resolutions to unite with us in carrying them into effect. . . ." The paper went on to admit: "Senator Douglas was frequently interrupted in reading these resolutions by loud cries of 'Good, good,' 'That's the doctrine,' and vociferous applause."—*ed.*]

You not only adopted that platform in regard to Slave States and the Fugitive Slave Law [federal law guaranteeing the return of runaway slaves, anathema to abolitionists but adopted as part of the Compromise of 1850—*ed.*], but you pledged yourselves one to another never to vote for a man for office in the State or Federal government, who was not committed to this proposition.

A Voice. Exactly. [Cheers. —*Tribune*]

Judge Douglas—Yes, you say exactly; you were committed to them. The same resolutions were adopted in the next Congressional District below, and when I get down below I intend to show him what their platform then was. The same resolutions were in substance adopted in your County Convention here, and now with the admission you make that these resolutions were your platform, that they embodied your sentiments then and embody them now, what do you think of Mr. Lincoln who is your candidate, and who is attempting to dodge the responsibility of this platform because it was not adopted in the right spot [a taunting reference to the "Spot Resolutions" introduced by young Congressman Lincoln in 1848, demanding that President Polk justify the Mexican War by identifying the exact spot of American soil on which American blood had supposedly first been shed; although Lincoln subsequently voted for bills that equipped the troops, his initiative was much mocked by his enemies at home, earning him the derisive sobriquet "Spotty Lincoln"—*ed.*] [Shouts of laughter, hurra for Douglas, &c. —*Times*] I thought it was adopted in Springfield, but it turns out that it was adopted at Rockford, and when I get down into the next district, I will show you that it was the platform there, and so on until I shall nail it on the back of all the Black Republicans throughout the State.

Voices—White! White! White Republicans! [Three cheers for Douglas. A Voice: "Couldn't you modify and call it brown?" Laughter. —*Times*]

Judge Douglas—No, I could not modify it a bit. I did think at one time it was getting a little brown, when your members all voted for the Crittenden-Montgomery amendment [the House of Representatives' alternative to the Lecompton Constitution bill, which ordered the Constitution resubmitted to the Kansas electorate; it was later supplanted by the compromise English Bill—*ed.*], but since you have gone back, its black, and not brown. [Laughter. —*Tribune;* Shouts of laughter, and A Voice: "Can't you ask him another question?" —*Times*] Now, gentlemen, having shown you that this was the platform in your own Congressional District—that it was the platform in the north, through all the counties where the Black Republican party had a majority in 1854, I want to call your attention to the action of your Representatives in the Legislature, when they got together. In the first place you must remember that they [this] was the organization of a new party. It is so expressed in the resolutions. They were then going to dissolve all old political ties, and make a new party called the Republican party. The old Whig party was to have its throat cut and be destroyed. The Democratic party was to be annihilated and be blotted out of existence and in lieu of them this Republican party was to be organized with this abolition platform. We know who the chief leaders in breaking up and destroying those two great parties were. Lincoln on the one hand and Trumbull on the other hand being disappointed politicians, [laughter, —*Times*] and having retired and been driven by their constituents into obscurity, because of their political sins, formed a scheme to abolitionize the two parties, and lead the old line Whigs and Democrats, bound hand and foot, into the abolition camp, having Fred. Douglass, and Chase, and Giddings ready to christen them whenever they brought them into the Abolition camp. [Great laughter. —*Times*] Lincoln went to work to dissolve the old Whig party. Clay was dead, although the sod was not green on his grave. He understood to bring into disrepute those great compromise measures of 1850 with which Clay had been identified. Up to 1854, the old whig party and the old Democratic party had stood on a common platform, so far as this slavery question was concerned. We differ—you Whigs and Democrats differed about a Bank, about a tariff, about distribution, about a specie circular, about the Sub-Treasury, but we agree upon this slavery question, and the true mode of preserving the peace and harmony of the Union with it. The compromise measures of 1850, introduced by Clay, defended by Webster, supported by Cass, approved by Fillmore, and sanctioned by all the national men of both parties, constituted the common plank upon which Whigs and Democrats stood. Then again in 1852, the Whig party in its National Convention at Baltimore—the last Whig Convention ever held—endorsed and approved these Compromise measures of Clay. So did the Democratic Convention do the same thing. And thus all the Old Line Whigs and Old Line Democrats stood pledged to the great principle of self-government, which guarantees to the people of each State and each Territory to decide the slavery question for themselves as laid down in the Compromise measures of 1850, and carried out in the Kansas-Nebraska bill in 1854. After the death of Clay and Webster, Mr. Lincoln, on the part of the Whigs, undertook to abolitionize the Whig party, dissolve it, and transfer the members of that party into the Abolition camp, and make them train under Giddings, Lovejoy, Farnsworth, and the other Abolition leaders. Trumbull undertook to dissolve the Democratic party by first abolitionizing it and then taking the old Democrats into the Abolition camp. Lincoln was aided in his efforts by many leading Whigs—old members of Congress— Washburne being one of the most active. [Good fellow. —*Times*] Trumbull on his part was aided by many renegades from the Democrats, such men as John Wentworth [Laughter. —*Times*], Tom Turner [speaker of the Illinois legislature, he was one of the moderators of this debate, according to the *Times*—ed.], and others familiar to you.

MR. TURNER—I drew these resolutions.

MR. DOUGLAS—Turner assisted in drawing these resolutions, too, he says. [Loud cheers. —*Tribune;* "Hurra for Turner," "Hurra for Douglas." —*Times*] That's right. Give Turner the cheers for drawing the resolutions, if you approve of them. If Mr. Turner drew these abolition resolutions he won't deny but what they are the creed of the Republican party.

MR. TURNER—They are our creed exactly. [Cheers. —*Times*]

JUDGE DOUGLAS—Turner says they are his—that is the Black Republican creed exactly, yet Mr. Lincoln denies that he stands upon them. ["Good, good," and laughter. —*Times*] Turner says that the creed of the Republican party here is, no more slave States; yet Mr. Lincoln says he would not like to be put in a position where he would have to vote on it. [More laughter. —*Times*] Well, now, all I have to say to Mr. Lincoln is that I don't think there is much danger of his ever being put in a position where he will have to vote on the admission of a slave State. I propose, out of mere kindness, to relieve him of the necessity of that vote. [Laughter. —*Tribune;* Renewed laughter and cheers. —*Times*]

But when this alliance between Lincoln and Trumbull was completed for the purpose of abolitionizing the Whig and Democratic parties in 1854, they spread over the State, Lincoln yet pretending to be an Old Line Whig—you know it would rope in the Old Line Whigs—Trumbull pretending to be as good a Democrat as he ever was, in order to coax the Democrats into the abolition camp. ["That's exactly what we want." —*Times*] Trumbull and Lincoln played the part in 1854 that a decoy duck does down on the Potomac. You know they make them an Artificial duck and send him out to decoy the wild ducks into the net, and Trumbull and Lincoln were the decoy ducks here to decoy the Old Line Whigs and Democrats into the Abolition camp, and when they got them there they elected a Black Republican Legislature, and when they got together, the first thing they did was to elect for Speaker of the House the very man that now boasts that he wrote the abolition platform on which Lincoln won't stand. ["Good," "hit him again," and cheers. —*Times*] I want to know of Mr. Turner if, when he was elected speaker, he was not a good embodiment of Republican principles.

MR. TURNER—I hope I was.

JUDGE DOUGLAS—He says he hopes he was. He wrote that platform and stands to-day upon it. [Applause and cries of, "Hurrah for Turner." —*Tribune* and *Times*] I admire Turner's honesty in that. Every man of you knows that what he says about that being the principles of the party is true, and you know that every one of these men who shuffles and tries to deny, is only trying to cheat the people out of their votes until after election. ["Good," and cheers. —*Times*] There is the platform of the party.

I promise now to trace this matter a little further, and see how much evidence there is to fasten this Black Republican revolutionary platform upon them. When the Legislature got together there was a United States Senator to be elected in the place of Shields, and before they would proceed to the election of the Senator the Republicans or Abolitionists in the House insisted upon laying down certain principles by which to govern the party. It has been published to the world, and satisfactorily proved, that there was at the time the alliance was made between Trumbull and Lincoln to abolitionize the two parties an agreement that Lincoln was to take Shields' place in the United States Senate, and Trumbull was to take mine as soon as I could be got rid of conveniently [laughter. —*Tribune*]; and when Mr. Lincoln was beaten for Shields' place, in a manner I will refer to in a few minutes, Lincoln felt very sore, and his friends grumbled, and some of them came out and charged that there was bad faith and treachery, that there was the most infamous treachery in the world—that the bargain was, that Lincoln was to have Shields' place and Trumbull mine, but that Trumbull, having the votes of a few Abolition Democrats under his control, would not let them vote for Lincoln, but kept them back until they finally drove the rest into voting for Trumbull. And Trumbull having thus cheated Lincoln out of the place, Lincoln's friends made a great deal of fuss, and in order to keep Lincoln quiet, they had to come forward and pledge themselves in advance in the State Convention that they would be for Lincoln and nobody else. Lincoln could be satisfied [the *Times* substituted "silenced"—*ed.*] in no other way, and you Black Republicans—[Loud cries of "White Republicans, White Republicans, sir!" —*Tribune;* "White, white," and great clamor. —*Times*] I wish to remind you that there was not a Democrat here vulgar enough to interrupt Mr. Lincoln when he was talking. [Great applause and cries of hurrah for Douglas. —*Times*] I know the shoe is pinching you when I am clinching Lincoln, and you are scared to death for the result. [Cheers. —*Times*] I have seen these men when they make appointments for joint discussion, and then the moment their man has been heard try to interrupt and prevent a fair hearing. I have seen your mobs before and I defy your wrath. [These remarks were followed by considerable disturbance in the crowd, ending in a cheer. —*Tribune;* Tremendous applause. —*Times*] Don't cheer; I need my whole time. Their object is to occupy it, so that I shall not go through with the evidence showing this double dealing of the Black Republican party.

When the legislature got together and were going into the election of Senator of the United States, Lovejoy offered some resolutions which I hold in my hand. I will read the resolution[s] and hand the preamble to the reporters, that they may publish the whole. [The preamble which Douglas chose not to read aloud contained the declaration that "human slavery is a violation of the principles of natural and revealed rights"—*ed.*]

Resolved, by the House of Representatives, the Senate concurring therein. That our senators in Congress be instructed, and our Representatives requested, to introduce, if not otherwise introduced, and to vote for a bill to restore such prohibition to the aforesaid Territories, and also to extend a similar prohibition to all territory which now belongs to the United States, or which may hereafter come under their jurisdiction.

Resolved. That our Senators in Congress be instructed, and our Representatives requested, to vote against the admission of any State into the Union the Constitution of which does not prohibit slavery, whether the Territory out of which such State may have been formed shall have been acquired by conquest, treaty, purchase, or from original territory of the United States.

Resolved. That our Senators in Congress be instructed, and our Representatives requested to introduce and vote for a bill to repeal an act entitled "an act respecting fugitives from justice and persons escaping from the service of their masters," and, failing in that, for such a modification of it as shall secure the right of *habeas corpus* and trial by jury, before the regularly constituted authorities of the State to all persons claimed as owing service as labor.

[Cries of "Good, good," and cheers. —*Times*] Now these resolutions were introduced by Lovejoy immediately proceding [*sic*] the election for Senator. These resolutions declare that the Wilmot Provision must be put on all country North of 36 deg. 30 min., and secondly, that it must be put on all territory South of 36 deg. 30 min., which we ever own or ever shall acquire—that no more Slave States shall be admitted into the Union under any circumstances whatever, no matter whether we acquire them by treaty, conquest, purchase, or any other manner. [The *Times* added: "A VOICE, 'That is right.' (DOUGLAS,) You say that is right. We will see in a moment—*ed.*] The next is for the unconditional repeal of the Fugitive Slave Law. They were opposed to any repeal, leaving no provision for carrying into effect that clause in the Constitution which guarantees the surrender of fugitives; but if they failed in the unconditional repeal, then they were to modify it in the manner therein pointed out. But they were opposed to any such law. If they could not get that, then get one as nearly useless as possible. Now I want to show you who voted for these resolutions. When the vote was taken on the first resolution, it was 41 in the affirmative, and 32 in the negative, and here are the votes, which I will hand to the reporter to copy.

Those who voted in the affirmative were: [The *Times* did not provide its readers with the list of names, so it was never thereafter included in the official transcripts of the debates—*ed.*]

Messrs Allen of Madison, Babcock, Beal, Brown of Knox, Courtney, Day, Diggins, Dunlan, Fods, Foster, Grove, Hackney, Henry, Henderson, Hills, Hollbrook, Jones, Johns, Lawrence, Lee, Little, Logan, Lovejoy, Lyman, McGuire, McClub, Parks of Logan, Parks of Will, Patton, Pinckney, Richmond of Cook, Riblet, Rice, Sargent, Strawn, Struck, Sullivan, Swan, Waters, Wheeler, Mr. Speaker.

Those voting in the negative were:

Messrs Allen of Williamson, Bennett, Baker, Bradford, Brown of Scott, Cline, Dearborn, Frankhouser, Gregg, Higbee, Hinch, Homer, Hopkins, Haliday, Kinney, Martin, Masters, McGillis, McClain, McDaniel, Morrison, Moulton, Preston, Pryler, Rawlings, Richmond of Montgomery, Richmond of Schuyler, Sams, Seeborn, Tanner, Trapp, Walters.

You will find that it is a strict party vote between the Democrats and the Black Republicans so far as I know their names, [Cries of "white, white," and clamor. —*Times*] and now the immediate point to which I want to call your attention is this, these resolutions were adopted on the 7th of February. On the 8th day of February they went into the election of United States Senator, and on that day every man who voted for these resolutions with two exceptions voted for Lincoln for the U.S. Senate. [Cries of "good," "good," and "give us their name." —*Tribune*]

JUDGE DOUGLAS—Yes, I will give them to you, if you want them, but I believe your object is to occupy my time. [Cries of "That is it." —*Times*] On the adoption of the next resolution the vote was 33 in the affirmative to 40 in the negative. On the next resolution the vote was 25 in the affirmative to 47 in the negative. The point to which I call your particular attention is that every man who voted for these resolutions, with two exceptions, voted for Mr. Lincoln the next day for United States Senator. Now bear in mind that these members who thus voted for the amendment were elected pledged to vote for no man for office under the State or Federal government who was not committed to this Black Republican platform as I read it at Ottawa. [Cries of "White, white," and "Good for you." —*Times*] They were pledged to that. Here were your members, among whom was Turner, who stands by me, and says he wrote the resolutions, and voted for Mr. Lincoln when he was pledged not to vote for Mr. Lincoln unless he was committed to these resolutions. Now, I ask Mr. Turner, did you violate your pledge in voting for Mr. Lincoln, or did Mr. Lincoln commit himself before you gave the vote? [The *Times* added: "Mr. Lincoln here started forward, and grasping Mr. Turner, shook him nervously, and said, 'Don't answer, Turner. You have no right to answer' "—*ed.*] Not only is the name of Turner here, but there are names from the adjoining counties. I could go through the whole list of the Black Republican party ["white, white." —*Times*] in the Legislature with two exceptions; for instance, here is the name of Porter Sargent, Willis [really Wallace—*ed.*] A. Little, of Jo Daviess, the name of Thomas J. Turner, of Stephenson, [William] Lyman, of Winnebago, Logan, [L. W.] Lawrence, of [Boone and—*ed.*] McHenry, [Hurlbut] Swan, from Lake, [the *Times* added to this recitation "Pinckney of Ogle County"—*ed.*], &c., and thus you see that every member from your Congressional District voted for Lincoln for the Senate, being pledged not to vote for him unless he was committed to this doctrine of no more Slave States, and the prohibition of slavery in the Territories, and the repeal of the Fugitive Slave Law. Yet Mr. Lincoln tells you to-day that he is not pledged to any such thing. Either Mr. Lincoln was then committed to these propositions, or Mr. Turner violated his pledge to you by voting for him. Either Mr. Lincoln was pledged to Mr. Turner, or else all the Black Republicans [Cries of "White, white." —*Times*] from this District violated their pledge of honor to their constituents by voting for him. Now, I ask you, which horn of the dilemma will you take? [VOICES; "We go for Turner." "We go for Lincoln;" "hurrah for Douglas," "hurrah for Turner." —*Times*] Will you hold Lincoln to the platform of the party, or will you believe that every member you had in the House of Representatives with two exceptions violated their pledges of honor to their constituents? So you see there is no escape for Mr. Lincoln on this pledge. He was committed to this proposition or your members violated their pledge. Take either horn of the dilemma—there is no dodging of the question.

Now, a word or two in regard to Mr. Lincoln's answers on this question. He says he was not pledged to the repeal of the Fugitive Slave Law. He was not pledged to it—doesn't quite like it—wouldn't introduce a law to repeal it—thinks there ought to be some law—didn't tell what it is, and upon the whole don't know what to do. That is the substance of his answer about the Fugitive Slave Law. I put the question, whether he indorsed that principle of entire abrogation and repeal. He answers, no. Then he will not tell what he will introduce—if he will introduce anything. If anybody else does do so, I ask how he will vote, and his answer comes to no answer at all. Why can't he speak out, and say what he is for, and what he will do? [Cries of "that's right." —*Times*] In regard to there being any more Slave States, he is not pledged on that. He wouldn't like to put himself in a position where he would have to vote either way. I pray you now, don't put him in a position to embarrass him so much. [Laughter. —*Times*] But if he goes to the Senate he may be put in that position, and I ask which way would he vote? Will he vote for or against the admission of a Slave State?

A Voice—How will you vote?

Judge Douglas—I will vote for just such a State as the people forming the constitution may want. If they want slavery they shall have it. If they want to prohibit slavery they may do it. They may do one thing or the other as they please, and I will receive them under the Constitution. ["Three cheers for Douglas." —*Times*] Why don't you Republican [the *Times* had "Black Republican"—*ed.*] candidates talk out as plain as that, when we put a question? [Cries of "good, good;" Here Deacon Bross spoke. —*Times*] I do not desire to deceive any man out of his vote. No man shall be deceived in my principles if I have the power to express myself in terms clear and distinct enough to convey my idea and meaning. Mr. Lincoln made a speech at Springfield, when nominated for United States Senate, which covers all of these abolition principles. He then lays down a proposition so broad in its abolitionism as to cover the entire ground. He says that:

"In my opinion this [slavery] agitation will not cease until a crisis shall have been reached and passed. 'A house divided against itself cannot stand.' I believe this Government cannot endure permanently half slave and half free. I do not expect the house to fall—but I expect it will cease to be divided. It will become all one thing or all the other. Either the opponents of slavery will arrest the further spread of it, and place it where the public mind shall rest in the behalf that it is in the course of ultimate extinction, or its advocates will push it forward till it shall become alike lawful in all the States—old as well as new, North as well as south."

Then [the *Times* substituted "There"—*ed.*] you find that Mr. Lincoln lays down the doctrine that this nation cannot endure divided as our fathers made it into free and slave States. He says they must all become one way or all the other—must all become free or all become slave; otherwise the Union cannot continue to exist. That being the case in his opinion, if we have any more Slave States, so that it would continue to be divided, it would dissolve the Union. [Cries of "Bring him out." —*Times*] I want to know whether Mr. Lincoln will vote for another Slave State, believing that the effect of it will be to dissolve the Union? He says the Union cannot exist divided—that the end will be to make them all Free or all Slave States. Hence he is for making them all free in order that the Union may exist. Yet he will vote for another Slave State, knowing that it would dissolve the Union if he did. [Great laughter. —*Times*] I ask you if this is fair dealing? The true intent and inevitable conclusion from his Springfield speech is, that he is opposed to the admission of any more Slave States under any circumstances. If so, why does he not say so? If he believes that this country cannot exist divided into Free and Slave States, if he believes they must all become free in order to save the Union, he is bound as an honest man to vote against any more Slave States. If he believes that, he is bound to do it. Show me that it is my duty under the Constitution, in order to save the Union, to do a particular act, and I will do it, if the Constitution does not prohibit me. [Applause. —*Times*] I am not for the dissolution of the Union under any circumstances. [Renewed applause. —*Times*] I will pursue no course of conduct to give just cause for the dissolution of the Union. The hope of the friends of freedom throughout the world rests upon the perpetuity of this Union. The friends of liberty in the old world—the down-trodden people under European despotism, all look with hope and anxiety to the American Union as the only resting place and permanent home of freedom and self-government; and not believing, as Mr. Lincoln says, that this Union cannot endure with Slave States in it, he will not tell you definitely whether he would vote for more Slave States and thus dissolve the Union, but he says he would not like to be put to the test. [Laughter. —*Times*] Well, I don't think he will be put to the test. [Renewed laughter. —*Times*] I don't think the people of Illinois desire a man to represent them who would not like to be put to the test in the performance of a high constitutional duty. [Cries of good. —*Times*] I will retire in shame from the Senate of the United States when I am not willing to be put to the test in the performance of my duty. [Applause. —*Tribune;* That is so. —*Times*] I have been put to several tests. I have stood by my principles in fair weather and foul—in the sunshine and in the rain. I have defended the great principle of self-government here among you, when Northern sentiment ran in a torrent against it. [A Voice,—That is so. —*Times*] I have defended the same great principle of self-government, when Southern sentiment come down with its avalanche upon me. I was not afraid of the test they put to me. I knew it was right—that the God of Heaven would smile upon me if I was faithful in the performance of my duty. [Cries of good, cheers and laughter. —*Times*] But Mr. Lincoln attempts to bolster up his charge of corruption against the Supreme Court of the United States and two Presidents of the United States and myself by pleading an offset, and saying I did the same thing on the Washington *Union*. Suppose I did make the charge of corruption against the Washington

Union when it was true, does that justify his making one against me and others where it is false? That is the question I want to put to him. He says that at the time the Nebraska Bill was introduced, before its passage, there was a conspiracy between the Judges of the Supreme Court and President Pierce and Mr. Buchanan and myself, pending the decision, to break down the barriers and establish slavery all over the Union. Gentlemen, he knows that charge is historically false as against Mr. Buchanan. He knows that Mr. Buchanan was at that time in England, representing this country with distinguished ability in the court of St. James, and had been there for a long time, and I [*sic*] did not come home for a year afterwards. He knows that fact, which proves the charge to be false in reference to Mr. Buchanan. [Cheers. —*Times*] Again I have called his attention to the fact that at [the] time the Dred Scott case was not pending before the Supreme Court at all. It had never been brought before the Judges. They knew nothing of it and had never heard of it in all probability. Thus the history of the country proves the charge false as to them. As to Mr. Pierce, his character as a man of integrity and honor is enough to protect him from the charge. [Laughter. —*Tribune;* laughter and applause. —*Times*] As to myself, I pronounce the charge an infamous lie, wherever and by whomsoever made. I am willing that Mr. Lincoln should rake up every act I have ever done—every report I have ever made—every speech I have ever delivered, and criticise them. But when he charges a corrupt conspiracy for the purpose of subverting the Constitution, I brand it as it deserves, and as I believe the history of the country proves it to be, false. But now he rakes up the Washington *Union*, because I made a speech against that paper. My speech against it was made simply because it advocated a doctrine revolutionary, by saying that the free States had not a right to prohibit slavery in their limits. Because I made that charge Mr. Lincoln says it was a charge against Mr. Buchanan. Suppose it was. Is Mr. Lincoln his peculiar defender? Is he in alliance with the Federal Administration that he is bound to defend it against any attack I have made? [Great laughter and cheers. —*Times*] I understand that the Washington *Union*, under the control of that most corrupt of all corrupt men, Cornelius Wendell, is advocating Lincoln's claims to the United States Senatorship. By the last Republican House of Representatives he was made the printer for the House, and he took the money he made by printing, and with it bought the Washington *Union*, and even in the name of the Democratic party he is advocating Mr. Lincoln's claims to the Senatorship, which Mr. Lincoln considers any attack on Wendell and his corrupt gang as an attack upon him personally. [Immense cheering and laughter. —*Times*] It only proves what I have charged, that there is an alliance between the Black Republicans and the Presidential aspirants out of the State to break me down at home. [A VOICE—That is impossible, and cheering. —*Times*] Mr. Lincoln feels bound to come to the rescue. In that speech discussing the Washington *Union*, I made the charge distinctly against the Union, and the *Union* alone. I did not go beyond that. If I ever have occasion to attack the President of the United States, I will do it in a way that will not be misunderstood. When I differed with the President, I spoke out so that you all heard me. ["That you did," and cheers. —*Times*] When that one question passed away and resulted in the triumph of my principles, by allowing the people to do as they pleased, there was an end of that controversy. ["Hear, hear." —*Times*] Whenever the great principles of self-government—the right of the people to make their own Constitution, and come into the Union with slavery or without it as they see proper, shall again rise, you will find me standing firm in defense of that principle, and fighting whoever fights it. ["Right, right." —*Tribune;* "Right, right," "Good, good," and cheers. —*Times*] If Mr. Buchanan stands, as I doubt not he will, by the recommendation in his message— by the principle that hereafter all Constitutions are to be submitted to the people before admission into the Union, you will find me standing by him firmly, shoulder to shoulder, in carrying out that principle. I know Mr. Lincoln's object. He wants to avoid a distinct avowal of opinion in order to elect himself to the Senate [the *Times* had: "he wants to divide the democratic party, in order that he may defeat me and get to the senate."—*ed.*]. [Applause. —*Tribune;* Mr. Douglas' time here expired; and he stopped on the moment. —*Times*]

MR. LINCOLN'S REJOINDER

[As Mr. Lincoln arose he was greeted with vociferous cheers. —*Tribune*]

My friends—It will very readily occur to you—It will very readily occur to you, that I cannot in half an hour notice all the things that as able a man as Judge Douglas could say in an hour and a half, and I hope, therefore, that if there be anything that you would like to hear something from me upon that I omit to say anything about, you will bear in mind that it would be expecting an impossibility. I can but take some of the points that he has dwelt upon, and employ my half hour on them.

The first thing that I think of saying to you is a word in regard to Judge Douglas' declaration about vulgarity and blackguardism in the crowd—that no such thing was shown by any democrat while I was speaking. Now, I only want by way of reply upon that subject, to say that while *I* was speaking *I* [emphasis added by *Tribune*—*ed.*] used no vulgarity or blackguardism toward any democrats. [Voices—"That is the principle." Elderly gentleman on the platform—"Apples of gold." —*Tribune;* Great laughter and applause. —*Times*]

Now, my friends, there is all this long portion of the judge[']s speech—I think, perhaps, an entire half of the speech, which he has indulged in, in regard to the various resolutions and platforms that have been passed in different counties and in different congressional districts and in the Illinois legislature, which he supposes are at variance with the position which I have assumed here before you to-day. Now, I think, that that is true—that many of those resolutions are at variance with the position which I have assumed here to-day. [Laughter and confusion. —*Times*] I think that is so. [Confusion. —*Times*] Let us talk reasonably about it, that is all I ask upon the subject, that we talk reasonably and rationally about it. I am quite sure, the judge's opinion to the contrary notwithstanding, I have never tried to conceal an opinion of mine from anybody—I never deceived anybody. I am sure that the judge may go and hunt out the members of the legislature, who voted for me [the *Tribune* added: "for United States Senator in 1855, after the election of 1854"—*ed.*] and who he supposes, to carry out their pledges, were bound to have pledges from me,—I will give him all these persons, and if he will find any one of these that will tell him that I gave him anything inconsistent with what I say now, I will resign now, and give the judge no further trouble. [Applause. —*Tribune*]

Now, the plain truth of the matter, it seems to me, is this way. At the introduction of the Nebraska policy many persons were induced to believe that the[re] was a new era being introduced upon the slavery questions, which was intended, or at least tended, if not intended, to the spread and perpetuation of slavery. We, however, in the degrees of our opposition, did not agree with one another. The people in the extreme north of the state were for extremer measures of opposition than we in the south. We were all opposed to the measure—we had that one feeling, that one sentiment, in common with one another. You here in the north met and held your conventions and passed your resolutions. We in the middle of the state and further south did not meet and hold such conventions and pass such resolutions, although we had in some things a common view and a common sentiment, so that all these resolutions and all these meetings that the judge has alluded to and read from were partial—were local; they did not spread to the extent of the state.

We at last met together, as we did in 1856, from all parts of the state, and we agreed upon a common platform. You who held more extreme notions in former times either yielded those notions, or, if you did not yield them, agreed to yield them practically, for the sake of combining the opposition that you held to the measures that the opposite parties were putting forward. We on the other side met you, and if anything was yielded—as I suppose there was—we agreed upon a platform for the entire republican party of the state of Illinois, and now I suppose we are all bound as party men, who belong to that party, to this platform; and I say, if it be true that any one of you expects that if I should be elected—as the judge thinks he is quite sure I will not—if any of you think that I shall do anything that is not indicated by the republican platform, and by my answers here to-day, I tell you you will be deceived. I do not ask for the votes of any one that thinks I have secret pledges, that I do not speak plainly upon.

Cannot the judge be satisfied? Does the judge think that [the *Tribune* added: "in the unfortunate case of my election" (laughter)—*ed.*] my going to Washington will not enable you to vote your sentiments? [The confusion at this time partly drowned the words of the speaker. —*Times*] [During the interruption, the *Tribune* finished the sentence thusly: "(and) enable me to advocate sentiments contrary to those which

I expressed when you voted for and elected me, I assure him that his fears are wholly needless and groundless. Is the Judge really afraid of any such thing?" (Laughter.)—*ed.*] I will tell you what the judge is afraid of. He is afraid that we will pull all together. [Laughter. —*Times;* Applause, and cries of "We will, we will." —*Tribune*] This is what the judge is afraid of. That is what is more alarming to him than anything else. [Laughter. —*Tribune*] Well, now, for my part, I do hope that all of us who entertain opinions adverse to his doctrines and to that which appears to us to be the tendency to perpetuate slavery, that we will waive minor differences and pull together. ["We will, we will," and loud cheers. —*Tribune*] If it be true that I occupy sentiments that are not fully up to yours, that are not such as some of you could wish, I shall still expect to have your votes. Nevertheless, if Judge Douglas holds opinions more in accordance with your views, then I am free to say to you go for him and not with me.

I hope to deal entirely fairly with Judge Douglas. I hope, at the least, that if I shall not be elected, that I shall go down with no real stain on my reputation, notwithstanding the hard opinions that Judge Douglas chooses to entertain of me. [Laughter. —*Tribune*]

The Judge has again addressed himself to the abolition tendency of a speech of mine which was made at Springfield. I have so often tried to answer what the Judge has said upon that subject, that I almost turn with disgust from the task of repeating an answer to it. I hope that most of this intelligent audience around me have really read that speech ["We have, we have." —*Tribune*], and if they have I might almost venture to leave it to them to inspect closely, to see whether there really be any of those bugaboos which Judge Douglas interestedly sees. [Laughter. —*Times* and *Tribune*] But there is one particular branch of this discussion to which I wish to ask the attention of this audience, more especially than to others, and which I have some apprehension of omitting; but still another smaller one occurs to me, and it is this: The Judge complained that I do not to-day fairly answer his questions. Gentlemen, if I have sense enough to fairly answer them, I have done so; if it could be pointed out to me, how I could more distinctly answer his interrogatories, I aver that I have not sense to see how it can be done. He says that I do not say that I would in any event vote for the admission of a slave State into the Union. When he shall see my speech in print, if it be fairly reported, he will see what I did answer to that. I did not merely say, as he represents it, I would dislike to be put to the test, but I said, if I should be put to the test, and if a new State, after a Territory that led to the new State, had been kept free from slavery until the time of the formation of her constitution should frame a slave constitution—a most extraordinary state of things, which I think is not likely to happen—but if it should happen—I did not see but that we should have to admit her. I said that in very plain language. The judge does not desire to see it or to know it, but when the papers shall put it in print the Judge will see it.

I aver that the Judge, when he says that if I voted for a slave State I would be in favor of a dissolution of the Union, the Judge is mistaken. I have said no such thing. I do say, I repeat it, in my opinion this government cannot endure permanently half slave and half free; and yet I have never said, and do not now say, and do not now believe, that the introduction of one slave State into the Union would permanently fix this as a universal slave nation or bring about a dissolution of the Union. I have never said any such thing. I have never thought any such thing. The Judge is very great in working up this quibble argument. [Laughter and cheers. —*Tribune*]

Before leaving this subject of answering of questions, I aver, as my opinion, and you will judge of it when you come to see it—when our speeches shall be read, every question he has asked has been more fairly, completely and fully answered than he has mine. [The *Tribune* added: "Is that not so?" (Cries of yes, yes.)—*ed.*] The two speeches shall be laid down side by side, and I will venture, before all impartial judges, that mine—his—have been more fully, fairly and completely answered by me, than mine have been by him.

And now, then, there is one subject to which I wish to call your attention. He says that he made a charge upon the editor of the Washington *Union* alone, of entertaining the purpose to rob the States of the power of excluding slavery from their limits. I say, and I make a direct issue on that, that he did not make that charge against the editor of the *Union* alone. [A voice—"What of that?" —*Times;* Applause. —*Tribune*]

I will occupy a portion of my time in trying to prove to this crowd that it was not the editor of the *Union* alone that he made it against; that is what he says it was. I will undertake to prove by the record here before I am done, that it was more than the editor of the *Union* alone that he made that charge against.

I am quite aware that he was shirking a little as to the form in which he put it, but I can make it manifest that it was more than the editor of the *Union* alone that he made his charges against.

Well, he again really dodges the argument as I made it, when he says I am the special friend of Mr. Buchanan. Not at all. Am I not making the same charge myself? [Laughter and applause. —*Tribune*] I am trying to show Judge Douglas that you are a witness on my side as to that charge. [Renewed laughter. —*Tribune*] That is what I am trying to show. I will tell Judge Douglas that when he made that charge he had an eye farther North than he has to-day. He was then fighting furiously against other people calling *him* a Black Republican [*Tribune*'s emphasis added—*ed.*] and an Abolitionist. It is all mixed up in that part of the speech, and I say that it is pretty fairly manifest that his eye was fixed farther North than it is to-day. [Cheers and laughter. —*Tribune*]

But the Judge says that although he made that charge such as it was that Mr. Toombs got up, and Toombs said that there was not another man in the United States (I don't know that I give the Judge's exact language), except the editor of the *Union*, who was in favor of the doctrine put forth by the editor of the *Union*, and, thereupon, I understand that the Judge withdrew the charge—that merely because Mr. Toombs got up and made a speech—simply because Mr. Toombs got up and made a speech—although he had taken extracts from newspapers to show that there was a fatal blow being struck, it all went to pot as soon as Mr. Toombs got up and told the Judge it was not so. [Laughter. —*Tribune*] He reminds me in that of John Phoenix's railroad survey that he published. John Phoenix [a California railroad surveyor—*ed.*], says he, started out with various modes of measuring when they were making the measurement from the plaza to the Mission San Dolores. One was an invention of chain and pins, and another was a go-it-ometer [the *Tribune* added: "an invention of his own—a three-legged instrument, with which he computed a series of triangles between the points"—*ed.*].

A VOICE—Turn this way.

Mr. LINCOLN—Well then, I shan't be this way! [The *Tribune* omitted this exchange—*ed.*]

At night he said when they had done their day's work, why, he turned to see the chain man to see what distance they had come, and he said that he found that the chainman had just drawn the chain along and stuck no pins. So he turned to the man with the go-it-ometer to see the number of paces marked, and found that it indicated four and a half miles, which he knew must be nine or ten times as far as they had come.

About that time, he being much perplexed, a drayman came by and he asked him how far it was, and the drayman said it was exactly half a mile, and he wrote that down in his book, just as Douglas did [the *Tribune* added: "after he had made his calculations and computations"—*ed.*] what Toombs said. [Great laughter. —*Tribune*] I think that Douglas is easily satisfied after he had arrayed his evidence as he had done upon that point by Toombs' speech; I think that he was satisfied as easily as the railroad surveyor was by the drayman's statement. [Renewed laughter. —*Tribune*]

There is another thing I believe is true about that editor of the *Union* that Douglas opposed. I believe it turned out that after all the opposition to him, that the Democratic party elected him. I think that the man that put forward that matter they really elected him printer.

Well, now, my friends, as I have got less time than I think I have, than I thought I had before I turned to the watch to see how it was, I will ask your attention, all of you to get a speech of Judge Douglas, made in 1858, on the 22d of March. You begin about the middle of page 21 in that speech, and read on till you get near the bottom of page 24, and you will find the entire evidence upon which I say that Judge Douglas did not make that charge alone against the editor of the *Union*. I had a notion to read it, but I can't stop to read it. [The *Tribune* added: "I will give it to the papers"; in the long extract printed only by the Republican paper, Douglas complained that any man who questioned the "several distinct propositions advanced boldly by the Washington *Union* editorially and apparently *authoritatively* . . . is denounced as an abolitionist, a Free-Soiler, a fanatic. The propositions are, first, that the primary object of all government at its original institution is the protection of property; second, that the Constitution of the United States declares that the citizens of each state shall be entitled to all the privileges and immunities of citizens in the several states; and that, therefore, thirdly, all state laws, whether organic or otherwise, which prohibit the citizens of one State from settling in another with their slave property, and especially declaring it forfeited, are direct violations of the original intention of the Government and Constitution of the United States; and fourth, that the emancipation of the slaves of the Northern States was a gross outrage on the rights of property, inasmuch as it was involuntarily done on the part of the owner. . . . When I saw that article in the *Union*," Douglas had concluded, ". . . that a State has no right to prohibit slavery within its limits, I saw that there was a *fatal blow* being struck at the sovereignty of the States of this Union." Lincoln then proceeded:] After he had quoted the article from the editor of the *Union* he then said:

"Mr. President—You here find several distinct propositions advanced boldly by the Washington *Union,* editorially and apparently authoritatively."

By whose authority, Judge Douglas? [Great cheers and laughter. —*Tribune*]
Again, he says in another place:

"It will be seen by these clauses in the Lecompton Constitution, that they are identical in spirit with this authoritative article in the Washington *Union* of the day previous to its endorsement of this constitution, and every man is branded as a Free-Soiler and Abolitionist who does not subscribe to them."

By whose authority? ["Renewed cheers." —*Tribune*] Who do you mean to say authorized the publication of this article? We all know that the Washington *Union* was the newspaper at Washington considered the organ of the administration, and I demand of Judge Douglas to say by whose authority he meant to say those articles were published. If he can say that he did not mean the President and Cabinet, who did he mean? How dare he say that he meant nobody but the editor of the Washington *Union?*

I have said I will prove that he meant more, and by his own speech. I defy him to say who he meant other than the President and his Cabinet. More than that, he says that the editor—that the articles in that paper and the provisions of the constitution are identical, and being identical, he argues that they are conspiring together; he don't use the word conspiring, but what other meaning can you put upon it? I ask you to read it yourselves.

More than that, he winds up with this:

"When I saw that article in the *Union* of the 17th of November, followed by the glorification of the Lecompton Constitution on the 18th of November, and this clause in the constitution asserting the doctrine that no State has a right to prohibit slavery within its limits,

I saw that there was a fatal blow being struck at the sovereignty of the States of this Union [the *Tribune* transcript of the quote ended here, but Lincoln continued from the platform:—*ed.*], a death blow to State rights, subversive of the Democratic platform and of the principles upon which the Democratic party have ever stood, and upon which I wish I will ever stand."

Now, I ask him if he made all these remarks—if he was talking about that fatal blow being struck by the editor of the Washington *Union* when he did not mean that anybody else was in it. It would be a terribly fatal blow that a single man could strike, when no president, no member of congress, no cabinet officers, no nobody else was assisting in the blow. That would be a terribly fatal blow. Out of respect for Judge Douglas' good sense we must imagine that he did not manufacture the idea of that fatal blow being struck by the contemptible editor of a paper, as he states him to be. I repeat here that if any man shall take these pages in his speech and carefully read them, he shall see that while Judge Douglas does not use the term, the fatal blow being struck; and he certainly means that to make that fatal blow which he sees being struck, it is by those who have the power to carry it into execution unless he resists it; and when he says it is authoritative it leaves us in no doubt who he means gives the authority, and we find it is distinctly announced. I would appeal to this audience, aye, to twelve democrats—Douglas democrats, on oath, to answer faithfully to the proposition that he made it not against the editor of the *Union* alone, but against the president, against the cabinet, against the framers of the Lecompton constitution, and against all its advocates in and out of congress. No man can examine those pages and fail to see that such was the fact. [The three previous, lengthy sentences went completely unreported in the *Tribune—ed.*] The Judge's eye is further south now [Laughter and cheers. —*Tribune*]—it was decidedly north then. His hope was very much then upon the idea of the evisceration of the black republican party, and the turning of it in and making it the tail of his new kite. [Great laughter. —*Tribune*] He knows that—he very well knows it—that he was then expecting to turn the republican party wrong end foremost, and place himself at one end of it, and thus fly the largest kind of a kite. He soon found that these despised black republicans understood and appreciated him better than that, and he has found that his security depends upon his crawling back into the ranks of the democratic party [the *Tribune* added: "with whom he now pretends to be at such fearful variance"—*ed.*]. [Loud applause and cries of "go on, go on." —*Tribune*, which reported that Lincoln responded: "I cannot, gentlemen, my time has expired."]

THE THIRD JOINT DEBATE AT JONESBORO

Wednesday, September 15, 1858

· THE SCENE ·

THEY CALLED THE REGION Egypt—perhaps because the throat of land here that jutted into the confluence of the Ohio and Mississippi rivers looked so much like the Nile Delta; possibly because its old Indian mounds resembled pyramids; or maybe only because its best-known town was named Cairo. No one knows for sure. What was indisputable, however, was that this was anything but Lincoln country—a bastion of pro-slavery, negrophobic sentiment nestled in rural isolation between two slave states, Kentucky and Missouri. Chicago was a distant 300 miles away, but the South was just across the river. And as historian Mark E. Neely, Jr., has pointed out, when Republican John C. Frémont ran for president in these precincts two years earlier, his electors failed to win even four percent of the vote.

Here, Douglas had boasted up north, was where he most eagerly looked forward to trotting down Lincoln and his so-called abolition doctrine. Here was where he would bring his opponent "to his milk," perhaps implying, prairie style, that Lincoln had gone dry on the truth. Douglas's warning prompted one Republican correspondent to complain, "Isn't this beautiful language to come from a United States Senator?"

In terms of its immediate impact, the third debate at Jonesboro proved a disappointment, not so much because the views expressed that day were empty but because the town itself was. Douglas may have owned the region's hearts, but he could not muster its bodies. Jonesboro proved simply too small and too remote to attract a large audience.

Only 800 people lived in the sleepy old village, and to many others it seemed practically inaccessible. A New York journalist who had convinced himself that he was covering a campaign on the prairies was horrified to find himself sweating in the humid air among its "hills and ravines . . . invested [sic] with forest," 400 feet above sea level. The railroad did not even stop here; the nearest depot had been built more than a mile away in a new town called Anna, which would soon surpass its stagnant neighbor in size and population. And the date for the debate had been as ill-chosen as the site. "Thousands of farmers," the Democratic *Times* explained apologetically, "were engaged elsewhere, at the State Fair" in nearby Centralia.

That left only a few diehards to plod into Jonesboro in the dog-day heat, and the Republican press could hardly contain its glee in reporting that most of these made their way slowly into town on old oxcarts that looked "as though they were ready to fall in pieces." One correspondent joked that the only demonstration of enthusiasm he observed came from "two yoke of steers" and a banner labeled "Stephen A. Douglas"—hanging "bottom upwards."

Lincoln arrived in Jonesboro the night before the debate, and spent a quiet evening with his eyes fixed on the clear night sky to observe the arrival of Donati's comet. "Mr. Lincoln greatly admired this strange visitor," wrote Horace White of the *Tribune:* he sat peacefully "for an hour or more in front of the hotel looking at it." Douglas's arrival the next morning was rather more dramatic. He brought with him a trainload of supporters, a large American flag, and a portable brass cannon that filled the air with "a loud noise and a bad smell."

At two p.m., a small but substantial audience of between 1,200 and 1,500 spectators—as at Ottawa and Freeport, roughly double the village population—gathered in a grove just outside town to hear the debaters. Eyewitnesses described the crowd as "orderly" and "lacking enthusiasm." As one wag put it: "They are a very *cool* set of people down here, notwithstanding the hot weather." Although the region boasted its share of "Danites"—the Douglas supporters' term for pro-Buchanan Democrats (the name referred pejoratively to the Mormons who followed prophet Joseph Smith regardless of morality or truth)—this was basically a Douglas crowd, and their response, such as it was, tilted heavily in his favor.

Douglas opened the encounter by reiterating his increasingly familiar charges that Lincoln was a dangerous "house divided" radical, his supporters abolitionists, and his views suspiciously more conservative the farther south he spoke. He retold his race-baiting Frederick Douglass anecdote, referred ominously to a "nigger" plank in an obscure New York State platform, and spent considerable time rehashing his old "conspiracy" theory, which held that Lincoln had once masterminded a covert deal to win a Senate seat, only to be jilted by his own friends. In his most ringing pronouncement, Douglas declared that he favored preserving the government only "for the benefit of white men and their posterity forever." There could be no justification ever, he insisted, for Negro equality.

To his credit, Lincoln did not use his rebuttal to play to the prejudices of his listeners. He acknowledged that the audience contained few "political friends," but addressed the crowd respectfully as "intelligent people." He denied that he had ever made a compact with cronies over mutual support for Senate seats. And he argued that Douglas's popular sovereignty position was no longer viable under the Dred Scott ruling which made it impossible legally to bar slavery from new territories. Calling up the ghosts of the heroes of the Revolution—still a potent political weapon in 1858—Lincoln asserted that the nation's founders had placed slavery "on the course of ultimate extinction." Douglas, he declared, was now thwarting their intentions. And he turned the tables on Douglas's charges of "Black Republican" abolitionist conspiracies by citing efforts by Illinois Democrats, some of whom Douglas had supported for election, to prevent the spread of slavery too.

Predictably, Democratic journals boasted that Lincoln had been "greatly embarrassed" at Jonesboro. "We fancy he has had enough of Egypt," said the Chicago *Times,* "and certainly Egypt has had enough of him." But the Republican press may have come closer to the truth by assessing his appearance there as "a decided triumph"—at least in the long run. Here, unlike at Freeport, Lincoln indeed played "a bigger game" by demonstrating his consistency to the broad newspaper-reading public outside overwhelmingly Democratic Egypt. He certainly swayed few voters in the Jonesboro area. Republicans running for statewide office would garner only fifteen percent of the vote in November, and Republican legislative candidates pledged to Lincoln for the Senate did not even bother running.

Following are the rival, unaltered texts of the Jonesboro confrontation.

Mr. Douglas' Opening Speech

[The brass cannon was subdued with difficulty and Mr. Douglas was introduced to the audience by Col. Hecker, Jr., after which —*Tribune*]

Mr. Douglas said: Ladies and gentlemen, I appear before you today in pursuance of a previous notice and an arrangement between Mr. Lincoln and myself, to devote the time to the discussion of the political topics that now agitate the country.

Prior to the year 1854 this country was divided into two great political parties, known as the Whig and the Democrat parties. Those parties differed about a bank, about the tariff and distribution, and the Sub-Treasury. On these issues they went before the country and discussed the principle and the object of the measures for the two great parties. Each of these parties could proclaim its principles in Louisiana as well as in Massachusetts—in Kentucky in the same manner that they were in Illinois. Since that period a great revolution has taken place in the formation of parties, by which they now seem to be divided by a geographical line—arraying the whole North, so far as it can be assembled under the Abolition or Republican banner, in hostility to the Southern States, southern people and Southern institutions.

It becomes us to inquire why was this transformation of parties from those of national principle to that of geographical limits in hostility, the one against the other. You remember that in 1850, when this country became agitated from centre to circumference about this slavery question, it became necessary for the leaders of the Whig party and the great Democratic party to bury, for the time being, their partisan dispute and unite to save the Union before we should quarrel as to the mode in which it was to be governed.

During the Session of '49 and '50, Henry Clay was the leader of the Union men, supported by Cass and Webster, by the leaders of the Democrats and the leaders of the Whigs, in opposition to Northern Abolitionists and Southern Disunionists. That great contest of 1850 resulted in the establishment of the compromise measures of that year, which measures rested on the great principle that the people of each State, and of each Territory of this Union, should be permitted to regulate their own domestic institutions in their own way, subject to no other limitation than that which the Federal Constitution imposes. I now ask your attention for a moment, whether or not that principle was right or wrong which guaranteed to every State, every community, the right to form and regulate their domestic institutions to suit themselves. These measures were adopted, as I have previously said, by the joint action of the Union Whigs and the Union Democrats, in opposition to Northern Abolitionists and Southern Disunionists. In 1852, when the Whig party assembled at Baltimore in national convention for the last time, they adopted the principle of the compromise measures of 1850 as their rule of party action in the future. One month thereafter the Democrats assembled at the same place to nominate a candidate for the Presidency, and declared the same principle as the rule of action by which the Democratic party was to be governed. The Presidential election of 1852 was fought on that basis. It is true that the Whigs claimed special merit for the adoption of those measures, because they asserted that their great Clay originated them and their God-like Webster defended them, and their [President Millard] Fillmore signed the bill. On the other hand, we Democrats claim special credit for the Democracy, on the ground that we gave twice as many votes in both Houses for the passage of those measures as the Whig party did. Thus you see that in the Presidential election of '52, the Whigs were pledged by their platform and their candidate to the principles of the Compromise measures of 1850. And the Democratic party were likewise pledged by their principles, their platform and their candidate to the same line of policy, to preserve peace and quiet between the different sections of the Union.

Since that period political parties have been transformed into a sectional party on the one side and a national party on the other. All sectional men, all men of Abolition sentiments and principles, no matter whether they were old Abolitionists or Whigs or Democrats, rallied now under the sectional, Republican, Abolition banner. And consequently all national men, all Union-loving men, whether Whigs or Democrats, or by whatever name they have been known, ought to rally under the stars and stripes in defence of the Constitution as our fathers made it. How, let me ask you, has this departure from the faith of the Democratic, from the faith of Whig party been accomplished in 1854[?] Certain restless mortals and discontented politicians throughout the land took advantage of the temporary excitement created by the Nebraska Bill to try to dissolve the old Whig party and the old Democratic party, and Abolitionize its members, and lead them bound hand and foot captives into the Abolition camp. In the State of New York a convention was held by which the platform was adopted, every plank of which was as black as night, each one relating to the nigger [the *Times* substituted "negro"—*ed.*] and not one to the interests of the white man. That example was followed throughout the Northern States trying to combine all the free States in hostile array against the slave-holding States. These gentlemen who thus thought to build up a great sectional party, and through its organization control the political destinies of this country, based all their hopes on the single fact that the North was the stronger division of the Union, and hence if the North could be combined against the South, a sure victory awaited their efforts.

In this State, I am doing more than justice to the truth of history when I say that Abraham Lincoln on behalf of the Whigs, and Lyman Trumbull on behalf of the Democrats, were the leaders who undertook to perform this grand object of abolitionizing the two parties to which they belonged. It is true according to the evidence and the history of the transaction, that they had a little private arrangement as to what was to be the political destiny of each of the contracting parties before they went into operation. That arrangement was that Mr. Lincoln was [to] take the Old Line Whigs with him, claiming that he was yet as good a Whig as he ever was, over to the Abolitionists. Mr. Trumbull was to run for Congress in the general [the *Times* had "Belleville"—*ed.*] district by claiming to be a good Democrat and thus coax the old Democrats into the Abolition camp, and when by the joint efforts of the abolitionized Whigs and the abolitionized Democrats united with the Old Line Abolition Free Soil party in this State, they should secure a majority in the Legislature. Mr. Lincoln was then to be Senator in Shields' place, and Trumbull was to stop in Congress until I should be accommodating enough either to die or resign in his behalf, and then he should go to the Senate. [Laughter, applause, and cries of "don't die." —*Times*] That was a very nice little arrangement so far as Lincoln and Trumbull were concerned, if the bargain had been carried out in good faith and my friend Lincoln had obtained the Senatorship according to contract. They went into that contest in every part of the State, calling upon all discontented politicians to join the crusade against the Democracy, and appealing to the prevailing sentiments and prejudices in each locality of the State. In all the northern counties, in the three Congressional Districts, certainly in the north end of the State, they adopted as the platform of this new party thus formed by Lincoln and Trumbull in connection with the Abolitionists,—they adopted as a platform, I say, principles, all of which aimed at the warfare by the North against the South. They declared in that platform that the Wilmot Proviso was to be applied to all the Territories of the United States, north as well as south of 36 deg. 30 min. [the Missouri Compromise line—*ed.*], not only as to the territory we then had, but as to all territory which in all time to come we should hereafter acquire. They then put in that platform a stipulation that no more slave States should be admitted into this Union, even if the people of such States desired slavery. They also incorporated the absolute and unconditional repeal of the Fugitive Slave Law, the abolition of the Slave trade between the different States, and in fact, every article of their creed related to this slavery question, and pointed to a northern geographical party in hostility to the southern States of this Union.

As they came a little further south, their principles bleached a little, and got paler just in proportion as the public sentiment was satisfied in this direction. They were Republicans or Abolitionists at the North; they were Anti-Nebraska men when they got down about Springfield, and down here they content themselves with talking about the impolicy and inexpediency of the repeal of the Missouri Compromise. [Shouts of laughter. —*Times*] In the extreme northern counties, they brought out men to canvass the State of the same complexion with their political creed, and hence you find Fred. Douglass, the negro, following Gen. Cass, the illustrious Senator from Michigan, and attempting to speak in behalf of Mr. Lincoln and Trumbull and abolitionism against that illustrious Senator. [Applause. —*Tribune;* Renewed laughter. —*Times*] Why they brought Fred. Douglass to meet me when I was addressing the people at Freeport as I am here, in a carriage with a white lady and her daughter in the carriage sitting by his side, and the owner of the carriage having the honor to drive the coach to convey the negro. [Applause. —*Tribune;* Shame. —*Times*] When I got through canvassing the northern counties and had made progress as far southward as Springfield, there I was brought into discussion on the one side against Mr. Lincoln, Lovejoy, Trumbull, Sidney Breese [Laughter. —*Times*], and Father Giddings, the high priest of Abolitionism, had just been there and Chase came about the time I left. ["Why didn't you shoot him?" —*Times*] [Illinois Supreme Court justice Sidney Breese, an anti-Douglas Democrat, had been rumored a third candidate for senator.

Back in 1841, Breese presided at the first case lawyer Lincoln ever argued on the slavery issue, contending that in the free state of Illinois, a black woman could not be sold to recover a debt; the following year Breese defeated twenty-nine-year-old Douglas in his first try for the Senate—*ed.*] Why I had to take a running shot at them, single handed against the crowd, and as they were so big a drove, white, black and mixed, I had to take a shot gun and fire at the crowd instead of taking them single handed with the rifle. [Laughter. —*Tribune;* Great laughter and cheers. —*Times*] Trumbull had for his lieutenant in abolitionizing the Democratic party, such men as John Wentworth, up at Chicago, and Governor Reynolds of Belleview and Sidney Breese of Carlyle, and John Dougherty of Union County [applause, —*Tribune;* "good," "good," "give it to them," &c., —*Times*], each moderating his opinion just in proportion to the locality, and I am told that Dougherty would not go much farther than to admit the inexpediency of the Nebraska Bill. Why, up there they went for negro citizenship and negro equality, putting the white man and the negro on the same basis under the law.

Now these men were then three or four years ago in that combination to break down the Democratic party. They are together this day for the same purpose. They do not raise the same flag, nor have the same opinion. They do not profess the same faith, but conceal it for the sake of policy. For instance, in the Northern Counties of this State now you find all the Conventions are called under the title of the Republican Convention. When you get down at Springfield they dare not call the Convention there as Republican, but they invite all the enemies of the Democratic party to unite. When you get down into Egypt Trumbull will issue his notice for the free Democracy to assemble to hear him discuss. [Laughter. —*Tribune*] Here is Trumbull's notice for the meeting that took place at Waterloo the other day, and I received it then: "A meeting of the free Democracy will take place in Waterloo Monday, September 13th when the Hon. Lyman Trumbull and John Baker will address the people upon the political topics of the day. Members of all parties are cordially invited to be present to hear and determine for themselves." (Signed) *"The Monroe Free Democrat."*

Now what is this name put forth for, unless to deceive the people and make them believe that they are not in the same party that raises the black flag of Abolitionism in the northern part of this State, and makes war upon the Democratic party throughout the State? When I put that question to them at Waterloo, one of them arose and said that they changed the name for political effect, in order to get votes. There was a candid admission that the object was in changing the name and the party organization and the avowal of their principles in different localities, to try to deceive and cheat some portion of the people out of their votes till after the election. Why can't a political party, conscious of the rectitude of its purposes and the soundness of its principles, avow these principles everywhere alike? I would disdain to hold any political principles that I can't avow in the same terms in Kentucky as well as in Illinois—in Charleston as well as in Chicago—in New Orleans as well as in New York. [Cheers. —*Times*] So long as we live under a Constitution common to all the States, our faith ought to be as broad, as liberal, as just as the Constitution itself, and ought to be proclaimed alike in every portion of the Union. [Hear, hear. —*Times*]. But we find that it is necessary for partisan effect to change those colors in different counties in order to catch the popular breeze, and with these discordant materials combine together a majority in the Legislature for the purpose of breaking down the Democratic party. Well, this combination did succeed in 1854, so far as to elect a majority of the confederates to the Legislature of the State. The first and most important act they had to perform was to elect a Senator in the place of the eminent and gallant Gen. Shields. His term expired in the Senate and he had to be crushed by this Abolition coalition for the simple reason that he would not join the conspiracy to wage war on behalf of the northern States against the southern States of this Union. That was the only objection to Gen. Shields. He had served you with ability in the Legislature of this State, he had served you with fidelity and ability as a financial officer, as Auditor of this State, he had performed his duties to the satisfaction of the whole country at the head office of the Land Department at Washington. He had covered the State and the Union with immortal glory upon the bloody valleys of Mexico, in defence of the honor and flag of the Union, and yet he had to be stricken down by this unholy combination, and for what purpose? Merely because he would not join a combination of the Northern half of the States of the Union to make war on the other half, after having poured out his heart's blood for all the States of the Union. Shields was stricken down by this unholy combination, and Trumbull was put in his place. How did Trumbull get there? Before the Abolitionists would consent to go into the election of an United States Senator, they required all the members of this combination to show their hands upon this question of Abolitionism. Lovejoy, the high priest of Abolitionism, brought in resolutions defining the Abolition creed, and required them to show their hand by voting on them under the ayes and nos. In that creed, as laid down by Lovejoy, they declared that the Wilmot Proviso must be put in all the Territories of the United States, north as well as south of 36 deg. 30 min., and that no more territory was to be acquired unless slavery was first prohibited therein. In the second place they declared that no more States should ever be received into the United States unless slavery was prohibited by the Constitution approved in such States; and third, they declared that the Fugitive Slave law must be unconditionally repealed; but if they failed in repealing it altogether, then such amendments were to be made as would render it useless and inefficient for the objects for which it was passed. The very day after these resolutions were voted upon, part of them carried and the others defeated, but being voted upon, the same men who voted for them with only two exceptions voted for Abraham Lincoln as their candidate for the United States Senate. He came within one or two votes of being elected [in the legislature—*ed.*], but he could not quite get elected, for the reason that his friend Trumbull, a party to the bargain by which Lincoln was to have Shields' place, had control of a few Abolition Democrats, and would not allow them to vote for Lincoln, thus worrying [the *Times* had "wronging"—*ed.*] him on each ballot, letting him almost be elected, but not quite, till he forced them to drop Lincoln and elect himself, in order to unite the party. [Immense laughter. —*Times*] Thus we find that although the Legislature was carried with the object and bargain between Lincoln, Trumbull and the Abolitionists uniting those discordant materials into the harmonious Abolition party, yet Trumbull violated the bargain, and played a Yankee trick on Lincoln the very first time they came to a division of the spoils. [Applause. —*Tribune;* Laughter and cheers. Mr. Lincoln greatly agitated, his face in his hands. —*Times*]

Perhaps you would like a little bit of evidence on this point, and if you want it, I will call Col. James H. Matheny, of Springfield, Mr. Lincoln's especial confidential friend for the last twenty years, and hear what he will say upon the subject of this bargain. Matheny is now the political [the *Times* had "Black"—*ed.*] Republican, Abolition candidate for Congress in the Springfield District against the gallant Tom Morris, and is now making speeches all over that portion of the State against him, in favor of Mr. Lincoln, in concert with Trumbull. He ought to be a good witness. Here is an extract from a speech that Matheny made in 1856 when he got mad because his friend Lincoln had been cheated, and it is only one of numerous speeches of the same tenor, with the same end, exposing this bargain between Lincoln and Trumbull and the Abolitionists. Mr. Matheny said [the *Times* version presented the exact text of Matheny's speech, which Douglas here paraphrased—*ed.*] that two years ago this fall the Whigs, the Abolitionists, the Know-Nothings, and the renegade Democrats made a solemn compact for the purpose of carrying the State against the Democracy, on this plan: first, they would all combine to elect Trumbull to Congress, and thereby carry his district for the legislature, in order to throw all the strength that could be obtained in[to] that body against the Democrats. Second. When the Legislature shall meet, the officers of that body, such as Speaker Clerks, Door-Keepers, &c., would be given to the Abolitionists. Third. That the Whigs were to have the United States Senator. That accordingly, in good faith, Trumbull was elected to Congress, and his district carried for the Legislature. When it convened, the Abolitionists got all the officers of that body, and so far the bond was fairly executed. The Whig party demanded the election of Abraham Lincoln to the U.S. Senate, that the bond might be fulfilled. The other parties to the contract have all secured all that was called for. "But," said Matheny, "in the most perfidious manner, they refused to elect Lincoln and the mean, low-lived, sneaking Trumbull succeeded in acquiring that office, thus forcing himself an excrescence from the rotten bowels of Democracy, into the United States Senate; and thus," said Matheny, "it has ever been that an honest man makes a bad bargain when he conspires or contracts with rogues." [Laughter. —*Tribune*] Thus Matheny thought that his friend Lincoln made a bad bargain when he consorted with such rogues as Trumbull and his Abolition associates of that campaign. [Applause. —*Tribune*; Great cheers and laughter; Lincoln looking very miserable. —*Times*] Mr. Lincoln was shoved off the track and you could have seen him and his friends looking sour, [laughter —*Times*] disposed to tell, but durs'n't. [Laughter. —*Tribune*; Shouts of laughter. —*Times*] And thus they stood for a long time, until the Abolitionists coaxed him back, and assured him that he should certainly have the Senatorship in Douglas' place. [laughter. —*Tribune*] In that way they were enabled to hold Mr. Lincoln in this Abolition cause up to this time and have brought him into fight against me to see whether he is again to be cheated. But Lincoln required them this time to toe the mark, and all give bond if not security that Lovejoy should not cheat him as Trumbull did.

[Laughter. —*Tribune;* Roars of laughter, Lincoln looking as if he had not a friend on earth, although Herr (Herman) Kreisman (German-born Chicago Republican and Lincoln supporter—*ed.*) whispered "Never mind" into his ear. —*Times*] And accordingly, when the Republican Convention assembled in Springfield, in June last, for the purpose of nominating officers only, they could not get Lincoln and his friends into it to act with them till they would pledge themselves that Lincoln should be their candidate for the United States Senate, and accordingly you find that that Convention framed a resolution unanimously declaring that Abraham Lincoln was the first, the last and the only choice of the Republicans for the United States Senate. He wasn't willing to have it understood that he was the first choice nor the last choice, but the only choice. The party had nobody else. Browning was nowhere. Governor Bissell was of no account. Old Archy Williams was not to be taken into consideration. John Wentworth was to be thrown overboard. John M. Palmer was to be discarded, and the Republican party presented the unusual and extraordinary spectacle of having but one—the first, last and only choice for the Senate. [Laughter. —*Times*] Suppose Mr. Lincoln should die, what a horrible condition would they be in. [Laughter. —*Tribune;* A groan from Lincoln and great laughter. —*Times*] They have no other choice, and it was necessary for them to put themselves before the world in the ludicrous, ridiculous attitude of having no other choice, in order to assure Lincoln that he should not be cheated again, and Lovejoy put in, as Trumbull was, before him by the trick then played. Well, gentlemen, I think they will have a nice time of it before they get there. I do not intend to give them any chance to cheat Lincoln at all this time. [Laughter. —*Tribune;* Cheers. —*Times*] I intend to relieve them from all anxiety on this subject, and save them from the mortification of having any more exposures of contracts made with rogues and cheating those who had pledged their honor. [Great applause. —*Times*]

But I wish to invite your attention to the chief points at issue between Mr. Lincoln and myself in this discussion.

Mr. Lincoln, knowing that he was to be the candidate of his party, by the arrangement of which I have already spoken, knowing that he would be nominated at that Convention as I have already stated, had his speech accepting the nomination all written and committed to memory, ready to deliver the moment the nomination was announced. Accordingly he rose and delivered it, a portion of which I will read in

order that I may state his political principles fairly by repeating them
in his own language:

"In my opinion it (the slavery agitation) will not cease until a crisis
shall have been reached and passed. A house divided against itself
cannot stand. I believe this Government cannot endure permanently
half Slave and half Free. I do not expect the house to fall, but I do
expect it will cease to be divided. It will become all one thing, or all
the other. Either the opponents of Slavery will arrest the further
spread of it, and place it where the public mind shall rest in the belief
that it is in the course of ultimate extinction, or its advocates will push
it forward till it shall become alike lawful to all the States—old as well
as new, North as well as South. [The *Times* version of the by-then-
famous quotation mangled the text somewhat—*ed.*]

There you have Mr. Lincoln's main proposition, upon which he
bases his claim, stated in his own language. He tells you this Republic
cannot endure permanently divided into slave and free States, as our
fathers made it. He says that they must all become free or all become
slave; must all be one thing, or all the other, or this government cannot
last. Why can't it last, if we will execute the government in the spirit and
on the same principles upon which it was made? Mr. Lincoln by that
proposition tells the South, "If you desire to maintain your institutions
as they now are, you must not be satisfied with minding your own
business, but you must invade Illinois and all the other Northern States,
and establish slavery here and make it universal." Then he tells the
North, "You must not be satisfied with regulating your own affairs, and
minding your own business, but if you desire to maintain your freedom,
you must invade the Southern States and abolish slavery everywhere,
in order to have them all the one thing or all the other." I say that these
propositions are the inevitable and irresistible result of Mr. Lincoln's
argument, inviting a warfare between the North and South, to be
carried out with ruthless vengeance. All the one section or the other
shall be driven to the wall and reduced as a victim to the rapacity of the
other. What good can be done by this system of warfare? Suppose the
North was to succeed in conquering the South, who will be the gainer?
Suppose the South should succeed in conquering the North, can the
Union be preserved in that way? And why is this sectional warfare to
be carried on between Northern and Southern States till there shall be

uniformity in all the institutions of the State? Because Mr. Lincoln says that "a house divided against itself cannot stand," and pretends that this scripture quotation, using the language of the Lord himself, is applicable to the American Union and the American Constitution. Washington and his compeers in the Convention that framed the Constitution, made this Government divided into free and slave States; made it composed of thirteen sovereign and independent States, each having sovereign authority over its local and domestic institutions, but all bound together by the Federal Constitution. Mr. Lincoln likens that law of the Federal Constitution's, joining free and slave States together, to a house divided against itself, and says it is contrary to the law of God, and hence cannot stand. Where did he learn and by what authority does he proclaim that this government made by our fathers is contrary to the law of God, and hence cannot stand? It has stood thus divided into free and slave States from the beginning of this government to this day. During that period we have increased from four millions to thirty millions of people. We have extended our territory from the Mississippi to the Pacific Ocean. We have acquired the Floridas and Texas, and other territory enough to double our geographical extent. We have increased in population, in wealth, and in naval and military power beyond any example on earth. We have risen from a week, feeble power, till we have become the terror and the admiration of the civilized world, and all this had been done under a constitution which Mr. Lincoln says, in substance, is a violation of the law of God, and under a union divided into free and slave States, and Mr. Lincoln says because of such division the house cannot stand. Surely Mr. Lincoln is a wiser man than those who made the government. Washington did not believe, nor his compatriots, that the regulations, laws and domestic institutions which were adapted to the Green Mountains of Vermont were suited to the rice plantations of South Carolina. They did not believe in that day that in a Republic as broad and extended as this, containing such a variety of climate, of soil and of interests, uniformity between the local institutions was very desirable or possible. They believed then, and our experience has proved to us now, that each locality having different interests, a different climate, and different surroundings, requires different local laws, local policy and local institutions corresponding and adapted to the interests of that locality. Thus our government was formed on the principle of diversity in the local institutions and laws, and not that of uniformity.

As my time flies, I must only glance at these points, in order to present, if I can, all of the topics I intend to touch upon for Mr. Lincoln to reply to.

He makes war on the decision of the Supreme Court, known as the Dred Scott decision. Now, my fellow citizens, I have no war to make on that decision or any other ever rendered by the Supreme Court. I am content to take it as having been delivered by the highest judicial tribunal on earth; a tribunal established by the Constitution of the United States, and hence that decision becomes the law of the land, binding on you, on me, and on every other good citizen, whether you like it or not, and hence I do not choose to go into an argument, or prove before this audience whether Chief Justice Taney understood better than Abraham Lincoln, or not. [Laughter. —*Times*] Mr. Lincoln objects to that decision, first and mainly because it deprives the negro of the rights of citizenship. I am as much opposed to his reason for that objection as I am to his objection itself. I hold that a negro is not and never ought to be a citizen of the United States. [Applause. —*Tribune*; Good, good, and tremendous cheers. —*Times*] I hold that this Government was made on the white basis; made by the white men, for the benefit of white men and their posterity forever, and should be administered by white men and none others. I do not believe that the Almighty made the negro capable of self-government. I am aware that all the Abolition lecturers that you will find travelling about through the country are in the habit of proclaiming and reading the Declaration of Independence, to prove that all men were created equal, and endowed by their Creator with certain inalienable rights, among which are life, liberty and the pursuit of happiness. Mr. Lincoln is much in the habit of following in the track of Lovejoy in that particular, by reading that portion of the Declaration of Independence to prove that the negro was endowed by the Almighty with the inalienable right of equality with white men. Now, I state to you my fellow citizens, in my opinion the Signers of the Declaration of Independence had no reference whatever to the negro, when they declared all men to have been created equal. The Signers of the Declaration were white men, of European birth and European descent, and had no reference either to the negro or to savage Indians, or the Feejee [*sic*], or the Malay, or any other inferior or degraded race, when they spoke of the equality of men. One good evidence that such was their understanding, is to be found in the fact that at the time every one of the thirteen colonies was a slaveholding

colony and every Signer of the Declaration of Independence represented a slaveholding constitution, and yet no one of them abolished
slavery, or at least conferred citizenship upon the slaves when they
signed and proclaimed the Declaration of Independence. And yet if
they had intended to declare that the negro was the equal to the white
man, and ought to be put on an equality by Divine right, they were
bound as honest men to put their negroes on an equality with themselves. [Cheers. —*Times*] Instead of that, with uplifted eyes they im-
plored the Divine blessing upon them during a seven years' bloody war
in carrying out the Declaration of Independence, never dreaming that
they were violating it by holding their negro slaves in bondage, and
depriving them of equality.

Thus, my friends, I am in favor of preserving the government on the
white basis, as our fathers made it. It does not follow by any means that
because the negro is not your equal or mine that hence he must
necessarily be a slave. On the contrary it does follow that we ought to
extend to the negro every right, every privilege, every immunity which
he is capable of enjoying consistent with the good of society. When you
ask me what those rights are that we should extend to them, I tell you
that is a question which each State in this Union must decide for itself.
Illinois has already decided that question. We have decided that the
negro must not be a slave within our limits. We have also decided that
the negro shall not be a citizen within our limits. He shall not vote, he
shall not hold office, he shall not exercise any political rights. I maintain
Illinois, as a sovereign State, had a right thus to fix her policy in
reference to the relation between the white man and the negro. But
while we have the right to decide that question for ourselves, we must
recognize the same right in Kentucky, and in every other State to make
the same decision or a different one to suit herself. Now having thus
made a decision fixing our own policy in reference to that race, we must
leave Kentucky, and Missouri, and every other State perfectly free to
make such decisions on that question as they see proper. Kentucky has
decided on that question for herself. She has said that within her limits
the negro shall not exercise any political rights. But she has also said
that a portion of the negroes under the law of that State shall be slaves.
She has as much right to fix that as her policy, as we have to fix the
contrary as our policy. New York has decided that in that State a negro
shall not vote unless he has $250 worth of property, and if he has that
much he may vote on an equality with the white man.

I, for one, am utterly opposed to negro suffrage anywhere, and under any circumstances, yet inasmuch as the Supreme Court of the United States have decided in the celebrated Dred Scott case that a State has a right to confer the privilege of voting suffrage on free negroes, I am not going to make war upon New York, because she has adopted a policy repugnant to my feelings. [That's good. —*Times*] And New York must mind herself, and not attempt to force it upon us. [Applause. —*Tribune;* Great applause. —*Times*] And so with the State of Maine. There they have decided that the negro may vote and hold office in an equality with the white man. I had occasion to say in a discussion with the Senator from Maine last session, that if they thought the white men within the limits of their State were no better than negroes, I would not quarrel with them, but they must not come to Illinois and say that my white constituents were no better than negroes [the *Times* added: "or we should be sure to quarrel"—*ed.*]. [Laughter. —*Tribune;* Cheers. —*Times*] The Dred Scott decision covers the whole question, that each State has a right to settle this question of suffrage for itself, and all questions on the relation between the negro and the white man. Judge Taney expressly lays down the doctrine. I receive it without comment as the law, and while these States are adopting regulations disgusting and abhorrent to my views, I will not make war upon them if they will mind their own business and let me alone. [Bravo, and cheers. —*Times*]

Now I come back to the question, why cannot this Union exist forever divided into free and slave States, as our fathers made it. It can thus exist if each State will act out the principles upon which our institutions were founded, to wit, the right of each State to do as it pleases, and then let its neighbours alone. Thus act on that great principle, and this Union can not only last forever, but it can extend and expand till it covers the whole continent, and makes this Republic one grand ocean-bound confederacy.

We must bear in mind that we are yet a young nation, growing with a rapidity unequalled in the history of the world—that our natural increase is great, and the flow of emigration from the old world is increasing, requiring us to expand and acquire new territory from time to time, in order to give them bread to live upon. If we will act upon the principle of State rights and State sovereignty, each State regulating its own affairs, and minding its own business and letting its neighbors alone, we can go on and expand indefinitely, just as fast as we will need the territory. The time may come, and has come, when our interests would be advanced by the acquisition of the island of Cuba. [Terrific applause. —*Times*] When we get Cuba we must take it as we find it, and leave the people of Cuba to decide the question of slavery for themselves without the interference of the federal government, or of any other State in the Union. So, when it becomes necessary to acquire any portion of Mexico, or Canada, or any island of the ocean, we must take them as we find them, and leave their people to do as they choose. I never have inquired, and never will inquire whether a new State applying for admission has slavery, if the constitution they present be the act and deed of the people and embody their will, and they have the requisite population. I will take them with slavery or without it, just as the people shall determine. [That's good. That's right, and cheers. —*Times*] My objection to the Lecompton Constitution did not consist in the fact that it was a slave State. I was as much opposed to it as a free State as I was as a slave State. I hold that that was a question the people had a right to decide for themselves, and no power on earth ought to interfere with their decision; but the question with me was that it was not the act and deed of the people of Kansas and did not embody their will, and the recent election just had in Kansas voting the Constitution down by nearly ten to one, shows conclusively that I was right in saying that that Constitution was not the act and deed of that people and did not embody their will.

If we wish to preserve our institutions in purity and transmit them unimpaired to our latest posterity, we must observe that just good faith [The *Times* had "preserve with religious good faith"—*ed.*], that great principle of self government which guarantees to every State, old and new, the right to make just such a Constitution as they desire, and establish just such a Constitution as its people want, and go into the Union with their own Constitution, and not with one palmed upon them. [Cheers. —*Times*] Whenever you sanction the doctrine that Congress may crowd a Constitution down the throats of an unwilling people against their consent you will subvert the great fundamental principles upon which all our free institutions rest. I say that our institutions rest on that great principle. In the future I have no fear that the attempt will ever be made. President Buchanan said in his last annual message that hereafter the rule of Minnesota requiring that the Constitution [the *Times* added: "(should) be submitted to the people,"—*ed.*] must be followed in all future cases. If he stands by that recommendation there will be no division of the Democratic party in the future.

Hence the great mission of the Democratic party is to unite the fraternal feeling of the whole country, and then restore peace and quiet to the country by leaving each State to mind its own business, regulate its own affairs, carry out the Constitution as our fathers have made it, and thus preserve the Union, and render it perpetual in all time to come. I would that we should do as our fathers did, who made this government. There was no sectional strife—there was no warfare between sections in Washington's army. They were brothers of a common Confederacy— fought under a common flag—they fought and struggled that they might impart to their posterity a common destiny, and to this end they poured out their blood in common streams, and shared in some instances a common grave. I am told my time is out.

[During Mr. Douglas' speech, the brass cannon was fired at intervals; and a young person on the stand with weak legs and fiery mustaches, who accompanies Mr. D. as a letter writer, shot in such expressions as "Hit him again," "Bully for you," &c. Not being strictly responses from the crowd, we have omitted them in the above report. —*Tribune;* Three hearty cheers for Douglas. —*Times*] [Douglas was by this time receiving much teasing in Republican journals both for traveling with a private secretary, and for taking with him to debates a small cannon which supporters detonated to punctuate—or, some charged, to ignite— crowd response to him—*ed.*]

Mr. Lincoln's Reply

[As Mr. Lincoln stepped forward, one of the numerous pedlars who haunt these meetings, mounted a seat and cried out in a feeble voice for three cheers for Lincoln, whereupon some five persons in the crowd halloed. —*Times;* Mr. Lincoln was then introduced to the audience by D. L. Phillips, Esq., and was greeted with three cheers, and then "three more"; after which he said —*Tribune*]

Mr. Lincoln said:—I hope you won't make fun of the few friends I have here. That is all I ask.

Ladies and Gentlemen—There are very many of the principles that Judge Douglas has stated that I most cordially approve, and there need be no controversy over them. In so far as Judge Douglas has insisted that all the States of the Union have a right to do exactly as they please about all their domestic regulations and institutions, including the question of slavery, I agree with Judge Douglas, and yet he places me wrong in spite of all that I can tell him. Again and again I have expressed my views upon this subject—I have made a great many speeches, some of which have been printed, and I state without hesitation, that it will be utterly impossible to read anything that I have ever put in print that will show anything to the contrary. I hold myself under the obligation to allow the people of other States—and to allow all the States to do as they please. I deny that I have any inclination to interfere with them even if there were no constitutional obstruction, and I say again that it is wrong to say that I entertain opinions other than these.

While I am upon this subject I will briefly answer some of the propositions that Judge Douglas has put forth. He says why cannot this Union endure permanently, half slave and half free. I have said I supposed it could not, and I will now, before this candid audience, try to give briefly some reasons for entertaining that opinion. Another form of his question is, why can we not let them stand as our fathers placed them. Therein consists the exact difference between us. I say that Judge Douglas and his friends have changed the policy from the way in which our fathers originally placed it. I say the way in which our fathers left this subject of slavery was in the course of ultimate extinction, and the public mind rested in the belief of its ultimate extinction. I say that when our government was first established it was the policy of the government to prohibit the spread or extension of slavery into the territories of the

United States where it did not then exist. I say that Judge Douglas and his friends have changed that policy, and placed it where it shall spread until it becomes alike lawful in all the States, old as well as the new, North as well as South. All that I have asked is that it should be put back on the basis that our fathers originally placed it on, and I have had no sort of doubt that it would there be extinguished in God's own time, if we could restrict it to the States where it exists, and prohibit it in the territories.

[Congressman Preston] Brooks, the man that had the difficulty with [the *Tribune* substituted "assaulted"—*ed.*] [Charles] Sumner upon the floor of the United States Senate [he had brutally caned Sumner into unconsciousness in 1856—*ed.*], was complimented by dinners and silver pitchers, I believe, and gold-headed canes, and a good many other things for that deed performed by him, and in one of the speeches he made about that time he declared that nobody had expected slavery to exist to this day, but that we have grown wiser than were our fathers, and he even went on to argue that the invention of the cotton gin made its perpetuation necessary. That is but an opinion, it is such an opinion as we cannot get from Judge Douglas, it is not an opinion that we can get from a Northern man that is in favor of slavery at all, but you can get it from a Southern man. He said that the perpetuation of slavery is a necessity, and he insisted on its being changed from the basis upon which our fathers left it to the basis of perpetuity and nationality, and I insist that Judge Douglas is helping it along, and that is where we differ. That is what I insist upon, and I insist upon its being placed back upon the basis upon which our fathers placed it.

I remember that Judge Douglas once said that he thought he saw evidence on the statute book[s] of this government of a policy of this government to divide the States by a geographical line, and he set about to place it upon that original basis that he thought it ought to be put upon, on principle at first, and in that speech he insisted that that was the policy of our fathers. [Applause. —*Tribune*] Now, when he asks me why we cannot put it upon that basis that our fathers put it upon he had better clear up the evidence that he has changed it. Any one who will read his speech of the 22nd March last, will not say that I was wrong when I say that he here put slavery upon a different set of principles. I think then that I fully answered him when he asks why this government cannot exist half slave and half free. [The *Tribune* has: "why we cannot let it alone upon the basis where our fathers left it, by showing that he has himself changed the whole policy of the Government in that regard"—*ed.*]

Now, my fellow citizens, in regard to this matter about the contract that was made between Senator Trumbull and myself, and all that long portion of Judge Douglas' speech on that subject, I wish only to say to you what I have said to him, that he cannot know whether it is true or not, and I do know that there is not a word of truth in it at all. [Voice in the crowd—"We all knew it wasn't true." —*Times*] [The *Tribune* added, "And I have told him so before." (Continued applause. "That's right." "Hit him again.")—*ed.*] I don't want any harsh terms indulged in here, at all, but I know not how to deal with that persistent telling of a story, when I do know that it is not true. I don't know how to meet that sort of an argument. I don't want to have a fight, and I know no way of working an argument upon it into a corn cob and stopping his mouth with it at all. [Laughter and applause. —*Tribune*] All I can say to that story—about the bargain between Trumbull and myself—is, that there is not one word of truth in it [Applause. —*Tribune*] and I can only ask Judge Douglas to show, by some evidence, that there is any truth to it all. Now, he brings forward what he says is a speech of James H. Matheny. Now, my own opinion is, that James H. Matheny did do that immoral thing of telling a story without knowing the truth of it, or anything about it, and I contradicted it at the time, and Trumbull has answered it at all times. I hope the Judge will not be angry if I have not the highest confidence in documents that he produces since he produced the Springfield resolutions [at Ottawa—*ed.*]. [Laughter and cheers. —*Tribune*] I don't know what to say of this, when a long story is brought on me, so I leave it in that way, insisting that he brings me proof of it. [The *Tribune* added: "That is all any man can do, and I leave it in that way for I know of no other way of dealing with it"—*ed.*]

The Judge leads off also with a long historical account of the old Whig and Democratic parties and it connects itself with this charge against Trumbull and myself. He says that they agreed upon the compromise measures of 1850. That the national convention of the National Democratic party agreed to stand upon the compromises of 1850, that resolutions were passed to abide by that compromise as a finality upon the question of slavery. He also says that the Whig National Convention agreed upon abiding by the compromises of 1850 as a finality. Now I understand the Judge to be all right about that. I understand that part of the history of the country to be entirely correct and remember that as a member of the old Whig party, I acquiesced in it. I recollect also that in the canvas following, that was when we had Gen. [Winfield] Scott up for President [he lost to Franklin Pierce in 1852—*ed.*], Judge Douglas was around branding us as abolitionists then. We could do nothing then, but it was abolitionism, as it is now. [The *Tribune* added: "I have often heard him. We could no nothing when the old Whig party was alive that was not Abolitionism, but it has got an extremely good name since it has passed away. (Laughter.)—*ed.*] But those compromises, I recollect, did nothing with the Missouri compromise, these compromises did not repeal the Missouri compromise, or propose to repeal the Missouri compromise. It became Judge Douglas' duty, as he thought, and I find no fault with that, as chairman of the Committee on Territories, to bring in a bill to organize one and afterwards two territories. When he brought in that bill he brought in such a bill as did upset and repeal the Missouri compromise. What, I ask, is the reason that he could not leave that alone? We had acquiesced in this settlement, and when he comes to form a government for a territory north of the compromise line, my question was, why could he not have left it alone? [Applause. —*Tribune*] Was it necessary in the organization of the territory? Not at all. Iowa had been organized as a territory north of that, and had come into the Union as a State without disturbing that compromise at all. There was no necessity to disturb that compromise in the organization of territory.

I know that it would take me an hour to meet all the quibbling arguments that it [the Missouri Compromise—*ed.*] was repealed by the compromise of 1850, and so on, but my opinion is, that Judge Douglas, at the time of the introduction of his famous Nebraska bill, first brought into Congress a bill, in which bill in its original form, he did not touch it, and he expressly stated that he had not done so because it had been forborne to be done by the compromise measures of 1850. I therefore close that part of the case by asking him why [the *Tribune* added: "when we had peace under the Missouri Compromise"—*ed.*] could he not have left it alone?

In complaining—and that is all I will say in regard to this—in complaining of the Springfield speech, in which he says I accepted the nomination of the convention—by the bye, he will find in that that he is at fault again, for I did not speak a word about accepting it at all—in complaining of this he said that there must be a variety in the institutions of the States. I agree to all that. Have these other matters ever produced any differences among us? Not at all. Have we ever had any quarrels at all over the fact that they had laws in Louisiana that are well adapted to the production of sugar, or, rather, to the commerce that follows from the production of sugar, and that we may have laws suitable to the nature of our soil, climate, and productions? Not at all. They don't make a house divided against itself. They are the props of the Union; they sustain and they really hold up the house. But has it been so with this subject of slavery? Have we not had quarrels and difficulties about it in all time, and when is it to be expected that we are to cease to have quarrels and difficulties about it? There has been peace save and except upon this question on which there has been difficulty whenever there has been an effort to spread it into new territories. Whenever it has been kept to the old territory there has been peace. This was the case in reference to the Missouri Compromise; it was so in reference to the annexation of Texas; it was the same during the Mexican war; and it has been so whenever there have been efforts made to extend it into new territories.

Now, I want to talk to this intelligent people—very few of whom I expect to be my political friends—I want to ask them if this agitation will cease with all the cause of agitation still existing. Do you expect that the Almighty will change the constitutions of men, or that the nature of men will be so changed that that same cause will cease to agitate them? Will Judge Douglas be able to persuade men to accept these views? Will Judge Douglas be able to persuade all these men so that this cause will cease to agitate?

Upon that subject I suppose that I have dwelt about as long as I ought, measuring and dividing my time as I best can. I have, therefore, supposed that when the institution of slavery is placed, as I think it is, upon a new basis—when that has taken away the whole hope of its ultimate extinction—when it takes the attitude of agitation and takes the attitude in which men have always been excited so far as has been my reading of history, what right have I to suppose that it will cease so to excite and agitate? What right have I to suppose that the agitation will come to an end until it shall be placed back where it did stand where the fathers of the government did place it, or until its advocates shall master all [the *Tribune* added "opposition"—*ed.*] and shall squat down under it? That is the view I entertain, and the view that I have expressed in the extract which Judge Douglas has read from a speech of mine.

There is one other thing that I feel myself under some sort of obligation to do. Judge Douglas has here, to-day, in a very rambling way, I
was about to say, spoken of platforms for which he holds me and those
who act with me, responsible, or seeks to do so. He says why can't we
speak out frankly. He reads an advertisement that he says was put up
for a speech to be made by Mr. Trumbull at Waterloo, and he says, why
cannot we speak out freely our sentiments as he and his friends do. How
can his friends speak out frankly and manfully his [the *Tribune* had
"their"—*ed.*] sentiments? A convention of his friends met on the 21st of
April, at Springfield. They passed a set of resolutions there and proclaimed them to the country and to the world as their platform, and it
is because he claims that they are his principles that he distinctly speaks
out his principles. Well, on the 9th of June, John Dougherty and Gov.
Reynolds and others, calling themselves national democrats, met at
Springfield, and passed resolutions as plainly stating a set of principles.
What is the reason the Judge cannot be willing that Dougherty and
Reynolds shall stand upon their platform as well as he upon his? Again,
when we came to our convention on the 16th of that same month of
June, the republicans of the State published to the world their platform
as distinctly and plainly as Judge Douglas. What is the reason that he
cannot let me stand on that platform? Why must he go around to find
that there is somebody supporting me that has said something against
these principles? If it turns out that he thinks the rule a good one, that
I must be responsible for every man that has ever said anything against
them—if that is a good rule for me; it is a good rule for him. But I think
it is not a good rule for either of us. [The *Tribune* added: "Do you think
differently, Judge?"

"MR. DOUGLAS—I do not."]

MR. LINCOLN—I am glad he thinks with me. Then I cannot see why
he rakes up old platforms passed five years ago [the *Tribune* added: "and
insisting they were my platform, notwithstanding my protest that they
are not, and never were my platform, and my pointing out the platform
of the State Convention which he delights to say nominated me for the
Senate."—*ed.*]. I cannot conceive what he means by parading these
platforms, unless he means to hold me responsible for them. [The
Tribune added: "If he says to me here, that he does not hold the rule to
be good, one way or the other, I do not comprehend how he could
answer me more fully if he answered me at greater length."—*ed.*] I must
be permitted to put in, in the course of this debate, what I, as a lawyer,

would call a good plea to a bad declaration. [Laughter. —*Tribune*] I have understood that it is a maxim with lawyers that a bad plea is a good answer to a bad declaration. I think that I am not responsible for these things, but if I can show the same thing of him, it will be a good plea to a bad declaration (the *Tribune* added: "and now I intend to try it"—*ed.*]

Now, at Freeport, he occupied a large part of his time in putting in documents in relation of some sort, as I understood, to make me responsible for them. I propose to do a little of the same sort of thing with him.

In 1850, a very good gentleman, Thompson Campbell, a friend of the Judge's, was the regular democratic candidate for Congress in the Galena district. He was interrogated as to his views—as to certain questions about slavery. I have here what I suppose to be the correct interrogatories and his reply. I will read them, and after that I have a few words of comment.

"1st. Will you, if elected, vote for and cordially support a bill prohibiting slavery in the Territories of the United States?

2d. Will you vote for and support a bill abolishing slavery in the District of Columbia?"

That is one and two. Now I read the answers to one and two.

"To the first and second interrogations, I answer unequivocally in the affirmative."

"3d. Will you oppose the admission of any Slave States which may be formed out of Texas or the Territories?

4th. Will you vote for and advocate the repeal of the Fugitive Slave Law passed at the recent session of Congress?

5th. Will you advocate and vote for the election of a Speaker of the House of Representatives who shall be willing to organize the Committees of that House so as to give the Free States their just influence in the business of legislation?

6th. What are your views not only as to the constitutional rights of Congress to prohibit the Slave Trade between the States, but also as to the expediency of exercising that right immediately?"

I read the answers, leaving out the first ones that I have read:

"To the third interrogatory I reply, that I am opposed to the admission of any more Slave States into the Union, that may be formed out of Texas or any other territory.

[']To the fourth and fifth interrogatories, I unhesitatingly answer in the affirmative.

[']To the sixth interrogatory I reply that so long as the Slave States continue to treat slaves as articles of commerce, the Constitution confers power on Congress to pass laws regulating that peculiar commerce, and that the protection of human rights imperatively demands the interposition of every constitutional means to prevent this most inhuman and iniquitous traffic.

T. CAMPBELL."

Now, I want to say here, that Thompson Campbell, on that platform, was elected to Congress as the Democratic candidate in the Galena district; he was elected to Congress over a very good man named Martin P. Sweet.

MR. DOUGLAS—Please to give the date of that letter.

MR. LINCOLN—The time he run [the *Tribune* corrected to "ran"— *ed.*] was in 1850. I have not got it on the paper, but my understanding— indeed I am quite confident of it that it was in 1850—some time in 1850, Mr. Campbell was elected to Congress. He went in and served out his term, I rather think, but I am not sure; a second term came and he was not re-elected; but at the end of his term of election upon this platform, his very good friend, Judge Douglas, got him a very high office from President Pierce, and sent him to California. Now, is not that so? I think that is so! That just at the end of his term our mutual good friend, Judge Douglas, got our mutual good friend, Thompson Campbell, a good office, and sent him off to California; and not only so, but Judge Douglas and myself, on the 22d of last month met at Freeport, and here was this same man, Tom Campbell, spoken of, as come back all the way from California to help Judge Douglas; and there was Martin P. Sweet "sneaking about"—I take back that ugly word (to the reporters), you must not put that in—doing all he could to help me along. [The *Tribune* omitted "sneaking about" as Lincoln requested, and added: "to help poor me get elected"—*ed.*] [Laughter. —*Tribune*]

Not only that—

On the 11th of September, 1850, a Democratic Congressional Convention assembled at Joliet to nominate a candidate for Congress. The convention nominated R. S. Molony for Congress, and unanimously adopted the following resolutions on the slavery question:

Resolved. That we are uncompromisingly opposed to the extension of slavery; and while we would not make such opposition a ground of interference with the interests of the States where it exists, yet we moderately but firmly insist that it is the duty of Congress to oppose its extension to territory now free, by all means compatible with the obligations of the constitution, and with good faith to our sister States: that these principles were recognized by the ordinance of 1787, which received the sanction of Thomas Jefferson, who is acknowledged by all to be the great oracle and expounder of our faith.

Subsequently, the same interrogatories, were propounded to Dr. Molony which had been addressed to Campbell, as above, with the exception of the 6th, respecting the inter-State slave trade, to which Dr. Molony, the Democratic nominee for Congress, replied as follows:

I received the written interrogatories this day, and as you will see by the La Salle *Democrat* and the Ottawa *Free Trader*, I took at Peru on the 5th and at Ottawa on the 7th the affirmative side of interrogatories 1st and 2d, and in relation to the admission of any more slave States from free territory, my position taken at those meetings as correctly reported in said papers was *emphatically* and *distinctly* opposed to it. In relation to the admission of any more slave States from Texas whether I shall go against it or not, will depend upon the opinion that I may hereafter form of the true meaning and nature of the resolutions on annexation. If, by said resolutions, the honor and good faith of the nation is pledged to admit more slave States from Texas when she (Texas) may apply for the admission of such State, then I should if in Congress, vote for their admission. But if not so PLEDGED and bound by sacred contract, then a bill for the admission of more slave States from Texas would never receive my vote.

To your fourth interrogatory, I answer *most decidedly* in the affirmative and for reasons set forth in my reported remarks at Ottawa last Monday.

To your fifth interrogatory I also reply in the affirmative *most cordially,* and that I will use my utmost exertions to secure the nomination and election of a man who will accomplish the objects of said interrogatories. I most cordially approve of the resolutions adopted at the union meeting held at Princeton on the 27th of September.

Yours, &c.

R. S. MOLONY

Now, all that I have got to say in regard to Dr. Molony is, that he was the regularly nominated candidate of the Democratic party for Congress in his district. He served his term. At the end of his term, I never heard of the instrumentality of Judge Douglas in it, but at the end of his term he was appointed to the land office, and I do know that when we spoke at Freeport, handbills were circulated to the effect that Dr. Molony would speak in behalf of Judge Douglas.

It is added here [the *Tribune* further added: "to this resolution"—*ed.*], and I believe truly:

"Among those who participated in the Joliet Convention, and who supported its nominee, with his platform as laid down in the resolution of the Convention and in his reply as above given, we cull at random the following names, all of whom are recognized at this day as leading democrats:["]

COOK COUNTY—E. B. Williams, Charles McDonell, Arno Voss, Thomas Hoyne, Isaac Cook, F. C. Sherman.

I reckon we ought to except Ike Cook. They are from Cook county. [Laughter. —*Tribune*]

WILL—Joel A. Matteson, S. W. Bowen.

KANE—B. F. Hall, G. W. Renwick, A. M. Herrington, Elijah Wilcox.

McHENRY—W. M. Jackson, Enos W. Smith, Neil Donnelly.

LASALLE—John Hise, William Reddick.

[The *Tribune* added: "William Reddick! another one of Judge Douglas' friends that stood on the stand with him at Ottawa, at the time the Judge says my knees trembled so that I had to be carried away! (Laughter.) The names are all here"—*ed.*]

DUPAGE—Nathan Allen.

DEKALB—Z. B. Mayo.

Now, again, there is another set of resolutions which, according to the custom that Judge Douglas has established, I believe that I will adopt, in handing to the reporter without reading:

On the 28th of February of the same year, a Democratic District Convention was held at Naperville, to nominate a candidate for Circuit Judge. Among the delegates were Bowen and Kelly of Will; Captain Naper, H. H. Cody, Nathan Allen, of DuPage; W. M. Jackson, J. M. Strode, P. W. Platt and Enos W. Smith, of McHenry; J. Horsman and others of Winnebago. Col. Strode presided over the convention. The following resolutions were unanimously adopted— the first on the motion of P. W. Platt, the second, on motion of William Jackson.

Resolved, That this convention is in favor of the Wilmot Proviso, both in principle and practice, and that we know of no good reason why any person should oppose the largest latitude in *free soil, free territory* and *free speech.*

Resolved, That in the opinion of this convention, the time has arrived when *all men should be free,* whites as well as others.

There is some portion of this that I will hand to the reporter to save time. There is only one other thing that I wish to comment upon.

[The *Tribune* added the following interruption: JUDGE DOUGLAS— What is the date of those Resolutions?

MR. LINCOLN: I understand it was in 1850, but] I will say here, ladies and gentlemen, that I don't know—I don't state a thing and say I know when I don't. I have the highest confidence that these things are all correct. I was not present at these conventions and do not know them to be true. It is not impossible that there is some error in it. I don't know of any way by which I could prove them to be true, but I believe they are all correct. I mean to put it no stronger than that.

Now, what I was going to comment upon is an extract from a newspaper published in DeKalb, and it strikes me as being rather singular, I confess, under the circumstances. There is a Judge Mayo in DeKalb county that it is said is a candidate for the legislature for the purpose of helping to elect Judge Douglas. He is the editor of a newspaper, and I saw in a newspaper purporting to be printed at his office, the exact article that I am going to read from. It was an article in which he was electioneering for Judge Douglas and against me. It is a curious article, I think, to be in such a newspaper. I agree to that, and the Judge may make as much as he can of it. He says:

> Our education has been such, that we have ever been rather *in favor of the equality of the blacks—that is, that they should enjoy all the privileges of the whites where they reside.* We are aware that this is not a very popular doctrine. We have had many a confab with some who are now strong Republicans, we taking the broad ground of equality and they the opposite ground.
>
> We were brought up in a State where blacks were voters and we did not know of any inconvenience resulting from it, though perhaps it would not work as well where the blacks are more numerous. We have no doubt of the right of the whites to guard against such an evil, if it is one. Our opinion is that it would be best for all concerned to have the colored population in a state by themselves [the *Tribune* added: "In this I agree with him"—*ed.*], but if within the jurisdiction of the United States, *we say by all means they should have the right to have their Senators and Representatives in Congress, and to vote for President.* With us, "worth makes the man and want of it the fellow." We have seen many a "nigger" that we thought much more of than some white men.

That is one of Judge Douglas' friends. Now, I don't want to leave myself in an attitude that I shall be misrepresented. I don't think the Judge is responsible for that, but I think he is as much responsible for it as I am for my friends.

I have a set of resolutions here which I will give to the reporter, passed by the Democratic State Convention, in the Judge's old native State of Vermont. [The *Tribune* listed five of them.—*ed.*]

A Voice upon the platform—Your time is half over!

MR. LINCOLN.—*I did not know that I was wasting time in that way.* I now understand that my time is half out. [The *Tribune* omitted this exchange—*ed.*]

At Freeport I answered seven interrogatories that had been propounded to me by Judge Douglas at the Ottawa meeting. The Judge has not thought fit at all to-day to find any fault with the position that I took in regard to those seven interrogatories, which were certainly enough in all conscience to cover nearly all the ground. In my answers to those interrogatories, which have been printed and which all have had an opportunity of seeing, I lay down my belief, and if I should be elected, those who elected me have no right to expect that I will do otherwise than according to those answers. I have a right to assume that Judge Douglas finds no fault with them, but he chooses still to force me onto some different ground without looking to those answers of mine, the obtaining of which cost him so much time and concern. I at the same time propounded four interrogatories to him, saying at the time that I claimed the right to propound to him a number equal to that which I answered. The Judge in answering me upon that occasion generally, put in what I suppose he intends as answers to all four of my interrogatories. The first one of these interrogatories I have before me, which is in these words.

The first one is: If the people of Kansas shall, by means entirely unobjectionable in all other respects adopt a State constitution, and ask admission into the Union under it, *before* they have the requisite number of inhabitants according to the English bill, to wit: ninety-three thousand—will you vote to admit them?

Now, as I read the Judge's answer in the newspapers, and as I remember it as he pronounced it at the time, he does not give an answer to that which is equivalent to yes or no. He answers it at very considerable length, rather quarrelling with me for asking the question, insisting that Trumbull had done something that I should say something about before asking the question, but finally coming out with something that leads me to infer that he would vote for the admission of Kansas—I only say that now that if he does not put a different construction upon it, I shall, from this time out, assume that he would vote for the admission of Kansas—he has a right to correct, and I only mention it now that I may assume that this is the true construction of his answer if he does not choose to correct me.

To the second interrogatory which I propounded to him, which is in these words:

2[.] Can the people of a United States territory, in any lawful way, against the wish of any citizen of the United States, exclude slavery from their limits prior to the formation of a State Constitution?

To that interrogatory the Judge answered that they can lawfully exclude slavery from the territory prior to the formation of a constitution, and he goes on to tell us how that can be done, as I have understood him, subject to correction, he holds that it can be done in any territorial legislature refusing to enact any legislation for the protection of slavery in the territory, and by unfriendly legislation to it. I state that again? That they can exclude slavery from the territory, first, by withholding what he assumes to be an indispensible assistance to it in the way of legislation, and by the enactment of unfriendly legislation. If I rightly understand him in regard to this, I wish to ask your attention awhile to this position of the Judge.

We understand in the first place that the Supreme Court of the United States has decided that any constitutional prohibition of slavery in a territory is unconstitutional. That they have reached this proposition as a conclusion from the former proposition that the constitution of the United States expressly recognizes property in slaves, and from the other constitutional provision that no person shall be deprived of property without due process of law, and hence they reach the conclusion that as the United States constitution expressly recognizes property in slaves, and as the United States constitution prohibits any person being deprived of property without due process of law, that to pass an act of Congress by which any man who owned a slave on one side of a line, if he took him on the other side is depriving him of that property without due process of law.

That I understand to be the decision of the court. I understand also that Judge Douglas stands to that decision. The difficulty in adhering to that decision is how there is power to exclude property from the territory unless it is by a violation of that decision.

In the Senate of the United States, in 1856, Judge Trumbull had, in a speech substantially, if not directly, put this same interrogatory as to whether the people of a territory had the lawful power to exclude slavery prior to the formation of a constitution. Judge Douglas then answered at considerable length, and his answer will be found in the *Congressional Globe,* under date of June 9, 1856. I am not sure that I have the page, but that is the date. At that time the Judge said that whether the people could exclude slavery prior to the formation of a constitution is a question for the Supreme Court—that it was a question to be decided by the Supreme Court. He put that proposition, as will be seen by reading the *Congressional Globe,* in a variety of forms, all running to the same substance, that that question is for the Supreme Court to decide. Now, I maintain that when he now says, after the Supreme

Court have decided that question, that he does not now virtually say that it is not a question for the Supreme Court, that he does shift his grounds. [Applause. —*Tribune*] He shakes his head! Now I want to appeal to these people, did he not say it was a question for the Supreme Court to decide? Has not the Court decided that question? Now does he not say that it is a question for the people? Does he not shift his ground? That is a very simple proposition, it is a fair and naked one. It seems to me that there is no difficulty in deciding on it. I have stated that the Judge stated it in a variety of forms, that it was a question for the Supreme Court to decide. He did not stop to tell Trumbull that the people could exclude slavery by unfriendly legislation; he did not make any such answer then, and [I] submit to this people whether the new state of the case has not induced Judge Douglas to shuffle [the *Tribune* substituted "sheer away"—*ed.*] from his original ground. [Applause. —*Tribune*]

This is not all with regard to that answer of his. I hold that the proposition that slavery cannot go into a country without friendly legislation is strictly false. I hold that the history of this country shows that slavery was originally planted upon this continent without such police regulations as the Judge thinks were necessary. But is here not another fact? Is there not this case of Dred Scott? How came this Dred Scott case? This came because the negro was led into that territory of Kansas [the *Tribune* had "Minnesota"—*ed.*] and was held there—that making the case which the court decided [the *Tribune* added: "because the act of Congress prohibited his being so held there"—*ed.*]. Will not the Judge hold that he was held in actual slavery without police regulations? There is one case, showing that there is vigor enough in the tendency to force slavery into a territory without positive police regulations. It takes not only law against it, but it takes the enforcement of law to keep it out when there is no law in its favor.

But not only so; I wish to ask some other questions.

Would not the courts of these United States, if there was an infringement of that property—would not the United States courts organized in these territories—would they not apply such remedy as would be necessary for the prevention of an infraction of these rights? It is a maxim of the courts that there is no right without a remedy.

Lastly, let me ask you, or any of you, my friends standing down there, when you are a member of a territorial legislature what is the first thing you have to do? Swear to support the constitution of the United States!

Suppose you believe, as Judge Douglas does, that the constitution guaranteed to your neighbor the right to hold a slave, can you take that oath and not give him the right to hold that slave? What is to support the constitution? Is it not to give such help to the rights given in the constitution as are practically needed, and can you have the help that the constitution establishes the right, clear your oath, without giving that support? Can you withhold it and not disregard your oath? I can conceive of nothing in the world there can be in the words "support the constitution," but to give all the rights accorded by it.

What I say would apply with more force to the Judge's [the *Tribune* added: "doctrine of"—*ed.*] unfriendly legislation. How could you, believing that the constitution gave the right to hold a slave, enact any unfriendly legislation? How could you? Why, that would be violating your own view of the constitution. Not only so, if you were to do so, how long would it take the constitution to hold your work unconstitutional and void? Not an instant.

And, lastly, I would ask this. Is not Congress itself under the obligation to give legislative support to any right that is established in the United States constitution?

A member of Congress swears to support the Constitution of the United States. He sees a right established by that constitution which needs specific legislative protection, can he clear his oath without giving that specific protection? How is it that many of us who are opposed to slavery give in our adherence to a fugitive slave law? Why do we give our support to it in passing, and then abide by it when it is passed? The constitution gives the right to reclaim fugitive slaves. I don't quote the words, but that right is rather a barren right unless there be some legislation to enforce it. The mere words of the constitution (quoted by speaker) ["No person held to service or labor in one State under the laws thereof, escaping into another, shall in consequence of any law or regulation therein be discharged from such service or labor, but shall be delivered up on claim of the party to whom such service or labor may be due," as quoted in full in the *Tribune* transcript—*ed.*] enforce no right. Now, on what ground is it that members of Congress, who are themselves opposed to slavery in the abstract, vote for a fugitive slave law, as I would do? On what ground? Because there is a constitutional right, and having sworn to support that constitution, I can not conceive that I do support it if I withhold necessary legislation to enforce the rights guaranteed by it. Is any one right any better guaranteed in the constitution than the other? Is there any argument why a member of Congress should give support to any one more than to any other? I think there is no distinction to be taken. I cannot see that if I should refuse to give support to slave property in a territory, if I could not give it with my view that the constitution established the right, but that I should be guilty of perjury. It would be that I deny that this decision properly construes the constitution. If I believed as Judge D. does, that this decision establishes slavery in the territory, I do not see but I should be a perjured man if I refused to give such legislation as is needed.

At the end of what I have said here, I propose now to give the Judge my fifth interrogatory, which he may take and answer at his leisure.

"QUESTION 5. If a slave-holding citizen of a United States territory should need and demand Congressional legislation for the protection of his (their) slave property in such territory, would you, as a member of Congress, vote for or against such legislation?"

[The *Tribune* added: "JUDGE DOUGLAS—Will you repeat that? I want to answer that question." Lincoln then restated his interrogatory—*ed.*]

I am aware that in some of the speeches that Judge Douglas has made, he has spoken as if he did not know or think that the court had decided that a territorial legislature cannot exclude slavery. Precisely what the Judge would say upon that subject—whether he could say definitely that he does not understand that they have decided it, or whether he could say that he does understand them to have decided it, I do not know, but I know that in his speech at Springfield he spoke of it as a thing that had not yet been decided. Now, I hold that if he does entertain that view, that it has not been decided, although he has not expressly said so, why then I think that he is mistaken, in so far as it can be said that the court has decided anything except jurisdiction. I know that the legal agreement [the *Tribune* substituted "argument"—*ed.*] can be made that when a court has decided that it cannot take jurisdiction, that this is the end of it. A plausible argument can be made in favor of that proposition, but I know that the Judge has said in a speech heretofore that the court went on and determined all the questions in the case, and if any of the points that were decided are *ex-cathedrally* decided, why then this one of the power to hold slaves in the territories is also; as was also the decision of the unconstitutionality of the Missouri Compromise. They are both *ex-cathedra* according as they may be made so by the fact that the court decided that they had no jurisdiction in the case, because of the want of capacity in the parties.

I want to show that the court did pass its opinion, and that is all that is important in the case, for if the court do not decide it they distinctly enough show us what they are ready to decide. After showing that Congress had no power to pass a law excluding slavery from a territory, they used language to the effect that if Congress could not pass such a law, certainly a territorial legislature, deriving its power from Congress can not. Thus expressing their opinion as unequivocally against the power of a territorial legislature to exclude slavery, as upon any other point of the case, and leaving us in a little doubt, as upon any point, that they really decided.

Now, my fellow citizens, for a little while longer will I detain you. I find a report of a speech made by Judge Douglas at Joliet since we last met at Freeport, taken, I believe, from the Mobile *Republican,* on the 9th of this present month. The Judge is speaking of me.

[Speaker quoted a paragraph to the effect that he had to be carried off the stand at Ottawa; that his knees trembled, and that, having seven questions propounded to him, he laid up seven days to concoct answers. We have no copy of the speech at hand, but give its substance. —*Times* The *Tribune* reprinted the extract as follows:

You know at Ottawa, I read this platform, and asked him if he concurred in each and all of the principles set forth in it. He would not answer these questions. At last I said frankly, I wish you to answer them, because when I get them up here where the color of your principles is a little darker than in Egypt, I intend to trot you down to Jonesboro. The very notice that I was going to take him down to Egypt made him tremble in the knees so that he had to be carried from the platform. He laid up seven days, and in the meantime held a consultation with his political physicians, they had Lovejoy and Farnsworth and all the leaders of the Abolition party, they consulted it all over, and at last Lincoln came to the conclusion that he would answer, so he came up to Freeport last Friday.]

Well, I know that sickness altogether furnishes a subject for philosophical contemplation [Laughter. —*Tribune*], and I have been treating it in that way, and I have really come to the conclusion (for I can reconcile it no other way), that the Judge is crazy. [Renewed laughter. —*Tribune*] If he was in his right mind, I cannot conceive how he could have risked disgusting the five thousand of his own friends.

Now, as to my having to be carried from the platform, there is not a word of truth in it.

A Voice—[The *Tribune* credited the interruption to Douglas himself—*ed.*] Did they not carry you?

Mr. Lincoln—Yes sir!! [The *Tribune* substituted "There"—*ed.*] Now that shows the character of this man Douglas. He smiles now, and says, "Did they not carry you?" You have said that I had to be carried. He sought to teach this country that I was broken down—that I could not get away; and now he seeks to dodge it. Why did you not tell the truth? [Great laughter and cheers. —*Tribune*]

Mr. Douglas—I did.

Mr. Lincoln—[Continued laughter. —*Tribune*] Then again, I "laid up for seven days." He puts this in print for people to read as a serious statement. I say again, if he had been in his right mind he would not have risked this statement in the face of his thousands of friends who heard me make speeches in Henry and all the surrounding counties, and then meet him at Freeport. I say there is no charitable way in the world but to say that he is crazy. [Laughter. —*Tribune*]

There is another thing in that statement that alarmed me very greatly, as he makes it, It is that he was going to trot me down into Egypt. He wants you to infer that I would not come to Egypt if he did not make me—that I would not come to Egypt at all, unless he, giant like, forced me [Laughter. —*Tribune*], and that [the *Tribune* added: "statement he makes, too"—*ed.*] in the teeth of my appointments to meet him, published to the world, and which appointments he was so reluctant to make. [Cheers and laughter. —*Tribune*]

Judge Douglas must, when he made that statement, have been crazy—he must have been out of his mind, else he would have known that the promises, and windy promises, of his power to annihilate Lincoln would not be sustained at all. Now, how much do I look like being carried away from here? Now, let the Judge come back on me in his half hour, and I want you, if I can't get away from here to let me sit here and rot, unless I am able to carry him to the tavern [the *Tribune* substituted "hotel"—*ed.*]. [Great laughter. —*Tribune*] Does any man know any other man that would make such a statement as that? [Cries of "No," "no," "Yes," "yes." —*Tribune*] What did the Judge think about trotting me here to Egypt and scaring me to death? Did he suppose that he would be able to make his friends turn on me and hurt me? I know this class of people better than he does. I was raised among this range of people, I am part of this people. The Judge was raised further North. He perhaps had some horrid notion about what they might be induced to do to him. [Roars of laughter and cheers. —*Tribune*]

But, really, I have talked over this matter perhaps longer than I ought to, and yet it is the most difficult sort of thing to deal with. The Judge has set about trying to make the impression that when we meet, that I am generally in his clutches, that I am a poor decrepit mouse, that I cannot do anything at all. I don't know how to meet that sort of thing. I don't want to call him a liar, yet, if I come square up to the truth, I do not know what else it is. [Cheers and laughter. —*Tribune*] I do not want to do any fighting—I want to reserve my fighting for a proper occasion.

I suppose my time is nearly out, and if it is not, I will give up and let the Judge set my knees to trembling [the *Tribune* added, "if he can"—*ed.*]

[The speaker retired having ten minutes to spare.]

Mr. Douglas' Rejoinder

[Three cheers for Douglas were called for and given, when Judge Douglas said: —*Tribune;* Mr. Douglas on again taking the stand was greeted with thundering applause. He said: —*Times*]

My Friends:—I am very grateful to you for the enthusiasm you exhibit but I will say to you in all frankness that your silence during my half-hour will be more agreeable than your applause, for so much would your applause deprive me of time to reply. [All right, go ahead, we won't interrupt, &c. —*Times*]

I will commence where Mr. Lincoln left off, and make a serious comment upon the serious complaint of his about my speech at Joliet. I did say then, in a playful manner, that when I put this question to Mr. Lincoln he failed to answer—that he trembled and had to be carried off from the stand and took seven days to get up his reply. [Laughter. —*Times*] That he didn't walk off the stand he won't deny; that when the crowd went away with me, a few persons took him on their shoulders and led him down. [Laughter. —*Tribune* and *Times*] And I wish to say this to you, whenever I degrade my friends or myself by allowing them to carry me on their backs through the public streets when I am able to walk, I will be willing to be deemed crazy. ["All right, Douglas," laughter and applause. Lincoln chewing his nails in a rage in a back corner. —*Times*] I did not say whether I beat him in the argument or whether he beat me. It is true I put those questions to him, not as idle questions, but I established that they had been adopted in nearly every county in Illinois, where the Black Republicans had a majority, and set forth as their platform; and then I simply asked him whether or not, he endorsed that platform of that portion of the State that he relied upon to elect him. He would not answer. When I reminded him that I was going to bring him into Egypt, and renew the questions if he did not answer; he then after consulting for a time got up those answers one week afterwards, answers which I may refer to after a while to show you how equivocal they were. My object was to get him to avow whether or not he stood by the platform of his party. That those resolutions I then produced had been adopted in the Galena Congressional District, in the Chicago Congressional District, in the Bloomington Congressional District, comprising a large majority of the counties in this State which give an abolition majority. Mr. Lincoln cannot and will not deny that they were in substance put forth in Lovejoy's resolutions, and voted for by a majority of his party, and some of them by nearly if not every man of his party, he will not deny either. Hence I held the foundation of putting these questions to him before I asked him whether that was or was not the platform of his party. He says he answered it. One of the questions was no more slave States are to be admitted into this Union. That was an article in the Republican creed. It was put forth in the Lovejoy resolutions; in the Legislature it was put forth, and passed in a majority of all the counties in the State which give Republican or Abolition majorities, or elect members to the Legislature of that school of politics. Hence I had the right to know whether he would vote for or against another Slave State in the event the people wanted it. He first answers that he was not pledged on the subject, and then says in regard to the other question of whether I am pledged to the admission of any more Slave States into the Union: "I state to you very frankly that I would be exceedingly sorry ever to be put in a position of having to pass on that question, ["No doubt," and laughter. Mr. Lincoln looks savagely into the crowd for the man who said "no doubt." —*Times*], and I should be exceedingly glad to know that there would not be another Slave State admitted into the Union." But at last he did say, that "if slavery should be kept out of the Territory during the territorial existence of any one given Territory and then the people having a fair chance and a clear field when they come to adopt the Constitution, do such an extraordinary thing as to adopt a slave constitution, uninfluenced by the actual presence of the institution among them, I see no alternative but to admit them into the Union."

Now analyze that answer. In the first place, he says he would be exceedingly angry to be put in the position so he would have to vote on the question of the admission of a Slave State. Why is he a candidate for the Senate, if he would be sorry to be in that position[?] I trust the people of Illinois will not force him into a position he would be so exceedingly sorry to occupy. ["There's no danger," &c. —*Times*] The next position he takes is that he would be glad to know that there would never be another Slave State, yet in such a contingency he would have to vote for it. What is that contingency? If Congress keeps slavery out by law, while it is a Territory, and then the people should have a fair chance and should adopt slavery uninfluenced by the presence of the institution, then he supposed he would have to admit it. Suppose Congress should not keep slavery out while it is a Territory, then how would he vote? That he didn't answer. That is just the case with every Territory we have now. In Kansas, slavery is not kept out by one act of Congress. I put the question to Mr. Lincoln, "Will you let them come in as they please, with or without slavery?" He won't answer. In Nebraska Territory slavery is not kept [out—*ed.*] by act of Congress. The Nebraska Bill authorizes them to do as they please about slavery. I ask him will he vote to let Kansas come in as she pleases. He won't answer. So with Washington Territory. He won't answer. And so with New Mexico, and you can't get an answer. And so with Arizona, he will give no answer, and so with the four new States from Texas. He answers only in regard to a certain contingency, knowing that it is a state of things that did not exist in any one territory of the Union, and he tries to give you to understand that he would allow the people to do as they please. Yet he dodges the answer as to every territory now in the Union. Why cannot Mr. Lincoln answer as to each of those territories[?] He has not done it—he won't do it. The Abolitionists up North understand that this answer is made as an evasion, not to commit himself on any one territory now in existence. It is so understood there. You can't extort an answer that applies to any one territory, or to the new States, which, by compact, we are obliged to admit out of Texas, when they have the required population, and apply for admission. I submit it to you whether he has made a single frank answer, so you can tell how he would vote in any one of these cases. He would be sorry to be put in the position. Why be sorry to be put in the position if his duty required him to give the vote[?] If the people of a Territory ought to be permitted to come into the Union with slavery or without, as they pleased, why not give the vote cheerfully[?] If they ought not to be permitted to come in with slavery when they want it, why not say he will cheerfully vote against it; but he would be sorry to vote that way which his conscience would compel him to do as an honest man.

Now in regard to the contract that he denies with Trumbull and the Abolitionists, I went on to show the history of the joint transaction between him and Trumbull, and Lovejoy, and Giddings, while Fred. Douglass, and [John] Hale [antislavery senator—*ed.*] and [Nathaniel P.] Banks [Republican speaker of the House and future Civil War general—*ed.*], and the other Abolitionists were traveling the States, and made speeches on the same side and in the same cause, and proved these facts. This charge was a notorious historical fact. He contents himself with a simple denial that any such thing occurred. Does he deny that he, and Trumbull and Breese, and Giddings, and Chase, and Fred. Douglass, and all those Abolitionists and deserters from the Democracy did make speeches in the same common cause? Does he deny that Jim Matheny was then and is now his confidential friend and wire worker?

MR. LINCOLN—Yes, sir.

JUDGE DOUGLAS—Does he deny that Matheny made the charge as to his own knowledge of the bargain? I have read it. Jim Matheny spoke of his own personal knowledge of that bargain existing between Lincoln, Trumbull and the Abolitionists. Jim Matheny is now his confidential friend, and is a candidate for Congress, canvassing for him in the northern part of the State. I assert that I can prove that charge to be true in detail, if I can ever get where I can summon and compel the attendance of witnesses.

MR. LINCOLN—If you will name the witnesses I will bring them to you. [The *Times* did not print Lincoln's comments—*ed.*]

JUDGE DOUGLAS—I have the statement of one man to the same effect, that I am not yet permitted to use, but Jim Matheny is a good witness on that point. The history of the country, too, is conclusive upon it, for Lincoln until then had been a Whig, then he undertook to abolitionize the Whigs and bring them into the Abolition camp. Trumbull, who had been a Democrat, undertook to abolitionize the Democrats. That they are both distinguished members of this Abolition Republican party, in full communion, is a fact that cannot be explained or denied, but Mr. Lincoln is not willing to be responsible for the creed of his party. He complains that I hold him responsible, and in order to defeat it, he attempts to show that individuals in the Democratic party many years ago expressed abolition sentiments. It is true that Tom Campbell published the letter which Mr. Lincoln read, in 1850, but I asked Mr. Lincoln for its date, and he could not give it. That date has been suppressed by their speakers wherever they have used it. I take it for granted that Mr. Lincoln don't know the date, but when he will inquire he will find it was written only two days before election and was never seen beyond the county and if it had been he would have been defeated. It is true that Molony did utter these sentiments, for the utterance of which good Democrats would not vote for him. I returned home from Congress after passing the Compromise measures, when I found Molony running under John Wentworth's tutelage [the *Times* added, "and on his platform"—*ed.*]. I declared he was not a good Democrat, and in my speech in Chicago, just before that election, I went before that infuriated people, and defended my principles, and I remember that the City Council had passed resolutions nullifying the act of Congress. I was the only man responsible for those measures in the city of Chicago, and I went before that crowd, and justified and defended those measures, and let it be said to the eternal glory of the people of Chicago, that when they were convinced by my defense of these measures that I was right and that they had been wrong in their opposition, they repealed their nullifying resolution, and declared their willingness to support the laws of the land. These are facts, and Mr. Lincoln can only set up individual witnesses, dating back five or six years, which are contradicted by the whole tenor of the Democratic creed. Mr. Lincoln does not want to be held responsible for the doctrine of "no more Slave States." Farnsworth, who is the candidate of his party in the Chicago district, made a speech in the last session of Congress, in which he appealed to God to palsy his right arm if he ever voted for another Slave State, whether the people wanted slavery or not. There is Lovejoy, too, making speeches all over the country for Lincoln, and declaring against the admission of any more slave States. There is [Elihu B.] Washburn in the Galena District [congressman and longtime Lincoln associate, although it had earlier been rumored he thought Douglas should not be opposed for reelection—ed.], making speeches in favor of this Abolition platform declaring no more slave States; and every man running for Congress in the Northern Districts takes that Abolition platform for his guide; but Lincoln will not avow this platform as he comes down to the Centre and Southern portions of your State in order to get your votes. [He can't get any. —Times] Let me tell Mr. Lincoln that his party in all the Northern end of the State do hold to that Abolition platform, and in the South and Centre his party presents the extraordinary spectacle of a house divided against itself, and consequently it cannot stand. [Hurra. —Times] I bring down upon him the vengeance of his own scriptural quotation, and give it a more prompt application than he did, when I say to you that his party in one end of the State is going for abolitionism and against it in the other, and it is a house divided against itself, and it cannot stand for it attempts to cheat the American people out of their votes, by dividing [the Times had "disguising"—ed.] their sentiments. [Cheers. —Times] Mr. Lincoln tries to get over his abolitionism by telling you he was raised a little east of here [Laughter. —Tribune and Times] over beyond the Wabash in Indiana, and he thinks that makes a mighty good man of him, and very sound on all these questions because he was raised in Indiana. I do not know that the place where a man was born or raised has much to do with his political principles. The worst Abolitionists I have ever known in Illinois were men who had sold their slaves in Alabama or Kentucky, and became Abolitionists while spending the money received for the slaves. [That's so, and laughter. —*Times*] I don't know that an Abolitionist from Kentucky or Indiana ought to have more credit because he was born and raised among slaveholders. [Not a bit, not as much, &c. —*Times*] I don't know that a native of Kentucky who was raised among slaves, and whose father and mother were nursed by slaves, is any more excusable when he comes to Illinois and turns Abolitionist, to slander the grave of his father and the institutions under which he was born and where his father and mother lived. True, I was not born out West here. I was born in the valleys of the Green Mountains [all right. —*Times*], with the high mountains all around; and I loved the old hills and the green valleys where I was born and where I played in my childhood. I came away to this State and went back for the first time for twenty years, and they treated me kindly and hospitably. There was then the commencement of the College; they invited me on the platform and conferred on me the title of L.L.D., the same as they did on old General Jackson when he went to a College commencement. When they had given me my degree, they read it to me in Latin, and I give you my honor that I understood just as much of that Latin as Old Hickory did. [Laughter. —*Tribune* and *Times*] When they got through that, they called for a speech from me, and while my heart was swelling with gratitude and emotions as I looked out on the mountains and valleys, I told my friends that Vermont was the most glorious spot on the face of the earth for a man to be born in, provided he emigrates when he is very young. [Roars of Laughter. —*Tribune;* Uproarious shouts of laughter. —*Times*] I did when I was very young. I came here when I was a boy, and I found that my mind was liberalized and my opinions enlarged as I got on those wide and expansive prairies, where only the heavens bound your vision, instead of having them bounded by the little narrow valley where I was born, and I discarded all those things at the land where a man was born. I wish to be judged by my principles, by those great principles upon which the peace, safety and prosperity of the government now rests.

Mr. Lincoln frames another question which he propounds to me, and desires me to answer. As I said to him at Ottawa, I have not put a question to him that I have not laid the foundation for, by showing that it was the platform of the majority of the party whose votes he is seeking, and adopted in the majority of the counties which he now hopes to carry. They are supported by the candidates of his party running in those counties. But I will answer his question. If the slave-holding citizens of a United States Territory should need or demand Congressional Legislation for the protection of their slave property in such territory, would you as a Member of Congress vote for or against such legislation? I answer him it is a fundamental article in the Democratic creed that there shall be non-interference, non-intervention by Congress in the States and Territories. [Cheers. —*Tribune;* Immense cheering. —*Times*] Mr. Lincoln could have found an answer to his question in the Cincinnati Platform. [Applause. —*Tribune* and *Times*] The Democratic party have always stood by that great principle of non-interference, non-intervention, by Congress with slavery in States and Territories alike. I stand on that platform now. [Applause. —*Tribune;* Cheer after cheer was here given for Douglas. —*Times*] Now I desire to call your attention to the fact that Mr. Lincoln himself don't define his own position on that question. How does he stand on that question? He put the question to me at Freeport, whether I would vote to admit Kansas into the Union before she had 93,420 inhabitants? I answered him at once, that it having been decided that Kansas had population enough for a Slave State, she had enough for a free State. ["Good; that's it," and cheers. —*Times*] I answered unequivocally, and I put the question to him, will you vote for or against the admission of Kansas before she had that population? He would not answer. To-day he has called my attention to the fact that my answer on that question was not quite plain enough, and yet he has not answered it himself; [Great laughter. —*Times*] and now he comes and puts the question in regard to Congressional interference in a State or Territory. I answer directly that he has not answered that question yet. I ask if a man has any right in common decency in these public discussions to put a question to his opponent that he won't answer himself when it is pressed home upon him? I put the question three times in his presence whether he would vote to admit Kansas when the people apply with a constitution of their own making and adoption under circumstances that are just, fair and unexceptionable. I can't get his answer, nor can I get his answer on this question about Congressional interference with slavery in the territories by making a slave code. It is true, he goes on to argue the question whether under the decision of the Supreme Court it is the duty of a man to vote for a slave code in the territory. Whether he thinks it is his duty under the decision that is made, and if he believes in that decision he would be a perjured man if he didn't go and vote. Now, I want to know whether he is not bound by a decision contrary to his opinion just as much as by one in accordance with his opinion. [Certainly. —*Times*] If the Supreme Court is a tribunal created by the Constitution to decide the question, and if its decision is binding and final, is he not bound just as much by it whether he be for or against it? Is every man in this land allowed to resist decisions he don't like, and only support those he does? What are your Courts worth, unless their decisions are binding on all good citizens? That is the fundamental principle of the Judiciary, that these decisions are final. The very object is, that when you can't agree among yourselves upon a disputed point, a Court shall decide, and their decision is binding, and every citizen must submit. That decision is the law of the land, just as much with Mr. Lincoln for it or against it. He contends that a man is perjured who is for that decision, if he don't vote for a slave code in each Territory of the Union. If you are not going to resist the decision, but obey it; if you [turning to Mr. Lincoln—*Times*] are not going to raise up mob law against the constituted authority, thus according to your own statement you must be a perjured man, unless you vote for it. My doctrine is, that while the decision is there recognizing the right to take slaves into the Territory, yet after they have got there, you need affirmative law to make that right of any value. That doctrine not only applies to slave property but to all other property. Chief Justice Taney places it on the ground that slave property is on an equality with all other property. Suppose one of your merchants should move to Kansas and open a liquor store, he has the right to take his liquors there and open a store, but the mode of selling them must be prescribed by local legislation. If the local legislation is unfriendly it drives you out just as effectually with your liquors as if there was a constitutional provision against liquors. So the absence of local legislation to protect slave property in a territory excludes it practically and as effectually as if there was a positive constitutional provision against it. Hence I assert that under that decision you cannot maintain slavery a day in a Territory against an unwilling people, without friendly legislation. If the people are opposed to it, your right is barren, worthless, and useless. If they are for it they will support and encourage it. Hence we come back to the practical question, if the people of a territory want slavery they will have it, but if they don't want it you can't force it upon them. That is a practical question. It is the great principle upon which our institutions rest. ["That's the doctrine." —*Times*] I am willing therefore, to take the decision of the Supreme Court as it is pronounced by that august body, not stopping to inquire whether I would have the decision the same way or not. I have had many a decision made against me when I was a practicing lawyer that I did not like, but I was as much bound by it as if I had liked it when it was adopted. Did you ever see a lawyer who lost his case and liked the decision, or a client defeated in court, who did not think the decision unjust. Yet you are just as much bound by it as if you were for it originally. In other words, in a government of laws like ours we must sustain the Constitution as our fathers made it, maintain the rights of the States as guaranteed under the Constitution, sustain the constitutional authorities as they exist, and then we will have peace and harmony between the different States and sections of this glorious Union. [Applause. —*Tribune,* which added: "Mr. Douglas spoke considerably over his time both in his opening and concluding speeches"; Prolonged cheering. —*Times*]

THE FOURTH JOINT
DEBATE AT
CHARLESTON

Saturday, September 18, 1858

· THE SCENE ·

FOR ABRAHAM LINCOLN, the fourth debate at Charleston was in
many ways a homecoming. Thirty years earlier, as a
nineteen-year-old pioneer boy, he had migrated to this region with
his family, negotiating a huge oxcart brimming with their crude
belongings. Here his aged stepmother still lived in a primitive cabin
not many miles from town. Following the debate, Lincoln would
spend a night in the home of his first cousin's son-in-law, no doubt
enjoying a nostalgic reunion with relatives and old friends.

A further reminder of Lincoln's intimate association with the
agricultural, onetime pro-Whig Coles County in east central Illinois
could be found this debate day on prominent display in downtown
Charleston. There supporters unfurled above the street between the
courthouse and the capitol building a huge, flag-festooned,
eighty-foot-long banner that featured a portrait of the young Lincoln
driving his oxteam into the area back in 1828. It was, again, a
forerunner of "railsplitter" image making to come. "Abe's Entrance

into Charleston Thirty Years Ago," proclaimed its boldly printed title, while on the reverse side, a large slogan predicted: COLES COUNTY—FOUR HUNDRED MAJORITY FOR LINCOLN.

Observers found additional Lincoln banners hanging from doors, displayed openly in shop windows, and floating from rooftops. Douglas took most of the favorite son display in stride, until he caught a glimpse of one particular caricature depicting a mighty "Old Abe" clubbing a cringing "Little Giant" to the ground. One eyewitness reported that at the sight of it, an enraged Douglas threatened to bolt from the parade transporting him to the debate. Lincoln passed without comment beneath an array of equally strident pro-Douglas banners.

Both candidates entered Charleston that day at the head of lengthy, impressive carriage processions that filed slowly into town, like conquering armies, along the dirt road from the town of Mattoon, some ten miles west. The Douglas entourage featured brass bands, gaudy signs, and thirty-two young women on horseback, representing the various states of the Union, each carrying an American flag. An endless line of teams "filled with men, women, and children" extended behind them "across the prairie as far as the eye could reach." One of the banners that welcomed Douglas into the flag-bedecked town proclaimed: "This government was made for white men—Douglas for Life."

The equally extravagant Lincoln procession, clogged with carriages, horsemen, and musicians, was dominated by a "mammoth car" draped in white silk and muslin, bedecked with wildflowers, and emblazoned with Lincoln inscriptions. His own symbolic delegation of thirty-two women rode inside, beneath a banner that read: "Westward thy star of Empire takes its way,/ Thy Girls *Link-on* to Lincoln,—/Their Mothers were for Clay." The other slogans adorning signs along the endless line of march could barely be seen "through the cloud of dust that accompanied them." By the time both candidates reached Charleston, observers noticed that the debaters were covered with prairie dust themselves.

The breathtaking display of pageantry ended up at the agricultural society fairgrounds, about a quarter of a mile west of town, where the debate began at two forty-five p.m. Between 12,000 and 15,000 spectators had flocked in by train, on horse or mule, on wagon trains, on freight trains, and on foot, many from neighboring

Indiana, and "some with their dinners." Now the "tide of humanity" jockeyed for position in a huge semicircle surrounding the speakers' platform, as Lincoln opened the debate.

The Republican challenger began by denying Douglas's persistent charges that he favored full equality for blacks. The fact that his listeners greeted these opening remarks with laughter—and then went on to applaud his subsequent call for a "superior position" in society for white people—shows vividly that those few favoring equal rights still remained very much isolated on the banks of the political mainstream in pre–Civil War Illinois. Lincoln proceeded to repeat the charge from his House Divided speech, that Douglas, together with President Buchanan and Chief Justice Taney, were conspiring now to nationalize slavery. Most of the remainder of Lincoln's first hour was devoted to the introduction of yet another conspiracy charge, this one suggesting that Douglas had reneged on his popular-sovereignty ethic in plotting, two years earlier, to ram through a Kansas constitution without allowing its voters to choose yes or no on slavery.

In his rebuttal, Douglas accused Lincoln of quibbling over diversionary issues in order to deflect attention from his undisguisable support for abolition doctrine that included black citizenship. He sought to unnerve Lincoln by suggesting that he, not his Republican rival, enjoyed closer links to the legacy of the great Whigs of the 1850s, including Henry Clay, Lincoln's "beau ideal." And he repeated his accusation that Lincoln had dishonored himself in Congress by voting against supplying American soldiers fighting in Mexico.

Lincoln's final half hour was devoted in part to yet another repudiation of the notion of equal rights for blacks. In again denying that he had opposed supplying U.S. troops during the Mexican War, he turned dramatically to a Douglas ally named Orlando Ficklin, who was on hand to hear the debate, and invited him to tell the audience what he remembered of Lincoln's position back in 1848. Ficklin, who knew Lincoln in his congressional days and still counted him as a friend, did not verify Lincoln's version of the record, but he did not refute it either.

The Illinois newspapers were filled with accounts of the encounter at Charleston. The pro-Republican *Sangamo Journal* thought Lincoln "drove his competitor to the wall." But the opposition *State Register* charged that Lincoln was now routinely spouting "ultra abolitionist" views in some areas and "conservative sentiment" in others, in order to "defraud conservative men of their votes."

After Charleston, Lincoln tried to steer clear of making definitive pronouncements on the subject of equal rights for blacks. Conceivably, he decided in retrospect that he had gone too far in the fourth debate, and now risked alienating his support among progressives in the northern reaches of the state. Regardless, Lincoln's comments at Charleston have since come to haunt his reputation, with many historians citing them to dispute his legendary status as an enlightened emancipator.

The following texts were published in the rival journals.

[Mr. Lincoln upon taking the stand was greeted with three cheers, he said: —*Times;* Mr. Lincoln took the stand at a quarter before three, and was greeted with vociferous applause; after which, he said: —*Tribune*]

LADIES AND GENTLEMEN.—It will be very difficult for an audience of the size of this to hear what is said, and consequently, it is very important that as profound silence be observed as is possible.

While I was up at the hotel to-day, an elderly gentleman called upon me to know whether I was really in favor of producing a perfect equality between the negroes and the white people. [Great laughter. —*Tribune*] While I had not proposed to myself upon this occasion to say much upon that subject, as that question was asked me, I thought I would occupy, perhaps, five minutes, in saying something in regard to it.

I will say then, that I am not nor ever have been in favor of bringing about in any way, the social and political equality of the white and black races [applause—*Tribune*], that I am not, nor ever have been in favor of making voters of the negroes, or jurors, or qualifying them to hold office, or having them to marry with white people. I will say in addition, that there is a physical difference between the white and black races, which I suppose, will forever forbid the two races living together upon terms of social and political equality, and inasmuch, as they cannot so live, that while they do remain together, there must be the position of superior and inferior, that I as much as any other man am in favor of the superior position being assigned to the white man. I say in this connection, that I do not perceive, however, that because the white man is to have the superior position, that it requires that the negro should be denied everything. I do not perceive because I do not court a negro woman for a wife, that I must necessarily want her for a wife [the *Tribune* correctly substituted "slave"; its version of the now-famous comment was: "I do not understand that because I do not want a negro woman for a slave I must necessarily want her for a wife."—*ed.*]. [Cheers and laughter. —*Tribune*] My understanding is that I can just leave her alone. I am now in my fiftieth year, and certainly never have had a black woman either for a slave or wife, so that it seems to me that it is quite possible for us to get along without making either slaves or wives of negroes.

I will add that I have never seen, to my knowledge, a man, woman, or child that was in favor of producing a perfect equality, socially and politically between the negro and white people, and I recollect of but one distinguished instance that I have heard of a great deal so as to be entirely confident of it, and that is the case of my friend Douglas' old friend, Col. Richard M. Johnston [former vice president whose long affair with a mulatto mistress was common knowledge—*ed.*]. [Laughter, and cries of "hurrah for Lincoln," and "hurrah for Douglas." —*Times;* Laughter. —*Tribune*]

I will add to the few remarks that I have made, for I am not going to enter at large upon this subject, that I have never had the least apprehension that I or my friends would marry negroes if there was no law to keep them from it [Laughter. —*Tribune*], but as my friend Douglas and his friends seem to be under great apprehension that may be they might if there was no law to keep them from it. I give him the most solemn pledge that I will to the very last stand by the law in this State that forbids the marriage of white folks with negroes. [Continued laughter and applause. —*Tribune*]

I will add one further word, which is this, I don't understand that there is any place where any alteration of the relation—the social and political relation of the negro and white man would be changed except in the state legislature, and in the Congress of the United States, and I do not really apprehend the approach of any such thing myself, but as Judge Douglas does seem to be in constant horror of some such thing I do recommend that the Judge be kept at home, and be placed in the next legislature to vote it off. [Cries of "hurrah for Lincoln," and "hurrah for Douglas." —*Times;* Uproarious laughter and applause. —*Tribune*, which added: "I do not propose dwelling longer at this time on this subject."]

When Judge Trumbull, our other Senator in Congress returned to Illinois, in the month of August, I believe it was, he made a speech at Chicago, in which he made what may be called a charge against Judge Douglas, which proved to be very offensive to Judge Douglas, as I understand. The Judge was at that time out upon one of his speaking tours through the country, and when the news of it reached him, as I understand, he denounced Judge Trumbull, as I understand, in rather harsh terms for having said what he had in regard to him. I was following along and speaking at the same place that Judge Douglas spoke at, but at a subsequent date to the time of his speaking, and when I heard of what Judge Trumbull had said of Douglas, and what Douglas had said back again, I felt that I was in a position that I could not remain entirely silent, and consequently upon two or three occasions I alluded to it, in no otherwise than to say that in regard to the charge that had been brought I personally knew nothing, and that I sought to say nothing in regard to it; that I did personally know Judge Trumbull, that I believed him to be a man of veracity, that I believed him to be a man of capacity sufficient to know pretty well whether an assertion that he was making as a conclusion upon a string of facts was true or false, and as a conclusion of my own, I stated as my belief, that if Judge Trumbull should be called upon he would prove everything he said.

Upon some subsequent occasion Judge Trumbull spoke again before an audience at Alton. He upon that occasion not only repeated his charge against Judge Douglas, but read the evidence which he said he relied upon to substantiate it, and the speech was published at length. Subsequently, at Jacksonville, Judge Douglas alluded to this matter, and in the course of his speech, and near the close of it, he said—but I will now read again a little note I have of it in regard to myself—"Mr. Douglas proceeded to remark that he should not hereafter occupy his time in refuting such charges made by Trumbull, but that Lincoln, having endorsed the character of Trumbull for veracity, he should hold him (Lincoln) responsible for the slander." I have done what I have stated to subject me to this invitation, to [the *Tribune* added "notice"—*ed.*] this charge, if that fairly subject me to it.

I now wish to say that it has not been my purpose to at all interfere about that matter. I had even dropped the fashion of speaking or alluding to it at all, but inasmuch as it seems to be the wish of Judge Douglas to make me responsible about it, then, for once in my life I will follow Gen. Jackson, and say, that to the just extent I take the responsibility. I say to the just extent I take the responsibility. [Great applause and cries of "good, good," "hurrah for Lincoln," etc. —*Tribune*]

Now, for the first thing. In the beginning I shall announce to you that I shall hand over to the reporter the entire portion of Trumbull's speech which is devoted to that subject, which was made at Alton. I shall, immediately in connection with that, hand over the entire portion of Judge Douglas' speech made in answer to it, at Jacksonville. I shall thereby furnish the reader of this debate the complete grounds occupied both by Judge Trumbull and Judge Douglas. I cannot read these. It would take me more, perhaps, than my first hour to do so. I can only make some comment upon them.

Trumbull's charge, as he published it—that last charge, is in the words which I will read—

"Now, the charge is that there was a plot entered into to have a constitution formed for Kansas, and put in force without giving the people an opportunity to pass upon it, and that Mr. Douglas was in the plot." [The *Tribune* declined to publish any of the excerpts handed to the reporters, explaining they were "too lengthy" and had appeared in print previously—*ed.*]

I stop without reading, knowing that all will have an opportunity of reading hereafter, that Judge Trumbull brings forward what he regards as sufficient evidence to substantiate this charge. He first shows, or at least he does show, whether first or not, that Senator [William] Bigler [Democrat from Pennsylvania—*ed.*], upon the floor of the Senate, had declared that there was a conference amongst the Senators, in which conference there was a determination, as he understood, to have a bill passed—an enabling act for the people of Kansas to form a constitution under, in which bill, it was agreed among them, it was best not to have a clause submitting the constitution to the vote of the people.

He then brings forward what he deems the evidence to prove that there was a bill which went into the hands of Judge Douglas, as chairman of the committee on territories [a chairmanship that Douglas, ironically, would lose after his reelection, because of his continuing feud with the Buchanan administration—*ed.*], which contained a provision in it for submitting the constitution that might be made to the vote of the people. He then brings forward evidence tending to show, and showing, as he deems it, that Judge Douglas reported that bill back to the Senate with that clause stricken out of it. He then brings forward evidence tending to show that there was a clause inserted into that bill brought back which would in its nature prevent the reference of the constitution back to the vote of the people, if, indeed, upon the mere silence of the law they had a right to so refer it.

These are the general statements. Now, after having made this general statement, I propose to examine the points in Judge Douglas' speech in which he answers that speech of Judge Trumbull. When you come to examine the points in Judge Douglas' speech you will find that the first point he makes is, "suppose it were true that there was such a clause in the bill and that I struck it out," and he argues from that that it does not follow that it was intended to prevent the people having the right to vote upon their constitution. His striking out such a provision, if there was one in the bill, he argues, does not establish or prove that it was stricken out for the purpose of robbing the people of that right. Well, I would say in the first place, that that would be the most manifest object of striking it out, as it would seem. It is true, as Judge Douglas states, that many territorial bills have passed without having such a provision in them, and I believe it as true, though I am not certain, that in certain instances constitutions framed under such bills have been submitted to a vote of the people, with the law silent upon the subject, but it won't follow that they once had their bill framed with an express provision for submission, and then struck it out when they did not mean to alter the effect of the law. That there have been bills that never had it in does not at all explain why it was taken out of one that it was in, and more especially does this evidence tend to prove the proposition that Trumbull puts, when we remember that in point of time that provision was stricken out of the bill almost simultaneously with the time that Bigler says that there was a meeting amongst Senators, and it was agreed that the bill should be passed [the *Tribune* substituted "framed"—*ed.*], lest difficulty should come out of the proposition to submit the constitution to the vote of the people. Judge Douglas altogether forgets in answering Judge Trumbull, to look to that conversation spoken of by Mr. Bigler. The Judge does not notice that. If you take that as one of the proven facts, and find out that simultaneously with it Judge Douglas did submit it and put the two points, the one in and the other out, I think it does not fall very far short of proving the proposition put by Judge Trumbull [the *Tribune* added: "(to) enter into a plot to put in force a Constitution for Kansas without giving the people any opportunity of voting upon it"—*ed.*].

But I must hurry on. The next proposition that Judge Douglas puts is, "But upon examination, it turns out that the Toombs bill never did contain a clause requiring the constitution to be submitted." [Georgia senator Robert Toombs had introduced legislation requiring federal commissioners to register Kansas voters before the election of delegates to a constitutional convention. It was passed in the Senate in 1856, but failed to win approval in the House—*ed.*]

Now that is a mere statement of fact, and, is one that can be determined by evidence. I only want to ask this question first—Why Judge Douglas did not say that the Toombs bill (for that is the bill that it is alleged that provision was stricken out of)—I want to ask this question, then. Why if the Judge wanted to make direct issue with Judge Trumbull, he did not take the exact provision which Judge Trumbull provided in his speech, and say that the provision was not stricken out? Mr. Trumbull has put down in his speech the exact words that were in the bill, and then he alleges that those words were stricken out. Now Judge Douglas does not say that these words were stricken out, but he says, "It turns out that the Toombs bill never did contain a clause requiring the constitution to be submitted." We see at once, then, that he is really making his issue, though he does not plainly say so, upon the meaning of the words. He is not undertaking to say that Trumbull tells a lie about these words being stricken out, but he is really, when he is pushed up to it, taking an issue on the meaning of words. Well now, I have here, if there be an issue on the meaning of words, or upon the question of facts, or whether these words were stricken out, why I have what I suppose to be a genuine copy of the Toombs bill in which it can be shown that the words which Trumbull says were in the bill, were in it. [The *Tribune* added: "If there be any dispute upon the fact, I have got the documents here to show they were there"—*ed.*] If, however, the controversy is upon the words, or the sense of the words, whether these words stricken out really constitute a provision for submitting the matter to a vote of the people, why, then, as this is a matter of argument, I think I may say I will use Trumbull's own argument upon that subject. Judge Douglas did not meet him at all on that, although he put it down fairly, but passes it off in the manner in which I have stated Trumbull says, "The provision is in these words."

> "That the following proposition be and the same are hereby offered to the said convention of the people of Kansas, upon when formed, for their free acceptance or rejection; which, if accepted by the convention, and *ratified by the people at the election for the adoption of the Constitution,* shall be obligatory on the United States, and upon the said State of Kansas," &c.

Now, Trumbull alleges that these last words were stricken out of the bill when it came back, and Trumbull's argument upon the subject, that it was a proposition, for submitting the constitution to a vote of the people, or a great portion of the argument, is this: "Would it have been possible to ratify the land provision at the election for the adoption of the constitution unless such an election was to be held? [Applause and laughter. —*Tribune*] That is Trumbull's argument. Now, Judge Douglas does not meet that at all; but he stands up and says that there was no provision in that bill for submitting the constitution to be framed to a vote of the people. Judge Trumbull admits that the language is not direct for the submission, but he asks how is it "possible to ratify the land proposition at the election for the adoption of the constitution unless such an election was to be held," and he goes on to show that it is not any less a law because it is in that indirect shape than it would be in a direct shape. But I presume that I have said enough to draw attention to this point. I pass by it also.

Another one of the points the Judge makes upon Trumbull at great length, is that Trumbull, while that bill was pending in the Senate, said he supposed the constitution, if made, would have to be submitted to the people, and he asks if Trumbull thought so what reason there is now for anybody thinking to the contrary. He asks if Trumbull thought in that way then, what ground there is for thinking any way differently now. Well now, fellow-citizens, this much may be said, that bill had been in the hands of a party to which Mr. Trumbull did not belong; it had been out in the hands of Judge Douglas in a committee at the head of which Judge Douglas stood. Mr. Trumbull perhaps had a printed copy of the original bill. I have no evidence upon that, except a sort of inference I draw from the usual course of business as I understand it, but what provisions for alteration were going on in the hands of the committee Mr. Trumbull had no means of knowing until the altered bill was reported back. Trumbull read it over hastily perhaps; has not seen precisely all the bearings that may be in the alterations; he is hastily run [the *Tribune* substituted "borne"—*ed.*] into a debate upon the subject, and it does not follow at all that because there might have been something that Judge Trumbull did not see then that it does not really exist. "More than that," is it true that whatever Trumbull did can have any effect upon what Judge Douglas did? [Applause. —*Tribune*] Suppose it was true that Judge Trumbull was in the plot, that he as well as these other men were in, would that let Judge Douglas out of it? [Applause and laughter. —*Tribune*, which added: "Would it exonerate Douglas that Trumbull didn't then perceive he was in the plot?"] I don't perceive that it would. He also asks the question why did not Judge Trumbull propose and amend the bill. Why did he not propose and amend the bill if he thought it needed any amendment. I may say generally that everything, I believe, that Judge Trumbull has proposed, particularly in connection with this question of Kansas and Nebraska, since he has been on the floor of the Senate, has been promptly voted down by Judge Douglas and his friends, and he had no promise, I believe, that any amendments of his offered to anything upon that subject would receive the slightest consideration or favor. Judge Trumbull did bring to the notice of the Senate at that time the fact as he understood, that there was no provision for submitting the new constitution to be made for Kansas to a vote of the people, and I believe I may venture to say that Judge Douglas made some reply to that speech of Judge Trumbull's, but never noticed that part of it at all. I think then that because Judge Trumbull offered no amendment does not throw much blame upon Trumbull, and if it did, it don't reach the question at all as to what Judge Douglas was doing. [Applause. —*Tribune*] I repeat, if Trumbull had previously been in the plot, it would not at all relieved [*sic*] the others that were in it—it would not touch the question at all. If I should be indicted for murder and upon the trial it should be discovered that I was engaged in that murder, but the prosecuting witness was in it to[o], it would be no relief to my neck that the discovery had come out.

Another one of the points that Judge Douglas makes against Trumbull is, that when he spoke at Chicago he made his charge to rest upon the fact that the bill had a provision in it for submitting the constitution to be framed to a vote of the people when it went into his (Judge Douglas') hands, and that it was taken out when he reported it to the Senate, and that he, in the published speech had subsequently said that the alterations in the bill made while it was in the committee were made on consultation between him (Judge Douglas) and Mr. Toombs. Let me not be misunderstood as saying specifically that he made these alterations with his own hand; but he said that "the alterations in the bill made while it was in the committee were made on consultation between him, (Judge Douglas) and Mr. Toombs.[']

The Judge goes on now and comments upon the fact that Trumbull in his Alton speech adduced the proposition that the bill not only came back with that proposition out of it, but it now came back with another proposition in it, saying—

I propose now to furnish that evidence. It will be remembered that Mr. Toombs' bill provided for holding an election for delegates to form a constitution under the supervision of commissioners to be appointed by the President, and in that bill as reported back by Judge Douglas, these words, not to be found in the original bill, are inserted at the close of the 11th section, viz:

"And until the complete execution of this act, no other election shall be had in said territory."

Which Mr. Trumbull argues was not only taking the proposition for submitting the constitution in a vote of the people away, but was putting an affirmative one in, that would prevent the people exercising that right, upon a bill that was merely silent upon that question. Now, in regard to that, he says Trumbull shifts the issue—shifts his ground—I believe he uses the term that the first charge being proved false, he shifts the ground. I call upon you all, when you shall examine Judge Trumbull's speech, to determine for yourselves whether Trumbull shifts his ground or not. I say he did not. I say he brought forward the same ground with more evidence. He made the charge precisely as he originally made it, and in addition thereto, he brought a new piece of evidence tending, as he thought, and as I think, to prove his proper position. That is—to illustrate by a trial—on one trial a man introduces as witnesses A and B to prove his case[;] on a second trial, he introduces those two witnesses who tell the same story that they told before, and he introduces another witness who tells something in addition that proves the main proposition. [The *Tribune* added: "So with Trumbull"—*ed.*] There was no conflict in the evidence.

But Judge Douglas says, that he himself in the Senate moved to strike out that last provision of the bill, and that on his motion it was stricken out, and a substitute put in the bill for it, and that I presume is the truth. I presume that is so. I presume that that last provision that was put in was stricken out by Judge Douglas. Trumbull has not said that it was not! He says, "I am speaking of the bill as Judge Douglas reported it back." It was amended some in the Senate before it passed. Now, when Judge Douglas parades the fact that he had that provision stricken out of the bill when it came back, he just meets nothing at all. Trumbull has said that he believes that he originally put it in. Did the Judge put it in? Trumbull says it was not in the Toombs bill when it went to the committee, and he says when it came back it was in, and Douglas said that the alterations were made by him after consultation with Mr. Toombs. He therefore believes that Judge Douglas put it in. Now, let

Judge Douglas not call Trumbull a liar, but let him show that he did not put it in. It is sometimes the case that a bear is hot pursued enough to drop a cub, and so I presume it was in this case. [Loud applause. —*Tribune*] I presume Douglas put [it] in and afterwards put it out. [Laughter and cheers. —*Tribune*] I presume that is the truth about it. Now, the question is, what did he put it in for? In the first place, why did he take the other provision out, and having taken that out, what did he put this one in for? I say that in the run of things it may have become apparent enough to any one that these were his cubs, but the question that Trumbull makes is, that Douglas put it in, and he does not meet Trumbull unless he denies it.

Near the close [the *Tribune* substituted "In the clause"—*ed.*] of Judge Douglas' speech upon this subject, he uses this language toward Judge Trumbull. He says, "he forged his evidence from beginning to end, and by falsifying the record he endeavored to bolster up his false charges." Well, now that is a pretty serious statement. "Trumbull forged his evidence from beginning to end." Now, upon my own authority, I say that is not so! [Great cheers and laughter. —*Tribune*] What is a forgery? Consider this evidence that Trumbull brought forward when you come to read his speech, and consider it briefly as you are able to do now, and then see whether he "forged his evidence from beginning to end." What was the evidence? I understand myself, although I don't read it from the speech, that Mr. Trumbull held up a bill or document in his hand like that, (holding up a bill) and he says that that is a copy of the Toombs bill, I believe it is the one as it was introduced, and went into Judge Douglas' hands. Does Judge Douglas say that is a forgery? That is one thing Judge Trumbull brought forward. That is the beginning! Does Judge Douglas say that is a forgery? Let him say it this evening and we will have a subsequent examination upon the subject. [Loud applause. —*Tribune*] Trumbull then says that he holds up another document like that, and he says that is an exact copy of the bill as it came back in the amended form out of Judge Douglas' hands. Does Judge Douglas say that is a forgery? He does say so in his general sweeping charge. [The *Tribune* added: "Does he say it now?"—*ed.*] If he does not, when then, if you take this Toombs bill, and this bill in the amended form, it only needs to compare them to see that the provision is in one that is not in the other, and it leaves the inference inevitably, that it was taken out. [Applause. —*Tribune*]

But while I am dealing with the question of the evidence, let us see what Trumbull's other evidence is—if I have time to do so. One piece of evidence I have already read. Trumbull says that there is in this original Toombs' bill the following provision:

> "That the following propositions be and the same are hereby offered to the said convention of the people of Kansas, when formed, for their free acceptance or rejection, which, if accepted by the convention, *and ratified by the people at the election for the adoption of the Constitution,* shall be obligatory on the United States, and upon the said State of Kansas," &c.

Now, if it shall be said that this is a forgery, he bringing it forward, I say it is in one of these papers. If Judge Douglas says it is a forgery, why we will open the papers and see if it is a forgery or not.

So, again, he says Senator Bigler made the following statement in his place in the Senate, December 9th, 1857, and then adds, "I read from Part 1, *Congressional Globe* of last session, page 21:

> "I was present when that subject was discussed by Senators, before the bill was introduced, and the question was raised and discussed, whether the constitution, when formed, should be submitted to a vote of the people. It was held by those most intelligent on the subject, that in view of all the difficulties surrounding that territory, the danger of any experiment at that time of a popular vote, it would be better that there should be no such provision in the Toombs bill, and it was my understanding in all the intercourse I had, that that convention would make a constitution and send it here without submitting it to the popular vote."

And then Trumbull follows on:

> "In speaking of this meeting again on the 21st December, 1857, (*Congressional Globe,* same vol., page 113) Senator Bigler said:
> "Nothing was farther from my mind than to allude to any social or confidential interview. The meeting was not of that character. Indeed it was semi-official, and called to promote the public good. My recollection was clear that I left the conference under the impression that it had been deemed best to adopt measures to admit Kansas as a State through the agency of one popular election, and that for delegates to

the convention. This impression was the stronger, because I thought the spirit of the bill infringed upon the doctrine of non-intervention, to which I had great aversion, but with the hope of accomplishing a great good and as no movement had been made in that direction in the territory, I waived this objection, and concluded to support the measure. I have a few items of testimony as to the correctness of these impressions, and with their submission I shall be content. I have before me the bill reported by the Senator from Illinois on the 7th of March 1856, providing for the admission of Kansas as a State, the third section of which reads as follows:

"That the following propositions be, and the same are hereby, offered to the said convention of the people of Kansas when formed, for their free acceptance or rejection; which if accepted by the convention, and ratified by the people at the election for the adoption of the constitution, shall be obligatory upon the United States and the said State of Kansas. The bill read in [its] place by the Senator from Georgia on the 25th of June, and referred to the Committee on Territories, contained the same section, word for word. Both these bills were under consideration at the conference referred to; but once the Senator from Illinois reported the Toombs bill to the Senate, with amendments, the next morning it did not contain that portion of the third section which indicated to the convention that the constitution should be approved by the people. The words 'and ratified by the people at the election for the adoption of the constitution,' had been stricken out."

Now, these, Mr. Trumbull says, were stated by Mr. Douglas upon the floor of the Senate on certain days, and are recorded in the *Congressional Globe* on certain pages. Now, does Judge Douglas say that that is a forgery? Does Judge Douglas say that there is no such thing in the *Congressional Globe* as that? What does he mean when he says that Judge Trumbull forges his evidence from beginning to end? So, again he says, at another place, page 15 of the *Congressional Globe*, wherein he, Judge Douglas, himself stated:

"That during the last Congress, I (Mr. Douglas) reported a bill from the Committee on Territories, to authorize the people of Kansas to assemble and form a constitution for themselves. Subsequently, the Senator from Georgia, (Mr. Toombs) brought forward a substitute for my bill, which, after having been modified by him and myself in consultation, was passed by the Senate."

Now, Trumbull says that that quotation of a speech from Douglas is reported and recorded in the *Congressional Globe!* Is that a forgery? Is it there or not? It may not be there; but I want the Judge to take these pieces of evidence and say that they are forgeries, if he dare do it. That is what I want him to do. [A voice—"He will."] You had better not commit him. [Cheers and laughter. —*Tribune*]

He gives other quotations. He gives a further quotation from Judge Douglas. He says:

> "I will ask the Senator to show me an intimation, from any one member of the Senate, in the whole debate on the Toombs bill, and in the Union from any quarter, that the constitution was not to be submitted to the people. I will venture to say, that on all sides of the chamber it was so understood at that time. If the opponents of the bill had understood it was not, they would have made the point upon it; and if they had made it, we should certainly have yielded to it, and put in the clause. That is a discovery made since the President found out that it was not safe to take it for granted that that would be done, which ought in fairness to have been done."

Now, Trumbull says that Judge Douglas made that speech and it is recorded. Does the Judge say that is a forgery, that it was not true? Trumbull shows somewhere—It will be found by any one who read this—shows a quotation of his own, that he did distinctly bring it to the notice of those engineering that bill, that it lacked that provision, and that he goes on to make another quotation from Judge Douglas:

> "Judge Douglas, he says, however, probably recollecting or being reminded of the fact, that I had objected to the Thomas bill when pending that it did not provide for a submission of the constitution to the people, made another statement which is to be found in the same column of the *Globe*, at page 29, in which he says:
>
> That the bill was silent [on] the subject is true, and my attention was called to that about the time it was passed and I took the fair construction to be, that powers not delegated were reserved, and that of course the Constitution would be submitted to the people."

Trumbull adds upon that—

"Whether this statement is consistent with the statement just before made, that had the point been made it would have been yielded to, or that it was a new discovery, you will determine; for if the public records do not convict and condemn him, he may go uncondemned, so far as I am concerned." [The *Tribune* inexplicably omitted the last twenty-one words—*ed.*]

I do not know in what shape Judge Douglas is going to sustain his position, that Trumbull's evidence is forged from beginning to end. I say here to-day, that these *Congressional Globes*—I have not got with me—they are big books—they are difficult to carry about—and I have not got them with me—and if Judge Douglas shall say that on these points where Trumbull has quoted from them, that there is no such proposition there, I shall not be able to prove they are; but I shall have another opportunity, however, whenever he points out and says that these things that Trumbull has quoted are not at the place that he says they are, then my attention will be drawn to it, and I will have another hour, and I state to you that I have not the slightest doubt that I shall find them exactly where Mr. Trumbull says they are.

Well, then, the question is, how can Judge Douglas make it out to be a forgery? What is a forgery? It is bringing forward some writing that is untrue. You came forward with a letter, write my name to it, which I never wrote—that is a forgery—with a thing in print, saying it is so, and so when it is not so, and that is a forgery; but how do you make out a thing to be a forgery when each piece is a copy of the genuine thing as it stands[?]

Now, I concede that Judge Douglas has a right to say these bills are false or forged—that he has a right to say that these extracts are false or forged—but until he does so say, specifically, we don't know how to get at him.

I presume that each one of these extracts that Trumbull has put in his speech will be found in the *Congressional Globe* exactly where Trumbull says they are. Then, I leave it to you if Judge Douglas in calling Trumbull's charge a forgery, from beginning to end, is meeting the argument at all. If it should turn out that one is a forgery it won't be me that will stick to it any longer. I have always wanted the Judge to deal that way between him and me. If I do accidentally upon any occasion say anything that is not strictly correct, and it is pointed out to me, I will withdraw it in a minute, but I don't choose to have Judge Trumbull's statements put down in clear terms, that they are forgeries from beginning to end[;] that is no fair way of answering a charge[,] at least it seems so to me, and I subject to Judge Douglas' friends and to all men to answer, if that is a fair way of answering a charge.

Now coming back, [the *Tribune* added: "—how much time do I have left? THE MODERATOR:—three minutes. MR. LINCOLN—"] I want to say the true point upon Judge Douglas is this, that unless he establishes that there is something of forgery, or that the bill that went into his hands had the provision in it which Judge Trumbull said it had, which Trumbull and I both say necessarily amount to a provision to submit the constitution to the people, that he took it out, that he says that he knows that the bill was silent; but I say that it was not silent—Judge Douglas, when you got it it was vocal—and now the direct question upon the Judge is, why did he silence it? If he had found the bill silent, if he had found the bill without that provision in it he might talk as he does now, that he supposed that it would be submitted to the people; and certainly these few words, making but two lines, did not encumber the bill. My question upon him is, why, finding the bill vocal with the provision— why he silenced it—what he took it out for; and although he took out the other provision, I ask him why he at first put it in—what he put it in for, if he did afterwards take it out?

Now, I ask him first to meet the question whether he took it out; I ask him what he did it for. It looks to us that he did it to alter the bill; if it looks different to him he can tell it; if he had a different reason from the plain and obvious reason, I insist upon having it [the *Tribune* added: "why he made the bill silent upon that point when it was vocal before he put his hands upon it"—*ed.*].

So of the subsequent provision. I was told before the last paragraph that my time was within three minutes of being out—I presume it is within one now, I therefore close. [Three tremendous cheers were given as Mr. Lincoln retired. —*Tribune*]

Mr. Douglas' Reply

LADIES AND GENTLEMEN:—I had supposed that we had assembled here to-day for the purpose of a joint discussion between Mr. Lincoln and myself upon the political questions that now agitate this whole country. The rule of all joint discussions is, that the opening speaker shall touch on all the points which he intends to discuss, in order that the one to reply shall have the opportunity of answering them. Let me ask you what questions of public policy has Mr. Lincoln discussed before you touching the welfare of the States or the welfare of the Union. [Cries of "None, none!" —*Tribune;* Great applause. —*Times*] Allow me to remind you that silence is the best compliment, for I need my whole time, and your cheers only occupy it.

Mr. Lincoln simply contented himself in the outset by saying that he was not in favor of social and political equality between the white and the negro; nor did he desire to have the law changed so as to make them voters or eligible to office. I am glad to have got an answer from him on that proposition, to wit: the right of suffrage and holding office by negroes, for I have been trying to get him to answer that point during the whole time that the canvass has been going on.

Passing, however, from that, I now propose to call your attention to the one question which he has occupied his entire time in discussing. He has occupied his whole hour in retailing a charge made by Senator Trumbull against me, originating two years ago, and prior to the last presidential election.

If that charge of Trumbull was true, why did he not make it in '56, when I was discussing the questions of that duty [the *Times* substituted "day"—*ed.*] all over this State with Mr. Lincoln and Mr. Trumbull. He was as silent as the grave on the question then. If that charge was true, the time to have brought it forward was the canvass of '56—the year when the Toombs bill passed the Senate; when the facts were fresh in the popular mind; when the Kansas question was a prominent one of the day, and when it would have a material bearing on that election, if true. Why did they remain silent then? Knowing that such a charge could be made and proved, if it was true, were they not false to you, false to the country, to have gone through that entire campaign, concealing the charge of this enormous conspiracy which Trumbull says he then knew and would not tell. [Laughter. —*Times*] Mr. Lincoln intimates in his speech a good reason why Trumbull would not tell, for he says it must be true, as I proved at Jacksonville, that Trumbull was also in the plot. Mr. Lincoln goes on to agree that if Trumbull was in the plot, that did not relieve me any more than if he was on trial for murder it would not relieve him if another man was detected during the trial to have been a party to the same crime. Well, if Mr. Trumbull then was in the plot and then concealed it in order to escape the odium upon himself, I ask, are you to believe him now when he turns State's evidence, and avows his own infamy in order to implicate me with him? [He is a liar, and a traitor. We couldn't believe Lyman Trumbull under oath, &c. —*Times*] I am amazed that Mr. Lincoln could come forward and endorse that charge, and occupy his whole time in rendering Trumbull's speech in support of it. Why, I ask, didn't Mr. Lincoln make a speech of his own, instead of occupying the whole time in reading from the speech at Alton[?] [Cheers. —*Times*] I had supposed that Mr. Lincoln was capable of making a public speech on his own account, or else I should not have accepted his banter from him for joint discussion, if I had supposed the whole time was to be occupied in reading Trumbull's speech instead of his own. [Applause. —*Times*]

A VOICE—Why don't you reply to the charge?

JUDGE DOUGLAS—Now, Sir, don't you trouble yourself, gentlemen; I am going to make a speech in my own way, and I trust that as the Democrats listened patiently to Mr. Lincoln, that his friends will not interrupt me when I am speaking.

Now, I propose to first state the charge in Trumbull's own language. Mr. Trumbull, returning from the East, landed at Chicago, and the first thing he did was to make a speech, wholly devoted to assaults upon my public character. I wish to call your attention to the fact that up to that time I had never alluded to Mr. Trumbull, directly or indirectly, nor to his course in Congress. Hence his assaults on me were entirely without provocation, without excuse, and since that he has been travelling from one end of the State to the other, repeating this same vile charge. I will read it now in his own language:

"Now fellow citizens, I make the distinct charge that there was a preconcerted arrangement plot entered into by the very men who now claim credit for opposing a Constitution formed and put in force without giving the people an opportunity to pass upon it. This my friends, is a serious charge, but I charge it to-night, that the very men

who traverse the country under banners proclaiming popular sovereignty, by design concocted a bill on purpose to force a Constitution
upon that people."

Again, speaking to some one in the crowd, he says:

"And you want to satisfy yourself that he was in the plot to force
a constitution upon that people? I will satisfy you. I will cram the truth
down any honest man's throat, until he cannot deny it and to the man
who does deny it, I will cram the lie down his throat till he shall cry
enough!" [The *Times* added: " 'It is preposterous—it is the most
damnable effrontery that man ever put on, to conceal a scheme to
defraud and cheat the people out of their rights and then claim credit
for it.' " The paper probably added these lines for the published
version—*ed.*]

Here is the polite language of Senator Trumbull applied to his
colleague when I was a hundred miles off. [That's like him. —*Times*]
Why didn't he apply it in the Senate and cram the lie down my throat,
when I did deny it to Bigler, and made him take it back? [Applause.
—*Tribune*] You all recollect how Bigler assaulted me when I was engaged in that hand to hand fight resisting a scheme to put a constitution
upon the people of Kansas against their will. Bigler then assaulted me,
and I turned upon him and made him take the back track and explain
his conduct to the country, and there was not an honest man in America
that would pretend it was true. [Hurra for Douglas. —*Times*] Trumbull
was then present face to face with me. Why didn't he then rise and
make the charge and say that he could cram the lie down my throat?
[Applause. —*Tribune;* He was afraid. —*Times*] I tell you that Trumbull
then knew it was a lie. He knew that Trumbull denied that there ever
was a clause in that bill when he brought it forward of the tenor of
which he now charges, and which he says required the Constitution to
be submitted to the people. I will now tell you all the facts in regard to
that question. I had introduced a bill to authorize the people of Kansas
to form a Constitution and come into the Union as a State whenever
they should have the requisite population for a member of Congress.
Toombs introduced a bill to authorize the people of Kansas to then,
with only 25,000 people, form a Constitution to come in at that time,
and the issue was whether we should allow them in with 25,000, or

whether we should require them to have the ratio for a member of Congress, to wit, 93,420. That was the point of debate in the committee. I was overruled; my proposition to have 93,000 was overruled, and Toombs' proposition to let them in was substituted in its place; and accordingly a bill to carry out Toombs' idea of immediate admission was reported as a substitute for mine, but the only point at issue was this question of population, and the fixing of proper safeguards as to frauds at the election. Now, Mr. Trumbull knew these to be the facts—the whole Senate knew them to be the facts, and hence he was silent at that time. But he waited until I was in the canvass with Mr. Lincoln, and found that I was showing up Mr. Lincoln's Abolitionism and Negro Equality. [Applause. —*Tribune;* Cheers. —*Times*] I was driving Mr. Lincoln to the wall until white men would not tolerate his rank Abolitionism, and they sent for Trumbull to come back, and they framed a system of charges against me to compel me [to] occupy my entire time in defending myself, so that I could not show up the enormity of the Abolition Black Republican party's principles [the *Times* omitted "Black Republican"—*ed.*]. Now, the whole object of this time today being occupied in an issue between Trumbull and me by Mr. Lincoln is to conceal from this vast audience the discussion of the questions that divide the two great parties. [That's it; and cheers. —*Times*] I am not going to allow them to take up much of my time by these transient matters. I have lived in this State twenty-five years. I, most of the time, have been in public life. My record is open to you all, and if that record is not enough to vindicate me against these petty, malicious assaults, I despair ever to be elected to office by slandering my opponent and traducing other men. [Cheers. —*Times*] Mr. Lincoln asks you to-day for your support in electing him to the Senate solely because he and Trumbull can slander me. Has he given any other reason [No, no. —*Times*] as to what he is going to do on any one question in Congress? [No, no. —*Times*] He attempts to ride into office not upon his own merits, or the merit and soundness of his own principles, but upon his success in fastening that stale old slander upon his opponent. ["That's the truth." "Hear, hear." —*Times*]

Now I wish you to bear in mind that up to the time of this Toombs bill and afterwards, there never has been an act of Congress for the admission of a new State which contained a clause requiring the constitution to be submitted to the people. The general rule was that the constitution be silent on this subject, taking it for granted that the people themselves would demand and compel a vote on the ratification of their constitution. Inasmuch as that had been the rule under Washington, and Jefferson, and Madison, and Jackson, and Polk, under the Whig Presidents, and under the Democratic Presidents, from the beginning of the Government down, nobody ever dreamed that the effort would be made to abuse the power thus confided to the people of a Territory. For these reasons, attention was not called to the fact of whether there was or was not a clause compelling submission: but it was taken for granted that the constitution would be submitted to the people, whether the law compelled it or not. And now I will read from the report made by me as chairman of the committee at the time that the Toombs bill was reported back. I reported back the substitute but, as I have said, it contained several clauses which I voted against in committee, but being overruled, I, as chairman, reported back all those agreed to, and one thing, and the main point I had been overruled is, was the question of population. In the written report containing the Toombs bill, I said:

"In the opinion of your committee, whenever a constitution shall be formed in any Territory preparatory to its admission into the Union as a State, justice, the genius of our institutions, the whole theory of our republican system imperatively demands that the voice of the people shall be fairly expressed, and their will embodied in that fundamental law without fraud or violence, or intimidation, or any other improper or unlawful influence and subject to no other restrictions than those imposed by the Constitution of the United States." [Cheers. —*Times*]

Here you find that the committee took it for granted that under that bill the Constitution was to be submitted to the people whether the bill was silent on the subject or not. Now, suppose I had reported it silent on the subject, following the example of Washington and Jefferson, and Monroe, and Adams, and Jackson, and Harrison, Tyler, and Polk, and Fillmore, and Pierce, would that fact have been evidence of a conspiracy to put a Constitution on the people against their will[?] [A unanimous "No!" —*Times*]

A VOICE—No, sir.

JUDGE DOUGLAS—If the charge be true that Mr. Lincoln makes against me, it is true against Millard Fillmore—true against Zachary Taylor, true against every Whig President as well as against every Democratic President. It is true against Henry Clay, who had been in the Senate and in the House for fifteen years, and advocated these very bills. No one of them ever contained a clause compelling submission to the people. Now are Messrs. Lincoln and Trumbull prepared to charge upon all these eminent men from the beginning of the government down to this day, that absence of a provision compelling submission is evidence of a corrupt design to force a Constitution on an unwilling people[?] ["We'll skin them if they dare to." —*Times*] I ask you to reflect on these things, for I tell you, here is a conspiracy to carry an election by slander or not by fair means. Mr. Lincoln's speech this day is conclusive evidence of the fact. He devotes the entire time to an issue between me and Trumbull, and not a word on the politics of the day. Are you going to elect Trumbull's colleague on an issue between Trumbull and me? [Laughter, and "No, no!" —*Times*] I thought I was running against Abraham Lincoln. [Laughter. —*Tribune*] I thought Mr. Lincoln intended to be my opponent. I thought Mr. Lincoln was discussing the public questions of the day with me; I thought he challenged me to such a discussion, and it turns out that his only hope is that he is going to ride into office on Trumbull's back and Trumbull is going to carry him by falsehood into office. [Cheers. —*Times*] Now, I will pursue this subject a little further. As I said before, the remainder of the record proves that Trumbull's charge was false that the Toombs bill originally required the constitution to be submitted to the people. The printed copy he shows declares that it required the last clauses, not the constitution, to be submitted; but taking it for granted that the people would order an election on the constitution, my report says that we take it for granted that the people would order an election. But there was no clause in the Toombs bill requiring the whole of the constitution to be submitted. Trumbull knew it at the time, and his speech made on the night of its passage discloses the fact that he knew it was silent on the subject; Lincoln pretends, and tells you that Trumbull has not changed his evidence in support of his charge since he made a second speech, and brought forward new evidence. What was the new evidence? The Chicago *Times* took up Trumbull's Chicago speech and compared it with the record, and proved all that part to be false declaring that the original bill required submission to the people. Trumbull saw that he was caught and exposed in his falsehood. He went right to Alton and under the very walls of the Illinois Penitentiary [Laughter, —*Times*], made a new speech, in which he predicated his assault on me on the allegation that I put into the bill a clause, and had it voted in, a clause which prohibited the convention from submitting the Constitution to the people. And he quoted what he pretended to be that clause— [the

Times added: "Now, has not Mr. Trumbull entirely changed the evidence on which he bases his charge?" ("Yes, yes!" "Lincoln's as big a liar as Trumbull," &c.)—*ed.*] the clause which he quoted in his Alton speech, and which he has published and scattered broadcast all over the State as evidence that the Toombs bill as amended by me and passed, contained these words, which I will read: "And until the complete execution of this act, no other election shall be held in said Territory." Trumbull said that the object of preventing any other election in said Territory by those words, was to prevent the Constitution from being submitted to the people by the Convention that had framed it. Now I will show you that when Trumbull made that statement at Alton, he knew it to be untrue. I now read from Trumbull's speech in the Senate on the Toombs bill, the day it passed. There he says: "There is nothing said in this bill, so far as I have discovered, about submitting the Constitution which is to be framed to the people for their sanction or rejection." [The *Times* added: "Perhaps the convention will have the right to submit it, if it should think proper, but it is certainly not compelled to do so according to the provisions of the bill"—*ed.*] Thus you see Trumbull said in the Senate when that bill was pending, that it was silent on the subject of submission, and that there was nothing in that bill one way or the other on the subject. In his Alton speech he says there was a clause in it preventing submission to the people, and that I put it in. Thus I convict him of falsehood and slander at Alton by quoting from his own speech as reported in the *Congressional Globe* in the Senate of the United States when the Toombs bill passed. Now what do you think of a man that will thus shift and make false charges and falsify the record to prove them. Now, in the next place, I will show you that the clause which Trumbull says was put in the bill on my motion, was never put in at all, and was stricken from the report of the Committee, and a substitute on my own motion put in its place. Sir, I call your attention to the *Congressional Globe*, page 795. Douglas said—"I have an amendment to offer from the Committee on Territories, on page 8, section 11, strike out the words, 'until the complete execution of the act, no other election shall be held in said Territory,' and insert the amendment which I hold in my hand." Thus you see here that I moved to strike out the very words that Trumbull said were put in, and they were never put in at all—but merely reported—the Committee overruling me as I stated and stricken out in the Senate on my motion and another clause put in its place.

On the same page you find the amendment was agreed to. That amendment being agreed to, I put in another clause, recognizing the right of the people of Kansas, under that bill, to order just such an election as they might see proper. Now I will read them. Page 796, Mr. Douglas said: "I have another amendment to offer from the Committee, to follow the other amendment which has been adopted. The bill reads now, 'and until the complete execution of this act, no other election shall be held in said Territory.' It has been suggested that it should be modified in this way, 'and to avoid all conflict in the complete execution of this act, all other elections in said Territory are hereby postponed until such time as said convention shall appoint' " [the *Times* added: "so that they can appoint the day in the event that there should be a failure to come into the Union. The Amendment was *unanimously* agreed to"—*ed.*]. This clearly and distinctly recognizes the right of the convention to order just as many elections as they saw proper in the execution of the act. Now Trumbull concealed in his Alton speech the fact that the clause which he quoted on me had been stricken out, and he concealed the other fact, that this clause had been put in, and then made the false statement that the bill contained a clause requiring submission. Now, I repeat my charge upon Trumbull upon that record that he did falsify the records of this country in making that charge. [Applause. —*Tribune;* "It's plain," and tremendous applause, —*Times*] And I tell Mr. Abraham Lincoln if he will look at that record he will then know that Trumbull falsified the public record in that charge. And Mr. Lincoln has this day endorsed Mr. Trumbull's veracity after he had my word for it that by the record his veracity was proved to have been forfeited and violated in this charge. It won't do for Mr. Lincoln, in parading his calumny against me, to put Trumbull between him and the odium and the responsibility that attaches to such calumny. I tell him I am as ready to prosecute the endorser as the maker of a forged note. [Applause. —*Tribune;* Cheers. —*Times*] I regret the necessity of occupying my time in these petty personal matters. It is unbecoming the dignity of a canvass for an office of the character for which we are candidates. When I commenced this canvass at Chicago I spoke of Mr. Lincoln in terms of kindness and respect as an old friend, and told you he was a man of respectable character, of good standing, and of unblemished reputation, and I had nothing to say against him. I repeated these remarks complimentary to him in my successive speeches, until he became the endorser for these and other slanders against me. If there is anything personally disagreeable, unkind or disrespectful in these personalities, the sole responsibility is on Mr. Lincoln, Trumbull and their backers. I will show you another charge made by Mr. Lincoln against me, as an offset in his expression of a willingness to take back anything that is incorrect, and to correct any false statement or misrepresentation into which he has fallen. Mr. Lincoln has made the charge several times against the Supreme Court of the United States, and President Pierce, and President Buchanan and myself, that at the time the Nebraska bill was introduced by me in June, 1854, at Washington City, there was a conspiracy between the Judges of the Supreme Court and President Pierce, President Buchanan and myself to have the Dred Scott case decided in such a manner as to establish slavery all over the country. He charged a conspiracy between us. I branded it as a falsehood and let it go. He repeated it, and asked me to answer and fetch the proof [the *Times* substituted "analyze its truth"—*ed.*]. I told him, says I, "Mr. Lincoln I know what you are after. You want to occupy my time in personal matters so I can't show up the revolutionary principles which the Abolition party, whose candidate you are, have proclaimed to the world!" But he wanted me to analyze his proof. Then I called his attention to the fact that at the time the Nebraska bill was introduced there was no such case as the Dred Scott case pending in the Supreme Court, nor was there for two years afterward, and hence it was impossible that there should be any such conspiracy between the Judges of the Supreme Court and the other parties involved. I proved by the record that it was false. What did he say to that? That he took it back like an honest man, and saw that he had been mistaken? No, he repeated the charge, and said that, although there was no such case then pending, yet there was an understanding between the Democratic owners of Dred Scott and the Judges and the other persons alluded to, that they would bring up such a case. I then demanded, and have since demanded, to know who those Democratic owners of Dred Scott were. But he could not tell; he did not know, for there were no Democratic owners of Dred Scott in this land. [Laughter. —*Times*] He was owned at the time by the Rev. Dr. [Calvin] Chaffee, an abolition member of Congress from Springfield [Massachusetts, not Illinois—*ed.*] and his wife [Applause. —*Tribune;* Immense laughter and applause. —*Times*] And Mr. Lincoln ought to know the fact that Dred Scott was thus owned by Dr. Chaffee and his wife, for the reason that as soon as the decision was announced by the Court Dr. Chaffee and his wife executed a deed emancipating Dred Scott, putting that deed on record. [Cheers. —*Times*] [Chaffee's brother-in-law, John Sanford, was Scott's official owner at the time of the 1857 Court decision, but Democrats like Douglas enjoyed embarrassing the New England abolitionist by linking him to the case. Precisely who owned Scott at the time remains a matter of dispute—*ed.*] Thus it was matter of public record that at the time that case was taken up, Dred Scott was owned by an abolition member of Congress, a friend of Mr. Lincoln holding him, in his own right, while the defense was conducted by abolition Congress [the *Times* substituted "lawyers"—*ed.*] on the other side. Thus the Abolitionists conducted both sides of the case. [Laughter. —*Tribune*] I have thus shown that this charge was false, and yet he won't withdraw that charge of conspiracy. I now submit to you how much confidence you can place in the fairness of a man who will, in making a charge proved to be false even by the record so shift his ground. I will state another fact to show how utterly reckless is this charge against President[s] Pierce and Buchanan. He says President Buchanan was a party to this conspiracy in 1854, when the Nebraska bill was introduced. Now the history of this Country shows that James Buchanan was at that time representing this country at the Court of London with distinguished ability and usefulness to his country. The history of the country shows that James Buchanan had not been in the United States for nearly a year previous, and never came here for about three years afterwards. [Laughter. —*Tribune;* Cheers. —*Times*] And yet Mr. Lincoln keeps repeating the charge of conspiracy against Buchanan, when the public record shows that it is untrue, and he ought to have known it. Having thus proved it false as to the members of the Supreme Court and false as to President Buchanan, I let it drop, leaving the public to say whether I by myself without other concurrence could have made a conspiracy with them. [Laughter and applause. —*Tribune;* Laughter and cheers. —*Times*]

But, my friends, you see that the object is clearly to conduct the campaign on personal matters, hunting me down, and making charge after charge, proven to be false by the public records of the country. I am willing to offer my whole public life and my whole private life to the inspection of any man, or of all men, who desire to investigate it and if twenty-five years of residence among you, and nearly the whole time a public man, exposed, perhaps to more assaults and more abuse than any man living of my age, or that ever did live, and if I have survived it all, and commanded your confidence thus far, I am willing to trust to your knowledge of me and my public actions, without making any personal defence against those assaults from my enemies. [Applause. —*Tribune;* Great cheering. —*Times*]

Now, my friends, I came here for the purpose of discussing the leading political topics which now agitate the country. I have no charges to make against Mr. Lincoln—none against Mr. Trumbull, for I was not aware that he was a candidate. [Laughter. —*Tribune*] And none to make against any man who is a candidate, except to repel their assaults on me. If Mr. Lincoln is a man of bad character, I leave it to you to find out. If his voting in the past was not satisfactory to you, I leave others to ascertain the fact, and if his course on the Mexican war was not in accordance with your opinions of patriotism and duty in defence of our country against a public enemy, I leave you to ascertain the fact. I have no assault to make against him except to place before you the history of the public question that now divides the country and engrosses so much of the public attention. You know that prior to 1854 this country was divided into two great political parties—the one Whig and the other Democratic. During that whole period, for twenty years prior to that time, I had been in public discussions in this State as an advocate of Democratic principles, and I can appeal with confidence to every Old Line Whig in the hearing of my voice if during all this time, I did not fight the Whigs like a man on every question that separated the Whig party from the Democratic party. I had the highest respect for Henry Clay as a gallant party leader, as an eminent statesman and one of the leading men [the *Times* substituted "bright ornaments"—*ed.*] of this country, and I conscientiously thought that the Democratic party was right on the question which separated Whigs from Democrats. Hence a man don't live that can say that I ever personally assaulted Henry Clay, or Daniel Webster, or any one of the leaders of that great party, while I was combating with so much energy the measures that they advocated. What did we differ about as Whigs and Democrats in those days? Did we differ about this slavery question? On the contrary, did we not, in 1850, Whigs and Democrats, unite to a man in favor of that system of Compromise Measures which Mr. Clay introduced, which Webster advocated, which Cass supported, and which Fillmore approved and made a law by his signature? While we agreed on these measures, we differed about a Bank, about the Tariff, and about Distribution, and the Specie Circular, and the Sub-Treasury, and other questions of that description. Now, let me ask you, what one of these questions, on which Whigs and Democrats then differed, now remains to divide the two great parties? Every one of these questions, about which Whigs and Democrats then differed, has passed away. The country has outgrown these, and they have become obsolete ideas, and have passed into history. Hence it is immaterial whether you did right or I did right on the Bank, or on the Tariff, or on Distribution, or on the Specie Circular, or on the Sub-Treasury, for they no longer continue living issues between parties. What then has taken the place of those questions about which we differ[?] The slavery question has now become the leading and controlling issue. That question on which you and I agreed, on which the Whigs and the Democrats were united, had now become the leading issues between the National Democracy on the one side and this Republican Abolition party on the other. Just recollect for a moment that memorable contest of 1850, by which this country was agitated from its centre to its circumference by slavery agitation. All eyes then turned to the three great lights that arrived from the days of the Revolution. They looked to Clay, then in retirement at Ashland, to Webster, then in the Senate, and to Cass, also a member of the U.S. Senate. Clay had retired to Ashland, having, as he supposed, performed his mission on earth, and was prepared for a better sphere of existence in another world. And in that retirement he heard the discordant, harsh, grating sounds of sectional strife striking upon his ears. He armed and came forth from his retirement and resumed his seat in the Senate of the United States, that great theater of his great deeds. From the moment that Clay arrived among us he became the leader of all Union men, whether Whigs or Democrats. For nine months we assembled each day in the council chamber, with Clay in the chair, and Cass upon his right hand, and Webster on his left, and the Democrats and the Whigs arrayed on the one side and on the other, all forgetting their partisan differences, and all animated by one patriotic sentiment, and that one to devise means and measures that could defeat the main revolutionary schemes of Northern Abolitionists and Southern Disunionists. [Applause and cries of "Good." —*Tribune;* Cheers. —*Times*] We did devise means. Clay brought them forward; Webster advocated them; Cass defended them; the Union Democrats and the Union Whigs voted for them; Fillmore signed them, and they gave peace and quiet to the country. These compromise measures of 1850 were founded on the great fundamental principle, that the people of each State and of each Territory ought to be left free to form and regulate their own domestic institutions to suit themselves, subject only to the Federal Constitution. [Cheers. Applause. —*Tribune;* Hear, hear. —*Times*] Now let me ask every Old Line Democrat and every Old Line Whig, within the hearing of my voice, if I have not truly stated the issues as they then presented themselves to the country. You recollect that the Abolitionists raised a wild bowl of vengeance and destruction against the Democrats and the Whigs both, who supported those compromise measures of 1850. When I returned home to Chicago that year, I found the city infuriated and inflamed with vengeance against the author of these great measures. Being the only man in that city who was held responsible for affirmative votes on each of these measures, I went forward and faced the assembled inhabitants of the city of Chicago and defended each and every one of Clay's compromise measures as they passed the Senate and the House and were approved by President Fillmore. Previous to that time, the City Council had passed resolutions nullifying the acts of Congress and instructing the police to withhold all assistance in their execution. But the people of Chicago listened to my defence, and like candid, frank, conservative men, when convinced that they had done injustice to Clay, Webster, Cass and the other great statesmen who had supported those measures, they repealed these nullifying resolutions, and declared that the law should be executed, and the supremacy of the Constitution maintained. Let it always be recorded in history, to the immortal honor of the people of Chicago, that they had a sense of justice to take the back track when they found they were wrong, and did justice to those whom they had blamed and abused unjustly. When the Legislature of this State assembled that year, they proceeded to pass resolutions approving the Compromise Measures of 1850. When the great Whig party assembled in 1852 in Baltimore, in National Convention for the last time, and nominated Scott for the Presidency, they adopted as a part of their platform the Compromise Measures of 1850. That was the cardinal plank upon which every Whig would stand, and by which he would regulate his future conduct. When the Democratic party assembled at the same place one month afterwards and nominated Mr. Pierce, we adopted the same plank, so far as these Compromise measures were concerned, and agreed that we too would stand by Clay's Compromise measures, as a cardinal article in the Democratic faith. Thus you see that in 1852 all the old Whigs and all the old Democrats stood on a common plank, so far as this slavery question was concerned, but different in other measures.

Now, let me ask you, how is it that since that time so many old Whigs have wandered from the true path marked out by Clay, and carved out broad and wide by the great Webster? How is it that so many old line Democrats have abandoned the old faith of the party, and joined with the Abolitionists and Free Soilers to overturn the platform of the old Democrats and the platform of the old Whigs[?] ["What a pity Douglas bolted." —*Tribune*] You can't deny but what since 1854, there has been a great revolution on this one question. Let me ask how has it been brought about. I answer, no sooner was the sod green on the grave of the immortal Clay—no sooner were the roses planted on the tomb of the godlike Webster, than many leaders of the old Whig party, such as Seward of New York, and his followers, attempted to abolitionize the old Whig party, and transfer you all bound hand and foot into the abolition camp. Seizing hold of the temporary excitement produced in this country by the introduction of the Nebraska bill, the disappointed politicians in the Democratic party united with the disappointed politicians in the Whig party, and attempted to form a new party of abolitionized Democrats and abolitionized Whigs, who were all Abolitionists banded together on an Abolition platform. And who led that crusade against Union principles in this State? I answer that Abraham Lincoln in behalf of the Whigs and Lyman Trumbull in behalf of the Democrats formed a scheme by which they would abolitionize the two great parties of the country; then that Lincoln should be sent to the Senate of the United States in the place of General Shields, while Trumbull should go to Congress from the Belleville District until I would be accommodating enough either to die or resign for his benefit, and then he would go to the Senate of the United States too. Now, you remember that during the year 1854, these two worthy gentlemen, Mr. Lincoln and Mr. Trumbull, one an old line Whig and the other an old line Democrat, were hunting for votes to elect a Legislature against the Democratic party. I canvassed the State that year from the time I returned home till the election came off, and spoke in every county that I could reach during that period. In the northern part of the State, I passed Lincoln's ally there, in the person of Fred. Douglass, the negro [the *Times* printed his name and race in capital letters—*ed.*], preaching revolutionary principles, while Lincoln was discussing the same principles down here, and Trumbull a little further down attempting to elect members of the Legislature, and acting in harmony each with the other. I have witnessed the effort made in Chicago by Lincoln's then associates and new supporters to put Fred. Douglass on the stand at a Democratic meeting, to reply to the illustrious Gen. Cass, when he was addressing the people there. [Shame on them. —*Times*] They had that same negro hunting me down, the same as they have a negro canvassing the principal counties of the North in behalf of Lincoln. [Hit him again; he's a disgrace to the white people, &c. —*Times*] Mr. Lincoln knows that when we were at Freeport, at a joint discussion, there was a distinguished colored gentleman there, [laughter —*Tribune* and *Times*] who made a speech that night and the night after, a short distance from Freeport, in favor of Lincoln, and showing how much interest his colored brethren felt in the success of their brother, Abraham Lincoln, [the *Times* substituted "Abe"—*ed.*]. [Laughter. —*Tribune* and *Times*] I have with me now, what I could read if necessary, a speech made by Fred. Douglass in Poughkeepsie, N.Y., to a large convention, in which he called upon all who were friends of negro equality and negro citizenship to rally as one man around Abraham Lincoln, as the chief embodiment of their principles, and by all means to defeat Stephen A. Douglas. [Laughter. —*Tribune;* It can't be done. —*Times*] Thus you find that this Republican party in the northern part of the State had colored gentlemen for their advocates in 1854, as they have now in concert with Lincoln and Trumbull. When, in 1854, I came down to Springfield in October, to attend a State fair, I found the leaders of this party all assembled under the title of an anti-Nebraska meeting. It was Black Republican up North, anti-Nebraska at Springfield, and I found Lovejoy, the high priest of Abolitionism, and Lincoln, one of the leaders who was to call the old line Whigs into the Abolition camp, and Sidney Breese and Gov. Reynolds, all making speeches against the Democratic party, and myself at the same place and on the same occasion. [The *Times* substituted "in the same cause" (They're all birds of a feather, shun them.)—*ed.*] The same men who are now fighting the Democratic party, and other regular Democratic nominees in this State were fighting us then. They didn't then acknowledge that they had become Abolitionists, many of them deny it now.

Breese, and Dougherty, and Reynolds, were then fighting against the Democratic party, under the title of anti-Nebraska Democrats. Now they are fighting against the Democratic party, pretending to be Simonpure Democrats [Laughter. —*Times*], and saying that they are to have every office-holder in Illinois beheaded who prefers the election of Douglas to that of Lincoln, or of the Democratic ticket to this Abolition ticket, either for State office, for the Legislature, for Congress, or for any other office in the State. They canvassed the State against us in 1854, as they are doing now, holding different principles in different localities, but having a common object in view. That was the defeat of all the men holding Union principles in opposition to this Abolition Sectional party. When they assembled at Springfield, having carried the Legislature in their favor, they proceeded to elect a United States Senator. All voted for Mr. Lincoln as their choice, with one or two exceptions. But they couldn't quite elect him. And why couldn't they elect him? Had not Trumbull agreed that he should have Shields' place? Had not the Abolitionists agreed to it? Was not that a solemn compact? Was not that the condition upon which Lincoln was to abolitionize the old Whigs, that he should be the Senator? But still Trumbull, having control of a few abolition Democrats, wouldn't allow them all to vote for Lincoln at any one time, and thus they could run him up almost to election, but not quite[,] and then run him again and drop him down until they wearied him and his friends so that they dropped Lincoln entirely and elected Trumbull in violation of the bargain. [Cheers. —*Times*] Now I desire to offer a bit of testimony, in confirmation of that notorious fact. Col. Jas. H. Matheny of Springfield is, and for twenty years has been, the confidential, personal and political friend and manager for Lincoln. Matheny is at this very day a candidate of the Republican-Abolition party against the gallant Major Thomas L. Harris, in the Springfield district, and is making speeches for Lincoln against me. Now let me read you the testimony of Matheny about this bargain between Lincoln and Trumbull, when they undertook to abolitionize the Whigs and Democrats, only four years ago. Matheny, in a public speech two years ago, being mad because Trumbull played a Yankee trick on Lincoln, explained the whole bargain in a speech which I will read, and the correctness of which Lincoln will not deny. Matheny says:

The Whigs, Abolitionists, Know-Nothings and renegade Democrats, made a solemn compact for the purpose of carrying this State against the Democracy on this plan. 1st, That they all combine and elect Mr. Trumbull to Congress and thereby carry his District for the Legislature in order to throw all the strength that could be obtained into that body against the Democrats. 2nd, That when the Legislature should meet, the officers of that body, such as speaker, clerks, door-keepers &c., would be given to the Abolitionists; and 3d, That the

Whigs were to have the United States Senator. Thus, accordingly, Trumbull was elected in good faith to Congress and his District carried for the Legislature, and when it convened the Abolitionists got all the officers of that body and thus the "bond" was fairly executed. The Whigs on their part demanded the election of Abraham Lincoln to the United States Senate, that the bond might be fulfilled, the other parties to the contract having already secured to themselves all that was called for. But, in the most perfidious manner, they refused to elect Lincoln, and the mean, low-lived, sneaking Trumbull succeeded by pleading all that was required by any party, in thrusting Lincoln aside and foisting himself, an excrescence from the rotten bowels of the Democracy into the United States Senate; and thus it has ever been that an honest man makes a bad bargain when he conspires or contracts with rogues.

Now Lincoln's confidential friend, Matheny, thought that Lincoln conspired and contracted with such rogues as Trumbull and the Abolitionists. [Laughter. —*Tribune;* Great Laughter. —*Times*] I would like to know whether Lincoln thought as well of Trumbull's veracity at the time that Trumbull agreed to go for him for Senator, and then cheated him, as he does now [Renewed laughter. —*Times*] when Trumbull comes forward against me. You could not prove this at that time. You could not prove Trumbull a nice man either by Lincoln or Matheny, or any of Lincoln's friends. They charged everywhere that Trumbull had cheated him in the bargain, and then Lincoln found out, sure enough, [the *Times* added: "that it was a *bad bargain*"—*ed.*] to conspire and contract with rogues. Now, I will explain to you what has been a mystery all over this State and Union, in regard to the reasons for Lincoln's being nominated for the United States Senate by the [the *Times* added: "Black"—*ed.*] Republican State Convention. You know it never was usual for any party in State Conventions to nominate a candidate for Senator. The first time it was ever done was probably this year by the Republican Convention. The Convention was not called for that purpose. It was called to nominate a State ticket, and nearly every man was disgusted when they nominated Lincoln. Archy Williams thought he was entitled to it. Browning felt that he deserved it. John Wentworth thought he must have it. [Ebenezer] Peck thought he deserved it. [Norman] Judd was sure to have it. Palmer was expecting it. To the astonishment of all, Lincoln was nominated by the Convention. [Laughter. —*Times*] He was not only nominated, but he received it unanimously by a resolution declaring that Abraham Lincoln was the first, the last and only choice of the party. How was that? Because they couldn't get Lincoln and his friends to make another bargain with rogues [Laughter. —*Times*] unless the whole party would come up as one man and pledge their honors this time that they would stand by Lincoln first and last and all the time, and that Lovejoy shouldn't cheat Lincoln this time as Trumbull did before. [Laughter. —*Tribune*] And thus it is by the passing of that resolution Lincoln received the universal support of the Abolitionists. Lovejoy is for him. Farnsworth is making speeches for him. Giddings is for him—they are all for him. The negroes are making speeches for him, and he is sure not to be cheated this time, for he would not go into the arrangement until he got the bond for it. And thus you find that Trumbull is compelled now to come out on the stump and get up those false charges against me, and travel all over the State to elect Mr. Lincoln, in order to keep him and his friends quiet about that bargain in which Trumbull cheated them two years ago. Now you see why it is that Lincoln and Trumbull are so mighty fond of each other. [Laughter. —*Tribune;* Tremendous laughter. —*Times*] They have entered into that conspiracy to hunt me down by these attacks on my public character, in order to draw my attention from a fair exposure of the mode by which they attempted to abolitionize the old Whigs and the old Democrats and lead them captive into the Abolition camp. [That's so, and hear, hear. —*Times*] Don't you remember that Lincoln was round here four years ago, making speeches to you, and telling you that you ought to go for that Abolition ticket, and swearing that he was then as good a Whig as he ever was? [Laughter. —*Times*] Trumbull went all over the State making speeches to the old Democrats, trying to coax them into the Abolition camp, swearing by his maker that he was still a good Democrat, and would never desert the Democratic party. [Laughter. —*Times*] But when he got your votes, the Legislature elected was an Abolition Legislature. They passed Abolition resolutions, and they passed Abolition laws, and supported Abolitionists for State and national offices. Now the same game is attempted to be played over again. You know that while Trumbull and Lincoln were thus making captive the old Whigs and Democrats, they had Giddings, the high priest of Abolitionists from Ohio to receive and christen them in the dark cause just as fast as they brought them in. [Hear, hear. —*Times*] Giddings found the converts were so numerous and were brought in from every part of the State, that he had to have assistance, so he sent off to John P. Hale, N. [Nathaniel] P. Banks and other Abolitionists, and they together with Lovejoy and Fred. Douglass made out to baptize the new converts just as fast as Trumbull, and Lincoln, and Breese, and Reynolds, and Douglass. Trumbull goes down to Monroe County; he went there the other day making a speech in favor of Lincoln, and I will show you under what notice the meeting was called. You see they are Black Republicans up north. In Springfield to-day, they daren't call their convention by the name of Republican Convention, but they call all men opposed to the Democracy. When they got down in Monroe County in lower Egypt, Trumbull had his notices in this way:—"A meeting of the Free Democracy will take place in Waterloo, Sept. 13th inst., where Hon. Lyman Trumbull and Jehu Baker will address the people on the political topics of the day. Men of all parties are invited to be present and hear and determine for themselves."—*Monroe Free Democrat.*

Now, did you ever hear of this new party called the Free Democracy? What is the object of changing their name in every county they come to? [To cheat people. —*Times*] One in the North, another in the centre and another in the South. When I used to practice law before my distinguished friend that I recognize in the crowd, and the proof showed that a man charged with horse-stealing had gone by one name in Stephenson County, a second in Sangamon, and was arrested under a third down in Randolph, we thought the fact of changing names was pretty strong proof that he was guilty of the charge made against him. Now, I would like to know why it is that this great Free Soil Abolition party are not willing to have the same name in all parts of the State. [They dare not. —*Times*] Why is it that if the Black Republican party believe that their principles are sound and their cause is just, that they do not have the same principles in the North and in the South—in the East and in the West, wherever the American Flag waves over American soil? [Cheers. —*Times*]

A VOICE—Don't call us Black Republicans.

JUDGE DOUGLAS—Why, sir, if you will go to Waukegan, fifteen miles north of Chicago, you will find a paper with Lincoln's name at the head, and you will find it said at the head of it, this paper is devoted to the cause of Black Republicanism. [Applause. —*Tribune;* Good, hit him again, and cheers. —*Times*] I had a copy of it to carry with me down here into Egypt to let you see by what name they went up there. And their principles vary as much up there as they vary from the name down here. Their principles up there are jet black; [laughter, —*Times*] when you get down into the centre they are a decent colored mulatto [Renewed laughter. —*Times*]; when you get down into lower Egypt they are almost white. [Laughter. —*Tribune;* Shouts of laughter. —*Times*] There were many white sentiments contained in Lincoln's speech down in Jonesboro, and I could not help contrasting them with the speeches of the same distinguished orator in the northern parts of the State. [Hit him again. —*Tribune*] Up there his party say they are for no more slave States under any circumstances; down here they pretend that they are willing to allow the people of each State, when they come into the Union, to do just as they please on the subject of slavery. Up there, you will find Lovejoy, their candidate for Congress in the Bloomington district, and Farnsworth, their candidate for Congress in the district of Chicago, and Washburne, the candidate in the Galena district, all pledged, never under any circumstances will they consent to admit another slave State in this Union, even if the people want it. [That's so. —*Times*] Thus while they there have one set of principles, down here they have another.

Here let me remind Mr. Lincoln of his scriptural quotations, which he has applied to the Federal Government, that a house divided against itself cannot stand. Does he expect this Abolition party to stand, when in one half of the State they advocate one set of principles, and in the other half repudiate them and advocate another? [Laughter. —*Tribune;* Laughter and applause. —*Times*]

I am told I have but eight minutes more. I want to talk about one hour more, but I will make the best that I can of that eight minutes.

Mr. Lincoln has said in his first speech that he was not in favor of the social and political equality of the negro and the white man; but I will now tell you what he has said everywhere at the north. He there said he was not in favor of the political and social equality of the negro, but he would not say up there that he was opposed to negro voting and negro citizenship. He declared his utter opposition to the Dred Scott decision, and advanced as a reason that the Court decided that it was not possible that a negro shall be a citizen under the Constitution of the United States.

Now, if he is opposed to the Dred Scott decision for that reason, he must be in favor of conferring the rights and privileges of citizenship upon the negro. I have been trying to get an answer from him on this point, but I have never yet obtained it, and I will show you why. In nearly every speech he made in the North, he quoted the Declaration of Independence to prove that all men were born free and equal, and that meant the negro as well as the white man; that their equality rested on the Divine law. I will read what he said upon this point.

"I should like," Mr. Lincoln said, "to know if you take this old Declaration which declares that all men are created equal and make exception to it, where will it stop? If one man says it don't mean a negro, why not another say it doesn't mean a white man?" [The *Times,* or Douglas, colloquialized this quotation, and omitted its ringing conclusion: "If that declaration is not the truth let us get the statute book in which we find it and tear it out!"—*ed.*]

Hence, Mr. Lincoln asserted that the Declaration of Independence declared that the negro was the equal of the white man, and that too by divine law, being endowed by his creator with certain inalienable rights. Now if he believes that by the divine law he was our equal, it was certain he should advocate negro citizenship. And when you grant negro citizenship, then you have put them on an equality under the law. [No negro equality for us; down with Lincoln. —*Times*] I say to you, gentlemen, in all frankness, that in my opinion a negro is not a citizen, cannot and ought not to be under the Constitution of the United States, I would not even qualify my opinion, although the Supreme Court in the Dred Scott case say that a negro descended of African parents and imported in this country as a slave is not, cannot and ought not to be a citizen. [That's the doctrine. —*Times*] I say that this Government was created on the white basis by white men for white men and their posterity forever, and should never be administered by any but white men. [Cheers. —*Times*] I declare that a negro ought not to be a citizen whether imported into this country or born here, whether his parents were slave or not. It don't depend upon the question where he was born, or where his parents were placed, but it depends on the fact that the negro belongs to a race incapable of self-government, and for that reason ought not to be put on an equality with the white man. [Applause. —*Tribune;* immense applause. —*Times*] Now, my friends, I am sorry that I have not time to pursue this argument further, which I could have done but for the fact that Mr. Lincoln compelled me to occupy a portion of time in repelling this gross, slanderous falsehood that Trumbull invented and circulated against me. Let me ask you, why should this country divide itself by a geographical line, arraying all men north of it into one great hostile party against all men south of it. Mr. Lincoln tells you in his speech at Springfield that a house divided against itself cannot stand—that the government cannot endure permanently divided into free States and slave States—that they must be all one way or all other, or this government cannot endure permanently. Why, let me ask, cannot this government endure forever divided into free and slave States, as our fathers made it? When this government was established by Washington and Madison and Jay and Hamilton, and the sages of that day, it was composed of free States and slave States, bound together by our common Constitution. We have existed and prospered from that day to this, divided into these free and slave States.

During that whole period, we have increased with a rapidity never yet known, in wealth, in the expansion of territory, in the elements of power and greatness, until we have become the first nation on the face of the globe. Why cannot we thus continue to prosper if we live and continue to execute the government in that spirit and in accordance with those principles upon which our fathers placed it[?] During that whole period Divine Providence has smiled upon us and showered upon this nation richer and more abundant blessings than were ever conferred upon any people on the face of the globe. [Loud applause. —*Tribune;* Mr. Douglas' time here expired, and he stopped on the minute, amidst deafening applause. —*Times*]

[As Mr. Lincoln stepped forward, the crowd sent up three rousing cheers. —*Tribune*]

FELLOW-CITIZENS: It follows, as a matter of course, that a half hour answer to a speech of an hour and a half can be but a very hurried one. I shall only be able to take hold of a few of the points that have been suggested by Judge Douglas and give them a rapid attention, while I shall have to omit others altogether for want of time.

Judge Douglas has said to you, I believe, that he has not been able to get from me an answer to the question as whether I am in favor of negro citizenship. So far as I know, the Judge never asked me the question before [Applause. —*Tribune*], and he will have no occasion to ever ask it again, for I tell him very frankly, I am not in favor of it. [Renewed applause. —*Tribune*] That furnishes me the occasion of saying a few words upon that subject. I mentioned in my Jonesboro speech, incidentally, that the Supreme Court had decided that the negro could not possibly be made a citizen, and without saying what was my ground of complaint in regard of it, Judge Douglas has from that thing manufactured nearly everything that he has said about me as to my disposition to produce equality among the black and white races. [Laughter and applause. —*Tribune*, adding: "If any one will read my speech, he will find I mentioned that as one of the points decided in the course of the Supreme Court opinions, but I did not state what objection I had to it."—*ed.*] Judge Douglas takes upon himself to tell the people what was my objection to it, when I did not tell them myself. [Loud applause and laughter. —*Tribune*] Now, my opinion is, that the different States have the power to make a negro a citizen under the constitution of the United States, if they choose. The Dred Scott decision decides that they have not. If the State of Illinois had that power I should be against the exercise of it. [Cries of "good," "good," and applause. —*Tribune*] That is all there is of that. That is the whole thing.

Now then, again. Judge Douglas has told you that he heard my speeches north and my speeches south; that he had heard me at Ottawa and at Freeport in the north, and he had recently heard me at Jonesboro in the south, and that there was a very different character in the speeches made in the north and south. I will not charge upon the Judge that he willfully misrepresents me about that, but I call upon any right

minded man to read those speeches, and I dare him to find any difference between the speeches [the *Tribune* added: "north and South"—
ed.].

While I am here, perhaps, I ought to say a word or two—may have
time to say a word or two in regard to this latter portion of Judge
Douglas' speech—by the way—that declaration [the *Tribune* substituted
"declamation"—*ed.*] in regard to my having said that I did not believe
this government could endure permanently half slave and half free. I
have said that I did not say it without having something to base upon
it that to me seemed reasonable. Let me ask a few questions. Do we
have any peace upon the slavery question? Do we have any peace upon
it? [No, no. —*Tribune*] When are we going to have any peace upon it
if it is kept up just now as it is? [Never. —*Tribune*] How are we going
to have peace upon it? Why, to be sure, if we will just keep quiet and
allow Judge Douglas and his friends to march on [the *Tribune* added: "in
their present career"—*ed.*] and plant slavery in all the States [*Tribune*
added: "and we acquiesce in it"] we shall have peace. [*Tribune* added:
"But let me ask Judge Douglas how is he going to get the people to do
that?" (Applause.)] They have been fussing over it for forty years in the
Missouri compromise, in the annexation of Texas, in the acquisition of
territory acquired from Mexico, in the war with Mexico, leaving [*sic*]
to the compromise of 1850, and when it was then settled forever, as
both great political parties said it was, that forever turned out to be two
[four—*ed.*] years [Laughter. —*Tribune*], when Judge Douglas re-
opened it in 1854. [Immense applause, cries of "Hit him again," &c.
—*Tribune*] When is it likely to come to an end? Why, he introduced his
measure then for the purpose of putting an end to slavery agitation; he
promised it would be settled, and he never made a speech [the *Tribune*
added, "since"—*ed.*] until he got into a quarrel with the President about
the Lecompton constitution, in which he has not declared that we were
just at the end of the slavery agitation. [Laughter and cheers. —*Tribune*]
He tells us again that it is all over now. The people of Kansas have voted
down the Lecompton constitution. How is it over? Why, that has only
put an end to one of the settlements of the slavery agitation. [The
Tribune added "one of these 'final settlements.' " (Renewed laughter.)—
ed.] Is Kansas in the Union? Has she got a constitution that she is likely
to come in under? Is not the slavery question to be settled yet? I know
that at this age of the world we can no more see where the end of the
slavery agitation is than we can see the end of the world itself. Since the

introduction of the Kansas-Nebraska bill, 4½ [years] have gone by, and if the end of it comes ever, we are just 4½ years nearer it, and so we are 4½ years nearer the end of the world, and we can as nearly see the end of the world as we can the end of slavery agitation, [Applause. —*Tribune*] for in point of fact, it is not wound up in Kansas. If Kansas was swallowed up, and only a large hole was left in her place, it would not be settled, and now I say there is no way to put an end to slavery agitation among us, but to put it back on the basis that our fathers put it on, [applause. —*Tribune*] restricting it to the old States and prohibiting it in the territories, [Tremendous and prolonged cheering; cries of "That's the doctrine," "Good," "Good," &c. —*Tribune*] thus the public mind being in the belief that it is in the course of ultimate extinction. [The *Tribune* added: "That is one way of putting an end to the slavery agitation." (Applause.)—*ed.*]

The other way is for us to surrender and let Judge Douglas and his friends plant slavery in all the States, and submit to it as one of the common matters of property among us, like horses and cattle. That would be another way to settle the question, but while it stands in the way of progress as now, I have ventured the opinion that I state again this evening [the *Tribune* added: "that we will have no end to the slavery agitation until it takes one turn or the other." (Applause.)—*ed.*].

I do not mean to say that when it takes a turn toward ultimate extinction, that is to come in a day or a year, nor do I suppose that it could be brought to ultimate extinction in less than a hundred years, it would be carried on as is best for the white and the black in God's own good time I have no doubt. [Applause. —*Tribune*] But, I am wasting more time on this than I intended to.

Now then in regard to this matter of Trumbull and myself making a bargain to sell out the entire Whig and Democratic parties in 1854. Judge Douglas brings forward no other evidence than a speech that James H. Matheny is said to have made in 1856, in which he told a "cock and bull story" of that sort on the same moral principle that Judge Douglas uses it to-day. [Loud applause. —*Tribune*] This is the third time that I have told Judge Douglas to his teeth [the *Tribune* substituted "face"—*ed.*] that there is not a word of truth in it. [Thunders of applause. —*Tribune*] He does not deal with me on that subject as Trumbull and I deal with him. He does not bring the record. There is no record for him to bring. [Cheers and laughter. —*Tribune*] He does not bring them at all. Now when he asks if I was ready to endorse

Trumbull's veracity when he broke a bargain with me—well if he had broken a bargain I should not perhaps be ready to endorse his veracity, but I am ready to endorse his veracity now, because neither in that thing nor in anything for the many years that I have known him, have I known Lyman Trumbull to prevaricate or tell a falsehood, large or small, on anything. [Great cheering. —*Tribune*] It is for that reason that I endorse Trumbull so as I believe the truth of that thing.

A VOICE [Mr. James Brown, Douglas Post Master—*Tribune*]—What does Ford say of him? [A reference to *History of Illinois from its Commencement as a State in 1818 to 1847,* an 1854 book by onetime Illinois governor Thomas Ford—*ed.*]

MR. LINCOLN—What does Ford say about him, some gentleman asks me. My recollection is that Ford speaks of him in very disrespectful terms, and a good deal worse of Douglas. [Roars of laughter and applause. —*Tribune*] I made that answer off-hand by my friend asking me a question, without having referred to Ford's history upon the subject. I refer you to the history for an examination. [Cheers. —*Tribune*]

Now Judge Douglas complains at very considerable length about a disposition there is upon the part of Trumbull and myself to attack him personally—to make some attack upon him personally. I want to attend to that a little. I don't want to be subject to the imputation of illiberality of dealing with an adversary. I would despise myself if I supposed that either in a court or a political discussion I was capable of dealing with less liberality than I was receiving.

You heard Judge Douglas come here to-day and make a reference, that he dare not make in specific shape, about the Mexican war. He knows, in regard to that Mexican war, the more respectable of the newspapers of his own party of the State have been compelled to take it back and say that it was a lie. [Continued and vociferous applause. —*Tribune*]

[Mr. Lincoln here stepped back, caught Colonel Ficklin by the left lapel of his coat, and literally dragged him to the front of the stand. —*Times; Tribune* substituted "led him forward and said."]

Now I did not dream to do anything with Mr. Ficklin more than to present him personally to your faces, and tell you that he knows it personally. He had a seat by the side of my own when I was in Congress, and he knows that whenever there was an effort made to approve the object of the war, I opposed it; I never denied that. And he knows that whenever there was a call for supplies for the soldiers, I gave the same vote that he and Judge Douglas gave. [Loud applause. —*Tribune*]

MR. FICKLIN—I wish to say this in reference to this matter: Mr. Lincoln and myself are just as good friends as Judge Douglas and myself. In reference to this Mexican war, my recollection is that on the Ashmun resolutions, in which it was declared that the Mexican war was unconstitutional, and commenced by the President of the United States, my friend Lincoln voted for the resolution.

MR. LINCOLN—That is the truth. Now you all remember that that was a resolution censuring the President for the manner in which the war was begun. Now, out of that some of our "personal friends" have been charging that I voted against the supplies, and thus starved the soldiers. The Springfield *Register* [also a Douglas organ—*ed.*] cautioned the Chicago *Times,* when the charge was first made, that the charge was made against me which should be brought against John Henry, who was in Congress before me, and now that same John Henry is making speeches most furiously for Douglas. [Loud applause. —*Tribune*]

I mention this for another purpose. He might have brought it forward as a sort of set-off to his reasoning because I had been dealing in something of the kind before. This is not the first time that he has said this thing, he did it in the opening speech that we made at Ottawa [the *Tribune* added: "the first time we met face to face; and in the opening speech that Judge Douglas made, he attacked me in regard to a matter"—*ed.*], it is ten years old; is not he a beauty to be whining about people making charges against him only two years old. [Cheers. —*Tribune*]

I know one other thing. The Judge thinks that it is altogether wrong that there should be—that I should have dwelt upon this matter of Trumbull's upon this occasion. I gave you my apology for doing so in the opening speech, perhaps I did not fix your attention. I said in the opening speech that when he had followed Trumbull at a place I had spoken at the next day, I had two or three times said I had a confidence in Trumbull's veracity, and had intelligence enough to investigate a question, and my opinion was he would be able to prove all that he stated. I said nothing more about it for weeks, nor merely for a day, and perhaps a month I had passed by that thing without saying one word at all. I find, at Jacksonville, Judge Douglas, in the plenitude of his power, is not willing to answer Trumbull and let me alone, but he goes on to say: that he will hold Lincoln responsible. But, what was Lincoln to do? [Laughter. —*Tribune*] What was Lincoln to do on that question? Did not Lincoln do right? I ask you if Lincoln did not do right, when the first opportunity he had he met Douglas here and told him he was ready for the responsibility? [Enthusiastic cheering, "good, good. Hurrah for Lincoln!" —*Tribune*, which added: "I ask a candid audience whether in doing thus Judge Douglas was not the assailant rather than I?" ("Yes, yes, hit him again!")] Having taken that responsibility, I ask the attention of this audience as to whether I have succeeded in sustaining that charge, ["Yes, yes, Hit him again!" —*Tribune*] and whether Douglas has succeeded in rebutting it? [Loud cries of "no, no." —*Tribune*]

You heard me ask him to tell me which of these pieces of evidence was a forgery. I asked him if it was the Toombs bill, ["No," "no." —*Tribune*] if it was his reported bill; ["No," "no," "no." —*Tribune*] I asked him if it was the quotation that Toombs made from Bigler; I asked him if it was the [*Globe—ed.*] quotations that Trumbull made from his, Douglas' speeches that were forgeries. Does he say it was, any word of it? [No, no, no. —*Tribune*, which added: "Does he say the quotations from his own speech are forgeries? ('No,' 'no,' 'no.') Does he say this transcript from Trumbull's speech is a forgery? (Loud cries of 'No, no' 'He didn't deny one of them.')"] Now, I would like to know where each piece of the story is true, how it come [*sic*] out that the whole is a lie in the end. [Great cheers and laughter. —*Tribune*] I take it these people have some sense, and I take it this people see that he is playing the game of the fish [the *Tribune* substituted "cuttle fish" (Laughter.)—*ed.*], that he is playing the game of a little fish that has no means of defence but by throwing out a little black fluid so that its enemies cannot see it. [Roars of laughter. —*Tribune*, which added: "Ain't the Judge playing the cuttle-fish?" ("Yes, yes," and cheers.)] I ask that you shall read the Judge's speech at Jacksonville as you will have an opportunity to do, that you will read his speech made here to-day, and you shall watch out and see which piece of evidence he denies, when he tells you that it is all a forgery. Then I come to the original question. If each is true, how is it possible that the whole is a falsehood? [Loud and prolonged cheers. —*Tribune*] That is what I want to know. He came up here to meet that charge of Trumbull, and reads from the *Congressional Globe* to show that on his motion it was stricken out. He need not have taken that trouble. I had told you that; it was in regard to that very thing that I told you he had dropped the cub. [Roars of laughter. —*Tribune*] Trumbull had showed you that by introducing it into the bill it was his cub. [Laughter. —*Tribune*], and now he comes up and calls Trumbull a liar, because he does not mention that he struck it out. [The *Tribune* added: "Suppose that were the case, does it answer Trumbull?" (No, no.)—*ed*.] It is like as if I say you are here to-day and you undertake to prove me a liar by showing that you were here [the *Tribune* substituted "in Matoon"—*ed*.] yesterday. [Laughter. —*Tribune*] The same as if I say you took your hat off your head and you prove me a liar because you put it on your head a minute or two afterwards. [Roars of laughter. —*Tribune*, adding: "That is the whole force of Judge Douglas' argument."]

Now, then, I want to come back to my original question. Trumbull says that Douglas got a bill in his hands that had a provision in it for submitting the constitution to be made to the vote of the people of Kansas. Does Douglas deny that fact? [Cries of "No, no." —*Tribune*] Does he deny that the provision that Trumbull reads as put in that bill, ["No, no." —*Tribune*] then Trumbull says that he struck it out. Does he deny that? ["No, no, no." —*Tribune*] Then I have a right to repeat the question upon Judge Douglas, why he took it out? [Immense applause. —*Tribune*] Bigler has said that there was a combination among certain senators—by which it was agreed to pass that bill and not have it submitted to the people. But we prove by another source that about that time Douglas came into the Senate with that provision stricken out of the bill. It is almost impossible not to believe that a thing done so agreeably to the thing agreed upon, was not done as agreed upon, and while we don't know that it was absolutely so, we say it looks so much like it that we have a right to call upon the man that did that thing to tell us what his reason was, [Great cheers. —*Tribune*] and if he will not tell us that true reason, he stands up in the attitude of a man accused of theft, who has recently stolen goods in his possession, who says he did not steal them, but who won't tell where he got them. [Immense applause. —*Tribune*] Not only this, but he tells us alterations or modifications in the bill had been made by him on consultation with Toombs, he says that he did it. To-day he says that there were certain modifications put in the bill in committee, that he did not vote for. We ask you to remember that whether certain amendments were made in the bill that he disapproved, by a majority of the committee, who put them there. We thank him to remember that he has told us that the alterations were made by him on consultation with Toombs. [Enthusiastic cheering. —*Tribune*] We had his word that the amendments and alterations were made by him and not by the committee. ["That's so," "good, good." —*Tribune*]

And now I ask you again, what is the reason that Judge Douglas is so exceeding chary about coming to the exact question? What is the reason that he will not tell you that that amendment was made by the committee over his head? What is the reason that he won't tell you how it was made, by whom it was made, or that it was made at all? He can explain all these things, and unexplained, I insist that we have the right to infer, as I do infer, that Judge Douglas did understand that it was the purpose of his party under that Nebraska matter, that a constitution should be formed and Kansas should come into the Union under a constitution without its being submitted to the people. ["That's it." —*Tribune*] If he will explain it and give a better reason, that explanation will be satisfactory, but until he does that—until he gives a more plausible reason than this one I suggest to him that it will not avail him at all if he stands up before an audience and swells himself and takes on dignity and calls people liars. [Great applause and laughter. —*Tribune*]

Why, sir, there is not a word in all Trumbull's speech that depends on Trumbull's veracity at all. Not one word. He has only arrayed the evidence and told you what he thinks follows as a matter of reasoning, there is not a thing in the whole speech depends on his veracity. [The *Tribune* concluded with: "If you have ever studied geometry, you remember that by a course of reasoning Euclid proves that all the angles in a triangle are equal to two right angles. Euclid has shown you how to work it out. Now, if you undertake to disprove that proposition, and to show that it is erroneous, would you prove it to be false by calling Euclid a liar? (Roars of laughter and enthusiastic cheers.)] They tell me that my time is out, and therefore I close.

The *Tribune* added: "When Mr. Lincoln had concluded, three cheers were given spontaneously by the crowd. . . ." In assembling his debates scrapbook, Lincoln here added (with the headlines in his own words): "Extract from Mr. Trumbull's Speech at Alton, Referred to by Lincoln in His Opening at Charleston," and "Extract from Mr. Douglas' Speech Made at Jacksonville, & Referred to by Mr. Lincoln in His Opening at Charleston." These long extracts were then published in the first book edition of the debates, and have appeared in most subsequent editions since. But they are omitted here because period newspaper transcripts did not include them.—*ed.*]

THE FIFTH JOINT
DEBATE AT
GALESBURG

Thursday, October 7, 1858

· THE SCENE ·

THE "IMMENSE" AUDIENCE that massed on the campus of Knox College in Galesburg for the fifth Lincoln-Douglas meeting was by some accounts the largest of the debates. It might have been even larger had not the perils of nineteenth-century rail travel conspired with the extremes of autumn prairie weather to inhibit attendance.

A twenty-two-car special train from Peoria, overflowing with 2,000 Galesburg-bound passengers, ran into mechanical problems that day, failing to arrive until the debate was nearly over. And after a day of downpours on October 6, the seventh dawned raw and cold. A strong sun failed to melt the "Arctic frost," and cold winds whipped banners into shreds and sent Lincoln and Douglas signs flying "pell mell all over town." But even bad weather, a journalist declared, failed to dampen the "political ardor."

By midday, between 15,000 and 20,000 spectators had converged on the college from all directions. An eyewitness recalled the outskirts of town cluttered with the "tents of farmers, who had come with their families and camped on the evening previous." As usual, they came aboard excursion trains, on horseback, on wagons, and on foot. The local population of 5,500 were roused at daybreak by the ringing of cannon, and students woke up early to put finishing touches on banners they planned to present to both of the candidates when they arrived.

Douglas entered the scene first, aboard an eleven-car train that pulled into the depot at ten a.m. Greeted by an artillery guard, he was ushered into Galesburg in a carriage drawn by six white horses. Lincoln followed two hours later in a procession of buggies and wagons "about long enough," one observer testified, "to reach around the town and tie [it] in a bowknot."

The war of words that afternoon was preceded by a war of images. "Lithographs of Douglas abounded," a journalist observed, but since the lesser-known Lincoln had not yet inspired mass-produced commercial portraits of his own, local artists filled the void with a dazzling display of original cartoon and caricature. One flattering portrait showed "ABE LINCOLN THE CHAMPION OF FREEDOM." Another depicted a mournful-looking Douglas, locked out of the U.S. Capitol on January 1 next, "blubbering": "Lincoln has got *my place.*"

Around two-thirty p.m., the speakers were driven to the college grounds aboard individual horse-drawn carriages riding side by side. The platform had been moved at the last minute from an open area on campus to a spot alongside the eastern front of the college building, to shield the speakers from the wind. According to legend, the candidates had to climb through the main-floor windows to reach the stand, prompting Lincoln to remark: "Well, at last I have gone through college!" Now both men looked out on a sea of faces, many of them young—students from both Knox College and Lombard University crowded the audience—and most of them pro-Lincoln. This northwestern Illinois village, midway between Peoria and the Iowa state border, was not only strongly Republican but an old stop on the Underground Railroad. Galesburg also boasted both a factory and a foundry, as well as two railroad lines. Proudly advertising the typical Lincoln coalition there, which Douglas had been ridiculing on the stump, one supporter held up a banner proclaiming: "Small-fisted Farmers, Mud Sills of Society, Greasy Mechanics, for A. Lincoln." A huge banner draped from the

building above the platform echoed: "KNOX COLLEGE FOR LINCOLN."
As Douglas surveyed the scene, he took a throat lozenge from a
small box and offered one to Lincoln.

As historian David Zarefsky has interpreted the oratory that
followed, "beginning in Galesburg, the debaters took on a new tone,
with candidates addressing matters of principle." The unedited
transcripts in fact show that the exchanges were sometimes shriller
than the polished reports afterwards indicated. But Zarefsky is
correct in pointing out that in the Galesburg encounter, moral
questions were given prolonged and revealing attention.

Douglas spent some of his opening hour on narrower issues,
protesting, for example, that he and his supporters had been
victimized by patronage punishment as a result of his break with the
Buchanan administration over Kansas. He reminded the antislavery
audience that Lincoln had earlier spoken out *against* negro rights in
Charleston, charging it proved that his rival regularly changed his
views to suit his audience. "His creed," taunted Douglas, "can't
travel."

Lincoln seized the high ground in his rebuttal by assailing
Douglas's own admission that he did not much care "whether
slavery is voted up or down" in the new territories. To promote
popular sovereignty without a moral rationale, he declared, revealed
Douglas as craven. Slavery, he countered, was "a moral and political
wrong." There was no inconsistency in his speeches at Jonesboro
and Charleston, Lincoln added, to cheers. He believed that "in the
right to life, liberty, and the pursuit of happiness," blacks were "our
equals."

Douglas reiterated in his rejoinder that Lincoln could not be held
to a "common standard in the different portions of the state." And
he continued to taunt Lincoln over his old, anti–Mexican War
"Spot Resolutions."

The Republican press hailed the Galesburg encounter as an
incontrovertible Lincoln victory. "Douglas actually foamed at the
mouth," laughed a pro-Lincoln paper from Quincy, the site of the
next debate, conceding: "It *may* have been the milk that he imbibed
while sojourning in Egypt." But the Democratic correspondents
hardly admitted to defeat at Galesburg. The *Times* informed its
readers in Chicago that Douglas had made a "great success" there,
while Lincoln supporters had been compelled to wrap their hapless

candidate "in flannels . . . to restore the circulation of blood in his almost inanimate body." One correspondent admitted that the strong winds buffeting Galesburg that day "rendered talking difficult" and made it impossible "for the speakers at times to make themselves heard at all." One young pro-Lincoln eyewitness claimed that even though Douglas tried to hold the crowd with displays of "violent" temper, "a white foam" gathering "upon his lips," the audience "gradually broke away and scattered" during his final remarks.

To the New York *Herald*, it hardly mattered. The discussion, they lamented, had by then "degenerated into the merest twaddle upon quibbles . . . and mutual recrimination of the most vulgar sort."

Galesburg press reports also reinvigorated the debate over conflicting transcripts, the Republican *Press and Tribune* charging three days later that Lincoln had been misrepresented on the pages of the rival *Times* by "two phonographic puffers imported from abroad." Douglas, they railed, "instructs them what to say and how to distort and pervert what his antagonist may say, and he pays them for these dishonorable services." A close comparison of the two transcripts, however, shows only that the respective papers presented the opposition in far more natural style than they did the candidate of their choice. Both papers missed an occasional sentence, and the *Tribune* failed to record rowdy crowd disturbances that interrupted both Lincoln and Douglas in midspeech. But even partisan stenographers could err. Whereas the *Times* heard Lincoln describe a group of Douglas supporters here as "cozy," the *Tribune* recorded it as "crazy." Preparing the Galesburg transcript for publication in book form, however, Lincoln reverted to the *Times* version, changing "crazy" back again to "cozy." In this case, the Democrats, not the Republicans, apparently heard him correctly.

Following are the *Tribune* version of Douglas's words and the *Times* version of Lincoln's.

MR. DOUGLAS' OPENING SPEECH

[When Senator Douglas appeared on the stand he was greeted with three tremendous cheers. —*Times*]

LADIES AND GENTLEMEN—Four years ago I appeared before the people of Knox County for the purpose of defending my political action upon the Compromise measures of 1850, and the passage of the Kansas–Nebraska Bill in 1854. Those of you who are now present will bear in mind that I placed my defense on the support of these two measures upon the fact that both rested upon a great fundamental principle, that the people of each State, each Territory have the right, and should be permitted to exercise the right, of regulating their own domestic affairs in their own way, subject to no other limitation than that which the Constitution of the United States imposes upon them. I then called upon the people of Illinois to decide whether that principle was right or wrong. If that great principle of self-government be right, then the Compromise measures of 1850 were right, and consequently the Kansas Nebraska Bill, based on the same principle, must necessarily have been right. [That's so, and cheers. —*Times*] The Kansas Nebraska Bill declared in so many words that it was the true interest and meaning of the act not to legislate slavery into any State or Territory, nor to exclude it therefrom, but to leave the people thereof perfectly free to form and regulate their own domestic institutions in their own way, subject only to the Constitution of the United States. For the last four years I have devoted all my time in private and in public to commend that principle to the whole American people. Whatever else may be said in condemnation or support of my political course, I apprehend that no honest man will doubt the fidelity with which under all circumstances, I have stood by that principle. During the last year a question arose in the Congress of the United States whether or not that principle was not being violated by the admission of Kansas into the Union under the Lecompton Constitution. In my opinion, the attempt to force Kansas into the Union under that Constitution was a gross violation of the principle enunciated in the Compromise measures of 1850, and the Kansas–Nebraska Bill in 1854. For that reason I led off in the fight against the Lecompton Constitution—conducted that fight until the effort was abandoned of forcing Kansas into the Union under it. During the whole of the fight, I can appeal to all men, friends and foes,

Democrats and Republicans, northern men and southern men, that I carried the banner aloft, and never allowed it to trail in the dust, and never lowered the flag until victory perched upon our banner [the *Times* substituted "arms"—*ed.*]. [Cheers! —*Times*]

When the Lecompton Constitution was defeated, then the question arose in the minds of those who then defended it what they should next resort to in order to carry their views. They devised the measure known as the "English Bill." They then granted political pardon and general amnesty to all men who had fought against the Lecompton Constitution, provided they would support the English Bill. I for one did not choose to accept the pardon nor to avail myself of the amnesty granted on that condition. The fact, however, that the supporters of the Lecompton Constitution were willing to forgive all differences of opinion up to that time in the event of supporting the English Bill, is an admission that to be opposed to Lecompton did not quite impair a man's position in the Democratic party.

Now the question arises, what was the English Bill which certain men now attempt to make a test of political orthodoxy in this country? It provided in substance that the Lecompton Constitution should be sent back to the people of Kansas, and subjected to vote in August last on the question of admission under that constitution, and in the event the people of Kansas rejected the Lecompton Constitution, Kansas was to be kept out of the Union until she had 93,420 inhabitants. I was in favor of sending the constitution back in order to enable the people of Kansas to say whether or not it was their act and deed—whether it embodied their will. But the other proposition, that they should be punished for rejecting the Lecompton Constitution by being kept out of the Union until they should double and treble their inhabitants, I never did and never would sanction by my vote. The reasons why I could not sanction that proposition is to be found in this fact, that by the English bill, if the people of Kansas would only have agreed to come into the Union as a slaveholding State, under the Lecompton Constitution, then they were to be admitted with 35,000 people. But if they insisted upon having a free State, as they had a right to do, then they were to be punished by being kept out of the Union until they had nearly three times that number. I then said in my place in the Senate what I now say to you—whenever Kansas has population enough for a slave state, she has enough for a free State. [That's it, and cheers. —*Times*]

A Voice—Good for you.

JUDGE DOUGLAS—I never yet have given a vote, and I never intend to record a vote by which I will make an odious and unjust distinction between the different States of the Union. [Applause. —*Times*] I hold it to be a fundamental principle in our republican form of government, that all States of this Union, old and new, free and slave, stand on an exact equality. Equality among the States is the cardinal principle on which all of our institutions rest. Whenever, therefore, you make an odious distinction by which you say that a slave State may be admitted into the Union with 35,000, but a free State does not come in until it has 93,000 or 100,000, you are throwing the whole weight of the federal government into the scale of one class of States against the other. Nor do I sanction the doctrine that a free State may be admitted with 35,000, but a slave State should be kept out until it has the 93,000. I am willing now, I have always declared my willingness in the Senate, to adopt the rule that no Territory shall ever become a State until it has the requisite population for a member of Congress, according to the then existing ratio. But while I was willing to adopt that general rule, I was not willing and would not consent to make an exception of Kansas as a punishment for her obstinacy in demanding the right to do as she pleased in the formation of her constitution.

It is proper that I should here remark that my opposition to the Lecompton Constitution did not rest upon the ground of the peculiar provision it has upon the subject of slavery. I held then, and I hold now, that if the people of Kansas wanted a slave State, it was their right to make one, and be received into the Union under it. If, on the contrary, they wanted a free State, it was their right to do so, and no man should have opposed them on that account. I hold to that great principle of self-government which asserts the right of every people to decide for themselves the nature and character of the institutions and the fundamental law under which they are to live. But the effort was made, and is now being made by certain postmasters and other federal office-holders, to make a test of faith on the support of the English Bill. They are making speeches—these postmasters are—all over the State against me, and in favor of Lincoln, either directly or indirectly, because I would not sanction that odious discrimination between free and slave States by voting for the English Bill.

But while that English Bill is made a test in Illinois for the purpose of breaking down the Democratic organization in this State, how is it in other States? Go to Indiana, and there you find that Mr. English himself, the author of the English Bill, has been forced by public opinion, as a candidate for re-election, to abandon his own daring project, and pledge himself to vote for the admission of Kansas at once, whenever she forms a Constitution in pursuance of law, and ratifies it by the votes of her own people. Not only is that the case with English himself, but I am informed that every Democratic candidate in the State of Indiana takes the same ground. Pass to Ohio, and there you find that [William S.] Groesbeck, and [George H.] Pendleton, and [Samuel S.] Cox [all congressmen—*ed.*] and all the other anti-Lecompton Constitution men who stood shoulder to shoulder against that Lecompton Constitution, and who voted for the English Bill, now repudiate it, and take the same ground that I do on that question. So it is with the Joneses [Congressmen Jehu G. Jones and Owen Jones—*ed.*] and others in Pennsylvania. And so it is with every other anti-Lecompton Democrat in all the Free States of America. They now abandon that darling project, and come back to the true Democratic platform which I proclaimed at the time in the Senate, and upon which the Democracy of Illinois now stands. And yet you are told that while every other Democrat in America, Lecompton and Anti-Lecompton—I mean in the Free States—has abandoned the English Bill, yet it is to be a test on me, while the power and patronage of government is all exerted to elect men opposed to it in the other States. My political offence, then, consists in not having first pledged myself by voting for that English Bill to keep Kansas out until she had ninety-three thousand inhabitants, and then come home, turn round and violate the pledge, and repudiate the law, and take the opposite ground. I did not choose to give that pledge, because I did not intend to carry out that principle. I never intend, for the sake of conciliating the friends of power, to pledge myself to do that which I do not intend to perform. And now I submit the question to you as my constituency, whether I was not right in resisting the Lecompton Constitution, and consequently in resisting the English Bill? [Cries of "Yes, yes." —*Tribune;* An universal "Yes," from the crowd. —*Times*] I repeat, that I opposed the Lecompton Constitution because it was not the act and deed of the people of Kansas. I opposed it because it was not the will of that people. I deny the right of any power on earth, under our system of government, to force a constitution on an unwilling people. [Applause. —*Tribune;* Hear, hear; that's the doctrine and cheers. —*Times*]

There was a time when some men could believe that the Lecompton

Constitution was the will of the people of Kansas, but that time has passed by. The question was referred to the people of Kansas last August, and there at the polls, at a fair election, the people rejected the Lecompton Constitution by eight or ten to one against it. Since the Lecompton Constitution was voted down by that overwhelming majority, no man can hereafter pretend that it ever was the act and deed of that people. [That's so; and cheers. —*Times*] And yet I submit the question to you whether if it had not been for me, that Constitution could not have been crammed down the throats of that people against their consent. ["That's so," and applause. —*Tribune;* It would, it would. Hurra for Douglas; three cheers for Douglas, &c. —*Times*] While you would all, at least ninety-nine out of every hundred of the people here present, would agree that I was right in defeating that project, yet you can use the fact that I did defeat it by doing right, as a means of trying to break me down, and put another man in my place in the Senate of the United States. [Applause. —*Tribune;* No, no, you'll be returned; three cheers, &c. —*Times*] The very men that acknowledged that I was right in defeating the Lecompton Constitution now form an alliance with the postmasters, with the federal officers, with the professed Lecompton men to defeat me because I did right. [It can't be done. —*Times*] My political opponents have no hope on earth. Mr. Lincoln would never dream that he had a chance of success but for the aid he is receiving from the federal officers, that is exerted against me in revenge for my having defeated the Lecompton Constitution. Now let me ask you what do you think of a political organization which will try to make an unholy and unnatural combination to beat a man merely because he was right. [Shame on it. —*Times*] Yet you know such to be the fact. You know the axe of proscription [the *Times* had "axe of decapitation and terror of proscription"—*ed.*] is suspended over the head of every Democratic office holder in Illinois, unless he goes for the Republican ticket against me and my Democratic associates. [Applause. —*Tribune;* The people are with you. Let them threaten, &c. —*Times*] I could find instances in Galesburg and at every other post office in this vicinity where men were stricken down for having first discharged their duties faithfully and secondly, supported the regular Democratic ticket in this State in the right. My friends, I know that political parties are prone to avail themselves of all the means in their power to carry the elections when they think they have got a chance, and the Republican party, if this one chance was taken from them, they would never have another, and their hopes would be blasted.

Now let me ask you whether or not this country has any interest in sustaining this organization known as the Republican party? That Republican party is unlike all other political organizations in this country. All other parties have been National in their character. All others have avowed their principles alike in the free States and in the slave States, and avowed them in Kentucky as well as in Illinois, in Louisiana as well as in Massachusetts. Such was the case with the old Whig party; such was the case, and now is, with the Democratic party. Whig and Democrats could proclaim their principles boldly and fearlessly in the North and in the South, in the East and in the West, wherever the American Constitution ruled, or the American flag waved over American soil. But now you have a sectional organization, a body appealing to the Northern section against the Southern section, a party appealing to Northern hopes, Northern spirits, Northern ambition and Northern prejudice, against Southern people, and Southern States, and Southern institutions. They hope to be able to connect the Northern States into one great sectional party, and inasmuch as the Northern section is the stronger, that the stronger section will out-vote and control and govern the weaker section. And hence you find that the Republican leaders now make speeches advocating principles and measures which cannot be advocated in any slaveholding State in this Union. What Republican from Galesburg can travel into Kentucky and carry his principles with him across the Ohio River? [No. —*Times*] What Republican from Massachusetts can visit the Old Dominion without leaving his principles behind when he crosses Mason and Dixon's line?

Now, permit me to say to you in all good humor, but in all sincerity, that no political creed is sound which cannot be proclaimed fearlessly in every State of this Union wherever the American Constitution is the supreme law of the land. ["That's so," and cheers. —*Times*] And we find that this Republican party is unable to proclaim its principles alike in the North and in the South, in the free States and in the slave States, but they cannot proclaim them in the same sense, and give them the same meaning in all parts of the same State. My friend Lincoln, here, finds it extremely difficult to manage a debate in the central part of this State, where there is a mixture of men from the North and the South. In the extreme North he can advocate as bold and radical Abolitionism as even Giddings, or Lovejoy, or Garrison have enunciated. When you get down South he claims then to be an old line Whig, [laughter

—*Tribune;* great laughter, —*Times*] that he is the disciple of Henry Clay, ["Singleton says he defeated Clay's nomination for the Presidency," and cries of "That's so," —*Times*] [Illinois Democrat James W. Single-ton was a former Whig—*ed.*] adhering to the old Whig creed, and has nothing whatever to do with Abolitionism, or with Negro citizenship ["Hurrah for Douglas." —*Times*] or Negro equality. I once hinted this same remark in a public speech, and Mr. Lincoln at Charleston defied me to show that his speeches in the North and in the South were not alike and in entire harmony with each other. I will now call your attention to two of them, and let you see whether you believe the same man ever uttered them. [Applause. —*Tribune;* Laughter and cheers. —*Times*] In a speech at Chicago in July last, replying to me, Mr. Lincoln, on this subject of equality of the negro with the white man, used the following language:

> "I should like to know, if taking this old Declaration of Indepen-dence, which declares that all men are equal upon principle, and making exceptions to it, where will it stop? If one man says it does not mean a negro, why may not another man say it does not mean a German [the original Lincoln text had "another man"—*ed.*]? [Loud cheers. —*Tribune*] If that Declaration is not the truth, let us get the statute book, in which we find it, and tear it out! Who is so bold as to do it? If it is not true 'let us tear it out!' "

There you find that Mr. Lincoln said if the Declaration of Indepen-dence declaring all men to be born equal did not include the negro and make him equal to the white man, then he says, "let us take the Statute book and tear it out." [Applause. —*Tribune;* Laughter and cheers. —*Times*] He then took the ground that the negro race was included in the Declaration of Independence as the equal of the white race—that there could be no such thing as distinction in races, making one superior and the other inferior. I read now from another portion of the same speech:

> "My friends, I have detained you about as long as I desired to do, and I have only to say, let us discard all this quibbling about this man and the other man, this race and that race and the other race, and the other race being inferior, therefore they must be placed in an inferior position. Discarding our standard that we have left, let us discard all

these opinions [the original Lincoln text had "things"—*ed.*] and unite as one people throughout this land, until we shall once more stand up declaring that all men are created equal."

A VOICE—That's right.

JUDGE DOUGLAS—Yes, I have no doubt you think it's right, but the Lincoln men down in Coles, and Tazewell, and Sangamon [counties—*ed.*] don't think it is right. [Applause. —*Tribune;* Immense applause and laughter. Hit him again, &c. —*Times*] In the conclusion of the same speech, Mr. Lincoln says, in talking to the Chicago Abolitionists: "I leave you, hoping that the lamp of liberty will burn in your bosoms until there shall no longer be a doubt that all men are created free and equal." [Cries of "good," "good." —*Tribune;* Good, good, shame, &c. —*Times*] Now you say, "good" on that, and are going to vote for Mr. Lincoln because he holds that doctrine. [Cries of "Yes, that's so," and applause. —*Tribune;* "That's so." —*Times*] Now I am not going to blame you for supporting him on that ground, but I will show you in immediate contrast to that, what Mr. Lincoln said, in order to get votes down in Egypt, where they didn't hold that doctrine. [Applause. —*Tribune*] "I will say, then, that I am not, nor never have been in favor of bringing about in any way the social and political equality of the white and black races. [Cheers. —*Tribune*] That I am not, nor ever have been, in favor of making voters or jurors of negroes, nor of qualifying them to hold office, nor to intermarry with white people; [cries of "good," "good," hurrah for Lincoln —*Tribune*] and I will say in addition on this that there is a physical difference between the white and black races which will ever forbid the two races living together on terms of social and political equality. And inasmuch as they cannot so live, while they do remain together, there must be the position of superior and inferior. I am as much as any other man [the original Lincoln text had "white man"—*ed.*] in favor of having the superior position assigned to the white race." ["Hurrah for Lincoln." —*Tribune;* Good for Lincoln. —*Times*] [The cheers were apparently offered as Douglas read the text—*ed.*] Yes, here you find men who hurrah for Lincoln, and say he is right when he discards all distinction between races, or when he declares that he discards the doctrine that there is such a thing as a superior and inferior race; [They're not men. Put them out, &c. —*Times*] and Abolitionists are required and expected to vote for Mr. Lincoln because he goes for the equality of the races, holding that in the

Declaration of Independence, the white man and the negro were declared equal, and endowed by Divine law with equality. And down South with the Old Line Whigs, with the Kentuckians, the Virginians, and the Tennesseeans, he tells you that there is a physical difference between the races, making the one superior, the other inferior, and he is [in] favor of maintaining the superiority of the white race over the negro. [The above section was substantially refined in the *Times* transcript—*ed.*]

Now, let me ask you, how can you reconcile these two positions? He is voted for in the South as being a Pro-Slavery man; he is to be voted for in the North as being an Abolitionist. ["Give it to him." "Hit him again." —*Times*] Up here, he thinks it is all nonsense to talk about different races. He says we must discard all quibbling about this man and the other man—about this race and that race and the other being inferior and therefore they must be placed in an inferior position. That decision is to be discarded in the North, to be adopted as the creed of his party in the South. And hence you find that their political meetings are called by different names in different counties. From here north, they can call the meetings as Republican meetings. Go over into old Tazewell, where Mr. Lincoln made a speech, last Saturday I think it was, but perhaps it was Monday, and they don't have any such thing as Republican meetings.

MR. LINCOLN.—Nor Democratic here. [Interruption not reported in the *Times*—*ed.*]

JUDGE DOUGLAS.—There they gave a notice calling all the Lincoln men together. [Laughter —*Tribune;* Great laughter. —*Times*] Not a word about Republicans there, because Tazewell is filled with old Virginians and Kentuckians, part of whom are Whigs and part Democrats, and if you called a Republican or Abolition meeting, Lincoln could not get any votes. [Laughter. —*Tribune* and *Times*] Then go down into Egypt and you find he even discords [*sic*] that, and gives a different name there [the *Times* substituted: "he and his party are operating under an alias there"—*ed.*]. When I was in Monroe County a few weeks ago, addressing the people on this question, I saw the handbill of one of Trumbull's meetings, where he was going to make a speech for Mr. Lincoln. And what do you think it was? The Free Democracy were requested to meet. [Laughter. —*Tribune;* Great laughter. —*Times*] Trumbull and Jehu Baker to address the Free Democracy of Monroe County! [Laughter. —*Tribune*] And it was signed "Many Free Democrats." The reason he adopted that name down there, was this: That was always an old-fashioned Democratic county. They have no old Whigs there, and hence it was necessary to make them believe down there that they were Democrats. [Laughter —*Tribune*] And they were appealing to them to vote for Lincoln as Democrats, down there. [That's it, &c. —*Times*] Go up to Springfield, where Mr. Lincoln now lives, and always has lived, and his conventions and meetings there dare not adopt the name of Republican. They call a convention and nominate men for the Legislature who are to support Mr. Lincoln, under the title of all opposed to Democracy. [Laughter and cheers. —*Times*] And thus you find that his creed can't travel even half the counties of this State. It has to change its color and its hues, getting lighter and lighter from the extreme North, until you get down into the extreme South. [That's so, it's true, &c. —*Times*]

Now I ask you, my friends, why can't public men avow their principles alike everywhere? I would despise myself if I thought that I were seeking your votes by concealing my opinions, or advocating one set of principles in one part of the State and a different class in another part of the State. If I do not truly and honorably represent your feelings I ought not to be your Senator, and I will never conceal my opinions, or modify them, or change them and waste breath in order to get votes. I tell you that in my opinion this Chicago doctrine of Mr. Lincoln's declaring that negroes and white men were included alike in the Declaration of Independence, made equal by Divine Providence, is a monstrous heresy. [That's so, and terrific applause. —*Times*] The signers of the Declaration of Independence never dreamed of the negro when they were writing that document. They referred to white men, men of European birth and European descent, when they declared the equality of all men. I see a gentleman here shaking his head. Let me remind him that when Thomas Jefferson wrote that Declaration he was the owner, and continued to the end of his life the owner of a large number of slaves. Did he intend to say that his negro slaves were created his equals by Divine law, and that he was violating the law of God every time [the *Times* substituted "day"—*ed.*] of his life by holding them as slaves? ["No, no." —*Times*] Bear in mind that when that Declaration was put forth every one of the thirteen Colonies were slaveholding Colonies, and every man who signed the Declaration of Independence represented a slaveholding constituency. Bear in mind that no one of them emancipated his slaves, much less put them on an equality with himself when he signed the Declaration. On the contrary, they continued to hold them as slaves during the entire Revolutionary war. Now do you believe that? Are you willing to have it said that every man who signed the Declaration of Independence declared the negro his equal, and then was hypocrite enough to hold him as his slave in violation of what he believed to be Divine law? [Cries of "No," "No." —*Tribune* and *Times*] And yet when you say that the Declaration of Independence included the negro you charge the signers of the Declaration of Independence with hypocrisy. Now I say to you frankly that in my opinion this Government was made by our fathers on the white basis. It was made by white men for the benefit of white men and their posterity forever, and was intended to be administered in all time to come by white men. ["That's so." —*Tribune;* "That's so," and cheers. —*Times*] But while I hold that under our Constitution and political system the negro is not a citizen—cannot be a citizen—ought not to be a citizen—yet it don't follow by any means that he should be a slave. On the contrary, it does follow that the negro as an inferior race ought to possess every privilege, every immunity which he can safely exercise consistent with the good of society where he lives. Humanity requires, Christianity commands that you shall extend to every inferior being and every dependent race all the privileges, all the immunities and all the advantages which can be granted to him consistent with the safety of society. Again you ask me what is the nature and extent of these rights and privileges. My answer to that question is this: It is a question which the people of each State must decide for themselves. ["That's it." —*Times*] Illinois has decided that question for herself. We have said that in this State the negro shall not be a slave, nor shall he be a citizen. Kentucky holds a different doctrine, New York holds one different from either. Maine is different from all the rest, Virginia differs in many respects from each of the others, and so on. There are hardly two States whose policy is precisely alike in regard to the relation of the white man with the negro. You cannot reconcile them and make them alike. Each must do as it pleases. Illinois has as much right to adopt the policy we have on this subject as Kentucky has to a different policy. The great principle of this government is that each State has a right to do as it pleases on all these questions, and that no other power on earth has a right to interfere with us or complain of us merely because our system differs from theirs.

In the Compromise measures of 1850, Mr. Clay recognized the great principle which I have asserted, and again in the Kansas–Nebraska Bill

of 1854, that this same privilege ought to be extended into the Territories as well as the States. But Mr. Lincoln cannot be made to understand, and those who are determined to vote for him, no matter which
side, whether in the North or South, whether for negro equality at one
end of the State or against it at another—you cannot make one of them
understand how it is that in a Territory the people can do as they please
on the slavery question under the Dred Scott decision. Let us see if I
cannot make all impartial men see how that is. Chief Justice Taney has
said in his opinion in the Dred Scott case, that the negro slave being
property, stands on an equal footing with other property and that the
owner may carry them to a United States Territory the same as he does
other property. [That's so. —*Times*] Now suppose two of you, neighbors, concluded to go to Kansas. Suppose one should have a hundred
negro slaves, and the other a hundred dollars' worth of mixed merchan-
dise including a quantity of liquors, you both, according to that decision, may carry your property to Kansas. When you get there, the
merchant with his liquors meets the Maine Liquor Law which forbids
him to use or sell his property when he gets it there. What is this right
to carry it there worth, if unfriendly legislation renders it useless and
worthless when he gets there? How can the owner of the slave be more
fortunate? The slaveholder, when he gets there, finds there is no local
law, no slave code, no police regulation supporting and sustaining his
right as a slaveholder, and he finds at once that the absence of friendly
legislation excludes him just as positively and irresistibly as a positive
constitutional prohibition could exclude him. Thus you find with any
kind of property in a Territory, that it depends for its protection on the
local and municipal law. Hence if the people of a Territory want slavery
they will make friendly legislation to introduce it. If they don't want it,
they will withhold all protection from it, and then it can't exist there.
Such was the view of Southern men when the Nebraska bill passed.
Read the speech of Mr. [James L.] Orr, of South Carolina, the present
Speaker of Congress, and there you find this whole doctrine argued out
at full length which I have now advanced. Read the speeches of other
Senators and Representatives, and you will find they understood the
Kansas-Nebraska bill in that way at that time, and hence slavery never
could be force[d] on a people who didn't want it. I hold that in this
country there is no power, there should be no power on the globe that
can force any institution on an unwilling people. The great fundamental
principle is that the people of each State and each Territory shall be left

free to decide for themselves what shall be the nature and character of our institutions. This Government was based on that principle. When this Government was made there were twelve Slaveholding States and one Free State in this Union. Suppose this doctrine of Mr. Lincoln and the Republicans of uniformity on the subject of slavery in the laws of all the States had prevailed when this Government was made. Suppose Mr. Lincoln had been a member of the Convention that made the Constitution of the United States and that he had risen in that august body and addressing the father of his country, had said as he did at Springfield, "a house divided against itself cannot stand, this Government divided into Free and Slave States cannot permanently endure, that they must be all free or all slave, all the one thing or all the other," what do you think would have been the result? (I don't pretend to quote his exact language but I give his idea.) [Lincoln restored his original language for the book version of the debates—*ed.*] Suppose he had made that Convention believe that doctrine, and they had acted upon that, what would have been the result? [Hurrah for Douglas. —*Times*] Do you think that one Free State would have out-voted the twelve Slaveholding States and have abolished slavery therefrom[?] [No! No! and cheers. —*Times*] On the contrary, would not the twelve Slaveholding States have out-voted the one Free State and under his doctrine have fastened slavery under a Constitutional provision on every inch of the American Republic[?] Thus you see that the doctrine which he advocated now, if proclaimed at the beginning of the government would have fashioned slavery everywhere throughout the American continent. Are you willing now since we have become the majority to exercise a power which we never would have submitted to when we were in the minority[?] ["No, no," and great applause —*Times*] If the Southern States had attempted to control our institutions, and made the States all slave when they had the power, I ask you would you have submitted to it? ["No, no." —*Times*] If you would not, are you willing now since we have become the majority under the great principle of self government which allows each State to do as it pleases, are you pre-pared now to force the doctrine on them?

My friends, I say to you there is but one path of peace in this Republic, and that is to administer this Government as our fathers made it, divided into free States and slave States, allowing each State to decide for itself whether it wants slavery or not. If Illinois will settle the question for herself, mind her own business and let her neighbors alone, we will be at peace with our neighbors. If Kentucky and every other Southern State will settle the question to suit themselves, and mind their own business and let others alone, there will be peace between the North and the South, and the whole Union. I am told my hour is up. [Loud applause. —*Tribune;* Nine cheers for Douglas. —*Times*]

Mr. Lincoln's Reply

[Mr. Lincoln, upon advancing to the front of the stand, was received with three cheers. He proceeded to say: —*Times;* Mr. Lincoln was received as he came forward with three enthusiastic cheers, coming from every part of the vast assembly. After silence was restored Mr. Lincoln said: —*Tribune*]

My Fellow Citizens: A very large portion of the speech which Judge Douglas has addressed to you has previously been delivered and put in print. [Laughter. —*Times* and *Tribune*] I did not mean that for a hit upon the Judge at all. [Renewed laughter. —*Tribune*] If not interrupted, I was going on to say that such an answer as I was able to make to a very large portion of it, had already been once made and put in print, and there is an opportunity already afforded—an opportunity has already been afforded, to see our respective views upon a large portion of the speech which has not been addressed to you.

I make these remarks for the purpose of excusing myself for not passing over the entire ground that he has gone over. I however desire to take some of the points that he has attended to, and ask your attention to them. I shall follow back upon some notes that I have taken, instead of beginning at the head and following them down.

He has alluded to the Declaration of Independence, and has insisted that negroes are not meant by the term "men" in that Declaration of Independence, and that it is a slander upon the framers of that instrument to suppose that they so meant. He asks you if it is possible to believe that Mr. Jefferson, who penned the Declaration of Independence would have supposed himself as applying the language of that instrument to the negro race, and yet have held a portion of that negro race in slavery, and not at once have freed them! I have only to remark upon this point, briefly, for I shall not detain you or myself upon it, that I believe the entire records of the world from the date of the Declaration of Independence up to within three years ago, may be searched in vain for one single declaration from one single man, that the negro was not included in the Declaration of Independence. I think I may defy Douglas to show that he ever said so, therefore, I think I may defy Douglas to show that any President ever said so—that any member of Congress ever said so—that any man ever said so until the necessities of the Democratic party had to invent that declaration [the *Tribune* substituted "affirmation"—*ed.*]. [Applause. —*Times;* Tremendous applause. —*Tribune*] And I will remind Judge Douglas and this audience, that while Mr. Jefferson was the owner of slaves, as he undoubtedly was, he, speaking on this very subject, used the strong language that he trembled for his country, when he remembered that God was just. I will offer the highest premium in my power to Judge Douglas, if he will show that he, in all his life, has ever uttered a sentiment akin to that sentiment of Jefferson's. [Applause. —*Times;* Great applause and cries of "Hit him again," "good," "good." —*Tribune*]

Another thing I will ask your attention to is the Judge's comments upon the fact, as he assumes it to be, that the Republicans cannot call their public meetings as Republican meetings throughout the State. He instances Tazewell county as one of the places where the friends of Lincoln have called a meeting and have not dared to entitle it a Republican meeting; and he instances Monroe county, where Trumbull and Jehu Baker addressed a meeting, calling themselves the free Democracy. I have the honor to inform Judge Douglas that he spoke in that very county of Tazewell last Saturday, and I there on Tuesday last, and when he spoke there he spoke under a call not venturing to call the meeting Democratic. [Applause. —*Times;* cheers and laughter —*Tribune*] Now [turning to Judge Douglas—*Tribune*], Judge, what do you think of yourself? [Laughter, and cries of "Hurrah for Douglas!" —*Times;* Immense applause and roars of laughter. —*Tribune*]

So again, there is another thing that I would ask the Judge's attention to upon that subject. In the contest of 1856 his party delighted to call themselves together as the National Democracy, but now, if there should be a notice put up anywhere for a meeting of the National Democracy, Judge Douglas and his friends would not go there; they would not suppose themselves invited; they would understand it to be a call of those hateful postmasters. [Applause, and cry of "A call of your allies, you mean" —*Times;* Uproarious laughter. —*Tribune*]

Now, then, a few words in regard to those extracts of speeches of mine, which Judge Douglas read, and which he supposes are in great contrast, the one with the other. They have been before the public for a long while, and if they have inconsistencies in them the public has been able to detect them. The Judge assumes—when he says that I make speeches of one sort for the North and of another sort for the South—he assumes that I do not understand that my speeches will be put in print. Now I have understood that the speeches that I made in

Chicago, at Jonesboro and at Charleston, would be put in print, and that all reading men might read them, and I have not at all supposed—I do not to-day suppose—that there is any conflict in them. ["They are all good speeches!" "Hurrah for Lincoln!" —*Tribune*] The Judge will have it, if we do not confess that there is a sort of inequality between the black and the white people, that lets us make slaves of the black, that we must make wives of them. [Loud applause, and cries, "Give, give it to him"; "Hit him again." —*Tribune*] Now, I have all the while made a wide distinction between this. He, perhaps, by taking two parts of the same speech might show as great a contrast [the *Tribune* substituted "conflict"—*ed.*] as he does here. I have all the while maintained that inasmuch as there is a physical inequality between the white and black, that the blacks must remain inferior; but I have always maintained that in the right to life, liberty, and the pursuit of happiness, they were our equals, [Long-continued cheering. —*Tribune*] and this declaration I have constantly made with reference to the abstract moral question which I suppose to be the proper question to consider, when we are legislating about a new country which is not at ready to be beset with the actual presence of slavery. I have insisted that in legislating for a new country where slavery does not exist, there is no just rule other than that of pure morality and pure abstract right; and with reference to legislating with regard to these new countries, this abstract maxim, the right to life, liberty, and the pursuit of happiness, are the first rules to be considered and referred to.

Now, there is no misunderstanding this except by men that are interested in misunderstanding. [Applause. —*Tribune*] I have to trust to a reading community to judge whether I advance just views, or whether I state views that are revolutionary or hypocritical. I believe myself guilty of no such thing as the latter; and of course I cannot claim that I am entirely free from error in the views and principles that I advance.

The Judge has also detained us a while in regard to the distinction between his party and our party; his, as he assumes, being a national party and ours a sectional one. He does this in asking the question of whether this country has any interest in maintaining the Republican party to prove that the country has not any such interest. He assumes that that party is altogether sectional, and he assumes that the party to which he adheres is national. His mode of argument is that no party can be a rightful party—can be based upon rightful principles unless it can announce its principles alike everywhere. Now, it is the first time, I believe, that I have ever heard it announced as being true, that a man could always announce rightful principles everywhere! I presume that Judge Douglas could not go into Russia and announce the doctrines of our national Democracy—he could not go there and denounce the doctrines of kings, emperors and monarchists, and it may be true in this country that he may not be able to announce a doctrine which is as clearly true as the truth of the Democracy, because of a sentiment so directly opposite to us that will not tolerate our doing so. Is it a true test of a doctrine that in some places people will not let you preach it! [No, no, no. —*Tribune*] Is that so? [No, no, no. —*Tribune*] I understand that a year or two ago the people of Chicago would not let Judge Douglas preach a certain doctrine! I commend it to his consideration whether he takes that as a test of the soundness of what he wanted to preach. [Loud cheers. —*Tribune*]

But there is another thing that I wish to ask your attention to in this connection. What is all this evidence that has been brought forward to prove that the Republican party is a sectional party? The main piece of evidence is that in the Southern States the people would not let the people preach the doctrine; that they have no supporters, or substantially no supporters in the slave States. They have not taken hold of our principles as we announce them, nor has the Judge now. We have a Republican platform laid down in Springfield in June last. We are now far advanced in this canvas. Judge Douglas and I have made, perhaps, forty speeches apiece; we have now met for the fifth time, face to face in debate, and up to this time I have not found Judge Douglas, or any one of his friends, laying his finger upon any one part of the Republican platform and showing that it is wrong. [Cheers. —*Tribune*] I ask Republicans to remember that! Judge Douglas turns away from that task. [Applause. —*Tribune*] Now, if he had great confidence that our principles are wrong, he would take hold of them and prove them to be so; but, instead of that he takes hold of the fact that there are people somewhere that will not allow us to preach our doctrines to them as if that were the way to prove them to be wrong. [The *Tribune* added: "I ask again, is that the way to test the soundness of a doctrine?" (Cries of "No," "No.")—*ed.*]

I ask the Judge's attention to another fact, that by his rule of nationality he is fast becoming sectional too. [Great cheers and laughter. —*Tribune*] I ask his attention to the fact that his speeches will not go so current South [the *Tribune* added "of the Ohio River"—*ed.*] as they have heretofore gone. [Loud cheers. —*Tribune*] I ask your attention to the fact that he felicitates himself on the fact that the entire Democratic party of the free States are with him. [Applause. —*Tribune*] If he has not thought of it I commend to him the evidence in his own declaration of his becoming sectional too. [Immense cheering. —*Tribune*] I see the day rapidly approaching, whatever the result of this ephemeral contest may be between Judge Douglas and myself—I see the day fast approaching when his epithets that he has been cramming down Republican throats, will be crammed down his throat. [Tremendous applause. —*Tribune*]

In regard to what Judge Douglas has said about the establishment of the compromise of 1850, which was the beginning of his speech, being the principles of the Nebraska bill, although I have often presented my views upon that subject I have not done so in this canvas, and if you please I will detain you a little while on that.

Now, I have always maintained so far as I have been able to do, that there was nothing in the Nebraska bill of the principle of the compromise measures of 1850—that in nothing could you find the principles of the compromise of 1850 in the Nebraska bill. If anywhere, you would find it in the two pieces of the compromise measures organizing the territories of Utah and New Mexico. It was expressly provided in those two acts, that when they came into the Union they should be admitted into the Union with or without slavery, according as they should choose under their constitution, and nothing was said as to what was to be done as to slavery during their existence as a territory, and Mr. Clay constantly gave his opinion that the old Mexican law[s] would govern that question during their existence as territories, and that the old Mexican law[s] excluded slavery. Now, how can it be said that during the territorial existence, as well as at the time of forming a constitution even, the people might have slavery [the *Tribune* added: "if they wanted"—*ed.*][?] I am not discussing whether it is right or wrong. But there was more than that; that they were at all the patterns for the Nebraska law. I maintain that the organization of the territories of Utah and New Mexico did not establish a general principle at all; it had no feature of establishing a general principle at all. They were parts of a compromise—they did not lay down what was proposed as a system for the organization of territories, but they were put in that shape because in another way—allowing them to go in that shape—they were paid for. Consider that that system of compromise measures included, if not quite, nearly half a dozen acts. It included the admission of California as a free State, which was kept out of the Union for half a year because it had formed a free constitution; it included the fixing of the boundary of Texas, which was a slavery question, because if you fixed it further west you made more slave territory, and if you fixed it further east you made more free territory; it included the abolition of the slave trade in the District of Columbia; and it included the passage of the new fugitive slave law. All these things were put together and although passed in separate acts as they were, they were nevertheless, as the speeches made upon them will show, made to defend the one or the other, and by this system of compromise, which gave name to the system of measures, these two bills for the organization of Utah and New Mexico were passed, and for that reason, as I say, they could not be taken as models to be used in the organization of new territories. I have an evidence of this as I think that Judge Douglas, when he first introduced a bill a year after for the purpose of organizing new territory, did not attempt to follow the New Mexico and Utah bills, and when he introduced the Nebraska bill he did not attempt to follow them. My opinion is that a thorough investigation will show plainly, first, that the Utah and New Mexico bills were one part of the compromise measures, and never intended as patterns for new bills, and if they were, this Nebraska bill don't follow them at all.

The Judge tells us in proceeding that he is opposed to making an odious distinction between the free and slave States. I am altogether unaware that the Republicans are in favor of making any odious distinction between the free and the slave States; but there still is a difference, as I think, between Judge Douglas and the Republicans in this vicinity of thought. For instance— [here some men running off to see some kind of a hubbub in the vicinity of the crowd—*Times;* not mentioned in the *Tribune—ed.*] Well, that is very beautiful—I suppose that the real difference between Judge Douglas and his friends, on the one side, and the Republicans on the other hand is, that the Judge is not in favor of making any difference between slavery and liberty, that he is in favor of eradicating, he is in favor of pressing out of view, and out of existence, all preference for free over slave institutions, and, consequently, every sentiment that he utters, discards the idea that he is against slavery, every sentiment that emanates from him discards the idea that there is any wrong in slavery. Every thought that he utters will be seen to exclude the thought that there is anything wrong in slavery. You will take his speeches and get the short pointed sentiments expressed by him, that he does not care if slavery is voted up, or voted down, and such like, you will see at once it is a perfectly logical idea if you admit that slavery is not wrong, but if it is wrong, Judge Douglas cannot say that he don't care for a wrong being voted up. Judge Douglas declares that if any community wants slavery they can have it. He can logically say that, if he admits that there is no wrong in it, but he cannot say that, if he admits that there is wrong in it! He insists, upon the score of equality, that the owner of slaves and the owner of horses should be allowed to take them alike to new territory and hold them there. That is perfectly logical if the species of property is perfectly alike, but if you admit that one of them is wrong, then you cannot admit any equality between right and wrong. I believe that slavery is wrong, and in a policy springing from that belief that looks to the prevention of the enlargement of that wrong, and that looks at some time to there being an end of that wrong. The other sentiment is, that it is no wrong, and the policy springing from it that there is no wrong in its becoming bigger, and that there never will be any end of it. There is the difference between Judge Douglas and his friends and the Republican party.

I confess myself as belonging to that class in the country that believes slavery to be a moral and political wrong. I feel, having regard to all constitutional guards thrown around it, that I do nevertheless desire a policy that shall prevent the enlargement of it. I do look to that point of time when it shall come to an end. [Great applause. —*Tribune*]

Judge Douglas has gone over for, I believe, the fifth time in my presence—if not the seventh—reiterating his charge of conspiracy or combination between the National Democracy and Republicans! What evidence Judge Douglas has upon that subject I know not, inasmuch as he never favors us with any. [Laughter and cheers. —*Tribune*] I have said upon former occasions, and I do not choose to suppress it now, that I have no objections to the division in the Judge's party. [Cheers. —*Tribune*] He got it up himself; it was all his and their work. The Judge had, I think, a great deal more to do with the steps that led to the Lecompton constitution than Mr. Buchanan had; [applause —*Tribune*] and at last, when they reached it, they quarreled over it, and are somewhat divided over it. [Applause. —*Tribune*] I am free to confess that I have no objection to the division, but I defy the Judge to show that I have in any way promoted that division, [loud applause and laughter —*Times*] unless he insists upon being a witness himself. [Laughter. —*Tribune*] I can give all the friends of Judge Douglas here to understand the views the Republicans take in regard to that division. Don't you remember, two years ago, that the opponents of the Democracy were divided between Frémont and Fillmore? ["Yes, sir, we remember it mighty well." Lincoln: "I guess you do." —*Tribune*] Now, any Democrat that is here will remember that he was very glad of that, [laughter, —*Tribune*] and then he will have the whole thing that there is between the Republicans and National [Democrats]—[the *Tribune* added: "What we now think of the two divisions of Democrats, you then thought of the Frémont and Fillmore divisions" (Great cheers)—*ed*.]— that is just all there is of it. We are glad of the division! But as the Judge does continue to put forward the declaration that there is an unholy and unnatural alliance between the National Democrats and the Republicans, I want to enter my protest against the Judge being received as an entirely competent witness upon that subject. [Loud cheers. —*Tribune*]

I want to call to the Judge's attention one fact he made upon me in the first one of these debates at Ottawa, on the 21st of August, I think it was. In order to fix extreme abolitionism upon me, Judge Douglas read a set of resolutions which he declared had been passed by a Republican State Convention held in October, 1854, at Springfield, Illinois, and that I, Lincoln, had taken part in that convention. It turned out that, although a few men calling themselves an anti-Nebraska State Convention, had met in Springfield about that time, that neither I took any part in it, nor did it pass the resolutions, or any such resolutions as Judge Douglas read. [Great applause. —*Tribune*] So apparent did it become that the resolutions that he read had not been passed at Springfield at all, not by a State convention anywhere, nor by any convention of any sort in which I had taken any part, that six days afterwards, at Freeport, Judge Douglas gave it up, but declared that he had been misled by Charles Lanphier, editor of the *Illinois State Register*, and Thomas L. Harris, member of Congress in that district; and he promised that when he should go to Springfield he would investigate the matter. Since then, Judge Douglas has been to Springfield, and I presume has made the investigation, but although a month has passed since he has been there, so far as I know he has made no report of the result of his investigation. [Great applause. —*Tribune*] I have waited sufficiently, as I think, for a report upon that investigation. I have some curiosity to see and hear whether the fraud [Applause. —*Tribune*] —an absolute forgery—was committed, and the perpetuation of it was clearly traced to the three (Lanphier, Harris, and Douglas), [Applause and laughter. —*Tribune*] or whether it can be shown in any way so as to exonerate any one of them. That is what Judge Douglas' report would probably show. [Applause and laughter. —*Tribune*]

It is true that the resolutions read by the Judge were published in the *Illinois State Register* on the 16th of October, 1854, as being the resolutions of an anti-Nebraska convention, which had sat during that same month of October at Springfield, but it is also true that the publication in the *Register* was a forgery then [cheers —*Tribune*]. The question is still behind, which of the three, if it was not by all, committed that forgery? [Great applause. —*Tribune*] The idea that it was done by mistake is absurd. The article in the *Illinois State Register* contains part of the real proceedings of that Springfield convention, showing that the author of the article had the real proceedings before him, and purposely threw out the genuine resolutions passed by that convention and fraudulently substituted the others. Lanphier then, as now, was the editor of the *Register,* so that there would seem to be but little reason for his escape; but then, it is to be borne in mind, that Lanphier had less interest in the object of that forgery than either of the other two. [Cheers. —*Tribune*] The immediate object of that forgery at that time was to beat [Richard] Yates and elect Harris to Congress, and that object was known to be exceedingly dear to Judge Douglas at that time. [Laughter. —*Tribune*] Harris and Douglas were both in Springfield when that convention was in session, and, although they both left before the fraud appeared in the *Register,* subsequent events show that they both had their *eyes* constantly fixed upon that convention. The fraud having been apparently successful upon that occasion, both Harris and Douglas has [*sic*] more than once been attempting to put it to new uses, as the woman said when her husband's body was brought home full of eels, and she was asked what should be done with him, she said take the eels out and set him again; [great laughter; —*Tribune*] and so Harris and Douglas have shown a disposition to take the eels out of that [the *Tribune* added "stale fraud by which"—*ed.*] they got by the first election, and set that fraud again more than once. [Tremendous cheering and laughter. —*Tribune*] On the 9th of July, 1856, Douglas attempted the repetition of it upon the floor of the United States Senate upon Trumbull, as will appear in the appendix of the *Congressional Globe* for that year. Later Harris tried it upon [Jesse O.] Norton [in the House of Representatives—*ed.*], as will appear from the *Congressional Globe,* and on the 21st of August, all three, Lanphier, Harris, and Douglas attempted it again upon me at Ottawa.

[Tremendous applause. —*Tribune*] It has been clung to, and played again and again as an exceedingly high trump by this blessed trio. [Roars of laughter and tumultuous applause, "Give it to him," &c. —*Tribune*] Now that it has been discovered publicly to be a fraud, why we find that Judge Douglas manifests no surprise at it at all. [Laughter, "That's it," "Hit him again." —*Tribune*] He makes no complaint of Lanphier, who must have known it to be a fraud from the beginning. Both he, and Lanphier and Harris are just as cozy now [the *Tribune* substituted "crazy," but Lincoln later corrected it to the *Times* version— *ed.*], just as active with the concoction of new schemes as they were before the general discovery of the fraud. All this is very natural, if they are all alike guilty of that fraud, [laughter and cheers, —*Tribune*] and it is very unnatural if any one of them is innocent. [Great laughter, "Hit him again," "Hurrah for Lincoln." —*Tribune*] Lanphier, perhaps, insists that the rule of honor among thieves does not quite require him to take all upon himself, [laughter, —*Tribune*] and consequently my friend Douglas finds it difficult to make a satisfactory report upon his investigation. [Laughter and applause. —*Tribune;* which added: "But meanwhile the three are agreed that each is *'a most honorable man'* " (Cheers and explosions of laughter.)] But, meanwhile, the three are all glad that an endorsement of his truths and honor by a re-election to the United States Senate, and he makes and repeats against me and against Judge Trumbull, day after day, charges which we know to be utterly untrue, without seeming to think for a moment that the unexplained fraud will be the least drawback to his claim to be believed. Harris ditto. Harris asks a re-election to the lower house without seeming to remember that he is in this fraud, and the Springfield organ, then, as now, the central organ of both Harris and Douglas, continues to make assertions without thinking at all that its assertions are at all lacking in title to belief.

After all, the subject of the fraud recurs, how did that fraud get into the *State Register*[?] Lanphier then, as now, was the editor of that paper. Lanphier knows. Lanphier cannot be ignorant of how and by whom it was originally concocted. It may be true that Lanphier insists that the two men for whose benefit it was concocted shall at least bear their share of it. How that is I do not know; but while it remain unexplained, after the express promise of Judge Douglas to investigate it, I hope I may be pardoned if I insist that Judge Douglas' making charges against me and against Judge Trumbull is not quite sufficient evidence of their truth. [Great cheering. "Hit him again." "Give it to him," &c. —*Tribune*]

While we were at Freeport, in one of these joint discussions, I answered certain interrogatories that Judge Douglas had propounded to me, and then in turn I propounded some to him, which he, in a sort of a way, at least as to some of them, answered. The third one of these interrogatories I have with me. I wish now to make some comments upon it. It was in these words: "If the Supreme Court of the United States shall decide that States can not exclude slavery from their limits, are you in favor of acquiescing in adopting, and following such decision as a rule of political action[?] To this interrogatory, Judge Douglas made no answer in any just sense of the word. He contented himself with sneering at the thought that it was impossible for the Supreme Court to ever make such a decision, and sneering at me for propounding the interrogatory. I did not propound it without some reflection, and I wish now to address to this audience some remarks upon it. In the second section of the sixth article, I believe it is of the Constitution of the United States, we find the following language: "This constitution, and the laws of the United States which shall be made in pursuance hereof, and all treaties made, or which shall be made under the authority of the United States, shall be the supreme law of the land, and the Judges in every State shall be bound thereby, anything in the constitution or laws of any State to the contrary notwithstanding." [The *Tribune* version substituted the exact phrasing of the article, which Lincoln apparently tried to recite from memory—*ed.*] The essence of the Dred Scott decision is compressed into the sentence which I will now read: "Now, as we have already said, in an earlier part of this opinion, upon a different point, the right of property in a slave is distinctly and expressly affirmed in the constitution." The right of property in a slave is distinctly and expressly affirmed in the constitution. What is affirmed in the constitution? Made firm in the constitution—so made that it cannot be separated from the constitution without breaking the constitution—durable as the constitution—a part of the constitution. Now remember, the provision of the constitution which I have read affirming that that instrument is the supreme law of the land, and that the judges of every State shall be bound by it, any law or constitution of any State to the contrary notwithstanding, and that the right of property in a slave is affirmed in it, is made firm in it, cannot be separated without breaking it, durable as the instrument, part of the instrument. What follows as a short, even syl[l]ogistic argument from that? I think that it follows, and I submit to the consideration of men capable of argumentation, whether, as I state the argument, it has any fault in it. Nothing in the law of any State can destroy a right distinctly affirmed in the constitution of the United States—the right of property in a slave is distinctly and expressly affirmed in the constitution of the United States—therefore nothing in the constitution or laws of any State can destroy the right of property in a slave. I believe that no fault can be pointed out in that argument. Assume the truth of the premises, and the conclusion, as far as I have capacity at all to understand it, the conclusion follows inevitably. There is a fault in it, as I think, but the fault is not in the reasoning, but the fault is the falsehood in fact of one of the premises. I believe that the right of property in a slave is not distinctively [*sic*] and expressly affirmed in the constitution, but Judge Douglas thinks it is. I believe that the Supreme Court of the United States, and the advocates of that decision may search in vain for the place in the constitution where the right of property is distinctively and expressly affirmed in the constitution. As I say, therefore, that I think that one of the premises is not true in fact, but it is true with Judge Douglas; it is true that the Supreme Court who pronounced it, they being estopped to deny it, and they being estopped to deny it, the syl[l]ogism follows that the Constitution of the United States, being the supreme law, no constitution or law of a State can interfere with it. It being affirmed in that decision that the right of property in a slave is distinctly and expressly affirmed in the constitution, the conclusion inevitably follows that no State law or constitution can destroy that right. I then say to Judge Douglas, and to all others, that I think it will take a better answer than a sneer to show that those who have said that the right of property in a slave is distinctly and expressly affirmed in the constitution are not prepared to say that no constitution or law of a State can destroy that right. I believe, I say, that it will take a far better argument than a mere sneer to establish, in the minds of intelligent men, that whoever have said that one will not affirm the other when the public sentiment will justify it. ["That's so." —*Tribune*] It is but an opinion—the opinion of one very humble man; but it is my opinion that the Dred Scott decision as it is, never would have been made in the form it is if the party that made it had not been sustained previously by the election; and my opinion is that the new Dred Scott decision deciding against the right of the people of States to exclude slavery will never be made if that party is not sustained by the

next election [Cries of "Yes, yes." —*Tribune*], and I believe, further, that
it is just as sure to be made as to-morrow is to come, if that party is
sustained by the election. ["We won't sustain it, never, never."
—*Tribune*]

I have said, upon a former occasion, and I repeat it now, that the
course of argument that Judge Douglas makes—I charge not his motive
in it—but the course of argument that he makes day by day is preparing
the public mind for that decision. I have asked him again to point out
to me the reason for his firm adherence to the Dred Scott decision. I
have turned his attention to the fact that Jackson differed with him in
regard to the political obligation of Supreme Court decisions; I have
asked his attention to the fact that Mr. Jefferson differed with him in
regard to the political obligation of Supreme Court decisions—that Mr.
Jefferson said that judges are as honest as other men, and not more so,
and substantially, that whenever, a free people should give up in absolute submission to any department of the government, retaining no
appeal from it, that their liberty is gone. I have asked the attention of
Judge Douglas to the fact that the Cincinnati platform, upon which he
stands, disregards a decision of the Supreme Court in the matter of a
United States Bank. I have asked the attention of the Judge to the fact
that he once opposed the Supreme Court of this State (the *Tribune*
added: "because it had made a decision distasteful to him"—*ed.*], his
opposition ending in the curious fact of his sitting down on the bench
[the *Tribune* added: "as one of the new Judges who were to overslaugh
that decision" (loud applause)] —he getting his name of Judge in that
very way. [Tremendous applause and laughter. —*Tribune*] I can get no
answer from the Judge on all this. I can get that far in the canvas and
no further. All I can get from him is that all of us who stand by the
decision of the Supreme Court are the friends of the constitution and
all you fellows that dare question it in any way, are enemies of the
constitution. [Continued laughter and cheers. —*Tribune*] Now, in this
very devoted position, in opposition to all the great political leaders that
he has held as great political leaders—now, in this adherence there is
something very marked, and there is something very marked in his
adherence to it—not adhering to it on its merits, for he does not discuss
it at all, but as being obligatory upon every one because of the source
whence it comes, as that which no man may gainsay, is another marked
feature of it. It marks it in this respect, that it commits him to the next
one as firmly as it does to this. As he will not investigate this, so he

commits himself to take the next without inquiring whether it is right or wrong [Applause. —*Tribune*], and as he teaches men—and he has a great power to teach men—he has a great power to make men say it is right if he says so, and because he has that so he is preparing the public mind to take the next, without inquiring whether it is right or wrong. In this, I argue the Judge is most ingeniously and most power-fully preparing the public mind to take that decision when it comes and not only so, but he is doing it in the other things that he does, in these maxims generally about liberty, in his maxims that he does not care whether slavery be voted up or be voted down; that whoever wants slavery has a right to have it; that upon the principle of equality it has a right to go everywhere. He is also, whether purposely or not, prepar-ing the public mind for making the institution of slavery national. [Cries of "Yes," "Yes," "That's so." —*Tribune*] I call to your minds—I repeat again, I don't charge that he means it so—but I call to your minds to inquire if you are to get the ablest instrument that you can think of and then set him to work to prepare the public mind, if you think of a single instrument so capable as Judge Douglas and one employed in so apt a way to do it. [Great cheering. Cries of "Hit him again," "That's the doctrine." —*Tribune*]

I have said once before, and I will repeat it now, that when Mr. Clay was once answering an objection to the Colonization Society, that it had a tendency to the ultimate emancipation of slavery, he said that those who would repress all tendency to liberty and ultimate emancipa-tion must do more than put down the benevolent efforts of the Coloni-zation Society; they must "go back to the hour ["era"—*ed.*] of our own liberty and independence, and muzzle the cannon that thunders its annual joyous return ["That's so." —*Tribune*]; that they must blow [the *Tribune* substituted "blot"—*ed.*] out the moral lights around us; that they must pervert the human soul, and eradicate the human soul and love ["light"—*ed.*] of liberty, and then, and not till then, they could perpetu-ate slavery in this country." [The last thirteen words of the Clay quote did not appear in the *Tribune* transcript—*ed.*]

I do think, and must repeat, because I think it—I do think that Judge Douglas and whoever teaches that the negro has no humble share in the Declaration of Independence, is going back to the hour of our own liberty and independence, and so far as in him lies, is muzzling the cannon that thunders its annual joyous return; ["That's so." —*Tribune*] that he is blowing out the moral lights around us, and perverting the human soul and eradicating from the human soul the love of liberty, and in every possible way, preparing the public mind with his vast influence for making that institution of slavery perpetual and national. [Great applause and cries of "Hurrah for Lincoln, that's the true doctrine." —*Tribune*]

There is, my friends, only one other point to which I will ask your attention in the remaining time that I have, and perhaps I shall not quite occupy the entire time that I have, as that one head [the *Tribune* substituted "point"—*ed.*] may not take me clear through it.

In the interrogatories that Judge Douglas propounded to me at Freeport, there was one in about this language: Are you opposed to the acquisition of any further territory by the United States unless slavery shall first be prohibited therein? I answered that, as I thought, in about this way: That I am not generally opposed to the acquisition of additional territory, and that I should support or oppose a proposition for the acquisition of additional territory according as I might suppose it was or was not calculated to aggravate this slavery question among us. I then propounded to Judge Douglas another interrogatory, which was co-relative to that, "are you in favor of acquiring additional territory in disregard of how it may affect us upon the slavery question?" Judge Douglas answered that in his way of answering, [Laughter. —*Tribune*] and I believe that although he took a good many words to answer it, it was a little more fully answered than any other. The subject of it was that this country must continue to expand, that it would need additional territory, that it was as absurd to suppose that we could continue upon our present territory, enlarging in population as we are, as it would be to hoop a boy of twelve years, I believe it was, and expect him to grow to man's growth, [the *Tribune* added: "without bursting the hoops" (Laughter.—*ed.*)], and that consequently he was in favor of the acquisition of territory so fast as we would need it, in disregard of how it would affect the slavery question. I don't say that this is his exact language, but that he would leave the question of slavery to be settled by the people of the territory.

A VOICE—That is perfectly right. ["That's the doctrine." —*Tribune*]

MR. LINCOLN—Maybe it is; let us consider it awhile. This will probably, in the run of things, become one of the concrete manifestations of this slavery question. If Judge Douglas, upon this slavery question succeeds and gets all opposition fairly laid down so that it ceases, the next thing he goes for grabbing Mexico and Central America, and the adjoining islands, each one of which promises an additional slave field, and it is to be left to the people that we get to settle the question of slavery in them. When we get Mexico, I don't know that the Judge will have a desire to let them settle that question for themselves, for the Judge has a great horror of mongrels, [laughter, —*Tribune*] and I understand that [the *Tribune* added: "the people of Mexico are most decidedly a race of mongrels" (Renewed laughter.)—*ed.*] not more than one out of eight are white. I don't know, but I don't suppose he is in favor of these mongrels settling this question, which would bring him somewhat in collision with this inferior race.

It is to be remembered that their power of acquiring additional territory is a power confined to the President and Senate of the United States—that is, the power is not in the control of the representatives of the people any further than they—the President and Senate—can be considered as the representatives of the people. Let me illustrate that a little. When we acquired territory from Mexico, in the Mexican war, the House of Representatives—the immediate representatives of the people—all the time insisted that the territory thus to be acquired should be acquired upon condition that slavery should be forever prohibited therein, in the terms and language that slavery had been prohibited in this country that we now inhabit. It was insisted upon constantly, and never failed, that that territory to be acquired should have that prohibition so far as the House of Representatives were concerned; but at last the President and Senate acquired the territory without asking the House of Representatives, and took it without that prohibition. They have that power, without the immediate representatives of the people being able to say anything about it. That furnishes a very powerful and apt means of bringing new territory into the country, and when it is brought into the country it involves us in this slavery agitation. It is, therefore, a very important consideration, I think, for the American people, whether the policy of bringing in an additional territory shall be brought in without considering at all how it will operate on the Union in reference to this one great disturbing element of the nation. You will bear in mind that it is to be acquired, in the Judge's view, as fast as we need it; and unfortunately, we have only the Judge and his class of men to decide how fast it is needed. We have no certain and apt mode of determining how fast territory is needed for the country. Whoever wants to go filibustering, thinks that territory is needed; whoever wants to extend slavery, thinks that territory is needed. It is just as easy as anything that is capable of demonstration, that territory is wanted; whatever the motive the man may have for wishing the annexation of new territory, it is as easy to say but it is impossible to prove, that we do not want it.

Now, I think that it is a great [*Tribune* had "grave"—ed.] question for the people of this nation to consider, whether, in view of the fact, that this slavery question has been the only one that has ever threatened or menaced a dissolution of the Union, that has ever disturbed us in such a way as to make us fear for our own liberty—I say in view of these facts, I think it it [*sic*] is an exceedingly important question for this people to consider, whether we shall enter upon a policy of the acquisition of new territory without regard to this question of slavery. The Judge's view has been expressed, and in my answer to his question I have expressed mine. I think it is going to become an important and practical question. Our views are before this public, and I am anxious that they should consider them, and that they should look through and turn them about, and arrive at a just conclusion whether it is or is not wise in the acquisition of new territory—whether it will do to overlook the one [and] only danger that has ever threatened the perpetuity of the Union, that has ever threatened our own liberty in the country. I say that I think it is extremely important that they should decide before entering upon this policy.

Now, having said the little that I wished to say—the little I desired to say on this head—whether I have occupied the time that I have or not, I will retire. I cannot enter upon any new topic without transcending my time, which I would not do.

[Mr. Lincoln gave way, having eleven minutes to spare. —*Times;* Three tremendous cheers for Lincoln from the whole vast audience were given with great enthusiasm, as their favorite retired. —*Tribune*]

Illustrator John D. Whiting (b. 1884) captured the striking difference in height between Abraham Lincoln and Stephen A. Douglas in this oil painting of their encounter at Ottawa, Quincy, or Alton—the three debates that occurred in town squares much like the one depicted here. However, the artist erred in depicting Lincoln in his presidential-style finery: eyewitnesses to the debates commented frequently on his "grotesque" appearance and ill-fitting clothes. (From the Frank J. and Virginia Williams Collection of Lincolniana; photograph by Mary Murphy)

Stephen Arnold Douglas (1813–1861), as he looked around the time of the debates with Lincoln, in a photograph by Mathew Brady. At five feet, four inches, "the Little Giant" made up for his small stature with a ferocious speaking style, a "deep horizontal wrinkle between his eyes, which was usually dark and scowling," and large, sparkling eyes that looked as if they were "shooting out electric fire," according to a journalist of the day. It was the fact that he was so short, a contemporary believed, that compelled him "to 'show himself' to his fellow men." (National Portrait Gallery, Smithsonian Institution, Washington, D.C.)

Abraham Lincoln (1809–1865) posed for this photograph two years after the debates to provide a model for a sculptor who proposed making a full-length statue of him. At six feet, four inches in height, a full twelve inches taller than his rival, "Long Abe" seemed to one journalist who covered the debates "indescribably gawky," especially when he employed "absurd, up-and-down and sidewise movements of his body to give emphasis to his arguments." Meeting him for the first time, future statesman Carl Schurz found him "ungainly," but marveled at his height. Although over six feet himself, Schurz had "to throw my head backward in order to look into his eyes." (Library of Congress)

Lincoln and Douglas Debate by artist Robert Marshall Root (b. 1863) portrayed Lincoln speaking at Charleston during the fourth debate, on September 18, 1858. Also visible here are the phonographic reporters, who can be seen on the platform in the near background transcribing Lincoln's words. From left to right are: ex-congressman Orlando Bell Ficklin (to whom Lincoln would unexpectedly pose a question during this debate); Dr. W. M. Chambers; Douglas; Horace White, the "color" reporter of the Chicago *Press and Tribune*; Robert Roberts Hitt, the *Tribune* stenographer; Lincoln; Henry Binmore, principal shorthand reporter for the Chicago *Times* (taking notes); Colonel J. T. Cunningham (arms folded), who welcomed Douglas to Coles County that day; James B. Sheridan, also of the *Times*; Usher F. Linder, another Douglas supporter, who had spoken on his behalf at the Jonesboro meeting; Congressman H. P. Bromwell, who gave the welcoming speech for Lincoln at Charleston; Elisha Linder; and Richard J. Oglesby, a Lincoln supporter destined to lose a race for Congress this year, but to win election as governor of Illinois during the Civil War. (Illinois State Historical Library)

The fifth debate, at Galesburg, was portrayed from the point of view of the dense throng of spectators in this illustration by Victor Semon Perard (b. 1870), a French-born artist for *Harper's* and *Scribner's* magazines. The "pushing and squeezing" of the immense crowd that day, the Missouri *Republican* reported "can be appreciated but not described." Lincoln can be seen in the distance, speaking from the platform that was put up alongside the Knox College building for the October 7, 1858, debate to shield the speakers from arctic northwest winds that day. (Library of Congress)

Six days before the Galesburg debate, on October 1, 1858, Lincoln gave a two-hour speech in Pittsfield, after which photographer Calvin Jackson took this ambrotype portrait. Observing him at one of his encounters with Douglas, an eyewitness described Lincoln's clean-shaven face as "almost grotesquely square, with high cheekbones." He looked "swarthy as an Indian, with wiry, jet black hair, which was usually in an unkempt condition." For this pose, Lincoln tilted his head down to hide the "long and sinewy" neck that Carl Schurz observed could barely be contained by "a white collar turned down over a . . . black necktie." (The Lincoln Museum, Fort Wayne, Indiana, a part of the Lincoln National Corp.)

On October 11, 1858, two days before the sixth debate at Quincy, Lincoln posed for this gloomy portrait by photographer William J. Thompson after speaking before a huge crowd in Monmouth. Chicago *Press and Tribune* correspondent Horace White observed of Lincoln around this time that when "addressing an audience . . . the dull, listless features dropped like a mask. The melancholy shadow disappeared in a twinkle . . . the whole countenance was wreathed in animation." But in repose, testified the humorist Petroleum V. Nasby, who saw Lincoln for the first time at Quincy, "I never saw so sad a face." (The Lincoln Museum, Fort Wayne)

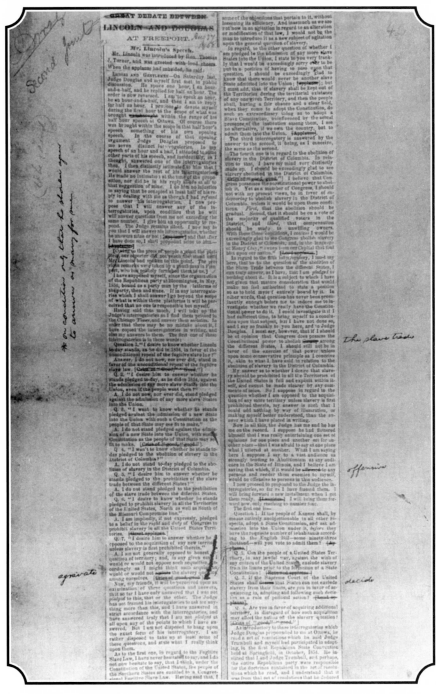

A page from Lincoln's personal scrapbook shows how he altered words, deleted crowd reaction, and added an entire new clause to the Chicago *Press and Tribune* account of his opening speech at Freeport before submitting his collection of debate records to Follett, Foster & Co. for publication in book form. The pro-Republican *Tribune* Lincoln transcript already showed him to better advantage than did that of the pro-Douglas *Times*, but Lincoln evidently thought it could be improved upon further. Despite the evidence, he maintained in an introduction to the 1860 volume that "the changes I have made . . . are verbal only, and very few in number." (Alfred Whital Stern Collection, Rare Books & Special Collections Division, Library of Congress)

Three years after Douglas's death at the age of forty-eight, the senator's widow, Adele Cutts Douglas, presented this *carte de visite* photograph of her late husband to President Lincoln, probably during a visit to the White House, "autographing" and dating the portrait herself. The Lincolns placed the picture in their family photograph album, where Douglas became the only Democrat, save for political renegades among their own relatives, to be included in their private collection. (The Lincoln Museum)

MR. DOUGLAS' REJOINDER

[When Senator Douglas rose to reply to Mr. Lincoln, six cheers were called for in the crowd, and given with great spirit. He said, quieting the applause: —*Times*]

Now, gentlemen, the highest compliment you can pay me during the brief half hour I have to conclude, is your entire silence. I desire to be heard rather than to be applauded. [Good. —*Times*]

The first criticism that Mr. Lincoln makes on my speech is, that it is in substance what I have said everywhere else in the State, when I have addressed the people. I wish I could say the same of his speeches. [Laughter. —*Tribune;* Good; you have him, and applause. —*Times*] The principal point of complaint I make of him is, that he makes one speech North and another South [That's so. —*Times*] —one set of sentiments in the Abolition counties, and another set in those counties opposed to Abolitionism. [Hit him over the Knuckles. —*Times*] The point of complaint is, that I cannot hold him to a common standard in the different portions of the State. He didn't pretend—no other man will—that I have one set of principles for Galesburg and another for Charleston. [No, no. —*Times*] He didn't pretend I have one set for Chicago and another for Jonesboro. I have proved that he has different sets of principles for each locality. [Cries of "It's not so," &c., and great confusion. —*Tribune*] Silence, if you please. All I could ask of him was to have delivered the speech that he has made to-day—that the speech he has made to-day, he would have delivered in Coles county, instead of old Knox. It would have settled the question between him and me in that doubtful county, if the speech delivered here had been made there. Here I understand him to re-affirm the doctrine of equality—that by the Declaration of Independence, the negro is declared equal to the white man. He tells you to-day that the negro was included in the Declaration of Independence, which says all men were created equal.

A VOICE—We believe it.

JUDGE DOUGLAS—You believe it. Very well! [The *Times* added: "Here an uproar arose, persons in various parts of the crowd indulging in cat calls, groans, cheers, and other noises, preventing the speaker from proceeding"—*ed.*] Gentlemen, I ask you to remember that Mr. Lincoln was listened to respectfully, and I have a right to insist that I shall not be interrupted in my reply.

[MR. LINCOLN—I hope that silence will be preserved. —*Times*]

He asserts to-day, as he did in Chicago, that that [*sic*] the negro was included in that clause of the Declaration of Independence which says that all men were created equal, and endowed by the Creator with certain inalienable rights, among which are life, liberty, and the pursuit of happiness. [Ain't that so? —*Times*] Then, if the negro was made his equal and mine, if that equality was established by Divine law, if that equality was an inalienable right, how came he to say at Charleston to those Kentuckians that the negro was physically inferior to the white man, belonged to an inferior race, and he was for keeping him always in that inferior condition? [Good. —*Times*] I wish you to bear those things in mind. In Charleston he says, the negro belongs to an inferior race, and that he is for keeping them in that inferior condition. There he gave them to understand that there was no moral question in it, because the inferiority being established, it was only a question of degree and not a question of right. Here to-day, instead of making it a question of degree he says it is a great crime to hold him in that inferior position. He holds that it was a great wrong to hold him in that inferior condition. [He's right. —*Times*] Is he right now, or was he right at Charleston? [Cries of "both," "both," "both." —*Tribune* and *Times*] This according to your doctrine, is right in one locality and wrong in another, so as to secure votes. All I desire is that he will declare the same doctrine in the North that he does in the South, and wherever the Constitution rules.

But did you notice how he answers my position that a man should hold the same doctrine throughout the length and breadth of this Republic? He says, would Judge Douglas go to Russia and proclaim the same principles that he does here? I remind him that Russia is not under the American Constitution. If Russia was a part of the American Republic under the same constitution, I would maintain the same doctrine that I do in the United States [the *Times* substituted "Illinois"—*ed.*]. [Applause. —*Tribune;* Cheers. —*Times*]

These slaveholders are under the same federal constitution with ourselves. Hence, any man's principles, to be in harmony with the Constitution, must be the same in the North as they are in the South, the same in the free States that they are in the slave States. And whenever a man advocates one set of principles in one section, and another in another section, his opinions are in violation of the Constitution which he has sworn to support, ["That's the doctrine." —*Tribune;*

"That's so." —*Times*] Suppose when Mr. Lincoln went to Congress in 1847, and put his hand on the Holy Evangelists, and took a solemn oath in presence of high heaven, he would be faithful to the Constitution, how did he mean—the Constitution as he explains it in Galesburg, or the Constitution as he explains it at Charleston[?] [Laughter. —*Tribune;* Cheers. —*Times*]

Mr. Lincoln has devoted considerable time to the circumstance of my having read at Ottawa a series of resolutions as having been adopted at Springfield, in this State, on the 5th of October, 1854. He has used hard names—has dared to talk about fraud [Laughter. —*Times*] and about forgery, and has insinuated that there was a conspiracy between Mr. Lanphier, Mr. Harris and myself to perpetrate a forgery. [Renewed laughter. —*Times*] Now bear in mind that he did not deny but what those resolutions were adopted by a majority of all the Republican party in the First Congressional District, in the second, in the third and in many counties in the north, and this became the platform of the party in a majority of the counties upon which he now relies for support. He didn't deny the truthfulness of the resolutions, but he takes exception to the spot where they were adopted. [Laughter. —*Tribune*] He makes a great merit that they were not adopted on the right spot, as he thought the Mexican war was unjust because it was not begun on the right spot. [Renewed laughter. —*Times*] He tries to make out that there was something very extraordinary simply on account of the place where the thing was done, and not of the thing itself. Now, I never believed before that Abraham Lincoln would have been guilty of what he has done this day in regard to those resolutions. [Applause. —*Tribune*] In the first place, the moment it was intimated to me that the resolutions were adopted at Bloomington and then at Aurora and then at Rockford, instead of Springfield, I did not wait for him to call my attention to it, but led off and explained in advance at my first meeting what the mistake was, and how it was made. [That's so. —*Times*] I would suppose that with every honest man conscious of his own rectitude, that explanation would have been sufficient. I did not wait for him when the mistake had been made to call my attention to it, but frankly explained it as an honest man would. [Applause. —*Tribune;* Cheers. —*Times*] (Here Judge Douglas turned round to Mr. Lincoln and talked to him.) I explained the authority also on which I made the statement, that having seen these transcriptions quoted by Major Harris in a debate in Congress as having been adopted by the first Republican State Convention in Illinois, I wrote to Major Harris asking him for the authority as to place and time of their adoption. Harris being extremely ill, Charles H. Lanphier called at his sick bed, received his answer, and wrote to me that it was adopted at Springfield on the 5th of October, 1854, and sent me a copy of the Springfield paper containing them. I read them from the newspaper just as Mr. Lincoln reads the proceedings of meetings years ago in the files of newspapers he finds. I made the explanation at the time. I did not believe that there was an honest man in the State of Illinois who did not believe that it was an error I was led into innocently in that way. I will say more, that I do not believe that there is an honest man on the face of this State that don't abhor with disgust his insinuations of my complicity with that forgery, as he calls it. [Applause. —*Tribune;* Cheers. —*Times*] Does he wish to push these things to the point of personal difficulties here? I began this contest treating him courteously, kindly, and spoke of him in words of respect. He seems now to try to divert the public attention from the enormity of his revolutionary principles by getting into personal quarrels, impeaching my sincerity and integrity. [Give it to him, and cheers. —*Times*] I desired to conduct the contest with him like a gentleman, but I spurn the insinuation of there being a complicity in a fraud merely because an editor of a newspaper had made a mistake as to the place where the thing was done, instead of the thing itself. These resolutions were the platform of the Republican party that year. They were adopted in the majority of all the Republican counties in the State, and it was those resolutions that I asked him to answer at Ottawa, and he won't answer. At Ottawa he himself believed that those resolutions were adopted at Springfield. He did not deny it, but said he wasn't there when they were adopted, but was attending Tazewell Court. He thought he had seen them published as having been adopted there just as I did. He knew that if there was a mistake I had nothing under heaven to do with that mistake. But yet you find in all these northern counties candidates running pledged to him for the Senate, yet adopting that political platform. One cardinal point in that platform which he shrinks from is that there should be no more Slave States admitted into this Union even if the people wanted them. Lovejoy stands pledged against any more Slave States.

A VOICE—So do I.

JUDGE DOUGLAS—So do you[, you] say[.] [John F.] Farnsworth too stands pledged against more Slave States. [Most right. —*Times*] [Elihu]

Washburne stands pledged against any more Slave States being received upon any condition. [Good, good. —*Times*] The candidate for the Legislature, who is running on Lincoln's ticket in Henderson and Warren Counties, stands pledged for the same thing, and I am informed, though I do not know the fact certainly, that your candidate stands pledged to the same thing.

A VOICE—Good for him.

JUDGE DOUGLAS—Now you Republicans all hallow "hurrah for him," and yet Mr. Lincoln tells you that his conscience won't enable him to sustain that doctrine. [Immense applause. —*Times*] Mr. Lincoln's complaint is that these resolutions which I have read, make him, as a member of the party, responsible for and sanctioning the doctrine of no more Slave States, while he won't be committed to it. Now you are one way, as you confess, and he pretends that he is the other, and yet you are both governed by principle, and you are governed by principle, I suppose, in your vote. Now if it be true that in all this north half of the State, the Republican party stands committed to the doctrine of no more Slave States, while that doctrine is repudiated by the Republicans in the other half of the State, I wonder if Mr. Lincoln and his party has not presented the case that he has cited in the Scripture, that a house divided against itself cannot stand. [Applause. —*Tribune;* Tremendous shouts of applause. —*Times*] I desire to find out what his principles are on that point. I want to know the principles of his party. I hold, and the party with which I am identified hold, and that [*sic*] the people of each State, old or new, have a right to decide this slavery question for themselves.

A VOICE—That's it sir. ["Right," and immense applause. —*Times*]

JUDGE DOUGLAS—When I used the remark that "I didn't care whether slavery was voted up or voted down," I used it in this connection—I was for allowing Kansas to do just as she pleased on the slavery question. I said, I care not whether they vote it up or vote it down, because they have a right to do as they please, and my action would not be controlled by their decision. [That's the doctrine. —*Times*] Why can't he, or the party with which he acts, speak out their principles, so that they would not be misunderstood, and not claim to be one way in one part of the State and another in a different part of the State? Whenever I advance these Abolition doctrines, which he complains of as being slanderous when applied to him—whenever I advance them up here, you halloo out "That's right," not knowing that your candidate is the other way. [You have them; and cheers. —*Times*]

Now I have a few words to say on the Dred Scott case, which has troubled the brains of Lincoln so much. [Laughter. —*Times*] He goes on and insists that the Dred Scott decision would carry slavery into the free States, notwithstanding the decision itself says the contrary. He made an argument to make me believe that I was in favor of and would sanction the doctrine that slaves could be brought here to Illinois as slaves, contrary to our State Constitution and laws. Now Mr. Lincoln knew the facts about that. He knew that but one newspaper in America, and so far as I know but one, ever asserted the doctrine, and that I was the first man in either House of Congress that read the article in a speech in the Senate, denouncing it on the spot as revolutionary. When the Washington *Union,* on the 17th of November, published an article to that effect I branded it, and hence the *Union* has been pursuing me ever since. Mr. [Robert] Toombs, of Georgia, replied to me by saying that there wasn't a man south of the Potomac River in all the Slave States that held any such doctrine. Mr. Lincoln knows that there is no member of the Supreme Court that holds that doctrine. He knows that every one of them in their opinions hold the reverse. Why then this attempt to bring the Supreme Court into disrepute among the people? It looks as if there was an effort to destroy public confidence in the highest judicial tribunal on earth. Suppose a man succeeded in destroying public confidence in the Court, so that the people would not respect its decisions, so that men will feel at liberty to disregard and resist the laws of the land, what will he have gained? He will have changed this Government from one of laws to that of a mob, in which the strong arm of power and violence will be substituted for the decisions of the courts of justice. ["Pretty good." —*Tribune;* "That's so." —*Times*] He complains that I don't go into the argument and review Justice Taney's opinions, and the other opinions of the different Judges, to determine whether their reasoning is right or wrong on the question of law. What use would that be? He wants to take an appeal from the decision of the Supreme Court to this meeting to decide whether a question of law was rightly settled. He is going to appeal from the Supreme Court to every town meeting, in the hope of exciting prejudice against the Supreme Court, and on the wave of that prejudice, ride into the Senate of the United States, when he couldn't get there upon his own principles or his own merits. [Laughter and cheers; "hit him again." —*Times*] Suppose he should succeed in getting into the Senate, what then will he have to do with the decision of the Supreme Court in the Dred Scott case? Can he reverse the decision when he gets there? Can he act upon it? Has the Senate any right to reverse or revise it? He will not pretend that. Then why drag it into this canvass, unless it is to make a false issue, upon which he can divert public opinion from the real issue. He then cites Gen. Jackson for his justification, in making war upon the decision of the Supreme Court. Mr. Lincoln misunderstands the history of the country, if he believes there is any parallel. It is true the Supreme Court once decided that if the Bank of the United States was a necessary financial agent of the government, it was constitutional; if it was not, it was unconstitutional; and whether it was necessary for that purpose, was a political and not a judicial question, for Congress to determine. Hence the Court would not declare the Bank unconstitutional. Jackson respected the decision and executed the law—obeyed it and carried it into effect during the whole existence of the law [that's so, —*Times*]. After the Bank expired, when there was a proposition to create a new Bank, Gen. Jackson said it is unnecessary, improper and not needed, and I will go against it on constitutional grounds as well as those of expediency. Is Congress bound to pass every act that is constitutional? There may be a dozen things constitutional, that are inexpedient and unnecessary, and hence you would not have them merely because you had the right to do so. Now because Gen. Jackson would not do a thing he had a right to do, Mr. Lincoln is to be justified in doing that which he had no right to do. [Laughter. —*Times*] I asked him whether he is not bound by the decision of the Supreme Court as well as I. The Constitution has created that Court to decide all constitutional questions in the last resort. When they had made a decision it becomes the law of the land, [that's so, —*Times*] and you, and I, and every good citizen is bound by it. Yet he assumes that I am bound by it, and he is not. [A laugh. —*Tribune*] He says the decision is binding on all Democrats, but not on Republicans. [Laughter and applause. —*Times*] Are not the Republicans bound by the laws of the land as well as the Democrats; and when the Court has fixed the construction of the Constitution upon the validity of a given law, is it not binding upon Republicans as well as Democrats? ["Yes, sir, certainly." —*Tribune;* It ought to be. —*Times*] Is it possible that you [the *Times* added "Republicans"—*ed.*] have a right to sway your party to raise mobs against [the *Times* added: "and oppose the laws of the land and"—*ed.*] the constituted authorities, and yet hold us bound by their decisions? I have only to say to you on that point, that I stand by the laws of the land. [That's it; hurrah for Douglas. —*Times*] I stand by the Constitution as our fathers made it, by the laws as they are enacted, and by the decisions of the Courts upon all points within their jurisdiction, as they are announced by the highest tribunal on earth, and any man that resists those must resort to mob law and violence, and overturn the government [the *Times* added: "of laws"—*ed.*]. [Applause. —*Tribune;* When Senator Douglas concluded, the applause was perfectly furious and overwhelming . . . —*Times*]

THE SIXTH JOINT DEBATE AT QUINCY

Wednesday, October 13, 1858

·THE SCENE·

LOCATED AT THE far western edge of central Illinois, just across the Mississippi River from the state of Missouri, Quincy was moderate in political sentiment, with a slight edge in support for the Democrats. In short, it was typical of the regions in which both candidates needed to broaden their appeal in order to win the election. Perhaps for just this reason, the debate here degenerated into one of the nastiest of the campaign. "It is certainly to be regretted," a journalist complained afterwards, "that the canvass in Illinois has turned so much on personal issues."

By midday, boats filled with spectators were steaming in from both Hannibal, Missouri, and Keokuk, Iowa, swelling the total crowd to between 10,000 and 15,000 people. The day was sunny and pleasantly cool, but visitors were forced to brave hazardous roads drenched in water and mud from days of incessant rain. Nonetheless, the usual array of partisans paraded in on carts, buggies, and carriages. Long before the scheduled commencement of debate at two-thirty p.m., a reporter described the town square as "pretty well filled up with a living, moving multitude." A visitor recalled "there was no end of cheering and shouting and jostling on the streets."

Douglas had entered town the previous night aboard his lavishly appointed special railroad car. As usual, the party newspapers provided wildly different descriptions of his reception. The Democratic reporters on the scene for his ten p.m. arrival noted an "extensive and brilliant torch light" procession, the grand illumination of the outside wall of the Quincy House hotel, and the proud display of a wreath-ornamented portrait of the Little Giant. To Republican observers, however, the demonstration was a "miserable fizzle," with the welcoming committee composed solely of "a small sized Irish mob"—an ethnic slur again designed to alarm voters who disliked Catholics and immigrants.

In turn, Democratic journals characterized Lincoln's entrance into Quincy with similar hostility. But Lincoln supporters insisted that their candidate's train from Macomb was met by a cheering crowd, a cannon salute, and an all-ladies' chorus singing a political song to the tune of "Columbia, the Gem of the Ocean." The highlight was a boisterous parade featuring a horse-drawn model of the U.S.S. *Constitution* piloted by "a live coon," the symbol of the old Whig Party. It was another reminder that in Quincy, and surrounding Adams County, there was a heated battle afoot for crucial middle-of-the-road support. (Lincoln had calmly occupied himself on the train journey greeting supporters and telling "all sorts of quaint stories.")

Banners and signs promoting both candidates filled the streets for the occasion, and while the partisan press claimed clear-cut crowd preference for their respective candidates, the German-born Lincoln supporter Carl Schurz probably came closest to the truth when he admitted that "the Democratic displays were much more elaborate and gorgeous than those of the Republicans," although he hastened to add: "Douglas had plenty of money to spend for such things." Douglas also wore his finest clothes for the meeting, while Lincoln came dressed in his usual wrinkled suit and battered hat. Earlier, Schurz had observed him carrying a gray woolen shawl, a "bulging" umbrella, and a worn satchel in his left hand, leaving the right one free for constant handshaking. He looked not only "lank" and "ungainly" but "uncouth" and "grotesque."

By debate time, the town was seething with people, and a loud, jostling crowd surrounded the "large, pine-board platform" built in Washington Square for the occasion. Predictably, before the speeches could begin, a few minor disasters delayed the proceedings. First, a railing along the stage gave way to the intense pressure, sending a dozen dignitaries and a large bench crashing to the ground. Then another bench, set up in front of the platform for the benefit of the ladies, collapsed under their weight, and several of the dazed victims had to be assisted from the area.

When order was restored, Lincoln opened the debate in a voice, Schurz admitted, that seemed "a shrill treble in moments of excitement." Sitting on the platform at Lincoln's invitation, he gazed into the crowd while Lincoln spoke, convinced nonetheless by "the looks of the audience . . . that every word he spoke was understood at the remotest edges of the vast assemblage."

Lincoln reiterated his view that "there is no reason in the world why the negro is not entitled to all the natural rights enumerated in the Declaration of Independence," and quoted from some of his earlier debate speeches to prove his consistency on the issue. After accusing Douglas of his own acts of inconsistency, Lincoln turned again to slavery, suggesting in the strongest terms he had yet used that the institution was "an evil so far as it seeks to spread itself."

In his hour and a half of rebuttal, Douglas again charged that Lincoln altered his views on Negro equality to suit southern and northern audiences. He persisted in his refusal to debate the right or wrong of slavery, and where the Dred Scott decision was concerned, declared more bluntly than ever that it was "the law of the land, binding on every citizen."

With this new opening before him, Lincoln used his rejoinder to suggest that Douglas's frank admission finally brought the candidates "a little nearer the true issue of this controversy." It was clearer than ever, he charged, that the Democratic party was conspiring to make slavery national and permanent. As for equality for blacks, Lincoln joked: "I, for my part, have lived some fifty years. And I never had a negro slave or a negro wife, and I think I can live fifty centuries for that matter without having either."

Carl Schurz marveled at how Lincoln changed the pace of the

debate for these final thirty minutes, hitting out at Douglas "with rapid thrusts so deft and piercing, with humorous retorts so quaint"—a technique vividly brought to life by these unedited transcriptions. His voice was "exceedingly penetrating," Schurz attested, granting that at best, its tone was "not positively disagreeable." As for Lincoln's manner of "enlivening a speech,"—"he would, to give particular emphasis to a point, bend his knees and body with a sudden downward jerk, and then shoot up again with a vehemence"—Schurz remembered that it made him look even "taller than he really was."

The Democratic press insisted that Douglas won the day by demonstrating "more than usual eloquence," while a Republican journal taunted that a "photographic agent" earlier seen hawking Douglas portraits during his rebuttal for seventy-five cents apiece reduced his price to sixty cents midway through the speech, and ended up pleading with customers to take them off his hands for only twenty-five cents each.

But Lincoln was learning that poor debate outings could do far more permanent damage to speakers later, if put into print unedited. Just before Quincy, he received word that the *Times* transcript of the first meeting at Ottawa—arguably his most desultory debate performance—had been published in a pamphlet. "There are about 10000 of this pamphlet in this place for circulation," wrote a worried supporter from Napierville. ". . . Your speech is in very poor type while Douglass' [*sic*] is good clear & large." Lincoln's section read so poorly that the admirer was certain it had been "badly mutilated." Of one thing he was certain: if broadly circulated, the "damnable document" would "work a great injury to yourself & our party's cause." Lincoln was even urged to call attention to the publication at his next debate, "enough to stamp it in the minds of all honest men with the title it deserves." He did not follow this advice, but as his later efforts to republish the "friendly" transcripts suggest, he appears to have learned from the experience.

Following are the transcripts reported in the rival press.

MR. LINCOLN'S OPENING SPEECH

[Mr. Lincoln took the stand, and received the welcome of three cheers from his friends; considerable of a mixture occurred in cheering. He proceeded to his remarks as follows: —*Times;* At precisely half past two o'clock Mr. Lincoln was introduced to the audience, and having been received with three cheers, he proceeded: —*Tribune*]

LADIES AND GENTLEMEN: I have had no immediate conversation with Judge Douglas, but I will undertake to say, that he and I are perfectly agreed that your entire silence when I speak, and when he speaks, will be most agreeable to us. [Cries of "Sit down in front," and considerable commotion. —*Times*]

In the month of May, 1856, the elements in the State of Illinois, which have since been consolidated into the Republican party, assembled together in a State convention at Bloomington. They adopted at that time what, in political language, is called a platform. In June of the same year the elements of the Republican party of the nation assembled together in a national convention at Philadelphia, and they adopted what is called a national platform. In June, 1858—the present year— the Republicans of Illinois re-assembled at Springfield in State convention, and adopted again their platform, as I suppose, not differing in any essential particular from either of the former ones, but perhaps adding something in relation to the new developments of political progress in the country. The convention that assembled in June last did me the honor—if it be one, and I esteem it such—to name me as their candidate for the United States Senate. I have supposed that in entering upon that canvass I stood, generally, upon this platform. We are now met together, on the 13th day of October of the same year, near four months from the adoption of the last platform, and I am unaware that in this canvass, from the beginning of it until to-day, any one of our adversaries has taken hold of our platform and laid his finger upon anything in it that he called wrong.

In the very first one of these joint discussions, between Senator Douglas and myself, Senator Douglas, without alluding at all to these platforms or any one of them of which I have spoken, attempted to hold me responsible [a voice, "hurrah for Douglas" —*Times*] for a set of resolutions passed long before the meeting of either of these conventions I have spoken of, and, as his ground for holding me responsible for those resolutions, he assumed, that they had been passed at a State convention of the Republican party, and, that I took part in that convention. It was discovered, afterwards, that this was erroneous— that the resolutions which he endeavored to hold me responsible for had not been passed by any State convention anywhere, and had not been passed at Springfield where he supposed they had, or assumed that they had, and had been passed by no convention in which I had taken any part. The Judge, nevertheless, was not willing to give up the point that he was endeavoring to make upon me, and he therefore sought to hold me to the point that he was endeavoring to make, by showing that the resolutions that he had read had been passed at a local convention in the northern part of the State, and that, although it was not a local convention that embraced my residence, nor one that reached nearer as I suppose, than 150 or 200 miles of where I resided; nor one in which I had taken any part at all. [Cries of "sit down in front" —*Times*] He also introduced other resolutions, passed at other meetings, and by combining the whole, although they were all antecedent to the two State and one National convention I have made mention of still ins[i]sted and now insists, as I understand him, that I am in some way responsible for them. At Jonesboro, at our third meeting, I insisted that I was no way rightfully to be held responsible for the proceedings of those meetings and local conventions in which I had taken no part, and in which I was in no way embraced, but I insisted to him, that if he thought that the rule was different, and that if he thought that I was responsible for every man, or set of men that was my friend, the rule worked both ways, and he ought to be responsible for the sayings and doings of all men and set of men that were his friends, and I gave him a pretty long string of resolutions by men who were his friends announcing doctrines which he does not approve.

This still does not satisfy the Judge. He still insists that I am responsible for what some of my friends in different parts of the State have done, yet he is not content that he should be held responsible for what his friends in different places have said and done.

But in addition to that, the Judge, at our meeting at Galesburg on Thursday of last week, undertook to establish that I am guilty of a species of double dealing with the public—that I make speeches of a certain sort in the north, among abolitionists, which I would not make in the south; and that I make speeches of a certain sort in the south which I would not make in the north. I apprehend, in the course that

I have marked out for myself, that I shall not have an opportunity to dwell at great length upon this topic. As this was done in the Judge's opening speech at Galesburg, I had an opportunity, as I had the middle speech there, of saying something in answer to it. He brought forward a quotation or two, perhaps three, from a speech of mine delivered at Chicago, and then took contrast with it from an extract from a speech of mine made at Charleston in which he insisted that I was greatly at variance, speaking one way at one time, and another way at another time. I wish only now—for I have not time to dwell upon it as long as I would like to do—I wish only now to quote that portion of my speech which the Judge quoted and then make some comments on it.

This he quoted from me as being delivered at Charleston, I believe correctly:

> "I will say then that I am not nor ever have been in favor of bringing about in any way the social and political equality of the white and black races: that I am not nor ever have been in favor of making voters of the free negroes, or jurors, or qualifying them to hold office or having them to marry with white people. I will say in addition that there is a physical difference between the white and black races which I suppose will forever forbid the two races living together upon terms of social and political equality, and inasmuch as they cannot so live that while they do remain together there must be the position of superior and inferior, that I as much as any other man am in favor of the superior position being assigned to the white man." ["Good," "Good," and loud cheers. —*Tribune*]

This I believe is the entire quotation, from the Charleston speech, as the Judge made it. His comments are as follows:

> "Yes, here you find men that hurrah for Lincoln, and say he is right when he discards all distinction between races, or when he declares that he discards the doctrine that there is such a thing as a superior and inferior race; and Abolitionists are required and expected to vote for Mr. Lincoln because he goes for the equality of the races, holding that in the Declaration of Independence the white man and the negro were declared equal, and endowed by Divine law with equality. And down South with the old line Whigs, with the Kentuckians, the Virginians, and the Tennesseeans, he tells you that there is a physical

difference between the races, making the one superior then the other inferior, and he is in favor of maintaining the superiority of the white race over the negro."

That is the Judge's comment. Now, I wish to show you that a month—or lacking only three days of one month, before I made the speech at Charleston which the Judge quotes from, he had himself heard me say substantially the same thing. That was at our first meeting at Ottawa, and I will say a word about where it was, the atmosphere it was in, after a while. At our first joint meeting at Ottawa I had read an extract from an old speech of mine, made four years ago, not in order to show my sentiments merely, but to show that my sentiments were long entertained and openly expressed, in which extract I had declared that my own feelings would not admit of there being brought about a political and social equality between the white man and the negro, and, if it were otherwise, then the sentiment in the public mind would not admit of it. That extract from my own speech the reporters, by some accident, never reported. I lay no blame on anybody. I suppose they thought they would get it from me and then went away without getting it of me. At the end of the quotation from my own speech I made the comments which were reported at the time, and which I will now read. I will ask you to notice that they are nearly the very same that the Judge quotes as having been too much so for good taste. After that reading I added these words:

"Now, gentlemen, I don't want to read at any great length, but this is the true complexion of all that I have ever said in regard to the institution of slavery and the black race. This is the whole of it, and anything that argues me into this idea of perfect, social, and political equality with the negro is but a specious and fantastic arrangement of words by which a man can prove a horse ches[t]nut to be a ches[t]nut horse. I will say here, while upon this subject, that I have no purpose directly or indirectly [to] interfere with the institution of slavery in the States where it exists. I believe I have no lawful right to do so, and I have no inclination to do so. I have no purpose to introduce political and social equality between the white and the black races. There is a physical difference between the two, which, in my judgment, will probably forever forbid their living together upon a footing of perfect equality, and inasmuch as it becomes a necessity that there must be a difference, I, as well as Judge Douglas, am in favor of the race to which

I belong having the superior position. [Cheers, "That's the doctrine." —*Tribune*] I have never said anything to the contrary, but I hold that notwithstanding all this, there is no reason in the world why the negro is not entitled to all the natural rights enumerated in the Declaration of Independence—the right to life, liberty, and the pursuit of happiness. I hold that he is as much entitled to these as the white man. I agree with Judge Douglas, he is not my equal in many respects—certainly not in color, perhaps not in moral and intellectual endowment; but in the right to eat the bread without leave of anybody else, which his own hands earns [*sic*], he is my equal, and the equal of Judge Douglas, and the equal of every living man." [Loud cheers. —*Tribune*]

I have chiefly introduced this for the purpose of meeting the Judge's charge, that the quotation he took from my Charleston speech was what I would say down south among Kentuckians, Virginians, and so on, and what I would not say to an audience where there was supposed to be more of the Abolition element. I now make this comment on it! That that speech which I have read from now, that speech was made away up north—was made in the Abolition district of this State *par excellence*— in the Lovejoy district—in the personal presence of Lovejoy, for he was on the stand when I made it that day, made and put in print, lacking three days only of a month ago, in that district, the like of which Judge Douglas thinks I would not make in the north.

In addition, I have but to say, that I am unconscious of double dealing any where. I believe, leaving many things unsaid—that I have but on one occasion said any thing which has seemed to be inconsistent, I deny it, at least so far as the intention has gone. [The *Tribune* version reads: ". . . upon one occasion I may say one thing and leave other things unsaid, and *vice versa;* but that I have said anything on one occasion that is inconsistent with what I have said elsewhere, I deny,— at least I deny it so far as the intention is concerned." The *Times* version made it appear that Lincoln was admitting to inconsistency—*ed.*]

I find that I have devoted to this topic a larger portion of my time than I intended to do in the discussion of this point. I wished to show, but I will pass it by for this occasion, that I am entirely borne out by our old Whig leader, Henry Clay. I have the book here, but as I have occupied more time on this subject than I desired to do, I pass by that topic.

Also, at Galesburg, I had tried to show that by the Dred Scott decision, carried to its legitimate consequences, slavery would be established in all the States as well as in the territories; I had done this because upon a former occasion I had asked Judge Douglas whether if the Supreme Court should make a decision declaring that the States had not power to exclude slavery from their limits, whether he would adopt and follow that decision as a rule of political action, and because he had not directly answered that question, but had merely contented himself with sneering at it, I again introduced it. I tried to show that the conclusion that I stated, followed inevitably from the decision that had already been made by the court. Judge Douglas had the reply upon me that time. Again he made no direct answer as to whether he would or would not sustain such a decision if made. I give him this third chance to say "yes" or "no!" He is not obliged to do either—probably will not do either—[Laughter. —*Tribune*] but I give him this third chance. I tried to show them that this conclusion inevitably followed from the point already decided by the court. The Judge in his reply upon me, again sneers at the thought of the court making any such decision and in the course of his remarks upon that subject he uses the language which I will now read. Speaking of me, the Judge goes on:

"He goes on and insists that the Dred Scott decision would carry slavery into the free States notwithstanding the decision itself says the contrary."

And he does more, he says—

"Mr. Lincoln knows that there is no member of the Supreme Court that holds that doctrine. He knows that every one of them in their opinions holds the reverse."

I especially introduce this subject again for the purpose of saying that I have the Dred Scott decision here, and I will thank Judge Douglas to lay his finger upon the place in that decision where the court in their opinion said the contrary, or to lay his hand upon a place in the entire opinions of the members of the court where any one of them said the contrary. It is very hard to affirm, with entire confidence, a negative. I say, however, that I have examined that decision with a good deal of care, a good deal like a lawyer would examine a decision, and so far as I have been able to do so the court has nowhere in its opinion said that States have the power to exclude slavery, nor used other language substantially that. I also say that so far as I can find, no one of the concurring Judges has said that any State can exclude slavery, or substantially that. I say that the nearest approach that any one of them has made to it, so far as I can find, was Judge Nelson, and the approach that he made to it was exactly the Nebraska bill, that the States have exclusive power over the question of slavery, so far as is not limited by the Constitution of the United States; and I ask the question, if the non-concurring Judges—McLean and Curtis—had asked to get an opinion into it, that the States could exclude slavery from their limits, what reason we have to believe that it would not be voted down, as the amendment of Chase was voted down by Judge Douglas and his compeers, when it was offered to the Nebraska bill. [Cheers. —*Tribune*]

I have yet to use half an hour.

Also, at Galesburg, I said something in regard to those Springfield resolutions that Judge Douglas had attempted to use upon me at Ottawa. I commented at some length upon the fact that they were, as presented, not genuine. Judge Douglas in his reply to me, seemed to be somewhat exasperated. He said he would never have believed that Abraham Lincoln, as he kindly called me, would have attempted such a thing as I had attempted on that occasion, and among other expressions that he used towards me was that I had dared to say forgery—that I had dared to say forgery! [Turning to Judge Douglas —*Tribune*] Well, yes, Judge, I did dare to say forgery. [Laughter and applause —*Times; Loud applause. —*Tribune*] But in this political canvass the Judge ought to remember that I was not the first who dared to say forgery. At Jacksonville Judge Douglas made a speech in answer to something said by Judge Trumbull [Lyman Trumbull, pro-Lincoln U.S. senator from Illinois who returned home in 1858 to campaign against Douglas—*ed.*] and at the close of what he said on that subject, he dared to say that Trumbull had forged his evidence from beginning to end. [A voice, "Hurrah for Douglas." —*Times*] And he said that he should not concern himself with Trumbull any more, but, thereafter he should hold Lincoln responsible for these slanders upon him. [Applause and cries of "Hurrah for Douglas." —*Times; Laughter. —*Tribune*] Well, I met him at Charleston after that, although I think I should not have introduced the subject if he had not said he should hold me responsible for it. I spread out before him a statement of the evidence that Judge Trumbull had used, and I asked Judge Douglas, piece by piece, to put his finger upon any piece of that evidence that he would say was a forgery, and when I went through each and every piece, Judge Douglas did not dare to say that any piece was a forgery. [Laughter, and cries of "good, good." —*Tribune*] So it seems that there are some things that Judge Douglas dares to do and some that he dares not to do. [Great applause and laughter. —*Tribune*]

[A VOICE—"That's the same way as you are." —*Times;* "It's the same thing with you." —*Tribune*]

MR. LINCOLN—Yes, sir, it is the same way with me! I do dare to say forgery when it was true, and I don't dare to say it when it is not. [Applause—cries of "hurrah for Douglas," "hurrah for Lincoln," "hit him again," and "you don't hit mighty hard." —*Times;* Thunders of applause. Cries of "Hit him again," "Give it to him, Lincoln." —*Tribune*] I will say here to this audience, and to Judge Douglas, that I have not yet dared to say that he committed the forgery, and I never shall until I know it; but I did dare to say and suggest to him that a forgery had been committed, which, by his own showing, was traced to him and two of his friends. [Applause —*Times;* Roars of laughter and loud cheers. —*Tribune*] I tried to suggest to him that he had expressly promised, in one of his public speeches, to investigate that matter, and I tried to suggest to him that there was an implied promise that when he had made that investigation that he would make the result known. I tried to suggest to him that he was not quite clear of all suspicion of that fraud, after he had been with his friends until, having an opportunity to make that investigation, yet he should make known the result. [Loud laughter. Cries of "Good, good," "Hit him hard." —*Tribune*] I dared to do that much, and I am not a very daring man, but I dared that much, and I am not much scared about it. [Applause and laughter. —*Times;* Uproarious laughter and applause. —*Tribune*] When the Judge says that he would not have believed that Abraham Lincoln would make such an attempt as that, it reminds me that he entered upon this canvass, with a purpose to treat me courteously, why it touches me some [Great laughter. —*Tribune*]—it sets me to thinking. I was aware, when it was first agreed that Judge Douglas and I were to have these seven joint discussions, that they were the successive acts of a drama, perhaps I shall say, to be enacted not entirely in the face of an audience like this, but in the face of the nation, and to some extent by my relation to him and not for anything in me, in the face of the world, and I was anxious that they should be conducted with a dignity and a degree of good temper that should be befitting the vast audience before which it was conducted. But when Judge Douglas got home from Washington, and made his first speech at Chicago, and I made the evening after, some sort of a reply to it; his second speech in Illinois was made at Bloomington, in which, in commenting upon my speech at Chicago, he said that I had used language ingeniously contrived to conceal my intentions, or words to that effect. Now, I understood that to be an imputation upon my veracity; I don't know what the Judge understood by it; but in our first discussion, at Ottawa, he led off there by charging a bargain somewhat corrupt in its character, upon Trumbull and myself, that we had entered into a bargain, one of the terms of which was, that Trumbull was to abolitionize the old Democratic party, and I, Lincoln, was to abolitionize the old Whig party, and that I, Lincoln, pretended all the while to be as good a Whig as ever. Now, the Judge may not understand that he implicated my truth, and my honor, when he said I was doing one thing and saying another, but I misunderstood him if he was treating me as a man of truth and honor, such as he now claims to have been disposed to treat me as.

Even now, even at Galesburg, when he brings forward an extract from a speech made by me at Chicago, and an extract of a speech made by me at Charleston, to set them in contrast to prove upon me that I am playing a double part—and to prove that I am trying to cheat the public that I may get votes upon one set of principles in one place, and upon another at another place, I do not understand but he does impeach my honor, truth, and candor, and because he does this I do not see that I am bound, if I see truthful grounds for it, to keep my hands off of him. I suggested, as soon as I learned that Judge Douglas was disposed to treat me in this way—I suggested then—that I should be obliged—should be driven—to draw upon the humble resources that I had, and to act on a different course toward him. I know that I will not be the first to cry hold. I think it originated with the Judge, and when he quits, I probably will. [Laughter and applause. —*Times;* Roars of laughter. —*Tribune*] But I shall not ask any favors at all.

He asks me, or rather, perhaps, asks the audience, if I wish to press this matter to the point of personal difficulty. I tell him no. He did not mis-state, in one of his early speeches, when he called me an amiable man, though, perhaps, he did when he called me an intelligent man. [A voice, "He did so." —*Times;* Laughter. —*Tribune*] It really hurts me to suppose that I have wronged any man on earth. I tell him no. I very much prefer, when this canvass shall be over, to continue to be on terms of friendship, let it result as it may.

A VOICE—"We don't want to hear your long yarns."

MR. L.—Now, is my friend entirely sure that these people agree with him. [Uproar. —*Times*] Don't waste my time.

The Judge has said, in his concluding speech at Galesburg, that I was pushing this matter toward a personal difficulty in order to avoid the responsibility for the enormity of my principles. Well, now, I say to the Judge, and to this audience, that I will again state our principles, as well as I hastily can in all their enormity and if the Judge hereafter chooses to confine himself to a war upon those principles, he will probably not find me departing from it.

We have in this nation this element of domestic slavery. It is a matter of absolute certainty that it is a disturbing element. It is the opinion of all the great men who have expressed opinions upon it that it is a dangerous element. Why keep up a controversy in regard to it? That controversy necessarily springs from a difference of opinion, and if we can learn exactly, reduced to the lowest element, what that difference of opinion is, we, perhaps, shall be better prepared for discussing the different systems of policy that we would propose in regard to that disturbing element. Now, I suppose—I suggest—that that difference of opinion, reduced to its lowest element, is no other than that between the man that thinks slavery wrong and those who do not think it wrong. I suppose that is the whole thing. It is the difference between those who think it wrong and those who do not think it wrong. We, the Republican party, think it wrong. We think it is a moral, a social, and a political wrong. We think it is a wrong, not confining itself merely to the person or to the States where it exists, but it is a wrong in its outspreading, that extends itself to the interest of the whole nation. Because we think it wrong, we propose a course of policy that shall deal with it as a wrong—we propose to treat it as any other wrong, in so far as we can prevent its growing any larger, and so that in the run of time there may be some promise of an end of it. [A voice, "Amen." —*Times*] We have due regard to the actual presence among us, to the difficulty of getting rid of it in any speedy and proper way, we have regard to all constitutional obligations thrown around it. We suppose that with reference to its existence under the constitutional obligations, that we have no right to disturb it in the States where it does exist, and we protest that we have no idea of disturbing it any more than we have the right to do it. We do more—we go further—we do not propose to go so far as the constitution would permit. We think that the constitution would permit us to disturb and abolish it in the District of Columbia, but we are unwilling to do that on the terms which we do not suppose the nation would agree to very soon—the gradual emancipation of the slave, with compensation to unwilling owners.

We also oppose it as an evil so far as it seeks to spread itself. We insist upon a policy that shall restrict it to its present limits. We do not suppose on doing this that we infringe upon the constitution, or anything due to the constitutional obligations thrown around us.

We oppose the Dred Scott decision in a certain way, on which a few words ought to be addressed to you. We do not propose that when Dred Scott is decided to be a slave, that we will raise a mob to make him free; we do not propose that when any one—or one thousand—or any number of men in his condition shall be decided by in a like manner, that we will disturb that decision, but we do oppose it as a political rule that shall be binding upon the man when he goes to the polls to vote, or upon the member of Congress, or upon the President, to favor no measure that does not actually tally with the principle of that decision. We do not propose to be bound by it as a political rule in that way; we propose, because we think that it lays the foundation not merely of enlarging and spreading that evil, but that it lays the foundation of spreading that evil into the States themselves—we propose to have that decision reversed, and to have a new true judicial decision spread upon the records of the country.

Now, I will add that if there be in the Republican party any man who does not believe that slavery is wrong in the three aspects in which I have mentioned it, that man is misplaced, and ought to leave us. If, on the other hand, there be any man in the Republican party who is impatient of the necessity springing from its actual presence, who is impatient of the constitutional obligations bound around it, he is misplaced, and ought to find [a] place somewhere else.

These, then, as well as I can hastily state them, are generally a statement of our principles in all their enormity.

I will say, now, that there is a sentiment in the country contrary to ours. There is a sentiment which holds that slavery is not wrong, and because it holds that slavery is not wrong, it goes for a policy that does not propose dealing with it as dealing with a wrong. That is the Democratic policy—that is the Democratic sentiment. If there be a matter of doubt in the minds of any one in this vast audience that that is the rule and the essential idea of the Democratic party in relation to this subject, I ask them to bear with me awhile to state a few things tending to prove that proposition. In the first place, the leading man—I think I may do my friend Judge Douglas the honor of calling him the leading man in the advocacy of the Democratic party—has never said that it is wrong. He has, I believe, the honor of never saying that it is right or wrong. [Laughter. —*Tribune*] If there be a man in the Democratic party that thinks it is wrong, I suggest to him in the first place that his leader don't talk like he does—he never says that it is wrong. In the second place, I say to him that if he will examine the policy proposed and carried forward, it carefully excludes the idea that there is anything wrong in it. If you will carefully examine the arguments made, you will see that each and every one of them carefully excludes the idea that slavery is wrong.

Perhaps that Democratic man that is as much opposed to slavery as I am says that I am wrong in this. Let him examine the thing and he will find that I am right. You say it is wrong—do you not object to anybody else saying so? You say it must not be opposed in the free States because it is not here, and it must not be opposed in the slave States because it exists there. It must not be opposed in politics because it will make a fuss; it must not be opposed in the pulpit because it is not religion; [Loud cheers. —*Tribune*] and in short, there is no suitable place to say anything against that thing that is wrong. You sometimes say that if the States or any State would free itself it would be all well enough, but consider awhile, Francis Blair [Free Soil elder statesman—*ed.*] and Gratz Brown [Missouri Free Soiler—*ed.*] tried it; they did all they could, they had an election later and they were beat and put down. You, Mr. Democrat, threw up your hats and said hurrah for Democracy. [Enthusiastic cheers. —*Tribune*] So I say again in regard to the arguments that are made when Judge Douglas says he don't care if slavery is voted up or voted down, whether he means it as an expression of sentiment, but only states it as a sort of view of the national policy, it is true to say it if he does not say that it is wrong, but if it be a wrong he cannot say that he would as soon see a wrong voted up as down. If Judge Douglas says that whatever community wants slaves has a right to have them, his logic is correct if he does not believe it a wrong. When he says that slave property, and horse and hog property ought to be allowed to go together to a territory upon principle, it is true if there is no difference between them, perhaps; but if one of them is right and the other wrong then there is no equality between right and wrong.

[A Voice—Douglas is right! —*Times*]

Mr. Lincoln—That is just the question that we are going to try.

So turn it in any way you can in all the arguments that sustain the Democratic policy, and in that policy itself there is a careful, studied exclusion of the idea that there be anything wrong in it.

Now, let me understand here that I have not been trying to prove that we are right and he wrong. I have been stating where we stand and where they stand; trying to show where the difference is between us. I now say that whenever we can get the question distinctly stated—can get all these men who believe the thing is in some of these aspects, wrong, to stand with us and to treat it as a wrong then, and not till then, I think we may see how we shall get to an end of this slavery agitation. [Prolonged cheers. —*Tribune*]

MR. DOUGLAS' REPLY

[Senator Douglas, in taking the stand, was greeted with tremendous applause. He said: —*Times*]

LADIES AND GENTLEMEN:—Unless entire silence is observed it will be impossible for me to be heard. My friends can do me no higher favor than to preserve entire silence during the whole of my remarks, omitting all expressions of applause or approbation. [We cannot help it, Douglas, &c. —*Times*] I desire to be heard rather than applauded. I wish to address myself to your reason, to your judgment, to your sense of justice, and not to your passions.

I regret that Mr. Lincoln should have deemed it proper for him again to have indulged in gross personality, and to have resorted to his insinuations and charges about those Springfield resolutions. Now I will call your attention for a moment to the facts, and submit to you what you think of the man who can predicate such a charge under those circumstances. I had seen the proceedings of the Congressional Convention held in Aurora—the Second Congressional District—in September 1854, purporting to be the platform of the Republican party. That platform declared that the Republican party was pledged never to admit another slave State into the Union and to prohibit slavery in all the Territories of the United States—not only all we then had, but all we should ever again acquire and to repeal unconditionally the Fugitive Slave law, to abolish slavery in the District of Columbia, and to prohibit the slave trade between the different States. These, and perhaps other articles against slavery, were contained in the platform adopted unanimously by the Republican Congressional Convention in that district. I had also seen that the Republican Convention in the Galena District the same year had adopted the same platform at Rockford. I had also seen that the Republican Convention at Bloomington, in the Third Congressional District, the same year, had adopted nearly word for word, the same platform, declaring it to be the platform of the Republican party. I had seen that Major Thomas L. Harris, member of Congress from the Springfield District, had referred to this, and said in his speech in Congress that they were also adopted by the first Republican Convention in the State. I wrote to Major Harris to know at what date that Convention was held to which he referred and to send me the proceedings. He having seen Charles H. Lanphier, answered my letter

by sending me the proceedings purporting to have been held at Springfield on the 3d Oct., 1854. I read those resolutions from that newspaper,
the same as you quote any fact from the files of newspapers. Afterwards,
Mr. Lincoln pretends that he had discovered that there was a mistake
about those resolutions having been adopted at Springfield. He don't
deny but that they were adopted by the Republican party at Bloomington, and also at Ottawa, and also at Rockford, and in nearly all the
counties in Northern Illinois where his party has a majority, and merely
because they were not adopted at the right spot [another taunting
reference to Lincoln's unpopular, anti–Mexican War "Spot Resolutions" years earlier in Congress—*ed.*], he chooses to quibble on the
place rather than to meet the merits of the resolutions themselves. I
stated when I quoted them, that I quoted them from that paper. I stated
my authority, and Mr. Lincoln believed at the time, as he has since
admitted, that they had been adopted at Springfield as published. Now
does he believe that I didn't tell the truth when I read those resolutions?
[Applause. —*Tribune*] He knows in his heart that I quoted them in good
faith, believing at the time that they had been adopted at that place. I
would consider myself an infamous wretch, if, under the state of facts,
I could charge any man with being a party to a trick or fraud. [Great
applause. —*Times*] And I tell him, too, that it will not do for him to
charge forgery on Charles H. Lanphier or Thomas L. Harris. No man
on earth that knows these men or Lincoln could believe Lincoln on oath
against either of them. [Applause. —*Tribune;* Cheers. —*Times*] There
are not two men in the State of Illinois who stand higher for truth, for
integrity, for moral character, for elevation of tone as gentlemen, than
those two men. Any man who attempts to charge them only marks
himself as a slanderer by the attempt to do it. [Vociferous applause.
—*Times*] Now, to show you that I acted with entire fairness, when it was
made known to me that there was a mistake, not about the truthfulness
of the resolutions, but about the spot where they were adopted, I did
not wait for Mr. Lincoln to find it out. The moment I discovered it, I
made a speech and published it to the world, correcting the error. I
corrected it myself, as a gentleman and an honest man, as I feel proud
always to do when I make a mistake. I wish Mr. Lincoln to show that
he has acted with that fairness and that truthfulness when I show that
he has been mistaken. I will give you an illustration. In that speech at
Springfield, Mr. Lincoln charged Chief Justice Taney and his associates, and Mr. Buchanan and myself, with having entered into a conspir-

acy, at the time the Nebraska bill was adopted, by which the Dred Scott decision was to be made by the Supreme Court in order to carry slavery everywhere under the Constitution. I called his attention to the fact, that at the time alluded to—to wit, the introduction of the Nebraska bill—it wasn't possible for such a conspiracy to have been had, for the reason that the case had never been taken to the Supreme Court, and was not for nearly a year afterwards. I then called on him to take back that charge against that court. Did he, let me ask, did he do it? I showed that it was impossible that the charge could be true. I showed it by the record, and called on him as an honest man to take back that false charge. What was his answer? Instead of coming out like an honest man, and taking it back, he charged again that although the case had not gone from the Missouri Court, yet the Democratic owners of Dred Scott had an understanding that they would take it up. I have since called on him to know who those Democratic owners of Dred Scott were. He could not tell. And why? Because there were no Democratic owners in existence. Dred Scott was at the time owned by Rev. Dr. Chaffee, an Abolition member of Congress from Springfield, Mass., in the right of his wife, and hence he was owned by one of Lincoln's friends, and not by Democrats at all. [Cheers. —*Tribune;* immense cheers, "give it to him," &c. —*Times*] On the other hand, Dred Scott was defended by Abolition lawyers, and hence that case was conducted on both sides, both by plaintiff and by defendant, by Abolition political friends of Mr. Lincoln. Notwithstanding that I thus found that the charge against the Supreme Court was false, yet instead of taking it back he resorts to another false charge to sustain the infamy of the first one. [Applause. —*Tribune;* Cheers. —*Times*] And he also charged President Buchanan with having been a party to the conspiracy with me when the Nebraska Bill was introduced. I called his attention to the fact that that charge could not possibly be true for the reason that at the time specified Mr. Buchanan was not in America. He was 3,000 miles off—was Minister representing the United States at the Court of St. James—had been there for nearly a year previous, and never returned for about three years afterwards. And yet I never could get Mr. Lincoln to take back that false charge; and yet, while I have called on him over and over again to take it back, he refuses to do it. He either remains silent or resorts to other tricks to try and palm the slander on the country. [Cheers. —*Times*] On the contrary (therein you will find the difference between Lincoln and myself), when I make a mistake I correct it without being asked, as an honest man is bound to. When he makes a false charge, he sticks to it and never corrects it. ["Don't spare him," and cheers. —*Times*] But one word more in regard to those resolutions. I quoted them at Ottawa only for the purpose of asking Mr. Lincoln whether he stood on that platform. That was the purpose for which I quoted them. I didn't think that I had a right to put idle questions to him without first laying a foundation by showing him that some portion at least of his friends had adopted it as their creed. Hence I read them and put those questions. He refused then to answer. [Laughter, "he was afraid," &c. —*Times*] Subsequently, one week afterwards, he did answer a part of the points, and on the other he has never answered to this day. [Great confusion. —*Tribune;* "No, and never will," "Never can," and cheers. —*Times*] My friends, if you are my friends, you will be silent, instead of interrupting even by your applause. ["We can't help it." —*Times*]

And now let me call your attention for a moment to the answer which Mr. Lincoln made at Freeport to those questions which I propounded to him, on the authority of having been adopted by a majority of all the Abolition counties which now, as then, support him. In regard to the question of any more slave States, Mr. Lincoln made this answer: He was not pledged against any more slave States; but he would be very sorry ever to be put in a position where he would have to vote for any—that he would be rejoiced to know that no more would be admitted into the Union, but that in the event that Congress should prohibit slavery in a given Territory during the whole time it was a Territory, and then they should adopt a slave constitution, he supposed that he would have to let the state in. [Laughter. —*Tribune*] Now, the point I want to know is this: Suppose Congress should not first prohibit slavery in the Territory, then how would he vote? He gave an answer that didn't apply to any Territory in America. I ask him [turning to Lincoln, —*Times*]: Will you admit Kansas into the Union with just such a constitution as her people want—with slavery or without, as they shall determine? He didn't answer. I have put the question to him time and time again—he won't answer it. I ask him again, will he vote to admit New Mexico, when she has the requisite population, with just such a constitution as her people want, either with slavery or without it, as they shall decide? He won't answer. [He's afraid, and cheers. —*Times*] I ask him about Oregon Territory? He won't answer. About Washington Territory? He won't answer. About the new states to be carved out of

Texas, in pursuance of the contract between Texas and the United States. He won't answer. He won't answer of any Territory now in existence; but he says in the event that Congress should prohibit slavery and then it should become a slave State, he supposed he would have to let it come. [Laughter. —*Times*] Now, I submit the question to you, whether his answer on that question don't justify me in saying that he has a fertile genius in devising language to conceal his own thoughts? [Good for you, hurrah for Douglas, &c. —*Times*] I ask you, is there an intelligent man in America that don't believe that that answer was made for the purpose of concealing what he intended to do? [No, no, and cheers. —*Times*] He intended to allow the Old Line Whigs to believe that he would stand on the doctrine of the Compromise measures, which required that the States might come in with slavery or without, as they pleased, while Lovejoy and his Abolition allies up north, explain to the Abolitionists that it is good Abolition doctrine, because it don't apply to any Territory in America. It was easy for him to have said: "I will let the people do as they please." Why didn't he do it? [He was afraid to. —*Times*] He won't give an answer on that question, for up north the Abolition creed provides that there shall be no more slave states. Down south, in Adams, in Coles, in Sangamon, he and his friends are afraid of that doctrine; hence an answer is given evasive, equivocal, to be construed one way in the North and another way in the South, and when analyzed don't answer at all to any Territory now in existence. ["Hit him on the woolly side," "Hurrah for Douglas" &c. —*Times*] But, my friends, Mr. Lincoln complains that in my speech the other day at Galesburg, I read an extract from his speech at Chicago, and then another from his speech at Charleston, and compared them, and showed that he had one set of principles in one part of the State, and another set in the other part of the State. How does he answer that charge? Why, he quotes his Charleston speech as I quoted it, and then quotes another one made at another place, which he says is the same thing, but he does not quote that Chicago speech by which I convicted him of that double dealing. [Applause. —*Tribune;* Cheers. —*Times*] I quoted his Chicago speech to prove that he held one thing to Abolitionists, and his Charleston speech to prove that he held another down South. His answer, passing over the Chicago speech entirely, and merely then arguing that he did the same thing at another place that he did at Charleston. Then if he did, I will show that he has twice, instead of once, held one creed in one part of the State and a different one in another. [He can't get out of it, and cheers. —*Times*] Now, up in Chicago, at the opening of the campaign, he replied to my reception speech, in which he undertook to answer my argument against negro equality. I had gone on to show that it was a falsification of the Declaration of Independence to pretend that it applied to the equality of negroes, when it said that "all men are created equal." What was Mr. Lincoln's reply? I read one from his Chicago speech—the one which he didn't quote—the one which he dare not quote in this part of the State. ["Good," "Hear, hear," &c. —*Times*] He said:

"I should like to know if taking this old Declaration of Independence, which declares that all men are equal upon principle and making exceptions to it, where will it stop? If one man says it does not mean a negro why not another say it does not mean a German? If that Declaration is not the truth, let us go by the statute book in which we find it and tear it out. Who is so bold as to do it? If it is not true, let us tear it out."

There you find Lincoln told the Abolitionists of Chicago, that if the Declaration of Independence was not true, in saying that the negro was created by the Almighty the equal of the white man, then we ought to take and tear it out. [Hurrah for Douglas. —*Times*]

And let me call your attention to another portion of the same speech. You know in his Charleston speech, which he has read, he says the negro belongs to an inferior race, and is physically inferior to the white man, and should always be kept in an inferior position, because he belongs to an inferior race. Now let me read to you what he said at Chicago on that point. He is at the conclusion of his speech within a sentence or two:

"My friends, I have detained you about as long as I desire, to do, and I have only to say, let us discard all this quibbling about this man and the other man, this race and that race and the other race, and the other race being inferior, therefore they must be placed in an inferior position. Discarding our standard that we have left, let us discard all these opinions and unite as one people throughout this land until we shall once more stand up declaring that all men are created equal."

Thus you see that in addressing the Chicago Abolitionists he declared that all distinction of race must be discarded—all distinction of men must be blotted out. He declared that the negro stood on an equal footing with the white man, and he said if one man would except the negro another man would except another being. Hence, he said, discard the difference between the negro race and other races, and declare them all created equal under the Declaration of Independence. Now let me ask you whether old [Joshua R.] Giddings [noted antislavery congressman from Pennsylvania—*ed.*], when he was down among you four years ago, ever preached more radical abolition than that? ["No, never." —*Times*] Did [Owen] Lovejoy [Illinois abolitionist minister-turned-congressman—*ed.*]? Did [William] Lloyd Garrison [noted abolitionist editor—*ed.*]? Did Wendell Phillips [Boston abolitionist—*ed.*], or Fred Douglas ever take higher Abolition ground than that? Mr. Lincoln told you that I had charged him with getting up those personal attacks to conceal the enormity of his principles. Then he went to talking about something else, omitting any hint of his Chicago speech as containing the enormity to which I alluded. He knew I alluded to this—to his negro equality doctrine—when I spoke of the enormity of his principles. Yet he didn't find it convenient to answer on that point. Now, having shown you what he said in his Chicago speech, about the negroes being born equal to the white men, and about discarding all differences between negroes and white men, I will read to you again what he said at Charleston in order that the two may go out side by side. Here is what he said at Charleston:

"I will say, then, that I am not, nor ever have been, in favor of bringing about in any way the social and political equality of the white and black races. That I am not, nor ever have been, in favor of making voters or jurors of negroes, nor of qualifying them to hold office, nor to intermarry with white people; and I will say in addition to this that there is a physical difference between the white and black races which will ever forbid the two races living together on terms of social and political equality. And inasmuch as they cannot so live while they do remain together, there must be the position of superior and inferior. I am as much as any other man in favor of having the superior position assigned to the white race."

[Cries of "That's good doctrine." —*Tribune;* A Voice—That's the doctrine. —*Times*]

Yes, that's good doctrine, but it won't suit the latitude of Chicago, where Mr. Lincoln hopes to get his votes. [Laughter. —*Tribune;* Cheers. —*Times*] That's good doctrine in all the Anti-Abolition counties, but his Chicago speech is good doctrine in all the Abolition counties. Hence I assert on the authority of those two speeches, that Mr. Lincoln does hold one set of principles in the Abolition counties, and a different and contradictory set in the other counties. ["That's so," and cheers. —*Times*] I don't question but what he did say at Ottawa what he quotes, but that only goes to convict him further of having done it twice instead of once. ["Good," and applause. —*Times*] Now I ask you why can't he avow his principles the same in the North and in the South, in every county, if he has the conviction that his principles are just? But he could not be a Republican if his principles would stretch alike all over the country. The party to which he belongs has principles limited to geographical lines. They cannot even cross the Missouri River in your own ferry boat. [Laughter. —*Tribune;* Immense applause. —*Times*] They can't even cross the Ohio River into Kentucky. Mr. Lincoln himself can't go [to] the land of his fathers, and the scenes of his childhood, and the graves of his ancestors, and carry his Abolition principles with him, as he declared them at Chicago. ["Hit him again," and cheers. —*Times*] This Republican organization appeals to the North against the South— appeals to Northern passion, Northern prejudice, and Northern ambition against Southern people, and Southern States, and Southern institutions. His only hope of success is by that appeal, and he goes on to justify himself in making war on slavery upon the ground that Frank Blair and Gratz Brown did not succeed in Missouri. [Applause. —*Tribune;* Laughter. —*Times*] Let us see what right Frank Blair had to believe he would succeed in Missouri. He was elected to Congress in August of 1856 as a Buchanan Democrat, and he turned Fremonter after the election, and thus belonged to one party before the election and another afterwards. What right had he to expect that his constituency would stand up to him whenever they got a chance at him at another election? ["None," "Hurrah for Douglas," &c. —*Times*]

Mr. Lincoln thinks it his duty to preach a crusade in the free States against slavery, because it ought to be extinguished, as he says, because it is a crime, as he believes, and because the slaveholding States would not abolish it themselves. How is he going to do it? Down here in the southern part of the State he takes the ground openly that he will not interfere with slavery where it exists. He says that he is not now, and never was, in favor of interfering with slavery where it exists in the States. Well, if he is not in favor of that, how does he expect by his policy to bring it into a condition of ultimate extinction? ["Hit him again." —*Times*] How can he extinguish it in Kentucky, in Virginia, in any slave State, by his policy, if he won't pursue a line of policy that would affect it in the States[?] ["That's so." —*Times*] But in his speech at Springfield, before an Abolition or Republican Convention, he declared his hostility to any more slave States in this language which I will read:

"Under the operation of this policy that agitation has not only not ceased, but has constantly augumented. It will not cease until a crisis shall have been reached and passed. A house divided against itself cannot stand. I believe this government cannot endure permanently half slave and half free. I don't expect the Union to be dissolved—I don't expect the house to fall, but I do expect it will cease to be divided. It will become all one thing or all the other. Either the opponents of slavery will arrest the further spread of it, and place it where the public mind will rest in the belief that it is in the course of ultimate extinction, or its defenders will push it forward until it shall become alike lawful in all the States, old as well as new, North as well as South."

Thus you see, Mr. Lincoln told his abolition friends that this government could not endure permanently half slave and half free as our fathers made it. They must become all free or all slave, otherwise this Union could not exist. How then does Mr. Lincoln propose to save the Union, unless it is by compelling the States all to be free, so that the house shall not be divided against itself? He is going to make them all free. He is going to preserve the Union in that way and yet he is not going to interfere with slavery in the States, nor anywhere else where it exists. How is he going to bring that about? Why, he is going to agitate and agitate until the South shall be worried out and forced to the abolition of slavery. Let us see the policy by which that is to be done. He first tells you that he would prohibit slavery everywhere in the Territories. He would thus confine slavery within its present limits.

When he gets it confined within its present limits, surrounded so that it cannot spread, the natural increase will go on until the increase will be so plenty that they cannot live on the soil. He will thus hem them in until starvation awaits them. Thus he will compel them to starve for the want of food, hemming them in, and thus put slavery in the course of ultimate extinction. If he is not going to interfere in the States, and is going to interfere to prohibit it in the Territories, and thus smother slavery out, it only follows that he can extinguish it by extinguishing the negro race, if he drives them to the position of starvation; and that is the humane remedy, the Christian remedy, that he proposes for the great crime of slavery. He tells you that I won't argue the question of whether slavery is right or wrong. I tell you why I can't do it. I hold that under the Constitution of the United States, each State of this Union has a right to do as it pleases on the subject of slavery. Hence we in Illinois have exercised that sovereign right by prohibiting slavery within our own limits, and I approve of the line of policy which Illinois has adopted on this subject. We have performed our whole duty in Illinois. We have gone as far as we have a right to go under the Constitution of our common country. It is none of my business whether slavery exists in Missouri or not. Missouri is a sovereign State of this Union, and has the same right to decide the slavery question for herself that Illinois had to decide it for herself. [Good. —*Times*] Hence, I don't choose to occupy the time that I have allotted to me in addressing you by discussing a question that we have no right to act upon. [Right. —*Times*] I thought you desired to hear those questions coming within our constitutional powers to act. Mr. Lincoln won't discuss those. What one has he discussed that comes within the power of a Senator to act upon? Why, he is going to discuss the rightfulness of slavery, when Congress cannot act upon it either way. He is going to discuss the merits of the Dred Scott decision, when under the Constitution a Senator has no right to interfere with the decisions of the judicial tribunals; and he wants you to devote your exclusive attention to those two, explaining and expounding what he has no power to act upon—a question that he could not vote upon if he was in Congress—questions that are not practical, in order to conceal your thoughts from those other questions which he might be required to vote upon if he was a member of Congress.

Mr. Lincoln tells you that he don't like the Dred Scott decision. Suppose he don't; how is he going to help himself? Why, he says he is going to reverse it. How will he do it? I know of but one mode of

reversing judicial decisions, and that is by appealing from the inferior
to the superior court; but I have never yet learned how you can appeal
from the Supreme Court of the United States. The Dred Scott decision
was pronounced by the highest judicial tribunal on earth. From that
decision there is no appeal this side of Heaven. Yet Mr. Lincoln says he
is going to reverse the decision. By what tribunal is he going to reverse
it? Is he going to appeal to the mob? Is he going to appeal to violence?
Is he going to appeal to Lynch law? Is he going to stir up strife and
rebellion in the land and overthrow the Court by violence? He don't
deign to tell you how he is going to reverse it, but he keeps appealing
each day from the Supreme Court of the United States to political
meetings of the country. [Laughter. —*Tribune* and *Times*] And he wants
me to argue with him the merits of each point of that decision before
this political meeting. I say to you, with all due respect, that I choose
to abide by the decisions of the Supreme Court as they are pronounced.
It is not for us to inquire, after the decision, whether I like it on all points
or not. When I used to practice law with Lincoln, I never knew him to
get beat in a case in the world, that he did not get mad at the Judge and
talk about appealing it. [Laughter. —*Tribune* and *Times*] And when I
got beat in the case, I generally thought the Court was wrong; but I
never dreamed of going out of the court house and making a stump
speech to the people against the Judges, merely because I found out I
didn't know the law as well as they did. [Great laughter. —*Times*] If the
decision did not suit me, I appealed until I got to the Supreme Court,
and then if that Court—the highest tribunal in the world—decided
against me, I was content, because it is the duty of every law abiding
man to obey the Constitution, and the laws, and the constituted authorities. He who attempts to stir up violence and rebellion in the country
against the constituted authorities, is stimulating the passions of men to
resort to violence and mobs, instead of to law. Hence I tell you, I take
the decisions of that Court as they have been pronounced, as the law
of the land, and I intend to obey them as such. But Mr. Lincoln says
I won't answer his question as to what I would do in the event the Court
should make so ridiculous a decision as he argues they would, by
deciding that the free State of Illinois could not prohibit slavery within
her limits. I told him, at Freeport, I would not answer such a question.
I told him there wasn't a man in America, lawyer or not, who ever
dreamed that such a thing could be done [Right. —*Times*]; and I told
him then, as I say now, by all the principles settled in the Dred Scott

decision, that it is impossible. I told him then, as I do now, that it is an
insult to a man's understanding. It was a gross calumny on the Court
to presume, in advance, that the Court was going to degrade itself so
low as to make a decision known to be in direct violation of the
Constitution. [A Voice.—The same thing was said about the Dred
Scott decision before it passed. —*Times*] Perhaps you think that they did
the same thing about the Dred Scott decision. I have heard men talk
that way before. The principles in the Dred Scott decision had been
affirmed previously in various other decisions. What judge ever
dreamed that a negro was a citizen? [Laughter. —*Times*] The State
Courts have decided that before, over and again; and the Dred Scott
decision only affirmed what every lawyer in America knew to be the
law. But I will not be drawn off in arguing the merits of the Dred Scott
decision. It is enough for me that the Constitution of the United States
created that Court to decide all disputed questions touching the true
construction of the Constitution, and that the decision, having been
pronounced, is the law of the land, binding on every good citizen. Mr.
Lincoln has a very convenient mode of arguing on that subject, and
holds that because he is a Republican he is not bound by the decision
of the Court, and because I am a Democrat, I am bound. [Laughter
and cheers. —*Times*] Well, it may be that Republicans don't hold
themselves bound by the laws of the land and the Constitution of the
country, as expounded by the courts. It may be an article of the
abolition creed that men who don't like a decision have a right to rebel
against it. When he goes to preach that doctrine I think he will find
some honest Republicans, some law-abiding men in that party who will
repudiate such a monstrous doctrine as that. The decision in the Dred
Scott case is binding on every American citizen alike, and yet Mr.
Lincoln argues that Republicans are not bound by it because they are
opposed to it. [Laughter. —*Times*] Democrats are bound by it because
they don't resist it. A Democrat cannot resist the constituted authorities
of his country. [Good. —*Times*] A Democrat is a law-abiding man. A
Democrat stands by the Constitution, by the laws, by the constituted
authorities, and relies upon liberty as protected by law, and not upon
mob or physical violence. I never yet have been able to make Mr.
Lincoln understand, nor can I make any man understand him who is
determined to support him right or wrong, how it is that under the Dred
Scott decision the people of a Territory as well as a State can have
slavery or not just as they please. I believe I can explain that proposition

to all law-abiding, Constitutional men in a way that they can't fail to understand it. Chief Justice Taney, in his opinion in the Dred Scott case, has said that slaves are property. Slaves being property, the owner of them has a right to take them into the Territory the same as he had any other property; in other words, that slave property, so far as that right is concerned, stands on the same footing with other property. Now, suppose that we grant that proposition. Then any man has a right to go to Kansas and carry his property with him; but when he gets there he must rely upon the local law to protect his property, whatever it may be. [That's so. —*Times*] Suppose then that three of you should concluded [*sic*] to go; one takes $10,000 worth of slaves, another $10,000 worth of groceries and another $10,000 worth of dry goods. When the man with his dry goods gets there, he goes to sell them, and he finds that he can't do it without license, and the license is so high as to destroy his profits; how is he going to help himself? The man with his liquors, when he goes to sell them, finds the Maine Liquor Law in force—yet what advantage is his right to go unless he can have that right protected if he goes there? [That's it. —*Times*] The man who goes there with his slaves, finds there is no law to protect him when he has arrived. There are no remedies if his slave runs away to another country. There is no slave code, there are no police regulations, and the absence of them excludes his slaves just as positively as a constitutional prohibition would. And such was the understanding of the Kansas Nebraska bill when pending in Congress. Read the speech of Speaker Orr, of South Carolina, in 1856, on the Kansas question. There you will find that he takes the ground, that while the owner of a slave has a right to go into a Territory, and carry his slave, yet he cannot hold him one day, or one hour, unless there is a slave code to protect him. He then tells you that slavery would not exist a day in South Carolina, or any other State, unless there were friendly people and friendly legislation. Read the speech of that giant intellect, Alexander H. Stephens, of Georgia [later vice president of the Confederacy—*ed.*], to the same effect. Read the speech of Sam. Smith, of Tennessee. Read the speeches of Southern men that they all understood the doctrine then as we understand it now. But Mr. Lincoln can't be made to understand it. Down at Jonesboro he went on to argue, that if it be the law that a man has a right to take his slaves into the Territory under the Constitution, then a member of Congress was perjured if he didn't vote for a slave code. Now I ask him if the decision of the Supreme Court is not binding on him as well as me. Then if so, holding that he would be perjured if he didn't vote for the slave code, will he do it? I have a right to an answer on that question, and I will tell you why he put that question to me. He put it with an air of triumph—he put it in about this form: "In the event that a slave-holding State or one of the United States Territories should need and demand a slave code to protect his [sic] slaves, will you vote for it?" I answered it that it was a fundamental article in the Democratic creed, as put forth in the Nebraska Bill and the Cincinnati Platform, the non-intervention by Congress with slavery in States and Territories. ["Good," "That's the doctrine," and cheers, —*Times*] Hence I would not vote for a code of laws either for or against slavery in any Territory by Congress. I will leave the people of each Territory to decide that question for themselves. [Cheers. —*Times*] But Lincoln and the Washington *Union* both think that is a monstrous bad doctrine. Neither Lincoln nor the Washington *Union* like my Freeport speech on this subject. The Washington *Union* in a late number, has been reading me out of the Democratic party because I hold that the people of a Territory, like those of a State, have a right to have slavery or not as they please. Just hear what the Washington *Union* says on that point. They devote three and a half columns to prove certain propositions. I will read one of them:

"We propose to show that Judge Douglas' action in 1850 and 1854 was taken with especial reference to the announcement of the doctrine and programme which was made at Freeport. The declaration at Freeport was, that in his opinion the people can, by lawful means, exclude slavery from a Territory before it becomes a State, and he declared that his competitor had heard him argue the Nebraska Bill on that principle all over Illinois in 1854, '55 and '56, and had no excuse to pretend to have doubts upon this subject."

The Washington *Union* there charges me with the monstrous crime of having, in 1850, in supporting Clay's Compromise measures, carried out the same doctrine that I now proclaim on the stump. The Washington *Union* charges that I am proclaiming the same doctrine that I did in 1854, in support of the Kansas Nebraska Bill. The Washington *Union* is shocked that now I should stand where I did in 1850, when supported by Clay and Webster and Cass, and the great men of that day, and the same as I did in 1856, when Mr. Buchanan was elected President. The *Union* then goes on to prove, and does succeed in proving from my speech in Congress on Clay's Compromise measures, that I then held the same doctrine I do now. It then goes on to prove that by this Kansas Nebraska Bill, I advanced the same doctrine that I now advance, and then it makes these remarks:

"Thus it will be seen that in framing the Kansas-Nebraska Bill, Judge Douglas framed it in the terms and upon the model of those of Utah and New Mexico and that in the debate he took pains extremely to revive the recollection in the vote which had taken place upon the amendments affecting the power of the territory legislation over the subject of slavery. In the bills of 1850, in order to give the same meaning, frame and act in the Kansas-Nebraska Bill on this subject, as had been given to those of Utah and New Mexico." [The *Times* transcript, as well as the official version of the debates published as a book in 1860, give far more extensive quotes from the *Union*, which Douglas may have supplied later—*ed.*]

Here are the propositions that the *Union* proves: First, that I sustained Clay's Compromise measures on the ground that they established the principle of self-government in the Territories, giving the Legislature the right to have slavery or not, as it pleased. Secondly, that I brought in the Kansas-Nebraska Bill on the same principles of Clay's Compromise measures of 1850; and Thirdly, that my Freeport speech is in exact accordance with these principles. Then what do you think is the objection that the Washington *Union* makes to me? The objection is this: The *Union* says that my Freeport speech is not Democratic—says I was not a Democrat in 1854, nor in 1850. Now is not that funny, [laughter —*Tribune;* Great laughter and cheers. —*Times*] that the author of the Kansas-Nebraska bill was not a Democrat when he introduced it, and the Washington *Union* says I was not a sound Democrat in 1850, nor in 1854, nor in 1856, nor am I in 1858, because I take the ground that the people of a Territory, like those of a State, have the right to decide for themselves whether slavery shall or shall not exist in a Territory? Now, I wish to state, for the benefit of the Washington *Union* and the followers of that sheet, one authority on that point, and I hope this authority will be deemed satisfactory to that class of politicians. I read from the letter of James Buchanan, accepting the Cincinnati nomination to the Presidency. You know that Mr. Buchanan, after he was nominated, declared to the Keystone Club, in a published speech, that

he was no longer James Buchanan, but he was the embodiment of the
Democratic Platform. In his letter to the committee accepting that
nomination, he defines the meaning of the Kansas-Nebraska bill and
the Cincinnati platform in these words:

> "The recent legislation by Congress respecting domestic slavery,
> derived as it has been from the original and pure fountain of legiti-
> mate political power—the will of the people—promises ere long to
> allay the dangerous excitement. This legislation is founded upon
> principles as ancient as free government itself, and in accordance with
> them has simply declared that the people of a Territory like those of
> a State shall decide for themselves whether slavery shall or shall not
> exist within their limits."

Thus you see that James Buchanan accepted the nomination at
Cincinnati on the condition that the people of a Territory, like those of
a State, shall decide for themselves whether slavery shall or shall not
exist within their limits. I sustained James Buchanan for the Presidency
on that platform; and now we are told by the Washington *Union* that no
man is a true Democrat who stands on that platform on which Mr.
Buchanan was nominated, as explained by himself. [Laughter.
—*Times*] We are told that a man is not a Democrat who stands on the
platform of Clay, Webster and Cass, and the Compromise measures of
1850, and the Kansas and Nebraska bill of 1854. Whether a man be a
Democrat or not on that platform, I intend to stand there, as long as
I have life. [Stick to it, and cheers. —*Times*] I intend to cling firmly by
that great principle of self-government which declares the right of each
State and each Territory to settle the question of slavery and every other
domestic question for themselves. I hold that if they want a Slave State
they have the right under the Constitution of the United States to make
it. If they want a Free State, they have a right to say so in their
Constitution. But the Washington *Union,* in advocating the claim of
Lincoln over me to the Senate, lays down two unpardonable heresies,
which he says that I advocate. The first is the right of the people of a
Territory, the same as a State, to decide for themselves the question
whether slavery shall exist within their limits, in the language of President Buchanan. The second is that a Constitution shall be submitted to
the people in order to find out whether it is the will of the people or not.
Now it so happens that on both of these heresies, for entertaining which

the Washington *Union* read me out of the Democratic church, Mr. Buchanan is pledged to both of them. In his annual message he said that he trusted that the example of the Minnesota case, requiring the Constitution to be submitted to the people, would be followed in all future cases. And to his letter of acceptance, he said the people of a Territory, the same as in a State, have a right to decide for themselves whether slavery shall exist within their limits. Thus you find that in both these heresies, for which the little corrupt gang that control the Washington *Union* wish to get Lincoln in the Senate in preference to me, they denounce the President in denouncing me. I say they are denouncing President Buchanan if he stands now by the principles he stood by when he was elected. Will they pretend to say that Mr. Buchanan don't stand by the principles on which he was elected? Do they hold that he has abandoned the Kansas Nebraska bill, the Cincinnati Platform, his own letter of acceptance of the nomination, the right of a people of a people [*sic*] of a Territory, the same as a State, to decide the question for themselves? I will not believe that he has betrayed or intends to betray the platform on which he was then elected. ["good" —*Times*] But if he does I will not follow him. ["Good again." —*Times*] I will stand by that great principle, no matter who desert it; I intend to stand by it for the purpose of preserving the peace between the North and the South, between the free and the slave States. ["Hurrah for Douglas." —*Times*] If each State of this Union will only agree to mind its own business, and let slavery alone, there will be peace forever between us. We in Illinois have tried slavery when we were a Territory; found it was not good for us in this climate with our surroundings, and hence we abolished it. We adopted then the free State, as we had a right to do. In this State we have declared by our policy that a negro shall not be a citizen. ["all right" —*Times*] We have also declared that he shall not be a slave. We have a right to adopt that policy. Missouri has just as good a right to adopt the other policy. I am now speaking of rights under the Constitution. I am not speaking of the moral and religious right. I don't discuss the morals of the people of Missouri, but let them settle that for themselves. I hold that the people of the slaveholding States are civilized men as well as we. They have consciences as well as we. They are accountable to God and to posterity and not to us, and it is for them to decide the moral and religious right of their slavery question for themselves within their own limits. But as to the constitutional question—I do decide, I say, they have as much right under the Constitution to adopt the system of policy which they have, as we have to adopt ours. Let each State stand firmly by that great constitutional right. Let each State mind its own business, and let its neighbors alone—then there will be no trouble on this question. If we will stand by that great principle, then Mr. Lincoln will find that this Republic can exist forever divided into free and slave States, as our fathers made it. Stand by that great principle, and then we can go on as we have done, increasing in wealth and in population, in power and all the elements of greatness until we shall be the admiration and the terror of the world. We can go on and enlarge as it becomes necessary, as our population increases, until we make this one ocean-bound Republic. Under that great principle, the United States can perform that great mission—that destiny which Providence has marked out for us. Under that principle we can receive, with entire safety, that stream of intelligence flowing from the Old World into the New, filling up the prairies, cutting down the forests, building up cities and towns, railroads and internal improvements, thus making this the asylum of the oppressed of the whole world. We have that great mission to perform. That mission can only be performed by adhering faithfully to those principles of self-government, in which our institutions were all established.

I repeat that those principles are the right of each State to decide its Slavery question for itself—to have slavery or not, as it pleases; and it don't become Mr. Lincoln, or anybody else, to tell the people of Kentucky that they have no conscience—to tell them that they are living in a state of iniquity—to tell them that they are cherishing the institution to their bosom, in violation of the law of God. Better for him to adopt the doctrine of "Judge not, lest ye be judged." [Good, and applause. —*Times*] Let him perform his own duty at home within our own limits, and then he will have a better fate in the future. I think there are objects of charity enough in the free States to exhaust the pockets, and the sympathies, too, of all the benevolent that we have, without going away in search of negroes of whose condition we know nothing. We have objects of charity at home—let us perform our own domestic duties. Let us take care of our own poor, our own suffering, and make them comfortable and happy, before we go abroad to intermeddle with other people's business.

My friends, I am told that my time is within two minutes of having expired. I have omitted many, very many topics that I would like to have discussed at length before you. There were many points touched by Mr. Lincoln that I have not been able to take up for the want of time. I have hurried over each topic that I have discussed as rapidly as possible, so as to omit as few as it was possible to do; but one hour and a half is not time sufficient for a man to discuss at length one-half of these great questions.

In conclusion, I desire to return you my grateful acknowledgements for the kindness and the courtesy with which you have listened to me. It is something remarkable that in an audience as vast as this, with men of opposite politics and passions highly excited, there should be such courtesy towards not only one another, but towards the speaker, and I feel that it is due to you that I should express my gratitude for the kindness with which you have treated me. [Loud applause. —*Tribune;* Nine cheers were here given for Douglas. —*Times*]

MR. LINCOLN'S REPLY

[Mr. Lincoln, on taking the stand, was again greeted with three cheers (During the course of his reply the reporter would here add, that his party kept up a perfect bedlam let loose. There was such a confusion even on the side of the platform occupied by the Republican marshals that great difficulty was experienced in hearing him.) —*Times;* On taking the stand, Mr. Lincoln was received with a tremendous cheer. —*Tribune*] He said:

MY FRIENDS: When Judge Douglas has said to you in his conclusion that he had not time in an hour and a half to answer all that I said in an hour, it follows of course that I will not be able to answer in half an hour all he has said in an hour and a half. [A voice Hurrah for Lincoln. —*Times;* Cheers and laughter. —*Tribune*]

I wish to return to Judge Douglas my profound thanks for his public announcement here to-day to be put on record, that his system of policy in regard to the institution of slavery contemplates that it will last for ever. [Voices, "Hit him again." —*Times;* Great cheers, and cries of "Hit him again." —*Tribune*] We are getting a little nearer the true issue of this controversy, and I am profoundly grateful for that one sentence. Judge Douglas asks why can't the institution of slavery, or the Union part free and part slave continue as our fathers made it, forever? Now in the first place I insist that our fathers did not make this nation half slave and half free, or part slave and part free. [Applause and "That's so." —*Tribune*] I insist that they found the institution of slavery existing here, and didn't make it so, but left it so because they did not know the way to alter it at that time, and that is all. ["Good, Good," "That's true." —*Tribune*] When Judge Douglas undertakes to establish that the fathers of the government as a matter of choice undertook to make the Union part slave and part free, he assumes to insist upon what is historically a falsehood, [applause—*Times;* Long continued applause —*Tribune*] and more than that, when the fathers of the government cut off the source of slavery they, by a bill, adopted a system of restricting it from the territories where it did not exist. When Judge Douglas asks me why it cannot continue forever as our fathers made it, I ask him and his friends, why they could not let it remain as our fathers made it? [A voice, "That's it." —*Times;* Tremendous cheering. —*Tribune*] That is precisely all I ask in relation to the institution of slavery, that it shall be placed upon the basis that our fathers placed it on. Brooks of South Carolina once said, and truly, that when this government was established no man expected the institution of slavery to last to this day and that the men who framed this government were wiser and better men than the men of these days; but the men of these days had experience and they had found that the invention of the cotton gin had made the institution of slavery a necessity. Judge Douglas could not let it remain where our fathers placed it, but he removed it and put it upon the cotton gin basis. [Roars of laughter and enthusiastic applause. —*Tribune*] That is the question, therefore, for him and his friends to answer—why they could not let it remain just as the fathers of the government placed it. [Cheers and cries of "Hurrah for Lincoln!" "Good!" "Good!" —*Tribune*]

Now, then I hope nobody has understood me as trying to maintain the declaration that we have the right to quarrel with the State of Kentucky or Virginia in regard to the institution of slavery so that Judge Douglas may make himself eloquent on that. Have I not expressed the belief that we have no right to interfere with them, but that the states of Kentucky and Virginia have a right to do what they please in behalf of the institution of slavery or any other institution. [Loud applause. —*Tribune*, which added: "Then what becomes of all his eloquence in behalf of the rights of States, which are assailed by no living man?" (Applause. "He knows it's all humbuggery.")]

I have to hurry, along. I have but half an hour. The Judge has informed me, or this audience, that the Washington *Union* is laboring for my election to the United States Senate. That is news to me, not very ungrateful. [Turning to Mr. W. H. Carlin, who was on the stand —*Tribune*] I hope Carlin will get elected to the State Senate and will vote for me for United States Senator. [William H. Carlin, Democratic candidate for state Senate, was the son of a former Illinois governor. In this period, voters did not directly elect U.S. senators. They chose state legislators like Carlin, who in turn elected the senator—hence Lincoln's lighthearted request for this Douglas supporter's future vote—*ed.*]

MR. CARLIN—Carlin don't fall in. [The *Tribune* substituted, "Mr. Carlin shook his head"—*ed.*]

MR. LINCOLN—Carlin don't fall in. [laughter —*Tribune*] I am glad of all the support I can get anywhere, if I can get it without practicing of any deception for it. In this large portion of Judge Douglas' speech in which he tried to show that in the controversy between him and the

administration party he is in the right, I don't feel myself at all competent or inclined to answer him. I say to Douglas, "give it to them
[laughter —*Tribune*] just all you can" [renewed laughter and cheers
—*Tribune*]. And on the other hand I say to Carlin and Jake Davis, and
our man Wagley up here [local politicians—*ed.*], give it to Douglas—
[roars of laughter —*Tribune*] just pour it into him. You know him and
he knows you. It is a fair fight, just clear the way and let them have it.
[Cries of "Hurrah for Douglas, for Jack Davis and Border Ruffian
Jake." —*Times;* Cheers and laughter—"Good for you," "Hurrah for
Lincoln!" —*Tribune*]

In regard to this matter of the Dred Scott decision, I have a word or
two to say. After all, the Judge will not say whether, if a decision is made
that the people of the State cannot exclude slavery, whether he will
support it. He obstinately refuses to say so, just as the Court as obstinately refuses to say whether they will do. You will bear in mind that
I had said that in Galesburg he said that the Court had already said that
the State couldn't exclude slavery, and I said that I would thank Judge
Douglas to lay his finger upon that portion of the decision. He has not
ventured to sustain his assertion [applause, —*Times;* Loud cheers.
—*Tribune*] and he never will. [Renewed cheers. —*Tribune*]

He is desirous of knowing how we are going to reverse the Dred Scott
decision. Well, now, Judge Douglas ought to know! Did he not, and his
political friends find a way to reverse a decision of that same court in
favor of the constitutionality of the United States Bank? [Cheers and
laughter. —*Tribune*] Did they not find a means to do that so far as the
decision is reversed practically[?] [Cheers, and cries of "good," "good."
—*Tribune*]

Another question I want to ask you is, did not Judge Douglas find a
way to reverse a decision of the Supreme Court of this State when it
decided that old Governor Carlin had not the power to limit the office
of Secretary of State [Great cheering and laughter. —*Tribune*] —did he
not go and make speeches in the lobby and show how it was villainous,
and did he not succeed in procuring the re-organization of the court
and did he not succeed in sitting on the bench, getting his name of
Judge in that way? [Thundering cheers and laughter. —*Tribune*] If
there is any villainy in opposition to Supreme Court decisions commend it to Judge Douglas' consideration. I know of no man in the State
of Illinois who ought to know so much about how much villainy it takes
to oppose a decision of the Supreme Court as our honorable friend S.

A. Douglas. [A voice—"Hurrah for Douglas then." —*Times;* Long continued applause. —*Tribune*]

Another declaration Judge Douglas makes—he says that I say that Democrats are bound by the Dred Scott decision and the Republicans are not. In the sense in which he argues it I have never said that. I will tell you what I have said and I will repeat it. I have said as they believe that decision to be correct, that the institution of slavery is fixed in the national constitution. They are bound to support it as such; but as we do not believe it is a correct decision we are not bound to support it as such. Gen. Jackson said that each man is bound to support it [the Constitution—*ed.*] in that way. Judge Douglas understands it in one way and he is bound to support it in that way. [Cheers. —*Tribune*] I understand it in another way, and consequently I am bound to support it in that way. [Prolonged applause. —*Tribune*]

Now, then, as Judge Douglas believes that decision to be correct, I will remark—let me take [talk to—*ed.*] some Gentleman who looks me in the face. You sir; you are a member of a territorial legislature. You believe that the right to take and hold slaves there is a constitutional right. The first thing you do is to swear to support the constitution. Your neighbor needs your decision to support his constitutional right. Now, I ask you if you refuse it if you do not commit perjury? [Cries of "Yes." —*Tribune*] I ask any reasonable [the *Tribune* had "sensible"—*ed.*] man if that is not a fact? [Voices—"Yes," "that is a fact," and "no." —*Times;* "Yes, yes"—"That's a fact." —*Tribune*] Does Judge Douglas mean to say that a territorial legislature or any legislature may, by the withholding of laws or by the passing of law, override a constitutional right? Does he mean to say that he means to ignore propositions long known and well established in law, that what you cannot directly do you cannot do indirectly? Does he mean that? The truth about all that matter is that Judge Douglas had sung paeans to his popular sovereignty doctrine until the Supreme Court decision had squatted his popular sovereignty out of the way. [Uproarious laughter and applause. —*Tribune*] To still keep up that humbug about popular sovereignty he has at last invented this sort of do-nothing sovereignty [renewed laughter —*Tribune*] of the people excluding slavery by doing nothing at all. [Continued laughter. —*Tribune*] I ask you is this not running down his popular sovereignty doctrine to death [the *Tribune* substituted "awfully" (Laughter.)—*ed.*], till it has got as thin as the homeopathic soup that was made by boiling the shadow of a pigeon that was starved to death? [Roars of laughter and cheering. —*Tribune*] But when you come to look at it there is not even that thin soup. In the demonstration of thought it is no other than to put the unphilosophical proposition that two bodies may keep the same position at the same time. The Dred Scott decision covers the whole ground and while it stands there is not room for even the shadow of a starved pigeon to occupy the same ground. [Great cheering and laughter. —*Tribune*]

[A Voice on the platform—"Your time is almost out." (Loud cries of "Go on, go on"—"we'll listen all day.") Lincoln: "Well, I'll talk to you a little longer" —*Tribune*]

Now Judge Douglas, in replying to what I have have said about having upon a previous occasion made the same speech that he took an extract from and that shows that I practiced the deception twice. Now my friends, are any of you obtuse enough to swallow that? ["No, no, we're not such fools." —*Tribune*] Judge Douglas had said that I had made a certain speech at Charleston that I would not make up North. I turned around and answered him by showing him that I had made the same speech up North—that I had made it at Ottawa—that I had made it in his hearing—that I had made it in the Abolition district—that I had made it in Lovejoy's district in the personal presence of Lovejoy—and that I made it in the same atmosphere as I made the Chicago speech that he complains on.

Now, in relation to my not having said anything about the Chicago speech. He thinks that is a terrible subject for me to handle. Why, I can turn round and show that the substance of that speech that I made down in Egypt, as he calls it, at Springfield. I have it in that book [probably his small scrapbook of printed speeches, notes, and the text of the Declaration of Independence—*ed.*], but I can't stop to read. [Cries of "read it" —*Times;* "Read it, read it." —*Tribune*] No, I am obliged to use my own judgement as to the use of my time. I want to show that in speaking of the Declaration of Independence that I only use the same language as Mr. Clay uses. Mr. Clay was one time called upon in Indiana to liberate his slaves. He made a written reply to that application in which are these words: "And what is the foundation of this appeal to me, in Indiana to liberate the slaves under my care in Kentucky? It is the general declaration in the act announcing to the world the independence of the thirteen colonies that all men are created equal. Now as an abstract principle there is no doubt of the truth of the declaration and it is desirable in the original construction of society[,] and in organized societies[,] to keep it in view as a fundamental principle." [Loud cheers. "Hurrah for Clay." —*Tribune*] Now, when I sometimes in relation to the organization of new societies in some new countries where the soil is clean and clear, advocate the policy of keeping it so in view, Mr. Douglas will insist that I want a Nigger [the *Tribune* text had "negro"—*ed.*] wife [Great laughter. —*Tribune*]; but never can he be brought to understand that there is any middle ground on this. Now I, for my part have lived some fifty years. And I never had a negro slave or a negro wife, [Cheers —*Tribune*] and I think I can live for fifty centuries for that matter without having either [Cheers and laughter. —*Tribune*], and I maintain yet that you may take Judge Douglas' quotations from my Chicago speech and my Charleston speech and as an honest man, I am willing to trust them to you and I deny, as you will, that there is any rascality or double dealing. [Great applause. —*Tribune*]

I suppose I have occupied about ten minutes. Well now, the Judge doesn't seem disposed at all to have peace. He is disposed, after all to have a personal warfare with me. He says my oath would not be taken against the bare word of Charles Lanphier or Thomas L. Harris. Well, that is a matter of opinion [Laughter. —*Tribune*], that is altogether a matter of opinion. It is not for me to vaunt my word against the oaths of these gentlemen: but I will tell Judge Douglas again what I dared to say[:] they proved a forgery. I pointed out at Galesburg and I call his attention to it now, that the publication of these resolutions in the *Illinois State Register* bore unmistakable evidence of the fact that the man who published them knowing that they were a forgery, that the writer had taken a part of the genuine proceeding, showing that he had those proceedings before him, and that taking one part of the resolution he substituted those fraudulent ones in their stead. I charged that his friend Lanphier was the editor of the *Register* at that time. He knows whether he did it or whether some of his friends had been allowed to do it. I pointed out to him that in his Freeport speech that he had promised to investigate the subject. Does he say he did not promise it? ["No," "No." —*Tribune*] If he does not delay it I have a right to ask him why he does not keep his promise[.] [Tremendous applause. —*Tribune*, which added: "I call upon him to tell here to-day why he did not keep that promise"—*ed.*] He has brought the fraud to Lanphier and Harris and there is little room for escape for Lanphier [Laughter. —*Tribune*]; and Lanphier is doing the Judge good service; and he desires Lanphier's word to be taken as a man of veracity, and he has alike with Harris, and when this thing lies between them he will not prosecute it to show where the guilt really belongs. Now as he has said that he would investigate it and implied that he would tell us how it is, I demand of him to tell why he did not investigate it, if he did not, and if he did I demand to know what was the result of that investigation. [Great cheers. —*Tribune*] I tell him another thing. That is the third time that he has assumed that he learned about those resolutions by Harris' attempting to use them against Norton [Representative Jesse D. Norton, Lincoln supporter from Joliet—*ed.*] on the floor of Congress. I tell Judge Douglas that the publication shows that he attempted to use it upon Trumbull a month before Harris tried them on Norton [Great applause—*Tribune,* which added: "—that Harris had the opportunity of *learning it from him,* rather than he from Harris. I now ask his attention to that part of the record on the case. My friends, I am not disposed to detain you longer in regard to that matter. I am told that I still have five minutes left."—*ed.*]

Well, there is another matter I will give some attention to. He says when he discovered that there was a mistake in that case that he magnanimously came forward and acknowledged it, without my calling his attention to it. I will tell you what that magnanimity was. When the newspapers of our side [the *Tribune* added: "had discovered and"—*ed.*] published it, and established that it was a fraud, he came forward and made a virtue of necessity. He said that I had a hand in passing them—that is what he said in his opening speech—that I was in the convention. Does he pretend that I had a hand in the resolutions which he says were passed? It strikes me that there is some difference between finding a thing a man had anything to do with and a thing a man had nothing to do with without holding him responsible for them. You will judge whether there is any difference in the spots or not. [Lincoln here turned his decade-old pejorative nickname of "Spotty" Lincoln against Douglas. It referred to his introduction of the "Spot Resolution" in Congress demanding to know the spot where American blood had been shed, igniting the Mexican War—*ed.*] [Laughter and cheers. —*Tribune*] And if he has taken credit for great magnanimity in coming forward and acknowledging what is proved on him, and proved upon him beyond even the capacity of Judge Douglas to deny, and he has more capacity in that way than any other living man. [Laughter and cheers. —*Tribune*]

He then wants to know why I won't withdraw a charge in regard to a conspiracy to make slavery national, as he has withdrawn the ones he has made. May it please his worship, I will withdraw it when it is proved false like that was proved false on him [shouts of applause and laughter. —*Tribune*] and I will do a little more than that. I will withdraw it whenever a reasonable man shall be brought to believe that the charge is not true. [Renewed applause. —*Tribune*] I have asked Judge Dogulas' attention to certain matters of fact tending to prove the charge of a conspiracy to nationalize slavery. He says now, that he convinces me that this is all untrue because Mr. Buchanan was not in the country at that time and because the Dred Scott case had not come into the Supreme Court and he says that I say that the Democratic owners of Dred Scott brought up the case. I never said so [Applause. —*Tribune*] and I don't now. I defy Judge Douglas to show that I ever said so or I ever did utter it. [Great confusion. —*Times;* One of Mr. Douglas' reporters gesticulated affirmatively at Mr. Lincoln. —*Tribune*] [The *Tribune* adds here that Lincoln then said to the reporter, who omitted it in his transcript: "I don't care if your hireling does say I did, I tell you myself that *I never said the 'Democratic' owners of Dred Scott got up the case.* (Tremendous enthusiasm.) I have never pretended to know whether Dred Scott's owners were Democrats or Abolitionists, or Free Soilers or Border Ruffians"—*ed.*] I have said that there is evidence about that case tending to establish that the case was a made up case, for the purpose of getting that decision. I have said that that evidence is very strong that the owner of him set him free showing that when he had the case tried, and had got the question settled for such use as could be made of the decision that he cared nothing about the property declared to be his by the decision. [Enthusiastic applause. —*Tribune*] [The *Tribune* added the conclusion: "But my time is out and I can say no more"—*ed.*]

[As Mr. Lincoln retired, a deafening cheer went up that was continued with unabated enthusiasm for some minutes.—*Tribune*]

THE SEVENTH JOINT
DEBATE AT ALTON

Friday, October 15, 1858

·THE SCENE·

IN TERMS OF PURE DRAMA, the Lincoln-Douglas encounter at Alton
paled before the memory of the violent confrontation that had made
the river village infamous twenty-one years before. Back in 1837,
abolitionist editor Elijah Lovejoy had been murdered here by a
violent pro-slavery mob while trying to protect his printing press
from destruction. The final debate of the 1858 Senate campaign
seemed tame by comparison.

Because of Alton's ugly history, however, and because the debate
there was the very last meeting between the candidates, the debate
at the Mississippi River town in southwestern Illinois was expected
to attract a considerable audience. Steamboats offered one-dollar,
round-trip discount fares from St. Louis, and the railroads advertised
attractive excursion rates of their own. A local newspaper predicted:
"There will be a great attendance." It was a beautiful day—"one of
the prettiest I have ever known in October," an onlooker
remembered—but although the usual retinue of spectators rolled in

on carriages and wagons, their numbers never exceeded 5,000, making the total crowd at Alton the second smallest of the series.

Nonetheless, by noon, the "whole town" seemed to one eyewitness "alive and stirring with large masses of human beings." Bands played, salesmen sold painkillers from the streets, little knots of boys and men marched up and down the public square shouting "hurrahs" for Lincoln or Douglas, and food emporiums and saloons overflowed with merry patrons. The competing banners floating high above the streets declared: "Popular sovereignty! Stephen A. Douglas, the People's Choice" and "Lincoln Not Trotted Out Yet."

For the first and only time, the debaters arrived in town together. Both men had remained at Quincy following their encounter on the thirteenth, and the following evening each booked overnight passage on the steamboat *City of Louisiana* for the 115-mile cruise down the Mississippi River to Alton, where they arrived at five a.m. on the fifteenth. The weary campaigners were then escorted to separate hotels, Lincoln by one account "a little despondent" when his own quiet welcome without "parade or fuss" was easily outdone by a "pompous" overture of martial music and artillery fire in Douglas's honor. Waiting for Lincoln was his wife, Mary, whom he described to a supporter as "dispirited" over his chances in the coming election. The Lincolns' eldest son, Robert, was also on hand for the final debate, in his role as fourth corporal in the Springfield cadets. His unit arrived by train in full uniform to observe the great event.

The debaters began promptly at two p.m., from a platform erected for the occasion alongside Alton's new city hall. The "whole arena," declared an eyewitness, "was crowded with thousands of people for several blocks in front of the stand." But the crowd was likely startled when they first saw the senator and heard Douglas's ragged delivery. Not only was his voice "completely shattered" by the long campaign, he also looked "bloated" and "haggard" to one observer. An eyewitness was certain he was heard only by "a small crowd gathered closely about the stand." By contrast, Lincoln looked sunburned, but "as fresh as if he had just entered the campaign." For both speakers a journalist noted "rather less than the ordinary amount of applause."

Neither candidate broke new ground in Alton; instead both used their time effectively to sum up the arguments they had introduced in the six meetings since August. Alton provided them their final opportunity to discuss the many additional issues facing the state and the nation. As in the first six debates, however, the focus here remained immovably fixed on slavery and union.

Douglas devoted his opening hour to an impassioned defense of popular sovereignty, and a renewed attack on Lincoln. He labored to distance himself from President Buchanan, a fellow Democrat, while endeavoring to identify himself more closely with Lincoln's hero, Henry Clay, a Whig. And he made a strong appeal for unified support for the Democrats, the only party, he declared, for "national men."

Conceding that the Alton audience enjoyed "strong sympathies by birth, education, and otherwise, with the South," Lincoln attempted again in his rebuttal to differentiate between favoring black equality and merely extending to blacks the blessings of the Declaration of Independence. And he scored Douglas for a lack of "statesmanship" for refusing to take a moral position of his own on slavery. In one of the soaring moments of his ten and a half hours in debate, Lincoln declared that their opposing views on the issue mirrored starkly "the two principles that have stood face to face, one of them asserting the divine right of kings, the same principle that says you work, you toil, you earn bread, and I will eat it."

Douglas did not sustain the elevated tone of debate in his final rejoinder. Instead he revived his attack on Lincoln's congressional voting record on the Mexican War, and sought to embarrass him for having turned against Henry Clay in 1848 to support a rival Whig, Zachary Taylor, for the presidency. Yet he ended dramatically with a searing attack on "agitators" who now assailed only slavery, but could as easily, he warned, wage war someday soon on "another domestic institution." As Douglas saw it, "the only remedy or safety is that we shall stand by the Constitution" and "obey the laws."

Republican leader Gustave Koerner, who had chaired the June convention that nominated Lincoln for the Senate, witnessed the debate and recalled that Lincoln's words "stirred my heart as nothing else did and made me a greater foe of the institution of slavery." Lincoln's performance in the final debate, he maintained, "sounded the knell of slavery" for the entire nation—although surely he exaggerated his candidate's impact on that small audience on

October 15, 1858. Years later, Koerner effused, the "tones of
Lincoln" were still "vibrating in my ears."

A Cincinnati journalist probably took the measure of the event
more accurately by observing that the small turnout at Alton proved
two things: that "the novelty had worn off" the Lincoln-Douglas
encounters, and that "the full reports of the previous debates" were
by then satisfying "the public curiosity." Few readers knew at the
time, or in the years that followed Lincoln's impending defeat, that
the "reports" on which they were relying bore scant resemblance to
the exuberant but unpolished stump performances that had
characterized the long, extraordinary war of words.

As for one who played a crucial role in creating that enhanced
record, he was as despondent over the results at the polls as he was
hopeful about the political future of his candidate. "I don't think it
possible for you to feel more disappointment than I do, with this
defeat," the *Tribune*'s Horace White wrote to Lincoln after election
day. But the candidate's loyal "friend in distress" remained certain
yet that "Abe Lincoln shall be an honored name before the
American people." In this assessment, for once, Horace White did
not exaggerate.

The following "rival" transcriptions were published a few days after
the final debate: the *Press and Tribune*'s unedited version of Douglas's
opening and closing statements appeared on October 18, and
the *Times*'s similarly unpolished version of Lincoln's rebuttal, on
October 17.

Mr. Douglas' Opening Speech

[Mr. Douglas, on being introduced was received with cheers. —*Tribune;* Long and loud bursts of applause greeted Senator Douglas when he appeared on the stand. As he was about to commence speaking, he was interrupted by Dr. Hope, one of the Danite faction (pro-Buchanan Democrats—*ed.*). —*Times*]

DR. HOPE, (in the audience.)—Judge, before you commence speaking, allow me to ask you one question, if you please. [The *Times* reported Douglas's initial reply: "If you will not occupy too much of my time," together with Dr. Hope's rejoinder: "Only an instant," and Douglas's answer: "What is your question?"—*ed.*] Do you believe that the Territorial Legislatures ought to pass laws to protect slavery in the Territories?

JUDGE DOUGLAS—You will get the answer in the course of my remarks. [Applause. —*Times*]

GENTLEMEN AND LADIES:—It is now nearly four months since these debates between Mr. Lincoln and myself commenced. On the 16th of June, the Republican Convention assembled at Springfield, and nominated Mr. Lincoln as their candidate for the Presidency and Senatorship [laughter, —*Tribune*] [The *Times* did not report this slip of the tongue—*ed.*] and he at the same time delivered a speech, in which he laid down what he insisted to be the Republican creed, and the platform upon which he proposed to stand during the canvass. The principal points in that speech of Lincoln's were, first—that this Government could not endure permanently divided into free and slave States, as our fathers made it—that they must all become free or all become slave— that they must all be one thing, or all be the other, otherwise the Union could not exist. I give you the substance of his position in almost, perhaps quite, his exact language. The next proposition was a crusade against the Supreme Court of the United States, because of their decision in the Dred Scott case, alleging [e]specially as a reason against that decision, that it deprived negroes of the rights and benefits of that clause in the Constitution of the United States which guarantees to the citizens of each and every State all the rights, privileges and immunities of the citizens of the several States. On the 11th [the *Times* corrected to "10th"—*ed.*] of July I returned home, and delivered a speech to the people of Chicago, in which I announced my purpose of appealing to the people of Illinois to sustain the course that I had pursued; and in that speech I joined issue with Mr. Lincoln on the points which he had presented. Thus there was an issue made up between us, clear and distinct, on these two propositions, by the speech at Springfield and my reply at Chicago. On the next day, the 11th of July, Mr. Lincoln replied to me at Chicago, explaining at some length, and re-affirming the positions which he had taken in his Springfield speech. In that speech at Chicago, he also went further, and uttered sentiments which he had often advanced previously in regard to the equality of the negro with the white man. [That's so. —*Times*] He then adopted the argument which Lovejoy and Giddings and the other Abolition lecturers had made for him to the northern and central portions of the State. He then took the ground that the Declaration of Independence having declared all men equal, and equal also by Divine right, that the negro equality was an inalienable right of which they could not be deprived. He insisted in that speech that the Declaration of Independence, declaring all men to be created equal, included the negro. And he went so far as to say that if one man was allowed to take the position that it didn't include the negro, others might take the position that it didn't include other men. Hence he said that all those distinctions between this man and that man, this race and that race, must be discarded, and we must stand by the declaration that all men were created equal. The issue thus being made up between Mr. Lincoln and myself, upon three points, we went before the people of the State. During the seven weeks that followed between the Chicago speech and our joint meeting at Ottawa, he and I had addressed the people in large numbers in many of the central counties, and in my speeches I held closely to these three propositions— controverting his proposition that this Union could not exist as our fathers made it, divided into free and slave States—controverting his proposition of a crusade against the Supreme Court on the Dred Scott decision and controverting his proposition that the Declaration of Inde- pendence included and meant negroes as well as white men, when it declared all men to be created equal. [Cheers for Douglas. —*Times*] I had supposed at that time that we had arrived at a distinct issue, that each was willing to be held to in every part of the State. I never intended to waver one hair's breadth from the issue either in the north or in the south, or wherever I should address the people of Illinois. I hold that whenever I can't proclaim my political creed in the same terms, not only in the north but the south part of Illinois, not only in the northern but in the southern States, wherever the American flag waves over American soil, then there must be something wrong in that creed. [Applause. —*Tribune;* "Good, good," and cheers. —*Times*] So long as I live under a common Constitution—so long as I live under a confederacy of sovereign and equal States, joined together as one, for certain purposes, I shall consider any political creed wrong which cannot be proclaimed in every State and in every action of that Union alike. Hence I took up his three propositions in my several speeches, analyzed them, and pointed out what I believed to be the radical error. The doctrines advanced by Lincoln in his Springfield speech were in violation of the declaration of the law of God, which says that a house divided against itself cannot stand. I repudiated it as a slander upon the makers of this government [the *Times* substituted "framers of our constitution"—*ed.*]. [Applause. —*Tribune*] I then said, and have often repeated it, and now again assert that in my opinion this government can endure forever divided into free and slave States as our fathers made it, each State having the right to prohibit, abolish, or sustain slavery, just as it pleases. ["Good," "right," and cheers. —*Times*] This government was made on the great basis of the sovereignty of the States—the right of each State to regulate its own domestic institutions to suit itself, and that right was conferred with the understanding and expectation that inasmuch as each locality had separate and distinct interests, each State must have different and distinct local and domestic institutions, corresponding to the wants and interests of each locality. Our fathers knew when they made this government that the laws and institutions which were well adapted to the Green Mountains of Vermont were unsuited to the rice plantations of South Carolina. They knew then, as well as we know now, that the laws and institutions which would be adapted to the beautiful prairies of Illinois would not be suited to the mining regions of California. They knew that in a Republic as broad as this, having such a variety of soil, of climate and of interests, there must necessarily be a corresponding variety in the local laws, and policy, and institutions of each State, adapted to its own wants and condition. For these reasons this Union was established on the right of each State to do as it pleased on the subject of slavery, and every other question, negativing the right of every other State to complain, much less interfere with such policy. ["That's good doctrine," "that's the doctrine," and cheers. —*Times*] Suppose this doctrine of Lincoln's and the abolitionists of this day had prevailed when the Constitution was made, what would have been the result? Only imagine for a moment that Lincoln had been then a member of the Convention that framed the Constitution of the United States, and when they were about to sign that immortal document, he had arisen in that Convention, as he did at Springfield this summer, and addressing himself to the President, had said, "a house divided against itself cannot stand [laughter —*Times*] —this government divided into free and slave States cannot endure— they must all be free or they must all be slave—they must all be the one thing, or all be the other; otherwise it is a violation of the law of God, and they cannot endure." Suppose Lincoln had convinced that body of sages that that doctrine was sound, what would have been the result, remembering that the Union was composed of thirteen States, twelve of which were slaveholding and one was free? Do you think that one free State would have out-voted the twelve slaveholding States, and thus have abolished slavery everywhere? [No, no. —*Times*] On the other hand, would not the twelve slaveholding States have out-voted the one free State, and thus have fastened slavery by a constitutional provision on every foot of the American Republic forever?

Thus you see that if the Abolition doctrine had prevailed when the government was made, it would have established slavery as a permanent institution in all the States, whether they wanted it or not. The question for us in Illinois to determine is, are we willing, when we have become the section which is in the majority, to enforce a doctrine on the minority which we would have resisted with our heart's blood, when we were in the minority? ["We never will," "good, good," and cheers. —*Times*] Now, how has the South acted and how have the free States increased in this Union, except under that principle which declares the right of the people in each State and of each Territory to form and regulate their own domestic institutions in their own way? Remember that it was under that principle that slavery was abolished in New Hampshire, Vermont, Connecticut, New York, New Jersey, and Pennsylvania. Under that principle one-half of the original slaveholding States became free. Under that principle we have increased from being one out of twelve, until we have become the majority of the whole Union, having the power in the House of Representatives, the power in the Senate, and consequently the power to elect a President by Northern votes without a Southern State. And having achieved this ascendancy under the operation of that great principle, are you now prepared to abandon that principle and assert, merely because we have the power, we will wage a warfare against the Southern States and their institutions, until we force them to abolish slavery everywhere? [Applause. —*Tribune;* No, never, and great applause. —*Times*] After having pressed home this argument on Lincoln for seven weeks, publishing several of my speeches, when I got him to the joint discussion [at] Ottawa, he began to flinch a little [the *Times* substituted "crawfish a little"—*ed.*] and back down. [Immense applause. —*Times*] I then propounded a certain question to him—whether he would vote for any more slave States, even in the event the people wanted them, and he would not answer. [Applause and laughter. —*Times*] I then told him if he didn't answer the questions there, I would renew them again in Freeport, and then after that I would trot him down into Egypt and put them to him again there. [Applause. —*Tribune;* Cheers. —*Times*]

Well, at Freeport, in dread of Egypt, knowing that that was the best joint discussion, he did answer the question of no more slave States in a mode that he hoped would accomplish an object. I will show you what that answer was. After saying he was not pledged on the subject, he declared that "in regard to that matter of whether I am pledged to the admission of any more slave States into the Union, I say to you very frankly that I would be exceedingly sorry ever to be put in the position of having to pass upon that question." Here permit me to remark that I don't think the people will ever force him into a position where he will have to vote upon it. [Applause. —*Tribune;* Great laughter and applause. —*Times*] Then he went on to say, "I should be exceedingly glad to know that there would never be another slave State admitted into the Union, but I must add that if slavery should be kept out of the Territory during its territorial existence—of any one given Territory—that the people having a fair chance and clear field when they come to adopt a State Constitution, did such an extraordinary thing as to adopt a slave constitution, uninfluenced by the actual presence of the institution among them, I see no other alternative, if we own the country, but to admit them." [Applause, and cries of "Hurrah for Lincoln," "Hurrah for Douglas." —*Tribune*] [The *Times* did not quote this Lincoln extract precisely, but it is possible that Douglas himself paraphrased it at Alton to heighten the effect of certain passages; ultimately it was reprinted exactly as Lincoln had originally said it for the book edition of the debates—*ed.*] Gentlemen, your silence is more acceptable than your applause, for I desire to address exclusively your judgment. That answer was supposed by Mr. Lincoln to be suited to the Old Line Whigs,

Kentuckians and Virginians down South. Now let me say what the answer is. I desired to know whether he would allow Kansas to come into the Union with slavery or not, as her own people desired. He would not answer. He said if Congress should prohibit slavery in a given Territory, and keep up the prohibition during the whole territorial existence, and then they should make a slave constitution, then he supposed he would have to let it come. But suppose Congress did not prohibit slavery while it was a Territory, as under Clay's Compromise measures of 1850, how will he vote? He must tell. I have put the question to him over and over again to get him to answer whether he will let Kansas do as she pleases on the slavery question, and he won't tell. [Applause. —*Tribune*; Laughter, "he'll answer this time," "he's afraid to answer," etc. —*Times*] I have put the question with reference to Nebraska and he won't answer. ["Put him through," "give it to him," and cheers. —*Times*] I have put it to him in reference to New Mexico, and I can't get a word out of him. I have gone through each Territory and put the question to him, and he won't say whether he would allow any Territory now in existence to come into the Union as she pleases, or not. He answers as to a state of things that don't exist, and won't answer as to any Territory now in existence. ["Hurrah for Douglas," "three cheers for Douglas." —*Times*] For instance, as to the compact [the *Times* substituted "contract"—*ed.*] with Texas to allow four more new States formed out of that State, to come into the Union as they pleased. I have put the question to him whether he would vote to redeem that pledge. I have put it to him three times in joint discussions, and he has not answered. He is silent as the grave on that point. [Laughter, "Lincoln must answer," "He will," &c. —*Times*] He would rather answer on a question he would never have to vote on, than one that would come up before him soon after he was elected. ["He'll never have to act on any question," and laughter. —*Times*] Now, why can't he say whether he is willing to allow the people of each Territory to have slavery or not, as they please, and then come into the Union when they have the requisite population, either as a slave State or as a free State, as they shall decide. I have no trouble in answering that question. I have said everywhere—I repeat to you now, if the people of Kansas want a slave State, they have the right under the Constitution to make it. I will let them come with slavery or without it, as they please. [Applause. —*Tribune*; "That's right," "good," "hurrah for Douglas all the time," and cheers. —*Times*] If the people of any other Territory desires [*sic*] it, let them have it; if they don't want it, let them prohibit it. It is their business, not mine. ["That's the doctrine." —*Times*] It is none of our business in Illinois whether Kansas is a free State or a slave State. It is none of your business in Missouri whether Kansas shall adopt slavery or reject it. It is her business, not yours. The people of Kansas have as much right to decide that question for themselves, as you have in Missouri, or we have in Illinois. ["That's what we believe," "We stand by that," and cheers. —*Times*] Here I will remark what I have said in every speech I have made in Illinois, and what I now repeat, that I will fight the Lecompton Constitution to the death, not because of the slavery clause in it, but because it was not the act and deed of the people of Kansas. [Applause. —*Tribune*] I said then, and say now, that if the people of Kansas wanted a slave State, they had a right to have it. If they wanted the Lecompton Constitution, let them have it. I was against it because I did not believe that it was the act of a majority of that people; but on the contrary, the act of a small pitiful minority coming in the name of the majority. At last that Constitution was sent back to the people for a vote in August last, for or against admission under the Lecompton Constitution, and at that election it was rejected by nearly ten to one, thus showing that I was right, when I said it was not the act and deed of the people of Kansas and did not embody their will. [Cheers. —*Times*] I hold that there is no power on earth which has a right under our system of government to ram a Constitution down the throats of an unwilling people. [That's so. —*Times*] Suppose there had been a majority of ten to one in favor of slavery in Kansas, and suppose there had been an Abolition President, and an Abolition Administration, and suppose in some mode the Abolitionists had got up an Abolition Constitution to be forced upon slaveholding people, would the people South have submitted to the act for an instant? [No, no. —*Times*] Well, if you of the South would not have submitted to it a day, how can you as fair-minded, honest men insist on putting a Slave Constitution on a Free State. ["That's so." —*Times*] Your safety and success depends upon both of us acting up to that great principle which asserts the right of every people to form and regulate their own domestic institutions to suit themselves, subject only to the federal constitution. ["That's the doctrine," and immense applause. —*Times*] Most of the men who denounce my course on the Lecompton question object to it, not because I was not right, but because it was expedient at one time, for the sake of keeping the party together, to do wrong. [Applause.

—Tribune; Cheers. *—Times*] I never knew the Democratic party to violate any one of its principles for the sake of policy or expediency, that it did not pay the debt with sorrow. There is no other safety except always to do right and trust the consequences to God and the people. And I am not going to depart from principle in that one instance, nor do I ever intend to do it. [Good. *—Times*] But I am told that it would all have been right if I had only voted for the English bill after the Lecompton was killed. [Laughter. *—Tribune;* Laughter and cheers. *—Times*] You know a general pardon was granted to all political offenders on the Lecompton [the *Times* added "question"—*ed.*] provided they would only vote for the English bill. I did not accept the benefits of that pardon for the reason that I was right in my opinion, and hence did not require any forgiveness. But let us see how the result was worked out. English brought in his bill referring the Lecompton Constitution back, with the declaration that if it was rejected, then Kansas should stay out of the Union until she had the full ratio for a member of Congress, thus in effect providing that if the people of Kansas would only consent to come into the Union under the Lecompton Constitution, and have a slave State when they didn't want it, then they might come in with 35,000; but if they were so obstinate as to insist upon having just such a Constitution as they wanted—insisted upon their right to make a free State if they desired, then they should be kept out until they had 93,420. I then said, and now repeat to you, that whenever Kansas should have people enough for a slave State, she had enough for a free State. [Applause. *—Tribune;* "That's the doctrine all over," "Hurrah for Douglas." *—Times*] I was willing to adopt the rule that no State shall ever come into the Union until it has the full ratio for a member of Congress, provided you make that rule universal. And I made that proposition in the Senate last winter, and they wouldn't take it. Then I said, if you won't take the general rule, I will not consent to make an exception of Kansas. I hold it is a violation of the fundamental principle of this Government to throw the weight of the federal power either into the scale of free States or slave States. Unity among all the States of this Union is a fundamental principle in our political system, and we have no more right to throw the federal government into the scale of the slaveholding State than we have in that of the free State. Least of all should our friends South consent for a moment that Congress should wield its power either way, when they know that there is a majority against them in both Houses of Congress. But how have

these supporters of the English bill stood up to their pledge not to let Kansas in until she had 93,000? The newspapers inform us that Mr. English himself voted against his own bill, in order to get re-elected. [Laughter and applause. —*Times*] We are informed that every candidate for Congress in all the States where elections have taken place recently, are pledged against the English bill, with perhaps one or two exceptions. Now, if I had only done as these Anti-Lecompton men did who voted for the English Bill, I would have had no trouble, that I pledged myself to stand by it, and then forfeit my pledge and go against it. You see the whole power and patronage of the Federal Government wielded in Ohio, Indiana and Pennsylvania, to elect Anti-Lecompton men to Congress, to elect men who voted for the English Bill, and then denounce the English Bill and go against it. [Good. —*Times*] My sins consist in not having given a pledge and then forfeited it, and for that reason in this State every postmaster, every route-agent, and every Federal office-holder in the State is removed the moment he expresses preference for the Democratic candidate [the *Times* inserted "against Lincoln and"—*ed.*] over his abolition associates. [Applause. —*Tribune;* That's so, and cheers. —*Times*] The Democratic Administration which we helped to bring into power deemed it consistent with its fidelity to principle and duty, to wield its power in this State in behalf of the Republican Abolition candidates in every county, in every Congressional district, against the Democratic party. All I have got to say on that point is, if they have not regard enough for principle, if they have not attachment enough to the creed of the Democratic party to bury forever their personal hostility to carrying out these principles [Good, good, and cheers. —*Times*] I have no personal difficulties with Mr. Buchanan or his cabinet. He chose to make certain recommendations, as he had a right to do, on the Lecompton Constitution. I could not vote for them. I had as much right to judge for myself how I should vote as he had as to how he should recommend. He undertook to say to me, if you don't vote as I tell you I will take off the heads of your friends. [Laughter. —*Tribune* and *Times*] I said to him to reply: "You did not elect me. I represent Illinois. I am accountable to Illinois as my constituency, and to God, but not to the President, nor any other power on earth." [Applause. —*Tribune;* Good, good, and vociferous applause. —*Times*] And this warfare is made on me because I wouldn't surrender my convictions of duty—because I would not abandon my constituency and receive orders from the Executive authority how I should vote under oath in the Senate of the United States. ["Never do it," "three cheers," &c. —*Times*] I hold that any attempt to control the Senate by the Executive is subversive of the principles of our Constitution. ["That's right." —*Times*] The executive department is independent of the Senate, and the Senate is independent of the President. On matters of legislation the President has a veto on the acts of the Senate, and in appointments and treaties the Senate has a veto on the President. He has no more right to tell me how I shall vote as to appointments than I have to tell him whether he shall veto a law that the Senate has passed. And wherever you recognize the right of the Executive to say to a Senator: "Do this, or I will take off the heads of your friends," you convert this Government from a Republic into a despotism. [Hear, hear, and cheers. —*Times*] Whenever you recognize the right of the President to say to a member of Congress, "vote as I shall tell you, or I will bring the power to bear against you," you destroy the independence of the Representative and convert him into a tool of Executive power. ["That's so," and applause. —*Times*] I resisted this invasion of the constitutional rights of the Senate; I intend to resist it as long as I have a voice to speak or a vote to give; and yet he can never get me to abandon one iota of Democracy out of revenge or personal hostility to his course. ["Good, good, three cheers for Douglas." —*Times*] I will stand on the platform of the Democratic party and by its organization, and support its nominees, and if they choose to bolt the ticket I will only show them that they are not as good Democrats as I am. [Applause. —*Tribune;* "That's so," "good," and applause. —*Times*]

My friends, there never was a time when it was as important for the Democratic party—for all national men—to rally and stand together as at this day. We find all sectional men giving up all past differences and combining on the one question of slavery. When sectional men unite on the one side, the national men should unite on the other hand. Such was the case in 1850, when Clay came out from his retirement in order to quell the sectional agitation and restore peace to the Union. Then we Democrats, with Cass at our head, welcomed the gallant Kentuckian as the man reserved by God for the times. He became our leader in the great fight. We then rallied around Clay as the Old Line Whigs in 1832 rallied around "Old Hickory," to put down nullification. [Cheers. —*Times*] Thus you see old Whigs and Democrats in old times fought fiercely about Banks and Tariffs, and the Specie Circular and Distribution and the Sub-Treasury. We united whenever the peace, or harmony, or integrity of the Union was imperiled. [Applause. —*Tribune;* Tremendous applause. —*Times*] Thus it was in 1829 [the *Times* corrected to 1850—*ed.*], when Abolitionism had so far divided the country north and south as to endanger the peace of the Union. Whigs and Democrats united in establishing the compromise measures of 1850. They rested on that great principle that people of each State and each Territory should be perfectly free to form and regulate their domestic institutions to suit themselves. You Whigs and we Democrats justified them on that principle. Now, in 1854, when it became necessary to organize the Territories of Kansas and Nebraska, I brought forward the bills on the same principle. In the Kansas–Nebraska bill you will find it declared to be the true intent and meaning of the act, not to legislate slavery into any State or Territory, or to exclude it therefrom, but to leave the people thereof perfectly free to form and regulate their domestic institutions in their own way. ["That's so," and cheers. —*Times*] Now, I stand on that same platform in 1858, that I did in 1850, '54 and '56. But the Washington *Union,* pretending to be the organ of the Administration, in the number of the 5th of this month, devotes three and a half columns to establish these propositions: first, that Douglas in his Freeport speech, avowed the same doctrine that he did when arguing the Nebraska bill in 1854. Second, that in 1854, Douglas justified the Nebraska bill on the same ground that he did Clay's measures of 1850—that he is the same now that he was in 1856, '54 and '50, and consequently never was a Democrat. [Applause. —*Tribune;* Great laughter. —*Times*] Now wasn't that funny that I was never a Democrat. [Renewed laughter. —*Times*] No pretense that I have changed a hair's breadth. The *Union* proves by my speeches that I expounded the Compromise Measures of 1850, just as I do now—that I advocated the Kansas-Nebraska bill in its passage, just as I do now—just as I did in my Freeport speech, and yet it says I am not a Democrat and cannot be trusted, because I have not changed during the whole time. Now it did occur to me that in 1854, the author of the Kansas-Nebraska bill was considered a pretty good Democrat. [Cheers. —*Times*] It did occur to me that in 1856, when I was exerting every nerve and every energy for James Buchanan, then standing on that identical platform I was on [the *Times* substituted "as I do now"—*ed.*], that I was a pretty good Democrat. [Renewed applause. —*Times*] But they did tell me that I am not a Democrat, because I assert that the people of a Territory, as well as those of a State, have the right to decide for themselves whether slavery can or cannot exist in such Territory. Let me read to you what James Buchanan said on that point, when he accepted the nomination for the Presidency in 1855. He said in his letter of acceptance as follows:

[The *Times* began with, although Douglas likely did not read, this sentence: "The recent legislation of Congress respecting domestic slavery, derived as it has been from the original and pure fountain of legitimate political power, the will of the majority, promises ere long to allay the dangerous excitement."—*ed.*] This legislation is founded upon principles as ancient as free government itself, and in accordance with them has simply declared that the people of a territory like those of a State shall decide for themselves whether slavery shall or shall not exist within their limits.

There, Dr. Hope, that is an answer to the question you put. [Applause. —*Tribune;* Vociferous shouts of applause. —*Times*] Of course no man considers it an answer who is outside the Democratic organization, bolts Democratic parties, and indirectly aids to put Abolitionists in power over Democrats. But whether he considers it an answer or not, James Buchanan has answered the question. The people of a territory, as well as those of a State, can regulate that question for themselves. I answer specifically, if you want it further, and say that under the new decision of the Supreme Court, according to the opinion of Chief Justice Taney, slaves are property, like all other property, and the owner can carry them to a territory the same as other property. Yet when they go there they are subject to local law, just like all other property. And you will find in a speech delivered in Maine the same construction given to that thing that I gave in my Freeport speech. [The *Times* substituted, although Douglas may not have read at the time: "You will find in a recent speech delivered by that able and eloquent statesman, Hon. Jefferson Davis (the future President of the Confederacy), at Bangor, Maine, that he took the same view of this subject that I did in my Freeport speech. He there said:"—*ed.*]

If the inhabitants of any territory should refuse to enact such laws and police regulations as would give security to their property or to his, it would be rendered more or less valueless in proportion to the difficulties of holding it without such protection. In the case of property in the labor of man, or what is usually called slave property, the insecurity would be so great that the owner could not ordinarily retain it. Therefore, though the right would remain, the remedy being withheld, it would follow that the owner would be practically debarred, by the circumstances of the case, from taking slave property into a territory where the sense of the inhabitants was opposed to its introduction. So much for the oft repeated fallacy of forcing slavery upon any community.

You will find that Mr. Orr of South Carolina, when Speaker of Congress, considered the Kansas-Nebraska Bill in the same way, in 1856. You will find that Alexander H. Stevens [*sic*], the great intellect of the South at this day, put the same construction on the Nebraska Bill in Congress that I do in my Freeport speech. The whole South are rallying to the doctrine, that if people of a Territory want slavery they have a right to have it; and if they don't want it, no power on earth should force it upon them. [Applause. —*Tribune*] I hold that there is no principle on earth more sacred to all the friends of freedom than that which says that no institution, no laws, no constitution, should be forced upon an unwilling people contrary to their wishes. I assert that under the Kansas-Nebraska Bill such is the case. It is the great principle contained in that bill. It is the principle on which James Buchanan was made President. Without that principle he never could have been President. And I will never violate nor abandon that doctrine, even though I stand alone. [Hurrah for Douglas. —*Times*] I have stood and resisted the blandishments and threats of power on the one side, and seduction on the other, standing immovable for that principle, fighting for it when assailed by Northern mobs, and fighting for it when denounced by Southern hostility. ["That's the truth," and cheers. —*Times*] I have defended it against the South and against the North. I will defend it against whoever assaults it, and I will follow it wherever its logical conclusions lead me. ["So will we all," "hurrah for Douglas." —*Times*] But I say to you that there is one, and but one, path of safety for this country, and that is to stand immovably by that principle which declares the right of each State, and each Territory, to decide this question for themselves. [Hear him, hear him. —*Times*] This Government was founded on that principle, and must be administered in that same sense in which it was founded.

But the Abolition party really think that the Declaration of Independence declared the negroes to be equal to white men—that negro equality is an inalienable right conferred by the Almighty, and hence that all human laws in violation of it are null and void. Well, with such men it is no use for me to argue. I hold that the signers of the Declaration of Independence had no reference to the negro at all, when they declared all men to be created equal. They did not mean negroes nor the savage Indian, nor the Fejee [*sic*] Islander, nor any other barbarous race—they were speaking of white men. ["It's so," "it's so," and cheers. —*Times*] They alluded to European men—of European birth and European descent—white men, and none others, when they declared that doctrine. ["That's the truth." —*Times*] I hold that this government is established on the white basis. It was established by white men, for the benefit of white men and their posterity forever, and should be administered by white men and none others. But it does not follow by any means, that merely because a negro is not a citizen, merely because he is not an equal, that therefore he should be a slave. On the contrary, it does follow that we ought to extend to the negro race and to all other dependent races, all the privileges, all the immunities which they can exercise consistently with the safety of society. Humanity requires that we should give them all of these privileges. Christianity commands that we should extend these privileges to them. Then the question is, what are these privileges—what is the nature and extent of them? My answer is this is a question which each State must decide for itself. We in Illinois have decided it for ourselves. We tried slavery—kept it up for twelve years, found it was not profitable and abolished it for that reason, and then became a free State. We now adopt the policy that in this state a negro shall not be a slave, nor shall he be a citizen. We have a right to adopt that policy. For my part, I think it is a wise and sound policy for us. You in Missouri must judge for yourselves whether it is a wise policy for you. If you choose to follow our example, very good. If you reject it, it is your business, not ours. Let Kentucky adopt her own policy to suit herself. If we don't like that, we will keep away from her. If she don't like ours, she can stay at home and let us alone. If the people of all the States will stand on that principle, and let each State mind its own business, attend to its own affairs and let their neighbors alone there will be peace between the North and the South [the *Times* added: "the East and the West"—*ed.*] and the whole Union. [Cheers. —*Times*] Why cannot we thus have peace? Why should we allow a sectional party to agitate this country and convulse it—array the North against the South, convert friends into enemies, merely that ambitious men may ride into power on a sectional hobby? How long is it since those ambitious, sectional, northern men wished to have a sectional organization[?] They never dreamed of a sectional party so long as the north was the weaker section. So long as the South was the stronger, they were all against a sectional party, but the moment, by the admission of California, the North became the strongest with a majority in the House and Senate, with the power to elect a President, Northern ambitious men formed a scheme of uniting the people of the North against the South, and making the people vote by sections, and the North being the most populous would out-vote the South, and consequently the leaders of the North would ride into office on that hobby.

I am told my hour is over. It was very short. [Loud applause. —*Tribune;* Cheer after cheer rose in the air for Douglas when he took his seat, and it was some time before sufficient silence could be restored to allow Mr. Lincoln to proceed. —*Times*]

Mr. Lincoln's Reply

[As Mr. Lincoln arose, there was a great confusion of cries and cheering. Among other cries we heard many "hurrahs for Douglas," with "cheers for Lincoln," and cries of "give him a chance," "let him have a sight," "hurrah for Lincoln," etc. The noise having somewhat subsided, Mr. L. proceeded to say: —*Times;* On being introduced to the audience, after the cheering had subsided Mr. Lincoln said: —*Tribune*]

LADIES AND GENTLEMEN:

A VOICE:—There are no ladies here.

MR. LINCOLN:—You are mistaken about that. There is a fine chance of them back here. [Laughter. —*Times;* the *Tribune* omitted this exchange—*ed.*]

I have been somewhat, in my own mind, complimented by a large portion of Judge Douglas' speech—by that portion of it which he addressed to the controversy between himself and the present Administration. [Laughter, and cries of "hurrah for Lincoln," and "hurrah for Douglas." —*Times;* Cheers and laughter. —*Tribune*] This is the seventh time that Judge Douglas and I have met in these joint discussions, and the Judge, upon that subject, has been gradually improving. [A voice, "that is so," and laughter. —*Times* and *Tribune*] In regard to his war with the Administration at Quincy last Wednesday—the day before yesterday—the Judge was a little more severe upon the Administration than I have heard him be upon any former occasion, and I complimented him for it, and I told him that I altogether commended him to a most vigorous prosecution of that war. I told him to give it to them with all the power he had; and, as some of them were sitting there present, I told them I would be much obliged to them if they would give it to *him* in about the same way [Uproarious laughter and cheers. —*Tribune*]; and I felt that as he has vastly improved upon the attack that he made then, that he has really taken my advice upon the subject, all I can say now is to recommend to him and to them what I then commended to him and them—the prosecution of the war in the most vigorous style. I say [the *Tribune* added "again"—*ed.*], "go it husband and go it bear." [Great laughter. —*Tribune*]

There is one thing, however, that I will mention before I leave this branch of the subject, although I do not consider that it is much of my business any how, and that is where the Judge undertakes to involve Mr.

Buchanan in an inconsistency. He reads something from Mr. Buchanan, and undertakes to involve him in an inconsistency, and he gets something of a cheer on doing so. I would only say to the Judge, now that he is valiantly fighting for the Nebraska bill and the repeal of the Missouri compromise, that it is but a little while since he was the valiant advocate of the Missouri compromise. [A voice—"That's so!" —*Times;* Cheers. —*Tribune*] Now I want to know if Mr. Buchanan has not as much right to be inconsistent as has Judge Douglas? [Loud applause and laughter; "Good, good!" "Hurrah for Lincoln!" —*Tribune*] Has Judge Douglas an exclusive right to be inconsistent? Has he a monopoly upon that subject? [Great laughter. —*Tribune*]

So far as Judge Douglas has addressed his speech to me, or about me, it is my business to pay some attention to it. I have heard the Judge two or three times state what he stated to-day,—that in a speech which I had made at Springfield, Illinois, I had in a very special manner complained that the Supreme Court, in the Dred Scott decision, had decided that a negro could never be a citizen of the United States. I have omitted heretofore by some sort of accident to notice that statement of the Judge. It has recurred to my memory to notice it now. In point of fact it is untrue as the Judge stated it. I never have complained of the Dred Scott decision because it decided that a negro could never be a citizen of the United States. I have the speech here, and I will thank him or any of his friends to find where I specially complained of the decision because it decided that a negro could never be a citizen of the United States. I have done no such thing! Judge Douglas' persistency in insisting that I have done so, has strongly impressed me with the belief of a predetermination on his part to misrepresent me. He could not get his foundation for insisting that I was in favor of negro equality anywhere else so well as in assuming that [the *Tribune* added "untrue proposition"—*ed.*] in regard to me.

Let me tell this audience what is true in regard to this, and the means by which they can correct me if I shall not correctly state it myself, to wit: by reference to the speech itself, I was endeavoring to prove that the Dred Scott decision was a portion of a system to make slavery national in the United States. I pointed out in that speech what points had been decided in that decision by the court. I mentioned that they had decided that a negro could not be a citizen, as a fact, and I mentioned that they had done so, as I supposed, to deprive the negro of all power of ever becoming a citizen, and claiming the rights of a citizen of the United States under a certain clause of the Constitution of the United States, which guarantees to the citizens of each State all the privileges and immunities of citizens in the several States. I stated that, without making any complaint of it at all. I adduced what other points they had decided, that the bringing of a slave into the State of Illinois, and holding him for two years, was a matter that they would not decide as to whether it would make him free or not; that they decided that taking him into a territory of the United States, where an act of Congress had made it free [the *Tribune* substituted "prohibited slavery"—*ed.*], did not make him free because the act was unconstitutional. I mentioned all these in a lump, and taken in connection with the Nebraska bill and the amendment of Chase, explanatory of the pretended objects of the bill, offered at the time, which was voted down by the friends of the bill, and combining these things together and offering them, I argued that they tended to prove a combination or conspiracy, tending to make the institution of slavery national in the United States.

In that connection, and in that way, I mentioned the decision that a negro could not be a citizen of the United States. Now, out of that Judge Douglas builds up his beautiful fabric [the *Tribune* substituted "fabrication"—*ed.*] of my purpose to introduce a perfect political, and social equality between the whites and the negroes, always adding, what is not true, that I made special objection that the decision said that a negro could not be a citizen of the United States.

As this has been alluded to, and as Mr. Clay has been alluded to, I desire to place myself, in connection with him, before this people as nearly right as I may. I know what is the object of Judge Douglas here to-day; he knows that we are before an audience with strong sympathies by birth, education, and otherwise, with the South; he desires, therefore, to place me in a strong Abolition attitude. He reads, on former occasions, and alludes to-day without reading, to a portion of a speech which I made at Chicago. In his quotations as he made them on former occasions, which were quotations made, as I suppose, bringing them within what is called garbling, that is to say, taking portions of a speech which when presented do not present the entire sense of the speaker as expressed at that time. I propose, therefore, out of that same speech from which he has presented some extracts upon former occasions, and to which he alludes to-day without presenting extracts, to show you an extract which he skipped over—ones before it and one after it—leaving the portion he has alluded to out. It will take me some little time, but still I think that I will occupy the time in that way.

You have heard him to-day frequently allude to my controversy with him in regard to the Declaration of Independence. I confess to you that I have had a struggle with Judge Douglas in the way of argument in regard to that matter and I will try to place myself right in regard to it briefly on this occasion. I said—and it is between those extracts that Judge Douglas has taken his extracts and put them in his published speeches—I said:

> "It may be argued that there are certain conditions that make necessities and impose them upon us, and to the extent that a necessity is imposed upon a man that [*sic*] he must submit to it. I think that was the condition in which we found ourselves when we established this government. We had slaves among us, we could not get our Constitution unless we permitted them to remain in slavery—we could not secure the good we did secure if we grasped for more, and having by necessity submitted to that much, it does not destroy the principle that is the charter of our liberties. Let that charter stand [the actual word from the Chicago speech is "remain"—*ed.*] as our standard."

Now, I have clearly and upon all occasions declared, as strongly as Judge Douglas, that we have no right to interfere with the institutions of slavery where it exists. You hear me read that from the same speech that he takes garbled extracts from, for the purpose of proving me to be inclined to establish perfect political and social equality between the whites and the negroes.

Let me show one other extract from a speech of mine made a year ago—more than a year ago at Springfield, in discussing this very same question, soon after Judge Douglas took his ground that the negro was not included in the Declaration of Independence. I said several things, some of which I will read. I said then:

> "I think the author[s] of that notable instrument intended to include all men, but they did not intend to declare all men equal in all respects. They did not mean to say all [men] were equal in color, size or intellect, moral development or social capacity. They defined with tolerable distinctness in what respect they did consider all men cre-

ated equal—equal with[in] certain inalienable rights, among which are life, liberty, and the pursuit of happiness. This they said and this they meant. They did not mean to assert the obvious untruth that all were then actually enjoying that equality, nor yet that they were about to confer it immediately upon them. In fact, they had no power to confer such a boon. They meant simply to declare the right so that the enforcement of it might follow as fast as the circumstances should permit. They meant to set up a standard maxim for free men [society] which should be familiar to all and revered by all, constantly looked to and constantly labored for, and even though never perfectly attained, constantly approximated and thereby constantly spreading and deepening its influence and augmenting the happiness and value of life to all people of all colors everywhere." [From Lincoln's address on the Dred Scott decision, delivered June 26, 1857—*ed.*]

There again are the sentiments that I have expressed in regard to the Declaration of Independence, upon a former occasion, which have been put in print, and have been read everywhere that anybody cared to know anything about what so humble an individual as myself might say in regard to it.

At Galesburg, the other day, I said in my speech, in answer to Judge Douglas, that three years ago there had never been a man, so far as I knew or believed, in the whole world that had declared that the Declaration of Independence did not mean the negro; that the term "all men" in the Declaration of Independence did not include the negro. I reassert that to-day. I assert to-day, that Judge Douglas and all his friends may search the whole of the records of the country, and it will be a matter of great astonishment to me if they shall be able to find that any one human being on earth, three years ago, had ever uttered that, to me, astounding sentiment, that the term "all men" does not include the negro.

Do not let me be misunderstood. I know that more than three years ago there were men that, finding that old documents [the *Tribune* substituted "these old assertions"—*ed.*] standing in their way in regard to their purpose of extending slavery, denied the truth of it—I know that Mr. Calhoun and the politicians of his school, more than three years ago, denied the truth of it—I know that it ran along through the mouths of several for years, ending in that rather coarse expression, as I have heard it, of [John] Pettit [U.S. senator—*ed.*] of Indiana, on the floor of the United States Senate, that the Declaration of Independence, in that respect, was a self-evident lie, rather than a self-evident truth; but I say still, that it is my opinion that three years ago there never had lived the man, who ventured in the sneaking way of pretending to believe in the Declaration then to say, that it did not mean to include the negro. [Cheers. —*Tribune*] I believe the first man that ever said that was Chief Justice Taney in the Dred Scott case, and the next to him was our friend Judge Douglas, [cries of "Good for Douglas," and applause, —*Times;* Cheers and Laughter. —*Tribune*] and now it is becoming the catch word of the entire party. I would like to call upon Judge Douglas' friends everywhere to consider how they have come to view that matter in so short a time, so entirely different from any view that they had of it before, and to consider whether, really, they are not being carried along in a current, whither they know not. [Great applause. —*Tribune*]

But in answer to this presentation of this proposition of mine at Galesburg last week, I see that some man in Chicago has gotten up a letter, addressed to the Chicago *Times,* to show, as he believes, that somebody had said so before, and he signs his name to his letter *"An Old Line Whig,"* as I remember it. Now, in the first place, I say that he was not an old line Whig. I am somewhat acquainted with the old line Whigs—I was with the old line Whigs from the origin of that party to the end of it, and I am somewhat acquainted with it, and I know that old line Whigs always had some sense, whatever else you could ascribe to them [Great laughter. —*Tribune*] —I know that there was no one of them but had more sense than to attempt to prove that, prior to the time I said, any one had said that a negro was not included in the term "all men" by such evidence as be produced.

I will reproduce his evidence. He brings forward part of a speech of Henry Clay, and the part of a speech from Henry Clay which I would myself bring forward to prove the contrary. [Laughter. —*Tribune*] Now, let us read that portion of Henry Clay's speech. I guess we are sur- rounded in some part here by old friends of Henry Clay, and they like to hear anything from him. [A voice—"Henry Clay was a mighty good man." —*Times*] In Indiana a man had presented a petition to Mr. Clay to liberate his negroes, and Mr. Clay made a speech in answer to him, which I suppose he carefully wrote out himself, and which was pub- lished, and which I have before me, and an extract from that speech is the evidence which this pretended old line Whig brought forward to prove what he asserted in contradiction of what I have asserted:

"And what is the foundation of this appeal to me in Indiana to liberate the slaves under my care in Kentucky? It is a general declaration in the act announcing to the world the independence of the thirteen American colonies' that all men are created equal. Now, as an abstract principle there is no doubt of the truth of that declaration, and it is desirable, in the original construction of society, and in organized societies, to keep it in view as a great fundamental principle. But then, I apprehend that in no society that ever did exist or ever shall be formed was or can the equality asserted among the members of the human race be practically enforced and carried out. There are portions of it, large portions, women, minors, insane, culprits, transient sojourners, that will always probably remain subject to the government of another portion of the community.

"That declaration, whatever may be the extent of its import, was made by the delegations of the thirteen States. In most of them slavery existed and had long existed, and was established by law. It was introduced and forced upon the colonies by the paramount law of England. Do you believe that in making that declaration, the States that concurred in it intended that it should be tortured into a virtual emancipation of all the slaves within their respective limits—would Virginia and the older [should be "other"—ed.] Northern States have ever united in a declaration which was to be interpreted into an abolition of slavery among them? Did any one of the thirteen States [colonies] entertain such a design or expectation? To impute such a secret and unavowed purpose would be to charge a political fraud upon the noblest band of patriots that ever assembled in council—a fraud upon the confederacy of the Revolution—a fraud upon the union of those States, whose Constitution has only recognized the lawfulness of slavery, but permitted the importation of slaves from Africa until the year 1808."

This is the entire quotation that was brought forward for the purpose of proving that somebody had said, prior to three years ago, that the term "all men" in the Declaration of Independence did not include negroes. How does it do it? What tendency has it to prove it? Mr. Clay says, it is true, that we cannot practically apply it in all cases, and he illustrates by bringing forward the case of females, minors, insane, culprits, and so on, but he says that it is true as an abstract principle, and it is desirable in the formation of new societies, and even in organized societies, that it should be constantly kept in view as an abstract principle.

Let me add a few words more which was not brought in. Mr. Clay says, a little further on:

> "I desire no concealment of my opinions in regard to the institution of slavery. I look upon it as a great evil, and deeply lament that we have derived it from the parental government, and from our ancestors. I wish every slave in the United States was in the country of his ancestors. But here they are, and the question is, how they can be best dealt with? If a state of nature existed, and we were about to lay the foundations of society, no man would be more strongly opposed than I should be to incorporate the institution of slavery among its elements."

These were the sentiments of Henry Clay[;] he says, "if a state of nature existed, and we were about to lay the foundation[s] of society, no man would be more strongly opposed than I should be to incorporate the institution of slavery among its elements." [The *Tribune* did not report this reiteration—*ed.*] Now, we have in this same book, this same speech that is brought forward for the purpose of trying to prove that Mr. Clay said prior to three years ago, that the negro was not intended in the Declaration of Independence—no such statement at all; but we have the declaration that it is a great fundamental principle that should be constantly kept in view in the organization of new societies, and in societies already organized, that all men are created equal. But, if I say a word about it—if I attempt, as Mr. Clay said that all good men should do, to keep it in view—if I ask attention to it—if in this organized society I ask to have the public eye turned upon it—if I ask in relation to the organization of new societies that the public eye should be turned upon it, forthwith I am villified [*sic*] everywhere.

What have I done in regard to the Declaration of Independence that I have not the license of Henry Clay to do? Have I done aught in reference to the organization of new societies, and in this organized society, but as he recommended, of holding up to public view that grand fundamental principle of free society? [Applause. —*Times;* Great applause and cries of "Hurrah for Lincoln." —*Tribune*] And when this new principle—this new proposition that no human being ever thought of three years ago is brought forward, I combat it as having an evil tendency, if not an evil design; combat it as having a tendency to dishumanize [the *Tribune* substituted "dehumanize"—*ed.*] the man [*Tribune* substituted "the negro"], to take away from him all right to be supposed or considered as human; I combat it, therefore, as being one of the thousand and one things doing [*Tribune* substituted "being done"] in these days for the purpose of preparing the public mind for making property and nothing but property of the negro in all the States of this Union. [Applause, and cries of "Hurrah for Lincoln!" and "Hurrah for Douglas!" —*Times* and *Tribune*] [The latter also reported shouts of "Hurrah for Trumbull"—*ed.*]

But there is a point that I wish, before leaving this, to ask your attention further to, which I have read, but I wish again to pass over it, to ask your attention to it. Mr. Clay says:

> "I desire no concealment of my opinions in regard to the institution of slavery. I look upon it as a great evil and deeply lament that we have derived it from the parental government and from our ancestors. But here they are and the question is, how they can be best dealt with? If a state of nature existed and we were about to lay the foundations of society, no man would be more strongly opposed than I should be to incorporate the institution of slavery among its elements."

Now, then, the principle that I had insisted upon, and all the principle[s] that I have insisted upon, from the Declaration of Independence, as applicable to this discussion and this canvas, is in relation to laying the foundation of new societies. I have never sought to apply this principle to those old States where slavery exists for the purpose of abolishing slavery in those States. It is nothing but gross perversion to assume that I have brought forth the Declaration of Independence to ask that Missouri shall free her slaves. I will propose no such thing at all; but when Mr. Clay says that in laying the foundations of new societies he would be opposed to the introduction of this element, I insist that in the speech of Mr. Clay we have his warrant, his license, for insisting upon the exclusion of that element which he declared in such strong and emphatic language was most hateful to him. [Cries of "good" and some applause, and a voice—"We want white men; we don't want niggers." —*Times;* Loud applause. —*Tribune*]

Judge Douglas, in this connection, has referred to a Springfield speech of mine, in which I said, "a house divided against itself cannot stand." Now, if you please, I will address myself for a little while to something that springs from that Springfield speech. The Judge has often made the entire quotation from that speech, and I can make it myself. I used this language:

> ["]We are now far into the fifth year since a policy was instituted [initiated—*ed.*] for the avowed object and with the confident promise of putting an end to slavery agitation. Under the operation of this policy the agitation has not only [not] ceased, but has constantly augmented. In my opinion it will not cease until a crisis shall have been reached and passed. A house divided against itself cannot stand. I believe this Government can not endure permanently half slave and half free. I do not expect the Union to be dissolved—I do not expect the house to fall—but I do expect it will cease to be divided. It will become all one thing or all the other. Either the opponents of slavery will arrest the further spread of it, and place it where the public mind shall rest in the belief that it is in the course of ultimate extinction; or its advocates will push it forward until it becomes alike lawful in all the States—old as well as new, North as well as South."

That quotation, and the sentiment expressed in it, have been extremely offensive to Judge Douglas. He has warred upon them as Satan does upon the Bible. [Laughter. —*Tribune*] He has never given it up, and his perversions upon it are endless. Now, hear my views for a little while in regard to that same thing. I said that we were "now far into the fifth year since a policy was instituted for the avowed object, and with the confident promise, of putting an end to slavery agitation." Is not that so? When did the Nebraska bill come forward? Four years ago the fourth day of January last, and we are far into the fifth year since then. Was not the avowed object of that bill to put an end to slavery agitation? We were to have no more agitation of the slavery question in Congress, no more in the States, and it was all to be confined to the territories. But here I will remark, as Judge Douglas is very fond of complimenting Mr. Crittenden about this time, that he said that there was a falsehood in it, that there was no slavery agitation at the time the bill was introduced, and that the bill was itself the means [the *Tribune* substituted "that very allaying plaster"—*ed.*] of stirring it up again. [Applause. —*Times;* Applause and laughter. —*Tribune*] But was it not introduced with the purpose and confident promise of putting an end to slavery agitation? Why, every speech that he (Douglas) made until he got into the *imbroglio*, I believe you call it, with the administration, was to the effect that it was the purpose of that bill to put an end to the agitation of the question of slavery—that the last kick of its tail [the *Tribune* substituted "the serpent's tail"—*ed.*] was just drawing out of sight. [Cheers and laughter. —*Tribune*] I have said that "under the operation of that policy, that agitation has [not] only not ceased, but has constantly augmented." Is not that true? When was that agitation ever so great as to day?

There was a collateral object which was to clothe the people of the territory with a power they had never had before. The first and main object of putting an end to slavery agitation has not succeeded. The second and collateral one of conferring a higher degree of self-government is a question of fact to be determined by you in answer to a question that I will put to you now: have you ever known of a people on the face of the earth that ever had as little to do with the application of this principle as in the first instance of its use, the people of Kansas, in the application of this same right of self-government in its main and collateral objects? [Loud applause. —*Tribune*] It has been nothing but a living, creeping lie from the time of its introduction to this day. [Applause. —*Times;* Loud cheers. —*Tribune*]

But I have said that "the agitation," as I think "will not cease until a crisis shall have been reached and passed." I have said in what way I suppose that crisis may be reached and passed. I have said that it may go one way or the other. I have said that it may be passed by arresting the further spread of it, and by bringing the public mind to rest in the belief that it is in course of ultimate extinction, and I have said, and I repeat, that my wish is that the further spread of it should be arrested, and that it should be placed where the public mind shall rest in the belief that it is in course of ultimate extinction. [Applause. —*Times;* Great applause. —*Tribune*] I have expressed that as my wish, and I have no disposition to shrink from it, but I have a disposition to be not misrepresented about it. I have a disposition to not have it believed by any honest man that I desire to go to war with Missouri. Not at all! I entertain the opinion upon evidence sufficient to my mind, that the fathers of this government placed the institution of slavery among them when the public mind did rest in the belief that it was in course of ultimate extinction. Let me ask you, if they did not, why did they make provision that the source of slavery—the African slave trade—might be cut off at the end of twenty years? Why did they make provision that in all the territories that were held at that time slavery should be inhibited? Why cut it off in one direction, and prevent its spread in another, if it was not that they placed [it] in the course of ultimate extinction. In the Constitution slavery is but referred to three times, and covert language is then used, as I suppose. What is the language in regard to the prohibition of the slave trade? It runs in this way:

"The migration or importation of such persons as any of the States now existing shall think proper to admit, shall not be prohibited by the Congress prior to the year one thousand eight hundred and eight, but a tax of duty may be imposed on such importation, not exceeding ten dollars for each person." [The reference to the ten-dollar tax was deleted by the *Tribune—ed.*]

The next allusion in the constitution to the institution of slavery and the black race, as I suppose, is as to the basis of representation, and there the language that they use is:

"Representatives and direct taxes shall be apportioned among the several states which may be included within this Union according to their respective numbers, which shall be determined by adding to the whole number of free persons including these bound to service for a term of years and excluding Indians not taxed, three fifths of all other persons."

No negro mentioned—no slaves mentioned, but the "three fifths of all other persons" can be applied to no other class of persons among us, and did mean slaves. Lastly, the provision for the reclamation of fugitive slaves. There it is said:

"No person held to service or labor in one State under the laws thereof escaping into another shall, in consequence of any law or regulation thereof, be discharged from such service or labor; but shall be delivered up on claim of the parties to whom such service or labor may be due."

There again there is no mention of the negro, or of slavery. In all three of these places, being the only allusions in the constitution to the institution of slavery at all—covert language is used—language is used not at all suggestive that slavery exists, or, that the black race of people is among us, and I understand the co[n]temporaneous history of the times to be, that that language was used with a purpose, and that purpose was that our constitution, which, it was hoped—and it is still read by intellectual [the *Tribune* added "and patriotic"—*ed.*] men—that there should be nothing on the face of that instrument that should suggest to the mind that we had negro slavery among us. [Enthusiastic applause. —*Tribune*] This being so, this is part of the evidence that the fathers of the government intended and expected the institution to come to an end. They expected and intended that it was, as they placed it, in the course of ultimate extinction, and when I say that I desire to see the further spread of it arrested, I only say that I desire to see that thing done that they then did; when I say that I desire to see it placed where the public mind will rest in the belief of its ultimate extinction, I only say that I desire to see it placed where they placed it.

It is not true, so far as I may understand it, that our fathers, as Judge Douglas assumes it, that our fathers made this government part slave, and part free. It is not true that they made it so in the sense that Judge Douglas put it.

He assumes that slavery, as a rightful thing within itself, was introduced by the framers of our Constitution. In that sense, then, it is not true that the framers of our Constitution made this government part slave and part free. The exact truth is that they found the institution existing among us and they left it as they found it, not making it so, with a thousand marks of disapprobation upon it. It is not true, as assumed, that our fathers made it so, but they found it that way and they left it among us, because of the difficulties and absolute impossibility of the immediate removal of it, and when Judge Douglas turns and asks me why it is that we cannot let it remain as our fathers made it, he asks a question based upon an assumption which is itself a falsehood, and I turn upon him and ask him when he found that policy which the fathers of the government had adopted—this policy among us, the best policy in the world, and the only policy that we can ever get upon that shall give us peace, unless it masters us all and puts us down, and becomes a lawful institution alike everywhere? I turn upon him and ask him why he could not leave it alone? [Applause. —*Times;* Great and prolonged cheering. —*Tribune*] I turn and ask him what is the reason he was driven to the necessity—what was the reason he was pressed to the necessity of introducing a new policy in regard to the matter, as he has himself said that he introduced a new policy—as he so said in his speech of 22d March, 1858?

I ask only in this controversy that we shall again place this institution upon the basis that our fathers placed it upon; I ask no more than that and now I ask you, where he infers that I am in favor of setting the slave and free States at war, the one with the other; does he not do me injustice? The institution being placed in that attitude by those who made the Constitution, did it make war? ["No, no," and cheers. —*Tribune*] If we had no war when it was thus placed, where is the ground of belief that we shall have war upon returning that policy? [The *Tribune* added: "Have we had any peace upon this matter spring-ing from any other basis? ("No, no.") I maintain that we have not"— *ed.*] I have proposed nothing more than this.

Now I confess very frankly that when I propose a certain measure of policy, that it is not enough for me to show that I do not intend a wicked and evil purpose; I have tried to show that it has not a tendency to that result. I have tried to show this by fair reasoning, and I think, in the minds of fair, reasoning men, I have shown that I propose nothing other that has [the *Tribune* had "but what has"—*ed.*] a most peaceful ten-dency.

It is part and parcel of the same thing, the quotation which I, in that Springfield speech, happened to make, that a [*sic*] "a house divided against itself cannot stand." That is exceedingly offensive to Judge Douglas. It is but part and parcel of the same thing. He tries to illustrate that variety in the different institutions of the several States is indispens-ible. I shall readily agree with him, that it would be very foolish in us to insist upon having a cranberry law in Illinois, where we have no cranberries, because they have one in Indiana, where they have cran-berries. [Laughter, "good, good." —*Tribune*] I should think it would be very foolish in us to insist that Virginia has no right to have an oyster law because we don't want an oyster law. [Renewed laughter. —*Tribune*] I understand that the variety in soil, climate, in the face of the country, and consequent variety in the people and institutions of the country, and further consequent variety in legislation are vast advan-tages. I understand as well as he, I repeat, that if we raise a barrel of flour more than we want, and Louisiana raises a barrel of sugar more than she wants, that it is a material advantage to both of us that we exchange them; it makes a mutual commerce, it makes us better friends, it brings us together, and I understand that these differences and varieties are the cement in part that bind this Union together, and instead of being things that divide the house, and tend to throw it down, they are the props tending strongly to hold it up; but when I have said all this, I ask if there is any parallel between these things and the institution of slavery among us? I ask if there is any parallel at all between the things? I ask you to consider well if we have any difficulty or quarrel among ourselves about the cranberry laws of Indiana, or the oyster laws of Virginia, or about the timber laws of Maine and New Hampshire, or about the fact that Louisiana produces sugar and we produce flour and not sugar. When have we had quarrels about these things? Never no such thing. On the other hand, when have we had perfect peace in regard to this thing, which I say is an element of discord in this nation? We have sometimes had peace, and when was that? We have had peace whenever the institution of slavery remained quiet where it was, and we have had turmoil and difficulty whenever it has made a struggle to spread out where it was not. I ask, then, if experience does not teach, if it does not speak in thunder tones, that that policy that gives peace being returned to, gives promise of peace again. ["Yes"; "yes"; "yes." —*Tribune*]

You may say, and Judge Douglas may say, that all that is said in regard to slavery is the mere agitation of office seekers—of northern men that want to get his place, I suppose. [Cheers and laughter. —*Tribune*] I agree that there is selfishness enough among office seekers. We are desperately selfish, I believe the Bible says, somewhere, and I believe that I should have discovered that fact if the Bible had not said it. I am not less selfish than other men, but I do claim that I am not more selfish than is Judge Douglas. [Roars of laughter and applause. —*Tribune*]

But is it new that all this agitation in regard to the subject of slavery springs from mere office seekers? How many cases of dangerous agitation have we had from that question? You go back to the Missouri compromise; to the compromise on the nullification question—at the bottom of which was this same slavery question; go back to the difficulties of the Texas annexation; go back to the difficulties of the times of the compromise of 1850, and you will find that the agitation sprang up upon the struggle of slavery to extend itself. But further, does it make disturbance nowhere but in political circles? Does it not enter into the church, please? What divided the great Methodist Church, North and

South? What makes the disturbance in every Presbyterian General Assembly that gets together? What made the disturbance in this city a few years ago in the Unitarian church? What set them by the ears in the great American Tract Society, not splitting it yet but surely to split it? Is this the thing that so operates upon the minds of men as to stir them up in all the relations of life [Applause. —*Tribune*], not merely in the political world, but in the moral and religious; is that, however, to be assuaged by pretending that it is an exceeding small thing and that we ought to quit talking about it? [Great cheers and laughter. —*Tribune*] Why, if you will get everybody else to quit talking about it I will quit before you have half done. [Renewed laughter. —*Tribune*]

But where is the statesmanship in saying that you can quiet that disturbing element menacing us with the only danger to our Union— where is the philosophy and statesmanship that rests upon the belief that we are to say and care nothing about it[?] This policy here in the North, here with Judge Douglas, at the head of which he stands is based upon the idea that we are to care nothing about it. [A voice, "that is true." —*Times*] Now, I ask if it is not a false philosophy and false statesmanship that undertakes to build up a system of caring nothing about a thing that everybody does care a great deal about ["Yes, yes," and applause. —*Tribune*] —that all experience has shown that every-body does care a great deal about. [Laughter and applause. —*Tribune*]

The Judge alludes very often in the course of his remarks to allowing the things to be decided exclusively by the different States for them-selves. I agree very readily that the different States have that right. He is but fighting a man of straw when he assumes that I am contending against the right of the States to do as they please about it. Our controversy with him is as to the new territory. We agree that when the States come in as States, they have entire power to do as they please about the question. We profess that we, as citizens of a free State—as members of the confederation, through the general government have no power to disturb it where it is; and we profess that we have no more inclination than power to disturb it in those States; yet we are compelled to defend ourselves against the assumption that we are warring upon it in the States.

We insist that it shall be kept from the territories. Judge Douglas insists that we have no right to say anything about that; but I think that we have some interest in that as white men. Do we not wish that our surplus population may have some outlet to go to? Do we not feel an interest, in going to that outlet that such institutions shall prevail as are pleasing to us? And it is not the sort of thing that can be divided. If you go to [a] new territory opposed to slavery, and another man goes there with slaves, as equals, it turns out that he has it all his way, and you have no part in the matter. A few going into a territory with their slaves make it a slave territory, and consequently a slave State.

Now, let me suggest this thing in another way. How many Democrats are here?

A VOICE—One thousand and one! [Laughter. —*Times*]

MR. LINCOLN—How many Democrats have professed to come into the State of Illinois, pretending that they desired to get rid of slavery? I guess that there are a thousand and one of that sort. [Applause. —*Times;* Laughter. —*Tribune*] Now, I will ask if your policy had prevailed in a time when this country had been in a state of existence similar to the territories to-day, where you would have gone to? [Applause. —*Tribune*] And when hereafter, for any cause, the free people of these States shall desire to find new homes—an outlet—if they wish to be rid of the institution of slavery, when will they find the place to go to? [Loud cheers. —*Tribune*] Now, irrespective of the moral question—irrespective of the question as to whether there be right or wrong in enslaving the negro, I am still in favor of the new territory being kept free, into which free white men may move, fix their homes and better their conditions in life. I am in favor of that—not merely—I must say it here as I say it elsewhere—not merely for our own people that are born among us, but I am in favor of an outlet for the free white people, for new homes in which all free white men from all the world may find place, and better their condition in life. [Applause. —*Times*]

I have stated upon former occasions, and I may as well do so again, what I understand to be the real issue in this controversy.

There has been no issue between Judge Douglas and I on the point of my wanting to make war between the free and slave States. I pray pass that. There has been no issue between Judge Douglas and I on the ground of my wanting to introduce a perfect social and political equality between the white and colored races. These are false issues that Judge Douglas has all the while tried to force this controversy upon without foundation. The real issue in this controversy, I think, springs from a sentiment in the mind, and that sentiment is this: on the one part it looks upon the institution of slavery as being wrong, and on the part of another class, it does not look upon it as wrong. The sentiment that contemplates the institution of slavery as being wrong, is the sentiment of the Republican party, it is the sentiment around which all their actions and all their arguments circle, from which all their propositions radiate. They look upon slavery as a moral, social, and political wrong, and while they contemplate it as being such, they nevertheless have due regard for its actual existence among us and the difficulties of getting rid of it in the States, and for all the constitutional obligations thrown around it; nevertheless, they do desire to see a policy instituted that looks to the thing not growing any larger; they insist upon a policy that shall treat it as a wrong and as the mildest policy to that end they look to the prevention of its growing larger [Loud applause. —*Tribune*], and to an end of it eventually [the *Tribune* added "as being wrong"—*ed.*]. All their sentiments, arguments and propositions, are brought within this range. Now I have said, and I repeat it here, if there be any man among us who does not think that the institution of slavery is a wrong—that it is not a wrong in any one of the aspects in which I have spoken, he is misplaced, and ought not to be among us; and, if there be a man who is so impatient of it as a wrong, as to disregard the difficulties of getting rid of it, or as to disregard the constitutional obligations thrown around it, that man too is misplaced; we disclaim sympathy with him in political action; he is not placed properly with us.

By the way, on this subject of treating it as a wrong, and limiting its spread, let me say a word. I have asked the question indirectly, what has ever threatened our own liberties and prosperity save and except this very institution of slavery? If this be true, how do you propose to amend it? By spreading it out larger, or making it bigger? You may have a cancer upon your person, and you may not be able to cut it out at once, lest you bleed to death, but you may not treat it as a wrong by spreading it over your whole body. So with this, the way is—is the peaceful mode to deal with it—to prevent the spread of it into new country. That is the old fashioned way of dealing with it, the example of which our fathers have set us.

On the other hand, I have said that there is a sentiment which treats it as not being a wrong. That is the Democratic sentiment of to-day. I do not mean to say that every man who stands within that range, positively asserts that it is right. That class will include all who do not say that it is right or wrong. This class all fall within the general class of those who do not look upon it as wrong; and now, if there be among you any one that supposes that he is a Democrat can consider and proclaim himself as being as much opposed to it as any body else, I would like to reason with him awhile. You never treat it as a wrong. What other thing that you consider wrong do you treat in that way? You, perhaps, say that it is wrong, but your leader does not say so, and you quarrel with every one else that says it is a wrong, although you say it yourself. We must not say anything about it in the free States because it is not here; we must not say anything about it in the slave States because it is there; we must not say anything about it in politics, because it will disturb the quietness of my ["]place["]; [Shouts of laughter and cheers. —*Tribune*] and you must not speak of it in the pulpit, because it is not religion. [Applause. —*Times*] There is no suitable place to oppose it; but finally you say that if they would adopt systems of emancipation in the slave States, you would approve of it—but don't deceive yourselves; Frank Blair and Gratz Brown and their co-laborers tried that thing in Missouri that you pretend that you would like here. Frank Blair and Gratz Brown tried that thing and were beaten and you threw up your hats and hurrahed for the democracy. [Applause. —*Times;* Great applause and laughter. —*Tribune*]

More than that, take all the arguments that are made in favor of the system. Take, first, the system itself that you propose, and it carefully excludes the idea that there is anything wrong in the system of slavery; the arguments that sustain that policy carefully exclude it, and even here to-day, you hear Judge Douglas quarrelling with me because I utter a wish that it might come some day to an end, although Mr. Clay can stand up and say that he wishes that every slave was in his own country, yet I am denounced as false to Henry Clay for expressing the wish that it may some time, in some way, come to an end. The democratic policy in regard to that institution will not tolerate the merest breath expressive of the slightest opposition to it. Try it by some of Senator Douglas' arguments. He says he don't care whether it is voted up or down. Now, I don't care whether that is intended to be expressive of his individual sentiment upon that subject or whether it is intended to be expressive of the national policy that he desires should be carried out; it is alike valuable for my purposes. I say that a man can logically say that if he sees no wrong in it, but he cannot say so logically if he admits that slavery is wrong. No man can say that he does not care if a wrong is voted up or down, he cannot say that he is indifferent as to a wrong; but he must have a choice between the right or wrong. He says that whatever community desires slavery has a right to it. He can say so logically if it is not a wrong, but if he admits that it is wrong, he cannot logically say that anybody has a right to do wrong. He says upon the score of equality, slaves should be allowed to go into the territories the same as other property. His argument is logical if the properties are alike, but if one is wrong and the other right, then he cannot say that, for there is no equality between the right and the wrong. I say that everything in the Democratic policy, in the shape it takes in legislation, in the Dred Scott decision, in their conversations, everyone carefully excludes the thought that there is anything wrong in it whatever.

That is the real issue! An issue that will continue in this country when these poor tongues of Douglas and myself shall be silent. These are the two principles that are made the eternal struggle between right and wrong. They are the two principles that have stood face to face [the *Tribune* added: "from the beginning of time; and will ever continue to struggle"—*ed.*], one of them asserting the divine right of kings, the same principle that says you work, you toil, you earn bread, and I will eat it. [Loud applause. —*Tribune*] It is the same old serpent, whether it come from the mouth of a king who seeks to bestride the people of his nation, and to live upon the fat of his neighbor [the *Tribune* substituted "the fruit of his labor"—*ed.*], or, whether it comes from one race of men as an apology for the enslaving of another race of men. It is the same old policy, and I expressed my gratification that the judge at Quincy announced that he looks to no end of this controversy. [Considerable confusion here arising among the crowd—much difficulty was experienced in hearing. —*Times*] [In the confusion, the *Times* did not hear Lincoln's next thoughts, as recorded, or supplied later, for the *Tribune:* "I re-express it here to Judge Douglas—that he looks to no end of the institution of slavery that will help the people to see where the struggle really is. It will hereafter place with us all men who really do wish the wrong may have an end"—*ed.*] Meanwhile, whenever that issue is clear, whenever we can get clear of those men that look to no end of it, when we can get those men out of that policy, and get them on the side of those who treat it as a wrong, there will soon be an end of it, it will then soon be in the course of ultimate extinction. When that issue can be made, and all extraneous matter can be removed from between the combatants, they can settle the matter, and it will be done peacefully, too. There is no war about it. There is no violation of the constitution, no violation of right, or, of the necessities that spring from the actual presence of the thing. We need but that policy again, that places it where the wisest and best men of the world originally placed it.

This man Brooks, of South Carolina, once declared that when this government was first established no one expected the institution of slavery to last until this day. When he said so, he stated a fact which I think is fully established by the history of the times; but, he said that though the men who framed this government were wiser and better men than the men of those days, that the men of these days had experience which their fathers had not, and that experience had brought them the invention of the cotton-gin which had made the perpetuation of the institution of slavery a necessity. I say that, willingly, or unwillingly, with purpose, or without purpose, Judge Douglas has been a most prominent instrument in the changing of the basis on which our fathers originally placed it, and putting it upon Brooks' cotton-gin basis [Great applause. —*Tribune*], placing it where he openly insists that he has no desire for the end of it. [Renewed applause. —*Tribune*]

I understand that I have ten minutes yet, and I will employ that time, or a portion of it, with that argument that Judge Douglas uses, while he holds to the Dred Scott decision, that the people of a territory can some way or other decide that question [slavery—*ed.*] for themselves.

The first thing that I say on that point is, that he frequently said before that decision that it was a question for the courts [Cheers. —*Tribune*], but now he virtually tells us that it is not a question for the church [the *Tribune* substituted, probably correctly, "Supreme Court," adding: "but for the people"; conceivably, Lincoln did hark back to "church" at the debate, but the reference was not understood—*ed.*]. [Renewed applause. —*Tribune*] But how does he state it? He says that it needs friendly legislation, and admits of unfriendly legislation, and that although he admits the right of the slave-holder to take a slave into the territory, that with unfriendly legislation the people can really exclude it. I look to the constitutional authority, and I take the gentleman who looks me in the face. We will say he is a member of the territorial legislature; like Judge Douglas, he believes that the right to take and hold slaves there is a constitutional right. The first thing he does is to swear he will support the Constitution; and suppose his neighbor needs legislation that he may be enabled to enjoy that constitutional right, can he withhold that legislation which his neighbor needs for the enjoyment of a right which is fixed in his favor in the Constitution of the United States, which you remember he has sworn to support without violating his oath, I ask? And more especially can he pass unfriendly legislation without violating that oath? Why, this is a monstrous sort of talk about the Constitution of the United States! [Great applause. —*Tribune*] There never has been such outrageous talk—such lawless talk—from any man of respectability, on the assumption, which he believes, that the right to hold slaves is a constitutional right. [Tremendous cheers. —*Tribune*] I don't believe it is a constitutional right. I believe the decision is improperly made, and go for reversing it. Judge Douglas is furious in his speech on those who go for reversing it, yet he goes for legislating from it all its force, while he leaves it standing. I affirm here that there never has, from the mouth of a respectable man on earth, been uttered so monstrous a doctrine. [Applause. —*Times;* Loud cheers. —*Tribune*] Why, I suppose that most of us, I know I myself, believe, the people of the southern States are entitled to a congressional fugitive slave law; that that right is fixed in the Constitution; that it cannot be made available to them without congressional legislation; that it is, in the Judge's language, a barren right, and that it needs legislation before it can be made efficient and valuable to the persons to whom it is granted, and we, such as I, agree that that legislation should be maintained for them. On what ground? We profess not to like that legislation, and perhaps have no great taste for running after [the *Tribune* added "and catching"—*ed.*] niggers[—]I profess to have none—and yet we do. At least, I yield my support to the fugitive slave law. Why? Because I do not understand that the Constitution which gives that right can be carried out if that legislation is withheld, and if I believed that the right to hold slaves in a territory was as firmly fixed as that is, why, on the same principle, I would be bound to give the legislation necessary to support it, and, I say, that no man can deny his obligation to give legislation for slave property in a territory, who believes that it is a constitutional right there. No man can make such an argument that will not give an Abolitionist a stronger argument to deny a fugitive slave law. Try it on and see; if that decision is correct, then that right of the slave power is as great a right as that the slaveholder shall have his slave returned to him, and the man who argues that by unfriendly legislation, in spite of that constitutional right, slavery may be driven from the territory, furnishes the argument, and cannot avoid the argument upon which the Abolitionist may deny the obligation, and may claim the power to furnish unfriendly legislation against the right of the slaveholder to claim his slave. I don't know how such an argument may take before a popular audience, but I defy any man to go before a court, or a class of men whose minds are accustomed to hearing arguments of this sort, and deny that there is a bit of difference between them [the *Tribune* elaborated: "between the constitutional right to reclaim a fugitive, and the constitutional right to hold a slave, in a Territory, provided this Dred Scott decision is correct." (Cheers.)—*ed.*]. I defy any man to go before such a class of men—to go and make an argument for adopting unfriendly legislation in the territories, that will not give an argument against the constitutional right to a fugitive slave law.

There is not such an abolitionist in all the States as Douglas [the *Tribune* added "after all"—*ed.*]. [Mr. Lincoln being run down, stopped, having several minutes to spare —*Times*; Loud and enthusiastic applause. —*Tribune*]

MR. DOUGLAS' REJOINDER

[Senator Douglas' re-appearance in front of the stand was the signal for a general yell of applause, which fairly shook the earth, and startled the old Mississippi which was rolling gently along in all its majesty within a few hundred yards of the stand. —*Times*]

Mr. Lincoln has closed his remarks by saying that there is not such an Abolitionist in all America as I am. If he could make the Abolitionists of Illinois believe it, he would not have much show for the Senate. [Laughter. —*Tribune* and *Times*] Make the Abolitionists believe the truth of that, and his political back is broken. [Laughter. —*Tribune;* Great laughter and applause. —*Times*] The back of his party is broken when Abolitionism is withdrawn. His first criticism on me is the hope that the war of the Administration will be prosecuted [the *Times* added: "against me"—*ed.*] with vigor. I have no doubt of it. His hope of success, and the hopes of his party depend upon it. They have no hope of destroying the Democracy except through the aid of the federal patronage in this State. ["That's a fact," "good," and cheers. —*Times*] He has all of the federal office-holders here as his allies ["That's so." —*Times*], running separate tickets against the Democracy to divide the party, but still the leaders all intend to vote directly the Abolition ticket, only leaving the green ones to vote for the separate ticket, who must go into the Abolition camp. [Laughter and cheers. —*Times*] And there is something really refreshing in the thought that Lincoln is in favor of prosecuting any war vigorously. [Laughter. —*Tribune;* Roars of laughter. —*Times*] It is the first war I ever knew him to be in favor of prosecuting. [Applause. —*Tribune;* Renewed laughter. —*Times*] It is the first one I ever knew him to believe to be either just or constitutional. [Laughter and cheers. —*Times*] When the Mexican war was waged and the American army was surrounded by the enemy in Mexico, he thought that was unconstitutional, unnecessary and unjust. [Laughter. —*Tribune;* "That's so," "you've got him," "he voted against it," &c. —*Times*] He thought it was not commenced on the right spot. [Laughter. —*Times*] When I made an incidental allusion to that in our joint meeting at Charleston, some weeks ago, Lincoln caught it up and said, "Douglas has charged me with voting against supplies," and then he reared up at full length, and said he did not vote against supplies—said it was a slander, and caught hold of Ficklin, who sat on the stand, and said, "Here, Ficklin, tell them it is a lie." [Applause. —*Tribune;* Laughter and cheers. —*Times*] Well, Ficklin stood up and told them that all he recollected about it was that Ashmun brought forward a resolution declaring the war as unconstitutional, unnecessary, and unjust, and that Lincoln voted for it. Lincoln said, "Yes, I did." Yes, he confesses that he voted that the war was wrong—that our country was in the wrong— that consequently, the Mexicans were in the right; and he said I had slandered him in saying that he had voted against supplies. I never charged him with voting against supplies in my life. I knew he was not there when they were voted. [Applause. —*Tribune;* Tremendous shouts of laughter. —*Times*] The war was commenced on the 18th of May, 1848, and on that day we appropriated ten millions of money, and fifty thousand men, to prosecute the war. During the same session we voted more men and more money. During the next session we again voted more men and more money, and thus gave men and money enough before Lincoln came to Congress. [Laughter and cheers. —*Times*] Getting there and being opposed to the war, and not being able to stop the supplies because they were all gone forward, all he could do was to follow the lead of Tom Corwin, and prove the war was not begun on the right spot; that it was unconstitutional, unnecessary, and therefore wrong. And remember, too, that this was done after the war began. It is one thing to be opposed to the declaration of war, and another thing to take the side of the enemy against your own country, for the war was commenced ["Good," and cheers. —*Times*], and our army was in Mexico at the time. Many bills had been voted—they were surrounded by the dangers, and the guns, and the poison of the enemy, and then it was that Corwin made his speech, stating that the American soldiers ought to be welcomed to hospitable graves with bloody hands, and Ashmun and Lincoln voted in the House that the war was unconstitutional and unjust, and Ashmun's resolutions and Corwin's speech and Lincoln's vote were sent to Mexico, and read to the army to prove to the army of the Mexicans that there was a Mexican party in the Congress of the United States. [Applause. —*Tribune;* "That's the truth," Lincoln's a traitor, etc. —*Times*] That the man who took the side of the common enemy against his own country in time [of] war would rejoice in the war being made on me now is very natural. [Applause. —*Tribune;* Immense applause. —*Times*] And in my opinion no other man would rejoice at it. ["Go it, Stephen. All right, my covey." —*Tribune;* "That's true," "hurrah for Douglas," and cheers. —*Times*]

Mr. Lincoln has told you a great deal to-day about his being an Old Line Clay Whig. ["He never was." —*Times*] Remember there are a great many Old Clay Whigs in this region. It is more agreeable here to talk about Old Clay Whigs than Abolitionists; but we don't hear much about this old Whig party up in those Abolition Districts. How much of an old Whig was he? Have you read Singleton's speech at Jacksonville. [Yes, yes, and cheers. —*Times*] You know Gen. [James Washington] Singleton. He was 25 years, the confidential friend of Henry Clay in Illinois. He testifies that in 1847, when the State Convention in this State was in session, the Whig members were invited to a Whig caucus by Lincoln's brother-in-law, and there, when they were organized, Lincoln made a speech in favor of throwing Clay overboard and taking up [Zachary] Taylor in his place, and gave as a reason that if the Whigs didn't take Taylor, the Democrats would. [Applause. —*Tribune;* Cheers and laughter. —*Times*] Singleton also testified that Lincoln in that speech urged as a reason for throwing Clay overboard, that the Whigs had voted long enough for principle and should now go for success. Singleton testifies that Lincoln's speech did have the effect to cut Henry Clay's throat, and that he and others withdrew from the caucus in indignation. He testified that when he went to the Philadelphia Convention, that Lincoln then was the bitter, deadly enemy of Clay, and tried to keep Singleton out of the Convention because he would vote for Clay [the *Times* added: "and Lincoln was determined to have Taylor" (Laughter and applause.)—*ed.*]. Singleton testified that Lincoln rejoiced with very great joy when he found the mangled remains of the murdered Whig statesman lying cold before him, and now he tells you he is an Old Line Clay Whig. [Applause. —*Tribune;* Laughter and cheers. —*Times*] Singleton testifies to these facts in a speech that has been printed and circulated broadcast for weeks, and offers to prove every fact, but not a lisp have we yet heard from Lincoln except that he is an Old Clay Whig. What part of Clay's policy did he ever advocate[?] He was in Congress in 1848 and '49, when this Wilmot Proviso warfare disturbed the peace and harmony of the country, until it shook from its centre to circumference. It was that sectional agitation that brought Clay forth from his retirement to the Senate of the United States to see if he could not, by his great wisdom and experience and the renown of his name, do something to restore quiet to the country. Who got up that sectional strife that Clay came there to quell? I have heard Lincoln boast in a public speech that he then voted 43 times for the Wilmot

Proviso, and as many more times to carry it. Lincoln is the man, in connection with Seward and Chase and Giddings and the other Abolitionists, that got up that strife that I helped Clay in putting down. [Tremendous applause. —*Times*] Clay came there in 1849 to see if he could not do something to restore peace to the country. All the Union Whigs and the Union Democrats welcomed him the moment he arrived as the man for the occasion. We believed that he of all men on earth had been preserved by Divine Providence to guide us out of these difficulties, and we Democrats rallied under Clay then as you Whigs rallied under the banner of old Jackson in Nullification times, forgetting party when the country was in danger, in order that we might have the country first and parties afterward. [Applause. —*Tribune;* "Three Cheers For Douglas." —*Times*]

And this reminds me that Lincoln has told you that the slavery question was the only one that ever disturbed the peace and harmony of the Union. Didn't Nullification once raise its head and disturb the peace of the Union in 1832? Was that the slavery question? Didn't this question raise its monster head through the last war with Great Britain? Was that the slavery question? ["Three cheers for Douglas." —*Times*] The peace of the country has been disturbed three times; once in the war with Great Britain, once on the Tariff question and once on the slavery question, thus his argument fails that this question of slavery is the only one that has created any disunion. It is true that agitators now are enabled in using the slavery question for the purpose of sectional strife. ["That's so." —*Times*] He admits that in all things else the principles which I advocate of leaving each State and Territory free to decide for itself ought to prevail. He instances his "Cranberry laws," [Laughter. —*Tribune*] —his "Oyster laws"—I might go through the whole list of them. I say the whole of them are local and domestic, and all local and domestic concerns should be left in each State and each Territory for itself, and if these agitators will acquiesce in that principle, there would never be any danger to the peace and harmony of the Union. ["That's so," and cheers. —*Tribune*] But he tries to avoid the main issue by denying the truth of the proposition that I made that our fathers made this government, divided into free and slave States, with the right of each to decide all local questions for itself. It is true they didn't make Slavery in the States, and make them free or slave, but finding 13 States, 12 of them slave and one free, they agreed to make a government uniting them together as they stood, although divided into free and slave States, and guaranteed for ever a right to each State to do as it pleased in the slavery question. [Applause. —*Tribune;* Cheers. —*Times*] Having thus made the government with the right of each to do as it pleased forever, I assert that this government can exist as they made it, divided into free and slave States, forever if any one State should retain slavery. [Applause. —*Tribune*]

He complains that I don't look forward to the time when slavery shall be abolished everywhere. I look forward to the time when each State shall be allowed to do as it pleases. [Applause. —*Tribune*] If it chooses to keep slavery forever, it is its business, and not ours. If it chooses to abolish, very good, it is its business and not mine. I care more for the great principle of self-government—the right of the people to rule themselves—than I do for all the niggers [the *Times* substituted "negroes"—*ed.*] in Christendom. [Applause. —*Tribune;* Cheers. —*Times*] I would not dissolve this Union; I would not endanger its perpetuity; I would not blot out the great inalienable rights of the white man for all the niggers [the *Times* again heard "negroes"—*ed.*] that ever existed. [Applause. —*Tribune* and *Times*] Then I say, let us maintain this Government on the principles that our fathers made it, with the right to each State to keep slavery as long as it pleases, and abolish it when it pleases. [Cheers. —*Times*] But Mr. Lincoln says that our fathers, when they made the Government, didn't look forward to this state of things that now exists, and therefore that the doctrine is wrong, is his inference. He quotes Brooks, of South Carolina, to prove that our fathers then thought that slavery would be abolished by each State acting for itself before this time. Suppose they did. Suppose they didn't foresee what has occurred. Does that change the principles of the Government? They didn't foresee, probably, the telegraph that transmits intelligence by lightning. They didn't foresee the railroads that are the bonds of union between the different States of the Union. They didn't foresee a thousand other inventions of benefit to mankind throughout the world; but do these facts change the principles of the Government? They made the Government on the principle I state—the right of the people to do as they pleased, and then let the people of each State apply it to each change of condition, to each improvement, as they may arise in all time to come. [Applause. —*Tribune;* Cheers. —*Times*] Mr. Lincoln goes on to tell you that he don't want to interfere with slavery in the States at all, nor does his party. I expected that he would say that down here. [Laughter. —*Times*] Let me ask him, then, how is he going to put slavery in the condition of ultimate extinction everywhere in the States, if he is not going to interfere with it in the States. [Applause. —*Tribune;* Renewed laughter. —*Times*] He says he will prohibit it in all the Territories and the inference is, then, that unless they make it a free State, he will keep them out. For mark you, he didn't say whether he would bring Kansas in with slavery or without it as they want. He didn't say whether he would bring in any new Territory now in existence on the principle of Clay's Compromise of 1850, with or without slavery as the people want, but I tell you he won't. [Applause. —*Tribune;* Give it to him, he deserves it, &c. —*Times*] His idea is to prohibit slavery in all the Territories and force them to become free States, and then surround the slave States with a cordon of free States, and hem them in, and then let them increase and multiply until they get so numerous that the soil on which they live wouldn't feed them, thus putting slavery in the process of ultimate extinction by starvation. [Applause. —*Tribune;* Cheers. —*Times*] He will extinguish slavery in the Southern States as the French General exterminated the Algerians—by smoking them out; and he is going to extinguish slavery by smothering, as you would smoke a fox out of his hole, and do it in the name of humanity and Christianity and in order to get rid of the terrible crime and sin entailed by our fathers of holding slaves. [Laughter and cheers. —*Times*] This is the line of policy that he marks out, and appeals to the moral sense and the justice and the Christian feeling of the North to sustain him. Then he says that those who hold the contrary doctrine to him are on the basis of kings who claim a government by divine right. Let us look for a moment and see on what principle they threw over the divine right of George III, who governed us. Didn't these colonies rebel on the principle that the British Parliament had no right to pass laws concerning our property and private and domestic institutions, without our consent? They demanded that the British Government should not pass such laws unless it gave us a full representation. The British said they would, and we went to war on that principle, that the home government should not control or govern these territories without representation. [Applause. —*Tribune*] Now what is the principle on which he proposes to govern the Territories? Give them no representation, and then call upon Congress to make laws controlling their property and domestic concerns, without their consent, against their will. Thus he asserts for his party the identical principle of the party of George III, and the Tories of the Revolution. [Applause. —*Tribune;* Cheers.

—*Times*] I hold that the people of a Territory like those of a State (I use the language of Mr. Buchanan in his letter of acceptance) have the right to decide for themselves whether slavery shall exist within their limits. ["That's the idea," "Hurrah for Douglas." —*Times*] The point upon which Chief Justice Taney expressed his opinion was, that slaves being property, stand on an equal footing with other property, and consequently the owner has the same right to carry that property into a Territory that he has any other, and of course subject to the same conditions. Suppose one of your merchants would take $100,000 [the *Times* had "fifty or one hundred thousand dollars"—*ed.*] worth of groceries to Kansas. You have a right to go there under the decision, but when you get there, you find the Maine Liquor Law in force. You cannot use it—cannot sell it. It is subject to the local laws, and that law is against you. What can you do with it?

A VOICE—You would drink it. [The *Times* did not report this bit of heckling—*ed.*]

JUDGE DOUGLAS—The best you can do is to bring it back to Illinois and sell it. If you take your negroes there, and as Col. Jefferson Davis says in his Bangor speech, you must take them there subject to the local law. If they want it, that will protect and encourage it; if they don't want it, they will withhold that protection. The absence of local legislation excluded it as completely as positive prohibition. ["That's so," and cheers. —*Times*] You slaveholders of Missouri understand practically that you cannot carry slavery where the people don't want it ["That's so." —*Times*], and all that you have a right to ask is that the people shall do as they please. If they want it, let them have it, and if they don't want it, let them refuse to encourage it.

No, my friends, if we will only live up to these great fundamental principles, there will be peace between the North and the South. Lincoln admits that all the domestic questions are left to each State under the Constitution in regard to all other questions except slavery, without the right to interfere with them. What right have we with slavery any more than with any other? But he says this slavery question is now the bone of contention. Why? Because agitators are banded together in the free States to make war on it. Suppose the agitators in all the States in one half of the Union should combine to make war upon the railroad system in the other half, you would have the same sectional strife. Suppose you should make war upon any other domestic institution, it would produce the same strife. The only remedy or safety is that we shall stand by the Constitution as our fathers made it; obey the laws as they are passed, while they stand on the statute book, and sustain the decision of the Supreme Court and the constituted authorities as they perform their duties under the Constitution. I am told my time is up. [Applause. —*Tribune;* For some minutes after he concluded, the applause was perfectly deafening and overwhelming. . . . —*Times*]

Appendix

Lincoln vs. Douglas: How the State Voted

NEITHER ABRAHAM LINCOLN nor Stephen A. Douglas "won" a popular election for the Senate in 1858. Neither of their names appeared on the ballot, and thus, citizens could not vote for either candidate directly. Under the rules governing Senate elections in nineteenth-century America, voters cast their ballots for local legislative nominees who in turn were empowered to choose senators, parliamentary-style. Douglas's party won more legislative seats than Lincoln's that year, and the Senator was thus returned to office, "defeating" Lincoln.

But at the same time, Lincoln's Republicans fared better than Douglas's Democrats in the key statewide popular vote held in 1858: the race for state treasurer. Republican candidates amassed more total votes in the state's nine congressional contests as well.

One question that has never been answered, however, is whether Lincoln or Douglas men did better among voters in counties in which their seven debates were staged. The statistics are presented here for the first time. The totals provide a clue, however imperfect, to the impact the debates had on the voting audiences who actually witnessed them. And what the numbers show is that Republican candidates did fare better—although only slightly so—in these areas. They amassed somewhat higher percentages of the popular vote in debate counties in both treasurer and congressional elections than they did in counties in which debates were not held.

It is risky, of course, to draw major conclusions from these statistics. For one thing, each debate attracted not only onlookers from the vicinity, but substantial out-of-county crowds as well. Besides, the strongest statement that any debate eyewitness could make at the ballot box, however inspired by a Senate candidate's performance, was an indirect vote for legislator, or a sympathetic one for treasurer or congressman.

Nonetheless, the numbers do lend credence to the prevailing assumption that Lincoln would have been elected to the Senate that year in a head-to-head popular vote, under twentieth-century rules. More to the point, Republican candidates' ability to run slightly ahead of state averages in those counties in which Lincoln met Douglas publicly, face-to-face, suggests the further, more intriguing possibility that he might have prevailed even under 1858 rules had Douglas agreed—as Lincoln originally proposed—that they debate dozens of times that season, and not just on seven occasions.

Do the statistics suggest, too, that Lincoln "won" the 1858 debates? Too many intangibles bar such an assumption. But if Lincoln men ran better in counties in which the candidates were seen and heard—and not just read—face-to-face, the results do tend to validate more than ever the crucial importance of the printed transcripts that offered the rest of the state's counties their sole access to the confrontations. The real winner of the 1858 race may have been the newspapermen, whose edited and embellished transcripts brought Abraham Lincoln and Stephen A. Douglas to voters in every region of Illinois—however imprecisely.

Following are statistical totals for the 1858 elections for state treasurer and Congress, comparing statewide votes to votes in those counties in which Lincoln and Douglas met in debate. All the records are from the 1859 *Tribune Almanac*.

The 1858 Popular Vote—Debate Counties

| DEBATE | | STATE TREASURER | | | CONGRESS | |
	COUNTY	REPUBLICAN	DOUGLAS DEMOCRAT	BUCHANAN DEMOCRAT	REPUBLICAN	DEMOCRAT	OTHER
Ottawa*	LaSalle	4,105	3,415	30	4,040	3,438	30
Freeport	Stephenson	2,160	1,483	16	2,140	1,489	16
Jonesboro	Union	61	584	462	65	819	—
Charleston	Coles	1,823	1,584	9	1,859	1,578	7
Galesburg	Knox	2,952	1,831	55	2,965	1,820	54
Quincy	Adams	2,986	3,408	78	3,004	3,280	136
Alton	Madison	2,030	2,221	29	2,054	2,185	31
TOTAL	7 COUNTIES	16,117 (51.5%)	14,526 (46.5%)	679 (2.0%)	16,127 (52.0%)	14,609 (47.1%)	274 (0.9%)
TOTAL	STATEWIDE	125,430 (49.9%)	121,609 (48.2%)	5,071 (1.9%)	125,668 (49.9%)	122,181 (48.5%)	4,111 (1.6%)
% DIFFERENCE IN DEBATE COUNTIES		+1.6%	−1.7%	−0.01%	+2.1%	−1.4%	−0.7%

*Lincoln fared even better in the two counties in which the Senate nominees addressed the same audiences separately, before formal debates were arranged. In Cook and Sangamon Counties, Lincoln's party won 52%, Douglas Democrats 46.2%, and Buchanan Democrats 1.8% in the Treasurer's race.

Notes

NOTES FOR THE GENERAL INTRODUCTION

1. Edwin Erle Sparks, *The Lincoln-Douglas Debates of 1858* (Collections of the Illinois State Historical Library III; Lincoln Series, Vol. I; Springfield, Ill.: Illinois State Historical Library, 1908), p. 319. The Sparks volume, cited frequently hereafter, contains extensive, complete descriptions of the debates from the pages of the period press. This account came from the New York *Evening Post,* September 21, 1858.

2. *Ibid.,* p. v; Don E. Fehrenbacher, *Prelude to Greatness: Lincoln in the 1850's* (Stanford: Stanford Univ. Press, 1962), p. 96.

3. Roy P. Basler, *et al.,* eds., *The Collected Works of Abraham Lincoln* (9 vols., New Brunswick, N.J.: Rutgers Univ. Press, 1953–55; cited hereafter as *Coll. Works of Lincoln*), II, p. 502; III. p. 84; Earl Schenck Miers, *et al.,* eds., *Lincoln Day by Day: A Chronology, 1809–1865* (3 vols., Washington, D.C.: Lincoln Sesquicentennial Commission, 1959; cited hereafter as *Lincoln Day by Day*), II, pp. 221–23; *Political Debates Between Hon. Abraham Lincoln and Hon. Stephen A. Douglas, in the Celebrated Campaign of 1858, in Illinois* . . . (Columbus, Ohio: Follett, Foster & Co., 1860), pp. 40–64; Author unknown, *Recollections of Lincoln and Douglas Forty Years Ago* (New York: n.p., 1899), p. 14.

4. *Lincoln Day by Day*, II, p. 221; *Coll. Works of Lincoln*, II, p. 504; Herbert Mitgang, ed., *Abraham Lincoln: A Press Portrait* (Chicago: Quadrangle Books, 1971), p. 105.

5. Fehrenbacher, *Prelude to Greatness*, p. 99; *Coll. Works of Lincoln*, II, p. 522; David Zarefsky, *Lincoln, Douglas, and Slavery: In the Crucible of Public Debate* (Chicago: Univ. of Chicago Press, 1990), p. 50.

6. *Coll. Works of Lincoln*, II, pp. 528–29.

7. *Ibid.;* Fehrenbacher, *Prelude to Greatness*, p. 100.

8. See James A. Smith, *The Christian's Defence, Containing a Fair Statement, and Impartial Examination of the Leading Objections Urged by Infidels Against the Antiquity, Genuineness, Credibility and Inspiration of the Holy Scriptures . . .* (Cincinnati: J. A. James, 1843); Thomas Lewis to J. A. Reed, January 6, 1873, in *Scribner's Monthly* 6 (July 1873): 339; Robert T. Lincoln to Isaac Markens, November 4, 1917, ms. in Chicago Historical Society; Paul M. Angle, "Lincoln and Religion" (ms.); *Coll. Works of Lincoln*, II, p. 530; John W. Forney, *Anecdotes of Public Men* (2 vols., New York: Harper & Bros., 1873), II, p. 179. Douglas actually made his remark when he first learned of Lincoln's nomination.

9. Reinhard Luthin, *The Real Abraham Lincoln* (Englewood Cliffs, N.J.: Prentice-Hall, 1960), p. 197.

10. William E. Baringer, "Campaign Technique in Illinois—1860," *Transactions* of the Illinois State Historical Society for 1931 (n.p., n.d.), pp. 212, 246; for further discussion of the political culture of the era, see Harold Holzer, Mark E. Neely, Jr., and Gabor S. Boritt, *The Lincoln Image: Abraham Lincoln and the Popular Print* (New York: Scribners, 1984), pp. 4–5; Harry V. Jaffa, *Crisis of the House Divided: An Interpretation of the Lincoln-Douglas Debates* (Garden City, N.Y.: Doubleday, 1959), p. 432.

11. Fehrenbacher, *Prelude to Greatness*, p. 101.

12. *Ibid.*, pp. 102–3; Sparks, *The Lincoln-Douglas Debates of 1858*, pp. 193, 197, 200; *Lincoln Day by Day*, II, p. 225; Herbert Mitgang, *The Fiery Trial: A Life of Lincoln* (New York: Viking Press, 1974), p. 42.

13. Sparks, *The Lincoln-Douglas Debates of 1858*, pp. 75–77.

14. *Ibid.*, pp. 80–92.

15. *Ibid.*, pp. 77–79; Otis R. Goodall, "Hon. Robert Roberts Hitt," *Phonographic Magazine* 7, No. 11 (June 1, 1893): 205.

16. Zarefsky, *Lincoln, Douglas, and Slavery*, p. 54; Sparks, *The Lincoln-Douglas Debates of 1858*, p. 79.

17. Sparks, *The Lincoln-Douglas Debates of 1858*, p. 79.

18. *Ibid.*, pp. 82–83; Mitgang, *Abraham Lincoln: A Press Portrait*, p. 110.

19. Sparks, *The Lincoln-Douglas Debates of 1858*, pp. 83–84; Chicago *Press and Tribune*, October 11, 1858.

20. Sparks, *The Lincoln-Douglas Debates of 1858*, p. 84; Chicago *Press and Tribune*, August 30, 1858; Robert S. Harper, *Lincoln and the Press* (New York: McGraw-Hill, 1951), p. 25.

21. Harper, *Lincoln and the Press*, p.82.

22. *Coll. Works of Lincoln*, III, p. 373; Henry Clay Whitney, *Life on the Circuit*

with Lincoln (Boston: Estes & Lauriat, 1892), p. 457; Sparks, *The Lincoln-Douglas Debates of 1858*, p. 595.

23. Emanuel Hertz, ed., *The Hidden Lincoln: From the Letters and Papers of William H. Herndon* (New York: Viking Press, 1938), p. 271.

24. Mitgang, *Abraham Lincoln: A Press Portrait*, p. 110; Sparks, *The Lincoln-Douglas Debates of 1858*, pp. 77, 594–95.

25. Sparks, *The Lincoln-Douglas Debates of 1858*, pp. 129–30; Saul Sigelschiffer, *The American Conscience: The Drama of the Lincoln-Douglas Debates* (New York: Horizon Press, 1973), p. 164; Forney, *Anecdotes of Public Men* II, p. 179; Robert W. Johannsen, *The Frontier, the Union, and Stephen A. Douglas* (Urbana, Ill.: Univ. of Illinois Press, 1989), p. 171; Isaac N. Arnold, *The Life of Abraham Lincoln* (Chicago: A. C. McClurg, 1906), pp. 141–42; Robert W. Johannsen, *Stephen A. Douglas* (New York: Oxford Univ. Press, 1973), pp. 640–41.

26. Rufus Rockwell Wilson, *Intimate Memories of Lincoln* (Elmira, N.Y.: Primavera Press, 1945), pp. 169–70; Horace White, "Abraham Lincoln in 1854," *Transactions* of the Illinois State Historical Society, 1908, No. 13 (Springfield, Ill.: Illinois State Historical Society, 1909): 32. For examples of surviving Lincoln fragments, see *Coll. Works of Lincoln*, III, pp. 97, 205, 326; Waldo W. Braden, *Abraham Lincoln: Public Speaker* (Baton Rouge: Louisiana State Univ. Press, 1988), p. 53; Hertz, *The Hidden Lincoln*, p. 20.

27. Wilson, *Intimate Memories of Lincoln*, pp. 174–75, 183–84; Johannsen, *Stephen A. Douglas*, p. 660.

28. Sigelschiffer, *The American Conscience*, p. 161; Carl Schurz, *Reminiscences* (3 vols., New York: McClure & Co., 1907), II, p. 95; George H. Putnam, *Abraham Lincoln* (New York: G. P. Putnam's Sons, 1909), pp. 44–45; Johannsen, *Stephen A. Douglas*, p. 660; William H. Herndon, *Herndon's Lincoln: The True Story of a Great Life* (3 vols., Springfield, Ill.: Lincoln's Herndon Publishing Co., n.d.), II, pp. 405–8; Jean Baker, *Mary Todd Lincoln: A Biography* (New York: W. W. Norton, 1987), p. 155.

29. Henry Villard, *Memoirs of Henry Villard, Journalist and Financier, 1835–1900* (2 vols., Boston: Houghton Mifflin, 1904), I, pp. 92–93; see also Sparks, *The Lincoln-Douglas Debates of 1858*, pp. 129–30.

30. Fehrenbacher, *Prelude to Greatness*, p. 100; Johannsen, *Stephen A. Douglas*, p. 655; Zarefsky, *Lincoln, Douglas, and Slavery*, p. 201; Baker, *Mary Todd Lincoln*, pp. 153–55; Schurz, *Reminiscences*, II, pp. 90–91.

31. Johannsen, *Stephen A. Douglas*, pp. 682–83. Historians Leon Litwack and Eric Foner observed that Lincoln's conservatism on race fit with the antiamalgamation sentiment of the general public. See Leon Litwack, *North of Slavery: The Negro and the Free States, 1790–1860* (Chicago: Univ. of Chicago Press, 1961), p. 278; Eric Foner, *Free Soil, Free Labor, Free Men: The Ideology of the Republican Party Before the Civil War* (New York: Oxford Univ. Press, 1970), pp. 261–67.

32. Don E. Fehrenbacher, *The Dred Scott Decision: Its Significance in American Law and Politics* (New York: Oxford Univ. Press, 1978), pp. 4–5; David M. Potter, *The Impending Crisis: 1848–1861* (New York: Harper and Row, 1976), p. 329; *Coll. Works of Lincoln*, II, p. 255.

33. Kenneth M. Stampp, *America in 1857: A Nation on the Brink* (New York: Oxford Univ. Press, 1990), pp. 290–93; Johannsen, *The Frontier, the Union, and Stephen A. Douglas,* pp. 233–35.

34. *Coll. Works of Lincoln,* II, pp. 461–68; Mario M. Cuomo and Harold Holzer, eds., *Lincoln on Democracy* (New York: HarperCollins, 1990), p. 105; Horace White, *The Lincoln and Douglas Debates: An Address Before the Chicago Historical Society* (Chicago: Chicago Historical Soc., 1914), p. 16.

35. Mark E. Neely, Jr., *The Abraham Lincoln Encyclopedia* (New York: McGraw-Hill, 1982), p. 80; James M. McPherson, *Battle Cry of Freedom: The Civil War Era* (New York: Oxford Univ. Press, 1988), p. 187.

36. Johannsen, *Stephen A. Douglas,* p. 660.

37. C. H. Ray to Elihu Washburne, quoted in Johannsen, *Stephen A. Douglas,* p. 665; Joseph F. Evans, "Lincoln at Galesburg," *Journal of the Illinois State Historical Society* 8 (January 1916): 563–64.

38. The best analyses of the complicated, nondefinitive election results can be found in Fehrenbacher, *Prelude to Greatness,* pp. 118–19; and Neely, *The Abraham Lincoln Encyclopedia,* p. 81.

39. *Coll. Works of Lincoln,* III, pp. 336–37, 339; Johannsen, *Stephen A. Douglas,* p. 678; Richard Allen Heckman, *Lincoln vs. Douglas: The Great Debates Campaign* (Washington, D.C.: Public Affairs Press, 1967), pp. 137–42.

40. *Coll. Works of Lincoln,* III, pp. 339, 342, 346.

41. See William E. Gienapp, "Who Voted for Lincoln," in John L. Thomas, ed., *Abraham Lincoln and the American Political Tradition* (Amherst: Univ. of Massachusetts Press, 1986), p. 62.

42. *Coll. Works of Lincoln,* IV, p. 93.

43. *Ibid.,* III, pp. 341, 343; Whitney, *Life on the Circuit with Lincoln,* p. 458; Robert W. Johannsen, *Lincoln, the South, and Slavery: The Political Dimension* (Baton Rouge: Louisiana State Univ. Press, 1991), p. 100; Gienapp, "Who Voted for Lincoln," pp. 59–63.

44. *Coll. Works of Lincoln,* III, pp. 347, 373; David C. Mearns, ed., *The Illinois Political Campaign of 1858: A Facsimile of the Printer's Copy of his Debates with Senator Stephen Arnold Douglas as Edited and Prepared for Press by Abraham Lincoln* (Washington: Library of Congress, n.d.), pp. 6–7.

45. Mearns, *Facsimile of the Printer's Copy of His Debates,* pp. 8–13. The Follett, Foster & Co. edition included the speeches Douglas and Lincoln had delivered in Chicago and Springfield before the formal debates got under way.

46. *Coll. Works of Lincoln,* III, p. 515.

47. *Ibid.,* III, p. 510.

48. Jay Monaghan, "The Lincoln-Douglas Debates," *Lincoln Herald* 45 (June 1943): 2; Robert W. Johannsen, *The Lincoln-Douglas Debates of 1858* (New York: Oxford University Press, 1965), p. v; James G. Randall, *Lincoln the President: Springfield to Gettysburg* (2 vols., New York: Dodd, Mead, 1945), I, p. 128; Albert J. Beveridge, *Abraham Lincoln, 1809–1858* (2 vols., Boston: Houghton Mifflin, 1928), II, p. 635; advertisement in *Political Debates Between Hon. Abraham Lincoln and Hon. Stephen A. Douglas,* p. iii.

49. Robert W. Johannsen, ed., *The Letters of Stephen A. Douglas* (Urbana, Ill.: Univ. of Illinois Press, 1961), p. 489.

50. Carl Sandburg, *Lincoln Collector: The Story of Oliver R. Barrett's Great Private Collection* (New York: Harcourt Brace, 1950), p. 152; Mearns, *Facsimile of the Printer's Copy of His Debates*, pp. 1–2; R. Gerald McMurtry, "The Different Editions of the 'Debates of Lincoln and Douglas,' " *Journal of the Illinois State Historical Society* 27 (April 1934): 95–107. Among the notable editions of the debates, after Sparks, have been: Paul M. Angle, ed., *Created Equal? The Lincoln-Douglas Debates of 1858* (Chicago: Univ. of Chicago Press, 1958), and Johannsen, ed., *The Lincoln-Douglas Debates of 1858*.

51. Mearns, *Facsimile of the Printer's Copy of His Debates*, p. 13; Waldo W. Braden used the term "earwitness" in *Abraham Lincoln, Public Speaker*, p. 198.

52. George S. Bryan, *The Great American Myth* (New York: Carrick & Evans, 1940), p. 54; *Lincoln Day by Day*, III, p. 26.

53. *Lincoln Day by Day*, III, p. 46.

NOTES FOR INDIVIDUAL DEBATE INTRODUCTIONS

OTTAWA

Chicago *Times*, August 22, 1858; Chicago *Press and Tribune*, August 23, 1858; Sparks, *The Lincoln-Douglas Debates of 1858*, pp. 85, 124–43; Neely, *The Abraham Lincoln Encyclopedia*, pp. 228–29; Sigelschiffer, *The American Conscience*, pp. 220–21, 223; *Coll. Works of Lincoln*, III, p. 37; New York *Tribune*, August 26, 1858; Johannsen, *Stephen A. Douglas*, p. 665; Henry Clay Whitney to Abraham Lincoln, August 26, 1858, and L. D. Whiting to Abraham Lincoln, August 23, 1858 (Abraham Lincoln Papers, Library of Congress).

FREEPORT

Wilson, *Intimate Memories of Lincoln*, p. 183; *Coll. Works of Lincoln*, II, p. 530; III, p. 336; Potter, *The Impending Crisis: 1848–1861*, pp. 336, 338; Sigelschiffer, *The American Conscience*, p. 238; Sparks, *The Lincoln-Douglas Debates of 1858*, pp. 188–211; Zarefsky, *Lincoln, Douglas, and Slavery*, pp. 133–34; Neely, *The Abraham Lincoln Encyclopedia*, pp. 117–18; J. H. Jordan to Abraham Lincoln, August 24, 1858, and Joseph M. Medill to Abraham Lincoln, August (?), 1858 (Abraham Lincoln Papers, Library of Congress); Robert J. Schmezle, *et al.*, *The Freeport Debate and Its Centennial Celebration* (Freeport, Ill.: The Lincoln-Douglas Society, 1959), pp. 171, 178–81; Johanssen, *The Frontier, The Union, and Stephen A. Douglas*, p. 235; Fehrenbacher, *Prelude to Greatness*, pp. 108–9, 122–27; Allen Thorndike Rice, ed., *Reminiscences of Abraham Lincoln by Distinguished Men of His Time* (New York: North American Review, 1888), p. 27; William

S. McFeely, *Frederick Douglass* (New York: W. W. Norton, 1991), pp. 187–88; Illinois *State Register,* September 1, 1858; Chicago *Press and Tribune,* August 30, 1858.

JONESBORO

The definitive account of this debate is found in John Y. Simon, "Union County in 1858, and the Lincoln-Douglas Debate," *Journal of the Illinois State Historical Society* 61 (Autumn 1969), pp. 267–92. See also Sparks, *The Lincoln-Douglas Debates of 1858,* pp. 144–45, 160–66; Sigelschiffer, *The American Conscience,* pp. 258–59; Chicago *Press and Tribune,* September 17, 1858; Chicago *Times,* September 17, 1858; Neely, *The Abraham Lincoln Encyclopedia,* pp. 167–68; Paul M. Angle, *"Here I Have Lived": A History of Lincoln's Springfield* (Chicago: Abraham Lincoln Book Shop, 1971), p. 227; Zarefsky, *Lincoln, Douglas, and Slavery,* pp. 59, 254.

CHARLESTON

Chicago *Press and Tribune,* September 21, 1858; Chicago *Times,* September 21, 1858; *Coll. Works of Lincoln,* II, p. 465; Sparks, *The Lincoln-Douglas Debates of 1858,* pp. 311–28; *Lincoln Day By Day,* II, p. 229; Zarefsky, *Lincoln, Douglas, and Slavery,* pp. 61–62; Sigelschiffer, *The American Conscience,* p. 280. For Lincoln's evolving views on Negro rights and colonization, see Don E. Fehrenbacher, "Only His Stepchildren: Lincoln and the Negro," *Civil War History* 20, No. 4 (December 1974), pp. 293–310; G. S. Boritt, "The Voyage to the Colony of Lincolnia," *The Historian* 37, No. 4 (August 1975), pp. 619–30.

GALESBURG

Chicago *Press and Tribune,* October 8, 1858; October 9, 1858; Chicago *Times,* October 9, 1858; Sparks, *The Lincoln-Douglas Debates of 1858,* pp. 371–88; Zarefsky, *Lincoln, Douglas, and Slavery,* p. 62; Neely, *The Abraham Lincoln Encyclopedia,* pp. 123–24; Sigelschiffer, *The American Conscience,* pp. 303–4; Joseph F. Evans, "Lincoln at Galesburg," *Journal of the Illinois State Historical Society* 8 (January 1916): 559–62; New York *Herald,* October 13, 1858.

QUINCY

Neely, *The Abraham Lincoln Encyclopedia,* pp. 249–50; Schurz, *Memoirs,* II, pp. 90–94; Zarefsky, *Lincoln, Douglas, and Slavery,* p. 64; Sparks, *The Lincoln-Douglas Debates of 1858,* pp. 435–48; Schurz, *Reminiscences,* II, p. 93; James G. Wright to Abraham Lincoln, October 11, 1858 (Abraham Lincoln Papers, Library of Congress).

ALTON

Sparks, *The Lincoln-Douglas Debates of 1858*, pp. 496–510; Neely, *The Abraham Lincoln Encyclopedia*, pp. 4–5, 175; Paul M. Angle, *The Lincoln Reader* (New Brunswick, N.J.: Rutgers Univ. Press, 1947), pp. 246–47; John Goff, *Robert Todd Lincoln: A Man in His Own Right* (Norman, Oklahoma: Univ. of Oklahoma Press, 1969), p. 20; Horace White to Abraham Lincoln, November 7, 1858 (Abraham Lincoln Papers, Library of Congress).

Index

The abbreviation A.L. represents Abraham Lincoln.